BREAKING THE CHAINS
SLAVERY AND ITS LEGACY IN THE NINETEENTH-CENTURY CAPE COLONY

EDITED BY

NIGEL WORDEN & CLIFTON CRAIS

WITHDRAWN

WUP

WITWATERSRAND UNIVERSITY PRESS

1994

Witwatersrand University Press
1 Jan Smuts Avenue
Johannesburg
2001
South Africa

ISBN 1 86814 267 1

First published in 1994

Typeset by Red Setter, Gardens, 8001
Reproduction by Cape Imaging Bureau, Woodstock, 7925
Printed and bound by Clyson Printers, Maitland, 7405

- CONTENTS -

- LIST OF PLATES -

- LIST OF MAPS -

- LIST OF TABLES -

- ACKNOWLEDGEMENTS -

We are grateful to the University of Cape Town Research Committee for supporting the original conference from which the idea of this book emerged; to Ken Behr for drawing the maps; to Jackie Loos, Karel Schoeman (South African Library) and Marion George (Cape Archives) for assistance with the pictures at very short notice; and to Glenda Younge for her meticulous editing and limitless patience.

– LIST OF CONTRIBUTORS –

Andrew Bank completed his MA at the University of Cape Town and is currently a doctoral student at St. John's College, Cambridge.

Vivian Bickford-Smith is Lecturer in History at the University of Cape Town.

Clifton Crais is Assistant Professor of History at Kenyon College, Ohio.

Wayne Dooling completed his MA at the University of Cape Town and is currently a doctoral student at St. John's College, Cambridge.

John Mason is Assistant Professor of History at the University of Florida.

Lalou Meltzer is Curator of the William Fehr Collection, Cape Town.

Susan Newton-King is Lecturer in History at the University of the Western Cape.

Robert Ross is Co-ordinator of Afrikanistiek at Rijksuniversiteit te Leiden.

Christopher Saunders is Associate Professor of History at the University of Cape Town.

Pamela Scully completed her doctorate at the University of Michigan.

Kerry Ward completed her MA at the University of Cape Town and is currently a doctoral student at the University of Michigan.

Nigel Worden is Associate Professor of History at the University of Cape Town.

- ABBREVIATIONS -

CA   Cape Archives
LMS   London Missionary Society
PRO   Public Record Office, London
SOAS   School of Oriental and African Studies, University of London
VOC   Vereenigde Oostindische Compagnie (Dutch East India Company)

- GLOSSARY -

bijwoonder/bywoner   a sub-farmer or sharecropper working part of another person's land giving either a share of the profits or labour or both in exchange.

burgerraad   burgher council.

burgher   citizen, with militia duties, of the Cape Colony.

ghoemaliedjies   literally 'drum songs', also known as 'straatliedjies' (street songs) or 'Malay picnic songs'. They originated as slave songs in Cape Town.

Heemraad/heemraden   district council assisting the Landdrost in the local court consisting of himself and three local burghers appointed as heemraden.

huisboorling(en)   child(ren) indentured to the farmer on whose land they were born and raised.

inboekseling(en)   child(ren), adult(s) or manumitted slave(s) who were 'ingeboekt' (registered) or apprenticed to a particular master for a certain number of years.

knecht   labourer or foreman, usually white and hired from the VOC (from Dutch 'servant').

krijgsgevangen(en)   prisoner(s) of war.

krijgsraad   council of war.

Landdrost   magistrate with jurisdiction over a particular district or *drosty*.

opgaaf records   annual register of burgher families, slaves and produce.

rixdollar   the monetary unit of the Cape under the VOC and in use until 1825.

sjambok   a heavy whip made of hide; to beat or thrash somebody with this.

strooijhuijs   farm labourer's hut built in traditional style.

tronk   jail.

veeboer(en)   stock farmer(s) or grazier(s).

veld(t)corporaal/veld(t)cornet   burgher appointed by the VOC as local militia officer.

veldwagtmeester   earlier designation of a veldcornet.

voorhuis   entrance hall of a Dutch house, usually large enough to be a general sitting-room.

vrouw   a married woman, usually Dutch; mistress of a household.

werf   area, often enclosed, including homestead, barns and other outbuildings; roughly equivalent to a farmstead or yard.

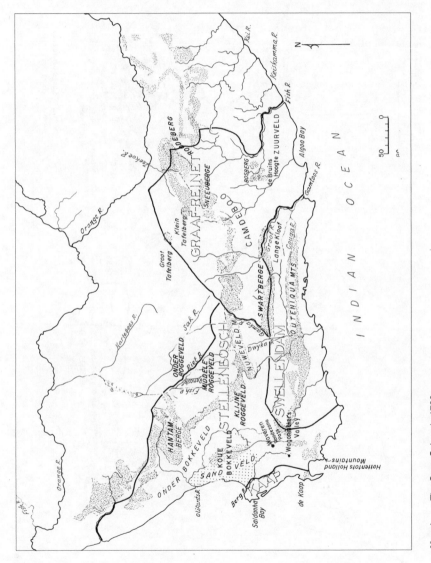

Map 1   The Cape Colony in 1786.

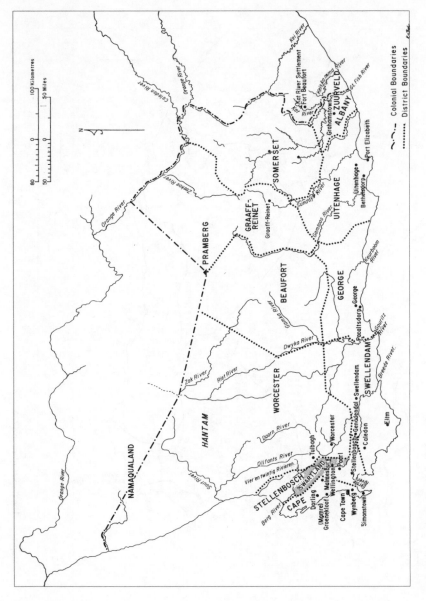

Map 2 The Cape Colony in 1830.

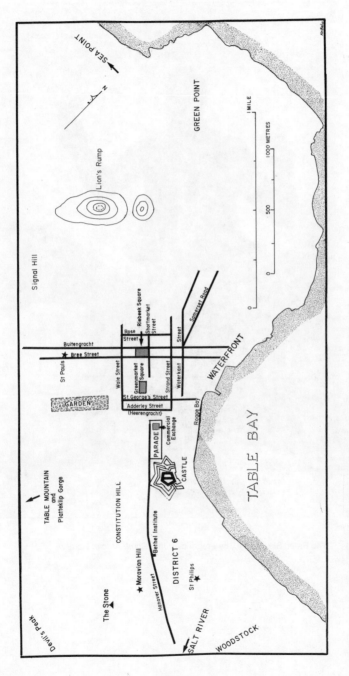

Map 3 Nineteenth-Century Cape Town.

XIII

Plate 1   The Freed Slave, 1840, by Frederick I'Ons. *South African Library.*

INTRODUCTION

− NIGEL WORDEN & CLIFTON CRAIS −

From the perspectives of popular memory and the scholarly literatures on the history of unfree labour and South Africa, slavery and emancipation in the nineteenth-century Cape Colony appears both undramatic and inconsequential. The wheat and wine estates of the western Cape, where the majority of slaves lived and laboured, paled in comparison with the sugar, tobacco and cotton plantations of the Americas. As far as Europe was concerned, the Cape, founded in 1652 as a refuelling stop for ships destined for the more interesting and more profitable East Indies, was never more than a two-bit player in an expanding capitalist world economy. In contrast to the West Indies, which provided an important market for the national economies of Europe, even in the best of economic times the Cape never played even a minor part in Europe's industrial revolution.[1]

The incorporation of the Cape Colony into the British Empire, first in 1795 and for a second and final time in 1806, maintained this slave economy at the southern tip of Africa. But in comparison to other slave societies in the early nineteenth-century Atlantic world, the Cape seems to be of little significance. Its slave population never exceeded 40,000. This was minuscule compared to the 167,000 slaves in Jamaica in 1768, the 1,700,000 slaves in Brazil in the 1850s, and, in the United States, the roughly 4,000,000 slaves on the eve of the great Civil War of 1862–7.[2] Focus by historians on the Atlantic slave trade has also marginalized the Cape, since most of the slaves imported in the oceanic trade to the Cape came instead from the Indian sub-continent and the Indonesian archipelago.

---

1   See E. Williams, *Capitalism and Slavery* (Chapel Hill, 1944); B. L. Solow, *Slavery and the Rise of the Atlantic System* (Cambridge, 1991); E. R. Wolf, *Europe and the People Without History* (Berkeley and Los Angeles, 1982), esp. pp. 195–231.

2   These numbers are taken from H. S. Klein, *African Slavery in Latin America and the Caribbean* (New York, 1986).

There was also little of the grand drama at the Cape that drives the
narratives of standard histories of slavery and emancipation in many other
regions. Until very recently the conventional wisdom has been that in the fair
Cape, with its production of the more genteel crops of wheat and wine,
slavery was somehow 'mild'. Unlike Brazil, Jamaica and, most notably,
Saint Domingue, where slaves staged a successful political revolution, there
were no major slave revolts in the Cape. And unlike the United States, the
ending of the 'peculiar institution' did not require a bloody war. According
to most of the general histories of South Africa written in the first seven
decades of the twentieth century, slavery began inconspicuously in 1658
with the importation of slaves from the west coast of Africa, and collapsed in
the 1830s with little more than a whimper of protest. Whereas in much of the
rest of the colonial world the ending of slavery was a time of high drama and
frequent tragedy, in the Cape slavery ended relatively inconspicuously.

Given this seemingly anaemic past, it is not surprising that very few comparative studies of slavery and emancipation even mention the Cape, let
alone engage in any extended discussion of it. Historians of South Africa
also have tended to look beyond the colonial world that created the bucolic
estates of the western Cape, where, today, tourists sip fine wine and the
descendants of slaves continue their work beneath the Cape sun. Early historians generally focused on the obstreperous and colourful frontier of the
eighteenth century, an area many scholars still believe was largely devoid of
a substantial population of slaves.[3] Subsequent historians generally followed
the lead of their predecessors, driving past the manor-houses of the slaveholding gentry, pressing beyond the Cape frontier, across the Orange River,
and on to the dramatic developments which followed the discovery of precious minerals at the end of the nineteenth century. So rapid was the pace of
historical change, so massive were the implications of the industrial revolution to the subsequent history of southern Africa, that the pre-industrial past
of the Cape seemed relatively insignificant. At best, a mere prologue to the
more interesting and more important and dramatic forging of a modern capitalist economy, slavery seemed economically inconsequential and emancipation historiographically irrelevant.[4]

This volume presents a different viewpoint. Our intent is not only to
resuscitate and make 'visible' the Cape's nineteenth-century history of

3   See, for example, W. G. James and M. Simons, *The Angry Divide: Social and Economic History of the
Western Cape* (Cape Town, 1989).

4   The literature on the mineral revolution is now immense. For a useful introduction see S. Marks and R.
Rathbone (eds.), *Industrialisation and Social Change in South Africa: African Class Formation, Culture
and Consciousness, 1870–1930* (London, 1982). An important collection of essays on pre-industrial
South Africa, published in 1980, made no reference to Cape slavery or to emancipation: S. Marks and A.
Atmore (eds.), *Economy and Society in Pre-Industrial South Africa* (London, 1980). But by the mid
1980s this neglect of the subject was beginning to be redressed. See, for example, R. Ross, *Cape of*

slavery and emancipation, but, as importantly, to suggest the ways in which an analysis of this era may lead to a rethinking of some of the most important developments in the history of South Africa. Throughout our discussions, research and writing, which have taken place over five years on three continents, we have been guided by a recognition that the history of labour in South Africa—whether slave or free—cannot be divorced from broader discussions of culture, ideology, and polity. We also have been guided by a critical engagement with the ways in which much of the social and economic history of modern South Africa has been the history of unfree labour. This point is not novel. Over the past two decades the history of labour has come to the centre of the exploration of South Africa's past. But despite the new attention to the study of labour, slavery (and the colonial era of which it was a part) has only recently come under closer historical scrutiny. As we shall outline at the end of this introductory essay, and as a number of the authors of the chapters in this volume will argue, this empirical and historiographical lacuna raises broader questions and issues concerning the periodization of modern South African history.

The essays in this volume focus not on the founding of a slave society during the late 1600s and its development in the subsequent century, but rather on the 'long' nineteenth century. This work has been informed by the new literature on the nineteenth century that has emerged in disciplines such as cultural history and literary theory, and on topics ranging from slavery to sexuality, the state and the body. Historians writing primarily on Europe have bracketed this 'long century' by the political revolutions of the late eighteenth century and the First World War of 1914–18. It was an era of great transformation, bearing witness to the rise of industrial capitalism and those important social and cultural shifts scholars typically include under that evocative and elusive term 'modernity'. As the historian of Jamaican slavery and labour, Thomas Holt, has written, this period was marked 'not so much by the calendar as by the transformations in the lives of human beings and human societies', a 'great watershed of human history, encompassing fundamental changes in how human beings relate to nature and to each other'.[5]

In South Africa, 1795 and 1902 are the more appropriate dates. The 'long century' arrived with the political investiture of British rule. This event marked the further incorporation of the Cape into the world economy, and

Torments: Slavery and Resistance in South Africa (London, 1983); N. Worden, *Slavery in Dutch South Africa* (Cambridge, 1985); R. Ross, 'The Origins of Capitalist Agriculture in the Cape Colony: A Survey', in W. Beinart, P. Delius and S. Trapido (eds.), *Putting a Plough to the Ground: Accumulation and Dispossession in Rural South Africa, 1850–1930* (Johannesburg, 1986), pp. 56–100.

5   T. C. Holt, *The Problem of Freedom: Race, Labor, and Politics in Jamaica and Britain, 1832–8* (Baltimore, 1992), p. 3.

was accompanied by a revolt of Khoikhoi serfs and peons and the dawn of a century of war along the colonial frontier in the eastern Cape. It ended with the carnage of the South African War of 1899–1902, the consolidation of an industrial capitalist economy, and the rise of new political élites and political movements among Africans and Afrikaners.

An age of great transformation, the 'long century' was also a time of paradox and hypocrisy. In Britain, this period saw the rise of liberalism and the emancipatory discourses of abolition, a heady ideological stew of evangelicalism, the new liberal political economy, and the domestic crises bequeathed by industrial capitalist development.[6] In the periphery, the late eighteenth and early nineteenth centuries bore witness to a massive expansion of slavery and the Atlantic slave trade. In Africa, Europe's great 'Age of Democratic Revolution' was a great age of servile labour and the traffic in human flesh. In the mid nineteenth century, European powers played a central role in the destruction of the slave societies they had created, but, in the process, abolitionism and the ending of the slave trade led quite directly to the creation of modern colonialism in Africa. Thus the great abolitionist, Thomas Fowell Buxton, would 'complain that our government has been too slow…in accepting territory' in Africa.[7] This association of enlightened practice with colonial expansion was especially true in South Africa. The first half of the nineteenth century saw the systematic and bloody extension of British colonial rule over once independent African communities along the Cape Colony's eastern frontier. By the late 1860s, the land between the Keiskamma and Kei rivers would be fully incorporated into the Cape Colony. In the 1840s the British annexed Natal. And, further in the interior, the Voortrekkers of the Great Trek of 1834–42 progressively extended their domination over African communities in Natal and what would late become the Orange Free State and the South African Republic.[8]

The paradoxes of liberal political contract and slavery, freedom and servitude, abolitionism and empire, were only a few among many in an age of contradiction and dilemma. There was another historical paradox that is especially apposite to students of South African history: the relationship between the ending of slavery and the rise of modern racism. For, as Nancy Stepan has written, 'just as the battle against slavery was being won by the abolitionists, the war against racism was being lost.'[9]

---

6   For the latest in an extensive literature on the English abolitionist movement and its ideological constructs, see D. Turley, *The Culture of English Antislavery, 1780–1860* (London and New York, 1991).

7   See T. F. Buxton, *The African Slave Trade*, 2 vols. (New York, 1840), vol. 2, pp. 163–8; D. B. Davis, *Slavery and Human Progress* (New York, 1984).

8   See C. Crais, *The Making of the Colonial Order: White Supremacy and Black Resistance in the Eastern Cape, 1770–1865* (Cambridge and Johannesburg, 1992); L. Thompson, *A History of South Africa* (New Haven, 1990), esp. pp. 31–69.

9   N. Stepan, *The Idea of Race and Science: Great Britain, 1800–1960* (London, 1983), p. 1.

The rise and decline of colonial slavery took place within the context of the consolidation of the capitalist world economy and of fundamental cultural and ideological shifts in the ways in which people conceived of the economy, labour and time. Where slavery was the dominant form of the organization of labour, emancipation 'threw open the most fundamental questions of economy, society and polity'.[10] However, in South Africa and throughout much of the colonial world, emancipation saw less the creation of free labour than the forging of new systems of coercion and exploitation which in many cases would endure well into the twentieth century.[11] Historians of slavery and emancipation working elsewhere, often from very different perspectives, have begun to notice the ways in which the debates over the 'peculiar institution' and the ending of slavery raised important questions concerning perceptions and practices of the private and the public, and the conduct and structure of the state. We are only just beginning to understand the ways in which, for instance, issues concerning the family, gender, and sexuality were entwined with the creation of modern economic classes and political institutions.[12]

At the political heart of the 'long century' was the creation of the modern state. This brute fact of political history is especially important for the history of South Africa because the first half of the nineteenth century essentially witnessed a transition from a world of personal rule to the rule of the state. Both the dominant and the subordinate sought access to state power. It was through the state that chattel labourers brought the entire system of slavery under greater scrutiny. And it was through the state that ex-slaveholders reasserted their control of the newly free in the creation of South Africa's first wage-earning working class. The century witnessed the legislative amelioration of slavery during the 1820s, the easing of the serf-like control over Khoi and San labourers in 1828, and the ending of chattel slavery between 1834 and 1838. But in the aftermath of these apparent breakings of the chains of bondage, new laws were promulgated which aimed at controlling black labour. Most infamous was the Masters and Servants legislation, first introduced in the wake of slave emancipation in 1841 and made increasingly restrictive as employers exerted a greater sway over the state in the mid and later nineteenth century. This was far more stringent than similar legislation in the British Caribbean and, in South Africa, it was only abolished over a century later, in 1974.[13]

---

10 E. Foner, *Nothing But Freedom: Emancipation and Its Legacy* (Baton Rouge, 1983), p. 1.

11 See Wolf, *Europe and the People Without History.*

12 See C. Hall, *White, Male and Middle Class: Explorations in Feminism and History* (Cambridge, 1992). For this approach at the Cape, see n. 31 below.

13 See C. Bundy, 'The Abolition of the Masters and Servants Act', *South African Labour Bulletin*, 2, 1 (1975), pp. 37–46.

The early and mid nineteenth-century Cape is rising from its historiographical slumber to emerge as a formative juncture in the modern history of South Africa. Here was created a labour-repressive economy where workers may not have been slaves, but where they were certainly not free. Modern racism arose in this complex reworking of domination at Africa's southern tip. The lines of these historical developments are only just beginning to surface in the on-going reconstruction of the South African past. But what is becoming increasingly clear is that the era that witnessed the ending of slavery in the Cape constitutes a kind of connective historical tissue uniting the beginnings of colonialism with the historical developments of the industrial era.

At the end of the 1980s the work available on slavery at the Cape focused primarily on the period of Dutch East India Company (VOC) rule in the seventeenth and eighteenth centuries.[14] This was the heyday of the slave system, associated with the evolution of a distinct settler society and economy. By the time the VOC relinquished control of the colony to the British in 1795, settler structures had spread geographically from their origins in the arable farming hinterland of Cape Town, to reach the dry lands of the Karoo and the pastoral farms of Graaff-Reinet in the east. Stratification of settler wealth accompanied the dispersal of European settlement, with slave ownership acting as a powerful measure of prosperity and status.[15] Increasing numbers of slaves were imported from elsewhere in Africa, and south and south-east Asia, but as the eighteenth century progressed, access to manumission and to land or independent status for those of non-settler origin was severely restricted.[16] Those indigenous Khoi and San who remained after the depredations of commando raids, disease and flight deeper into the interior of the continent, were steadily incorporated as labourers and servants into the bottom ranks of settler society.[17] Although their legal position theoretically may

---

14   Notably J. Armstrong, 'The Slaves, 1652–1795', in R. Elphick and H. Giliomee (eds.), *The Shaping of South African Society, 1652–1820*, 1st. edn. (London and Cape Town, 1979), pp. 75–115; Ross, *Cape of Torments*; Worden, *Slavery in Dutch South Africa*; Robert Shell 'Slavery at the Cape of Good Hope, 1680 to 1731', 2 vols. (Ph.D. thesis, Yale University, 1986). For an account of key developments in Cape slave historiography, see N. Southey, 'From Periphery to Core: The Treatment of Cape Slavery in South African Historiography', *Historia*, 37, 2 (1992), pp. 13–25.

15   R. Ross, 'The Rise of the Cape Gentry', *Journal of Southern African Studies*, 9, 2 (1983), pp. 193–217; L. Guelke and R. Shell, 'An Early Colonial Landed Gentry: Land and Wealth in the Cape Colony, 1682–1731', *Journal of Historical Geography*, 9 (1983), pp. 265–86; P. van Duin and R. Ross, *The Economy of the Cape Colony in the Eighteenth Century*, Intercontinenta, no. 5 (Leiden, 1985).

16   R. Elphick and R. Shell, 'Intergroup Relations: Khoikhoi, Settlers, Slaves and Free Blacks, 1652–1795', and R. Elphick and H. Giliomee, 'The Origins and Entrenchment of European Dominance at the Cape, 1652–c.1840', both in Elphick and Giliomee *The Shaping of South African Society, 1652–1840*, 2nd. edn. (London and Cape Town, 1989), pp. 184–239, 521–66; L. Hattingh, *Die Eerste Vryswartes van Stellenbosch, 1679–1720* (Bellville, 1981).

17   For recent work on this see S. Newton-King, 'The Enemy Within: The Struggle for Ascendancy on the Eastern Cape Frontier, 1760–99' (Ph.D. thesis, London University, 1992); N. Penn, 'Labour, Land and

have differed from that of imported slaves, in practice the Dutch Cape had produced a broad underclass of both indigenous peons and imported slaves.[18]

Despite important processes of local stratification and economic change, the VOC period was unified by the essential structures of its political economy. Ruled as an outpost of a commercial trading company which was concerned primarily with the extraction of meat and grain for the provision of ships from its more lucrative stations in the Indian Ocean, Cape settler society was little affected by the major booms and slumps of the world economy which dominated the colonial slave systems of the New World in the seventeenth and eighteenth centuries. The VOC's vision of the Cape settlement as a supplier, rather than a producer and manufacturer, crippled the emergence of a local mercantile community of the kind which flourished in Latin America and the northern American colonies by the middle of the eighteenth century.[19] And the VOC monopolized administration and government: there was no equivalent to the settler assemblies of the Caribbean or North America.

These features of the Cape's early colonial political economy have defined the way in which its slave system was analysed. Work over the past decade has revealed much about the economic role of slavery in the rural economy of the colony, the forms of overt and covert resistance which took place by the bonded, and the extent to which slavery provided an impetus for the rise of racial and class identities in the Dutch settlement. These concerns have raised broader issues and debates on the nature of the power and authority that owners exerted over their labourers, and especially the extent to which force, either overt or implicit, conditioned that relationship.[20] From the mid 1980s historians of Cape slavery had begun moving from an earlier concern with political economy and resistance to an engagement with

---

Livestock in the Western Cape During the Eighteenth Century: The Khoisan and the Colonists', in W. James and M. Simons (eds.), *The Angry Divide: Social and Economic History of the Western Cape* (Cape Town, 1989), pp. 2–19, and his forthcoming Ph.D. thesis, University of Cape Town; R. Viljoen, 'Khoisan Labour Relations in the Overberg Districts During the Latter Half of the Eighteenth Century, *c.*1755–95' (MA thesis, University of the Western Cape, 1993) specifically examines the position of Khoi labourers on western Cape farms.

18   R. Ross, 'The Changing Legal Position of the Khoisan in the Cape Colony, 1652–1795', *African Perspectives* (1979), pp. 67–87, and in R. Ross, *Beyond the Pale: Essays on the History of Colonial South Africa* (Hanover, 1993 and Johannesburg, 1994), pp. 166–80.

19   F.W. Knight and P.K. Liss (eds.), *Atlantic Port Cities: Economy, Culture and Society in the Atlantic World, 1650–1850* (Knoxville, 1991) reveals the full extent of this process.

20   Ross, *Cape of Torments* and Worden, *Slavery in Dutch South Africa* stressed the coercive aspects of the relationship. R. Shell has emphasized the incorporative role of the settler farm family, which treated slaves as children of the patriarchal unit; see 'The Family and Slavery at the Cape, 1680–1808', in James and Simons (eds.), *The Angry Divide*, pp. 20–30, and *Children of Bondage: A Social History of the Slave Society at the Cape of Good Hope*, 1652–1834 (Middletown, 1994). The debate is still far from concluded: for a historiographical critique of the issues, see P. van der Spuy, 'Gender and Slavery at the Cape of Good Hope with a Focus on the 1820s' (MA thesis, University of Cape Town, 1993), ch. 2.

questions of culture and society. At the same time there was also a shift towards the nineteenth century.[21] There were both practical and conceptual reasons for this changing focus. Although much remained (and still remains) to be written about bonded labour in the VOC era, the field of slave studies seemed unusually wide open for the last 40 years of its official existence. By the end of the 1980s there was an emerging consensus that fundamental changes took place in the slave society of the early nineteenth century which were to crucially shape the fabric of Cape society. These influences are still felt today.

International trends away from the study of slavery itself to the processes of emancipation and post-emancipation structures in other settler societies influenced Cape researchers. There was, however, an additional reason. For historians based in Cape Town, many of whom were students formulating research topics, these broader historiographical trends in the study of slavery and emancipation were unfolding at the height of the mass campaigns of the mid 1980s. The inequalities of race and class, and the increasing radicalization of consciousness and forms of resistance, were raising vital questions about the historical legacies of the region. Slavery, it seemed, was a key component of the past of this part of South Africa, and the legacy of its removal was still all too apparent.[22]

It was in this context that new researchers and the older first generation of revisionist slave historians began to ask new questions which vitally extended and developed our understanding of Cape slavery and its aftermath. This book is a presentation of the findings of their work. It stems from a conference held at the University of Cape Town in 1989, at which 26 papers were presented,[23] many of them describing work in progress. This volume is not merely a reproduction of disparate papers but rather reflects the considerable refinement and modification of initial ideas that has taken place in the four years since the conference was held. And although the contributions to this book are all individual essays in their own right, collectively they present a cohesive and novel view of the nature and significance of slavery to the Cape Colony and South Africa as a whole in the 'long century'.

21   Two important Ph.D. theses appeared during this period, unfortunately neither of them have been published: M. Rayner 'Wine and Slaves: The Failure of an Export Economy and the Ending of Slavery in the Cape Colony, South Africa, 1806–34' (Ph.D. thesis, Duke University, 1986), and J. Marinkowitz, 'Rural Production and Labour in the Western Cape, With Special Reference to the Wheat-Growing Districts' (Ph.D. thesis, University of London, 1985).

22   For further discussion of the increasing interest in slavery in relation to the events of the 1980s in the western Cape, see G. Cuthbertson, 'Cape Slave Historiography and the Question of Intellectual Dependence', *South African Historical Journal*, 27 (1992), pp. 35–6.

23   The conference entitled 'Cape Slavery—And After' is discussed in A. Bank, 'History Conference—Cape Slavery', *Southern African Discourse*, 1 (1989), p. 68. We are grateful to the University of Cape Town for the grant which made the conference possible. Several of the papers have been published elsewhere: N. Penn, 'Droster Gangs of the Bokkeveld and the Roggeveld, 1770–1800', *South African Historical*

The first five essays deal with the continuities, changes and realignments of Cape slave society in the period between the last decades of VOC rule and the eve of emancipation in the 1830s. They raise themes of the interconnections of economic, political and ideological factors which are developed throughout the volume.

Wayne Dooling sets the framework for this development. He shows that the role of law and the inter-relationship of the legal structures and the values and perceptions of the slaveowner community were vital. Cape slaveowners never had the absolute power of some of their New World counterparts. In contrast to many of the settler ruled colonies of the New World, the VOC local state operated a legal system to which they were, at least partially, subordinated. Roman law, even as modified at the Cape by Batavian and local statute, gave a theoretical universality of access to state law. However, the rule of VOC law was far from status-blind. The hierarchies of status and power in settler society were fundamental, and the subordination of servants and slave to master and owner was paramount in the maintenance of social order. What is important in this balance of universal access to law and maintenance of hierarchy, is the emphasis which the courts placed on the public reputation of slaveowners within the local community. The law upheld the social hierarchy, but not by unequivocally supporting all slaveowners. Settlers who, for instance, severely maltreated their slaves or servants, could be brought to check by the intervention of the law, and bonded workers could bring complaints or evidence against them. However this was not an automatic right. Dooling shows that it was those owners who had forfeited their honour and their reputation within the settler community by transgressing accepted notions of appropriate behaviour, who were most likely to be punished. In such cases, slaves often appealed to neighbours and even their owners' kin, in bids for redress against maltreatment and abuse.

In the course of the early nineteenth century, new perceptions of state intervention, law and authority began to emerge. There was a shift from a system which recognized status as a key determinant of access to law to one which, in theory at least, was 'no respecter of persons'. During the 1820s and 1830s a number of new 'ameliorative' laws sought to intervene more directly

Journal, 23 (1990), pp. 15–40; E. Bradlow, 'Mental Illness or Resistance?: The Case of Soera Brotto', Kleio, 23 (1991), pp. 4–16; R. Shell, 'The Synod of Dort and Cape Slavery, 1618–1838' and 'Tender Ties: The Women of the Slave Society', both in Children of Bondage; W. Dooling, 'Slavery and Amelioration in the Graaff-Reinet District, 1823–30', South African Historical Journal, 27 (1992), pp. 75–94; J. Mason, 'Hendrik Albertus and his Ex-Slave Mey: A Drama in Three Acts', Journal of African History, 31 (1990); R. Ross, 'The Etiquette of Race', in Ross, Beyond the Pale, pp. 111–21; C. Crais, 'Slavery and Freedom Along a Frontier: The Eastern Cape, 1770–1838', Slavery and Abolition, 17 (1991), pp. 190–215; P. Scully, 'Liquor and Labour in the Western Cape, 1870–1900', in J. Crush and C. Ambler (eds.), Liquor and Labour in Southern Africa (Athens, 1992), pp. 56–77; M. Adhikari, 'The Sons of Ham: Slavery and the Making of Coloured Identity', South African Historical Journal, 27 (1992), pp. 95–113.

in the relationship of owners and slaves by, for instance, prescribing levels of domestic punishment, food, clothing allowances and working hours. This was a much more assertive and intrusive regulation of the world of labour by the state than previously, prefiguring the decisive intervention of total emancipation by decrees of the Westminster and colonial authorities in the 1830s. Between 1826 and 1838 a succession of state officials, many from outside the colony, were appointed to redress slave grievances against owners who failed to uphold the new regulations. Dooling shows that this called the reputations of owners into question much more frequently, and with more rigidity, than previously. Nonetheless community norms and values still prevailed, particularly when, in criminal cases after 1827, the jury system allowed for judgement of slaveowners by their peers. The intervention of the 'public' British state into the 'private' world of owners and slaves thus formed part of a larger pattern of governance at the Cape. And although owners riled against state intervention into their private patriarchal world, and contradictions between law and honour emerged, the hegemonic function of maintenance of social hierarchy and order was not disturbed.

John Mason also examines the implications of this public intervention at the level of the private domestic sphere and argues for an important shift in the consciousness of both owners and slaves during the decades before final emancipation. Using cases of complaint brought by rural slaves against their owners in the 1820s and 1830s, he shows how the bonds of patriarchy and paternalism which knit together the owner-slave relationship were, at least partially, weakened by the interventions of new liberal laws and magistrates. Slaves now appealed to new authorities in assertion of their rights and were no longer, as under the VOC, dependent upon support from their owners' neighbours. At least some owners submitted to the supremacy of this external authority, sometimes to the extent of releasing their slaves (or apprentices as they were known from 1834 to 1838) from their bondage.

This was a change in degree rather than character from the situation at the start of the nineteenth century. As Mason emphasizes, although there were important shifts which challenged the chains which bound slaves to their owners, the old order of forced deference and the daily rituals which reinforced the unequal paternalism of settler labour relations continued to thrive in the farms and households of the colony. There was, thus, no single direction of change; both owners and slaves responded in widely differing ways to their situations. Women slaves, in particular, were less able to free themselves from the chains of dependency. But there were, nonetheless, clear signs that by the decade of formal emancipation, a degree of 'ideological confusion' had emerged which fundamentally challenged the assumptions of paternalism and power that had earlier underpinned the slave system of the colony.

Mason's exploration of the weakening of rural slaveholder *mentalité* in the twilight years of chattel slavery is paralleled by Andrew Bank's analysis of the structural erosion of slavery in the colony's only significant urban centre during the early nineteenth century. Dutch Cape Town relied heavily on slave labour. Important economic shifts in the subsequent decades of British rule ended this situation. The flow of slave imports to the town, which had increased during the last decades of the eighteenth century, was stemmed when the external slave trade was outlawed in 1807. In addition, a redeployment of slave labour from Cape Town to the vineyards of its hinterland was encouraged by the temporary opening of the British market to Cape wines as a result of preferential tariffs between 1813 and 1825.[24] The emergence of a new class of British-based merchant capitalists in the city, bringing with them ideas of the efficiency and reliability of wage labour, further weakened the hold that slave ownership had exercised over the labour market of Cape Town. As economic activity increased, and as wage labour became more prevalent, both the hiring out of slaves and their manumission became more widespread.

But the erosion of urban slavery was not solely economic. The 'ideological confusion' identified by Mason for the rural areas was even more acute in the city. Bank points to the problems of maintaining discipline and control over a servile labour force in the physically expanding city; the fragmentation of increasingly complex ruling classes—British/Dutch, slaveowner/non-slaveowner, merchant/non-merchant, although not all of these categories were self-contained—and the increasingly evident and assertive underclass culture which was shaping itself in the context of manumission and a higher ratio of locally-born slaves with the ending of imports. Together with transformation from above came challenges from below. Some, such as desertion, were overt. Others, such as growing conversion to Islam and construction of family kinship networks between free and unfree, were less immediately challenging but nonetheless significant. In Cape Town the chains of bondage were weakening before formal emancipation, and even more effectively than on the farms of the rural interior.

Internal ideological, economic and social changes thus undermined chattel slavery at the Cape before the axing of the institution by fiat of Westminster in 1833. Yet, as Christopher Saunders reminds us, freedom from formal slave status did not necessarily imply a greater measure of economic independence or social mobility. Taking as a litmus test the 'Prize Negroes' who were indentured at the colony after being rescued from foreign slavers, he demonstrates that the terms of their indenture and apprenticeship

---

24   Rayner, 'Wine and Slaves'.

differed little with regard to treatment and status from that of chattel slaves. Indeed contemporaries often referred to them as 'Prize Slaves'. Corruption by the officials appointed to distribute their services effectively annulled attempts by the state to oversee their welfare. And, as newcomers, they had less access to the urban underclass network of Cape Town than formal slaves, although there is evidence that in time many of them converted to Islam. The continued apprenticeship of Prize Negroes in the 1840s, after the end of slavery itself, blurred, as Saunders stresses, the distinction between slave and free and raises the question as to just how much of a turning point formal emancipation was for the labour structures of the colony. A pattern was beginning to emerge. Slaveowner power had never been absolute at the Cape, but it was being challenged further by the interventions of the state in the 1820s and by shifts in the economy as liberal and mercantile influences were felt. Yet the ending of slavery was not intended to produce any degree of social or economic opportunity for the labourers of the colony. The case of the 'Prize Negroes' had already demonstrated this before 1834 and merely confirmed the fact in the 1840s.

Ameliorative measures, the erosion of urban slavery, and the 'ideological confusion' initiated by the British in the first three decades of their rule in the Cape highlights the central four years from 1834–8 when slaves were 'apprenticed' to their owners. Nigel Worden shows how the ostensible purpose of this interval between slavery and formal freedom, this ambivalent loosening of the chains of slavery, was to prepare both employers and slaves for the realities of wage labour. In one sense this was a further intensification of state intervention in the domestic sphere of labour relations in the transition from the personal rule of patriarchal slavery to the rule of the bureaucratic state. And although coercive regulations demanded by colonists, such as a Vagrancy Law, were overruled by the Governor and by the Colonial Office, in many ways the apprenticeship period gave greater support to the continuity of a stable labour force under the control of settlers than had been the case in the 1820s and early 1830s. Apprenticeship regulations were frequently more coercive than those under the slave ameliorative legislation. And certainly the government did not intend to train apprentices for a future of economic or social independence. Rather the weight of the state was reorientated towards the production of a compliant and tractable labour force. Specially-appointed magistrates implemented a highly-regulated system of penalties against apprentices who resisted this moulding, and they used imprisonment extensively as a reforming and character-building punishment. Absolute authority over workers was still being taken out of the hands of their owner-employers. Nonetheless, slave 'apprenticeship' bore more relation to the indigenous patterns of coercive indenture of Khoi and Prize

Negroes than to the metropolitan notion of training for a skilled job.

The goals of emancipation were clearly revealed: the replacement of slaveowner arbitrary tyranny by a more powerful state regulation of labour, but one which would continue to ensure the maintenance of social hierarchy and inequality of race and class. Some colonists who lacked the status and capital to benefit from such a nurtured order, rejected emancipation by trekking out of the colony, but the majority were reconciled to the prospect of emancipation.

Yet the prospect of imminent freedom gave the apprentices the incentive to claim a new independence which went further than that asserted under the last years of slavery. In 1838 the contest of wills was ready to be played out between a state which planned the continuation of a stable and controlled labour force, differing only from that desired by settler producers in the extent to which it was prepared to endorse overt coercion, and the freed people, many of whom had other ideas of establishing themselves and their families in an independent livelihood. The literal chains of slavery were broken but it remained to be seen how far the less tangible markers of oppression were to be overcome.

The essays by Ross, Meltzer and Scully demonstrate the uneven outcome of such a contest. Robert Ross shows the dependence of the pre-emancipation Cape economy on unfree labour, both slave and Khoi, and outlines the vision of abolitionists both in Britain and the Cape for a stable wage labour force without disruption to rural production. Both Ordinance 50, releasing the Khoi from enserfment, and slave emancipation were the results. In terms of production levels in the decades after 1838, he demonstrates that the Cape was one of the few British slave colonies where abolitionist goals were fulfilled. In striking contrast to many Caribbean islands where the old slave plantation system collapsed, Cape producers who had depended on slaves were able to maintain, and even to slightly expand, their output. Nor did they obtain new external sources of indentured labour, as in Mauritius or Jamaica.[25] Ross's analysis of the post-emancipation rural economy eliminates several possible economic explanations for this survival of settler production methods. Wool production significantly expanded in the mid nineteenth century, but other sectors of the rural economy which had previously depended on slavery saw no significant expansion of external markets, increase in productivity or insertion of capital.

---

25   W. Green, 'The West Indies and Indentured Labour Patterns—The Jamaican Experience', in K. Saunders (ed.), *Indentured Labour in the British Empire, 1834–1920* (London and Canberra, 1984), pp. 1–41, and M.D. North-Coombes, 'From Slavery to Indenture: Forced Labour in the Political Economy of Mauritius, 1834–67', in Saunders, *Indentured Labour*, pp. 78–125; N. Worden, 'Diverging Histories: Slavery and its Aftermath in the Cape Colony and Mauritius', *South African Historical Journal*, 27 (1992), pp. 3–25, discusses the contrasts of the post-emancipation labour structures of the Cape and Mauritius.

The reasons for the stability of agrarian production after emancipation were twofold. Firstly the colonial state continued to protect and encourage the existing social hierarchy of landowner employers and landless servants. It vetoed overtly coercive legislation, such as the proposed Vagrancy Ordinance of 1834, and it backed down on anti-squatting legislation in 1850–1 when the threat of open underclass rebellion loomed. Eastern Cape settlers engaged in wool farming were especially concerned with the 'squatting problem'. By and large, however, the Masters and Servants Ordinance of 1841 effectively maintained the class control of landholders. 'Servants' were to receive contracts, thus obviating the arbitrary controls of slavery, but in return deference, corporal punishment for desertion or subordination, long working hours, poor living conditions, and low wages were entrenched in criminal law. Increasingly severe penalties were imposed when the ordinance was renewed in 1856 after settlers had obtained access to representative government and the code remained the linchpin of settler land and labour control until well into the twentieth century.[26] In other words, the state continued its practice of intervention into the domain of rural labour relations, controlling arbitrary individual tyranny but maintaining the existing social hierarchy. In this it was following the patterns laid down from the VOC period, and intensified under amelioration and apprenticeship.

This is not to say that there was no change at all in the patterns of post-emancipation rural labour. The second reason cited by Ross for the stability of output after 1838 was one which he describes as fortuitous rather than planned. Arable production, mainly grain and wine, had never required a full-time labour force throughout the year. Both sectors were highly seasonal. Under slavery this had been problematic: what were owners to do with large numbers of slaves which they only required for ploughing, harvesting and grape picking? They solved the issue by diversifying their crops, and by hiring out their slaves, or relying on hiring those from kin and neighbours.[27] After emancipation, Cape farmers could replace their slave holdings with a smaller permanent labour force, supplemented by seasonal reapers, shearers, and grape-pickers. Since the opportunities for fully independent subsistence for many freed people was limited by the lack of readily available fertile land, seasonal workers were readily recruited at low wages from the towns, villages and mission stations dotted over the landscape of the rural Cape.[28] In

26   Bundy, 'Abolition of the Masters and Servants Act'; R. Winstain, 'The 1841 Masters and Servants Ordinance and the Structure of Post-Emancipation Social Relations in the Arable South-Western Cape' (BA Hons. thesis, University of Cape Town, 1990), and L. Whittaker, 'In the Shadow of Slavery: Masters and Servants in the Worcester District, 1839–45' (BA Hons. thesis, University of Cape Town, 1992) discuss the formulation and implementation of the Ordinance in the immediate post-emancipation years.

27   Worden, *Slavery in Dutch South Africa*, pp. 25–7.

the 1840s a new rural division of labour emerged in what Ross describes as a 'bifurcated labour force'. Firstly there were permanent workers whose lives differed little in material terms from those of the slaves of the previous decades. Many of them continued to live on the same farm and in outhouses as they had done before emancipation. Secondly there were seasonal workers with a resident base in another community, urban or mission station, who were able to assert a greater degree of independence. This division enabled Cape farmers to maintain their production levels, but it produced a new division which was to be etched on the social landscape of the western Cape to the present. On the one hand, there emerged a landless rural proletariat living on settler farms and, on the other, a more mobile freed population, although one still dependent on the settler dominated economy for employment.[29]

Thus emancipation stabilized rather than disrupted the rural economy of most of the areas where colonists had depended on the exploitation of slave labour. This stabilization came at the expense of the independence of freed people and in terms which liberals and abolitionists supported and the colonial state dictated. Lalou Meltzer demonstrates that in Cape Town too the ending of slavery failed to disrupt the city's economy but rather gave it a vital injection. The mercantile community of the city, as represented most forcefully by John Fairbairn's newspaper, *The South African Commercial Advertiser*, was fully behind the transition from slave to wage labour. Yet, at the same time, Cape Town merchants had been closely involved in the slave economy of the colony. Some were slaveowners themselves. Many others supplied mortgages with slaves as collateral, or gave credit for slave purchases, particularly during the wine boom years of the 1820s.

The new mercantile capital of early nineteenth-century Cape Town was involved in the slavery of the colony, if not on a scale equivalent to that of its North American counterpart. Meltzer shows that they were thus well placed to benefit from the £1.25 million of slave compensation money that was paid out by the British government as part of the emancipation deal. In contrast to the conventional belief of South African historiography, that compensation was tied up in London and never benefited the colonists, Meltzer shows that Cape Town merchants were well placed to benefit from this new capital resource, not only as agents and pursuers of claims for rural slaveowners but

---

28 On the movement of freed slaves in 1838, see N. Worden, 'Adjusting to Emancipation: Freed Slaves and Farmers in the Mid Nineteenth-Century South-Western Cape, 1834–56', in James and Simons, *Angry Divide*, pp. 31–9; Marinkowitz, 'Rural Production and Labour', ch. 1.

29 Case studies of the immediate post-emancipation western Cape which demonstrate this dichotomy are: E. Host, 'Capitalisation and Proletarianisation on a Western Cape Farm: Klaver Valley, 1812–98' (MA thesis, University of Cape Town, 1992), and H. Ludlow, 'Missions and Emancipation in the South-Western Cape: A Case Study of Groenekloof (Mamre), 1838–52' (MA thesis, University of Cape Town, 1992). The contributions of Bickford-Smith, ch. 11, and Ward, ch. 12, later in this volume, show the working out of this scenario at the end of the nineteenth century.

also as individuals with investment and stakes in slave property themselves.
She argues that emancipation gave a general boost to the economy of Cape
Town through this inflow of capital, as well as the changing market conditions that it brought. In ways anticipated and devoutly wished by Fairbairn
and his like-minded mercantile associates, freed people became consumers
of small-scale goods. The benefits which emancipation would bring to the
market was a key theme of the *Commercial Advertiser's* discourse throughout the 1820s and 1830s. In addition, one of the places to which some of the
freed people who left the farms headed, after 1838, was Cape Town, seeking
work in the more fluid labour market of the city. Few found prosperity there,
and wage levels quickly fell, but the increased numbers of rural migrants led
to massive demands for cheap housing and provided a fillip for slum property building and landlordism.

In other words, both compensation money and the changing market provided by emancipation gave a boost to the urban economy which benefited
primarily the mercantile sector. In particular, new small-scale joint stock
companies were formed, many of them utilizing new sources of local, rather
than metropolitan, capital. The years 1838–9 saw an important expansion of
the economic base of a local commercial bourgeoisie which was to have a
major impact on Cape Town's municipal and national politics, when the city
became the centre of a representative settler government in the 1850s.[30]

Slave emancipation thus brought a breaking of the literal chains of
bondage, but the economic benefits of freedom in both the rural and urban
sectors of the economy went to the ex-owners and new commercial élites
rather than to the freed people themselves. Pamela Scully focuses our attention on their experience of freedom. By examining the central issue of the
family, she adds the crucial dynamic of gender to studies of Cape slavery
and emancipation.[31] Through a case study of the rural districts of Worcester
and Swellendam between the onset of apprenticeship in 1834 and the post-
emancipation decade of the 1840s, she shows how the family became a central site of struggle between freed people, settler farmers, and the missionaries under whose control many of the ex-slaves who had left the farms placed
themselves. The intervention of the central state into the private sphere of
master-slave relations by the amelioration legislation of the 1820s provided a
challenge to the absolute control of the slaveowner patriarch over slave family relationships by, for instance, permitting marriage and offering some

---

30   See D. Warren, 'Merchants, Commissioners and Wardmasters: Municipal Politics in Cape Town,
     1840–54' (MA thesis, University of Cape Town, 1986).

31   This is a vital new area of Cape slave and emancipation work. See esp. P. Scully, 'Liberating the
     Family?: Gender, Labor and Sexuality in the Rural Western Cape, South Africa, 1823–53' (Ph.D. thesis,
     University of Michigan, 1993); P. van der Spuy, 'Gender and Slavery' (MA thesis, University of Cape
     Town, 1993) and her historiographical critique in 'Gender and Slavery: Towards a Feminist Revision',
     South African Historical Journal, 25 (1991), pp. 184–95.

protection from the sale of children separately from their mothers. Yet its real significance was the battle that slaves, and particularly slave women, were prepared to fight to maintain the unity of their kin group. Under apprenticeship this struggle intensified, especially as a loophole in the apprenticeship regulations enabled farmers to indenture children born to apprentice women well beyond the period of their mothers' bondage.

After 1838 a prime response of freed people was to reunite their fragmented families, either on farms or mission stations. But the perceptions of the state and of the missionaries ensured that a new pattern of gender relations emerged which adds an important dimension to the bifurcation of the labour force outlined by Ross. In the aftermath of slavery, freed people elaborated a sexual division of labour in which men engaged in permanent work on farms and women avoided farm labour when possible. An analysis of the Masters and Servants legislation reveals the inherently ambiguous status of women workers, especially married ones. The law guaranteed a male labourer primacy over his family relations. Granting him the decision-making power over the labour of the family, labour legislation tied married women workers to their husbands and rendered wives a subcategory of workers who required special mention and protection.[32]

Emancipation thus led to the restructuring of economic relationships, but with little disturbance to the hierarchy of power, wealth and status in the regions of the colony where slavery previously had played a vital role. State intervention and continued settler-class power were crucial in this process.

The essays by Newton-King and Crais turn our attention to the eastern districts of the colony where formal slavery had played a less central economic and social role, but where racial and class inequalities were similarly shaped and perpetuated as the frontier regions of the colony were brought in line with the patterns of the post-emancipation south and west, with an even greater intensity.

Susan Newton-King depicts the process by which, in the later eighteenth century, settler farmers acquired control over a servile labour force in ways which differed from those of their western Cape counterparts. The latter obtained slaves who had already been forcibly removed from their homelands by others, or the offspring of slave women already in the colony. In the Graaff-Reinet district it was the settlers themselves who forcefully extracted a labour force in the 1780s and 1790s, primarily from San prisoners captured in commando raids and from the offspring of Khoi women living on settler-occupied lands. The process was one of heightened violence, not only in the

---

32 Slave labour was never completely ungendered, but the construction of new notions of appropriate male and female labour roles was apparent during the amelioration period of the 1820s, and was intensified during the post-emancipation restructuring. See Van der Spuy, 'Gender and Slavery', ch. 1, as well as Scully, ch. 8 in this volume.

capture of labourers, but also to ensure that they remained on settler farms. Unlike the imported slaves, San and Khoi labourers had access to the world from which they had been removed, both in cultural and geographical terms. There was no total alienation from the societies in which they had been nurtured.[33] These labourers were not chattel slaves, and they could maintain a semblance of family and kin links and were not subject to arbitrary sale. As with slaves, the VOC state allowed them the right to complain against the worst abuses, but the highly-coercive system that evolved bore much resemblance to chattel slavery. However, unlike slaves, the labourers of Graaff-Reinet had retained sufficient cultural unity to organize widespread resistance, and the eastern Cape Khoi rebellion of 1799–1801 marked the power of that resistance.

The revolt was finally crushed, and with firm results. The new British state ensured that Khoi and San labourers would be subjected to tight controls, tying them to settler farms. Under the 1809 Caledon Code, labourers were required to maintain a 'fixed place of abode'. They were also issued with passes by their masters or by a local official.[34] The legislation effectively controlled the access of Khoi and San to mission stations and waste land, and entrenched their servile status within the Cape's political economy. Indeed, by the 1810s Khoisan workers on settler farms were as firmly enchained as their slave counterparts.

In the course of the next few decades the pastoral economy of the eastern regions of the Cape expanded markedly and by the 1830s the region was actively engaged in commercial wool production, with the accompanying processes of land accumulation, settler wealth stratification, and incipient capitalist relations.[35] A variety of forms of unfree labour existed. Slaves were increasingly used, while the old apprenticeship indenture system was extended into a broader debt peonage. As Clifton Crais shows, a single class and sub-culture of unfree labour survived after the 1799 rebellion and strengthened in the course of the subsequent decades. These regions of the colony underwent the same process of removal of coercive labour controls as in the west, both through the releasing of Khoisan labour from indenture by Ordinance 50 and by slave emancipation. But in contrast to the arable rural regions of the south-west, these acts of legislated emancipation brought about a fundamental disjuncture in the labour system of the eastern districts. With access to land and flocks, and with a strong heritage of active

---

33   This argument is based on Patterson's theory that a universal definition of slavery was the 'natal alienation' that slaves experienced. See O. Patterson, *Slavery and Social Death* (Cambridge, Mass. and London, 1982).

34   R. Elphick and V. C. Malherbe, 'The Khoisan to 1828', in Elphick and Giliomee, *Shaping of South African Society, 1652–1840*, 2nd edn., pp. 40–1.

35   C. Crais, 'Gentry and Labour in Three Eastern Cape Districts, 1820–65', *South African Historical Journal*, 18 (1986), pp. 125–46.

resistance to serfdom and slavery, the labour of the pastoral districts deserted settler farms *en masse* and, in some cases, established peasant communities out of settler control. The colonial state was not prepared to reimpose forced labour, and in the process alienated many of the poorer and less commercially orientated farmers, some of whom left the colony in the celebrated process of the trek northwards in the mid 1830s. But the state was prepared to back the capitalist farmers in defence of commercial wool production. Crais shows how the 1840s were marked by active attacks by settlers on those ex-slaves and Khoi workers who sought to escape from proletariat status. Land alienation, enclosure and marked pressure on peasant communities, such as that established at Kat River, ensued. The result was another rebellion of the dispossessed in a final bid to resist the imposition of settler power over their land and labour. The uprising of 1851–3, which coincided with the resistance of the Xhosa to settler land encroachment, was crushed by the full weight of the British colonial state. Its defeat ensured that the future of the eastern districts would parallel that of the west: the domination of a white landed class over a black proletariat. By more dramatic means, the eastern frontier had been brought into line with the rest of the colony.[36] The chains of slavery and enserfment were replaced by the no less restrictive ones of class and racial subordination. Indeed, as Crais demonstrates, racial control was more overtly articulated in this period than under slavery itself.[37]

The last two essays in this collection provide case studies which reflect on the breaking of the chains of slavery from the perspective of the late nineteenth and early twentieth centuries. They reveal ways in which new roles and identities of the descendents of the unfree were shaped at the eve of the present century.

Vivian Bickford-Smith examines the position in late Victorian Cape Town. On the eve of the Mineral Revolution of the 1870s, the correlation of class and colour which had been evident in the city since the days of slavery was little altered. Slave and Khoi descendents lacked the capital or access to skills training to enable them to break free of the unequal economic power relations of the past. The Masters and Servants legislation, born in the aftermath of emancipation, dominated the division of employer and employed. The Mineral Revolution did offer some expansion of opportunity for the emergence of a small black middle class, but this was offset by the increasingly stringent racial segregation which developed in the city in the course of the 1880s and 1890s. In this context, freedom for the Capetonian underclass took on different meanings to that of unquestioned triumph and progress

---

36 Rumours of rebellion also spread in the western districts in 1851, but proved unfounded; Marinkowitz, 'Rural Production and Labour'; E. Bradlow, 'The "Great Fear" at the Cape of Good Hope, 1851–2', *International Journal of African Historical Studies*, 23 (1989), pp. 401–21.

37 Crais, *Making of the Colonial Order*.

with which it was viewed by the dominant classes of the city.

Bickford-Smith analyses several key examples of popular celebration and memory of slave emancipation, revealing the ambivalence of celebrations of liberation at a time of active struggle against segregation. In this context the promise of freedom which 1834 had provided, was sometimes bitterly reflected upon by slave descendents. Most strikingly, the battle against segregation subsumed the slave heritage under a new social and political identity of 'coloured' ethnicity. Kinship, occupational and community ties were being mobilized into an identity which fought for recognition in opposition to the highly discriminatory 'Native' Africans, and which brought the descendents of Khoi and slaves together in a new mobilizing force. To some extent this succeeded: Capetonians who adopted the identity of 'Coloured' avoided the worst markers of racial segregation, such as the forced removal and residential isolation which affected other black Capetonians in the early decades of the twentieth century, although this was not to be the case for long, and the hope of equality of acceptance by white Cape Town has still to be achieved.

Kerry Ward draws this collection of essays to a close by examining the history of inhabitants of Mamre mission station, in the Swartland grain-producing hinterland of Cape Town, from the time of emancipation into the twentieth century. Drawing on the archival research of Helen Ludlow for the emancipation era, she uses rich oral testimonies of present-day Mamre residents to reveal the changing identities and experiences of one rural community of slave descendents over a hundred-year period.[38]

Mamre was founded by Moravian missionaries in 1808, primarily for Khoi soldiers and their families who had fought for the British, but it was also a key place of refuge for freed slaves after 1838, who were drawn to it by the prospect of land and by kinship ties. Ludlow's recreation of the origins of Mamre newcomers in the 1830s substantiates Scully's claim that the desire to constitute nuclear families by the freed people was allied to missionary perceptions of family structure. To kinship links were added the acceptance of Moravian Christianity and church membership as markers of Mamre community membership. Nonetheless, as Ross has shown in general terms, mission inhabitants were never cut off from the surrounding community. The need to find outside wage labour ensured that continued links were retained with the surrounding farms.

As Mamre became more crowded, and as divisions of wealth which marked the growth of the community developed amongst its inhabitants, many males were dependent on seasonal farm work to maintain themselves

---

38 Ludlow, 'Missions and Emancipation'. The full analysis of oral testimonies is given in K. Ward, 'The Road to Mamre: Migration, Memory and the Meaning of Community, c.1900–92' (MA thesis, University of Cape Town, 1992).

and their families. Ward shows how this web of rural ties began to weaken in the later nineteenth century as opportunities for work on road and railway building projects emerged and, in particular, as nearby Cape Town developed a manufacturing economy requiring factory workers. Many Mamriers migrated to Cape Town from the turn of the century, including increasing numbers of women who were employed as domestic servants. Yet despite this shift to full-time work outside the mission, they retained their sense of belonging to the mission community. Family links were retained and earnings remitted. Regular return visits were made. And even in Cape Town, Mamriers retained a separate identity by their membership of the Moravian Hill Church in the centre of the town. Many retired to Mamre. An identity as Mamriers was thus formed which spanned both the countryside and the city.

Ward's interviews with present-day Mamriers revealed that this identity is still strong. Yet in the process the heritage of slavery has been eclipsed from the popular memory of the community. Other identities—that of Mamre itself, or more broadly that of being 'coloured' in a segregated society—have overridden memories of the slave past. As in the broader 'coloured' community of the Cape, analysed by Bickford-Smith, slave roots are hidden beneath layers of other identities. Yet as Ward comments at the end of her essay, as the Cape now moves into a new era of its history as part of a restructured South Africa, new questions about the inheritance of slavery are emerging.[39] For as this book has shown, the chains of slavery and the results of their breaking have deeply marked the social and political landscape of the Cape. The challenge is to bring an awareness of this legacy to an analysis of the issues which face the region today.

Of all the forms of domination in the pre-industrial world created by European overseas expansion—serfdom, peonage, indentureship, contract labour—slavery was the most complete and unequivocal. But as the essays in this volume demonstrate, slavery was more than an exploitative economic system; it was also a social and cultural one. A piece of property bought, sold and traded, the slave was also a person who, even under the most oppressive master, actively participated in the production of culture and history. The struggle over the family, analysed by Scully, the recollections of the people of Mamre recounted by Ward, and the story told by Crais of the rebel Kautgong who—some 140 years ago—declared that he would rather die than return to bondage, highlight the ways in which the struggles of slavery and emancipation extended well beyond the chains of economic

39 Popularization of academic work on Cape slavery and emancipation has begun but, as yet, has made little impact on popular consciousness. See Juanita Pastor, 'The History of Cape Slavery: Changing Perceptions?' (BA Hons. thesis, University of Cape Town, 1990); N. Southey, 'Making Southern Africa's Early Past Accessible: Alternative Histories for Schools', *South African Historical Journal*, 23 (1990), pp. 168–83; N. Worden, *The Chains that Bind Us* (Cape Town, 1994).

exploitation.

A decade ago the study of the nineteenth-century history of slavery and emancipation in the Cape was, at best, a backwater in the reconstruction of the South African past. This volume questions older conventional wisdoms, about slavery and emancipation in particular and, more generally, about how historians have periodized the modern history of South Africa. Our collective goals have thus been not only to fill in an empirical lacuna, but also to begin to raise more general historiographical questions. The proverbial 'more work remains to be done' is applicable here. Fortunately, a surprisingly large number of advanced students have initiated research projects into slavery, emancipation, and South Africa's 'long century'. This volume, then, is one small preliminary contribution to a far larger emerging literature.

It is still too soon to determine where the new research and writing on slavery and emancipation will lead a new generation of historians. Two possibilities seem especially hopeful. The essays in this volume thus point the way forward for historians of not only the Cape but of the sub-continent. From Luanda to Inhambane, from the trade routes along the Zambezi to the port of Lourenço Marques, throughout this region and beyond, the late eighteenth and early nineteenth century witnessed both a tremendous rise in the capture and sale of slaves and a proliferation and intensification of a variety of systems of unfree labour.[40] The story of the Cape Colony during this period thus forms just one small part of a history that embraced the entire subcontinent. Certainly an acknowledgement of the expansion of slavery beyond the Boland raises significant questions concerning the emergence of the frontier and the relationships between colonists and the African communities with which they came into contact.

Indeed, a number of historians have now suggested that the *mfecane*, which had once been seen solely as the result of the rapid expansion of the Zulu kingdom, has to be placed within a context that incorporates slavery and the rising market for human beings as a motor force in the generation of instability. The on-going revision of the *mfecane* has produced lively discussion and debate. What is becoming increasingly clear, however, is that in the Cape there existed an illegal and, especially from the end of the eighteenth century, an expanding internal market for slaves and other dependent labourers. The ways in which the development of colonialism at the southern tip of Africa formed part of a far wider set of historical processes may well become one of the most exciting avenues of research on South Africa.[41]

40   In particular, the massive growth of the Atlantic trade from west-central Africa and the slave raiding and exports of the south-eastern part of the continent which spawned the oppressive labour systems of the *prazero* agricultural estates of the Zambezi. See J. Miller, *Way of Death: Merchant Capitalism and the Angolan Slave Trade, 1730–1830* (Madison, 1988); P. Lovejoy, *Transformations in Slavery: A History of Slavery in Africa* (Cambridge, 1983) pp. 228–30; M.D.D. Newitt, *Portuguese Settlement on the Zambesi: Exploration, Land Tenure and Colonial Rule in East Africa* (London, 1973).

A second possibility ultimately revolves around questions of politics and ideology. The British colonial state and the liberal ideology that informed it was enormously Janus-faced. The ending of slavery was about human freedom, but it was also about power and control. The very era that ended bonded labour and, in 1853, established a non-racial franchise, also saw the emergence of new forms of unfree labour and, perhaps most tragically, the emergence of modern racist ideologies in South Africa. Historians recently have noted that there never emerged in the Cape 'any explicit racist defence of slavery based on...the supposed innate inferiority of other races'.[42] If so, how do we begin to understand the ideological shifts that allowed for a transition from master and slave to black and white in South Africa?

41 See J. Cobbing, 'The Mfecane as Alibi: Thoughts on Dithakong and Mbolompo', *Journal of African History*, 29 (1988), pp. 487–519; E. A. Eldredge, 'Sources of Conflict in Southern Africa, *c.*1800–30: The "Mfecane" Reconsidered', *Journal of African History*, 33 (1992), pp. 1–35.

42 A. du Toit and H. Giliomee, *Afrikaner Political Thought: 1750–1850*, vol. 1 (Cape Town, 1983), p. 32; R. L. Watson, *The Slave Question: Liberty and Property in South Africa* (Hanover, 1990).

Plate 2   The Drosty at Stellenbosch, 1800, by Lady Anne Barnard. *Cape Archives.*

'THE GOOD OPINION OF OTHERS'
LAW, SLAVERY & COMMUNITY IN THE CAPE COLONY
c1760-1830[1]

— WAYNE DOOLING —

In 1830 Abraham Benjamin de Villiers appeared before the Stellenbosch circuit court on a charge of ill-treating his slave, Arend. It was alleged that he had put Arend's hands and feet in irons and flogged him with quince 'twigs'.[2] By 1830, it was by no means unusual for slaveholders to face charges brought against them by their slaves. In the 1820s and 1830s large numbers of slaves, encouraged by new openings which the legal structure permitted, took legal action against their masters.[3] De Villiers appeared in court under laws (replicated elsewhere in the empire) aimed at the 'amelioration' of slavery. The early decades of the nineteenth century were years of considerable flux in the colony, primarily stemming from the replacement of the moribund VOC at the end of the eighteenth century by a British colonial government. Britain, the leading colonial and industrial force of the era, brought with it completely novel notions of rule, government and empire. As far as the administration of the law was concerned, the British held that it was 'especially necessary that [the] administration and application [of the law] be effected with unbiased judgment, and without respect of persons.'[4] This differed markedly from the principles enunciated by the VOC: 'the distinction of persons is one of the essential points by which the degree of

---

1 This paper has benefited from seminars held at Northwestern and Cambridge Universities. I am also grateful to Nigel Worden, David William Cohen, and John Iliffe for their comments on various drafts.

2 Cape Archives (CA), 1/STB 2/31, Circuit Court Cases, 2 Sept. 1830, no. 14.

3 J.E. Mason, 'The Slaves and Their Protectors: Reforming Resistance in a Slave Society, the Cape Colony, 1826–34', *Journal of Southern African Studies*, 17, 1 (1991), pp. 103–28; W. Dooling, 'Slavery and Amelioration in the Graaff-Reinet District, 1823–30', *South African Historical Journal*, 27 (1992), pp. 75–94; P. van der Spuy, 'Slave Women and the Family in Nineteenth-Century Cape Town', *South African Historical Journal*, 27 (1992), pp. 50–74.

4 Address of Chief Justice J.A. Truter on the occasion of the first assembly of the court in the new Court House, 19 Jan. 1815, in Du Toit and Giliomee, *Afrikaner Political Thought: Analysis and Documents, Volume I: 1780–1850* (Cape Town, 1983), p. 101.

punishment is measured in most civilized nations.'[5] It is thus not surprising that historians have regarded these years as initiating fundamental change in the history of slavery at the Cape.[6]

What makes De Villiers's case of particular interest, however, is his response to the charges brought against him. In his defence, he made no attempt to deny the punishment and 'relied for an acquittal on the character of humanity and good treatment of his slaves' which he received from the Civil Commissioner and magistrate of the district.[7] This case is instructive in a number of ways. De Villiers's plea suggests that he believed that non-legal considerations should prevail over strictly legal ones. He sought to emphasize the personal over the legal and his reputation over his deeds. The plea illuminates the extent to which slaveholders, in their interactions with their slaves, were in the presence of a broader slaveholding community and that they sought to justify their actions in its eyes. Even more remarkable, is the fact that De Villiers could make this plea in 1830. For the early decades of the nineteenth century, as noted above, saw significant changes in the content of the laws regarding slavery. But De Villiers's case, being heard at a time when slaves theoretically enjoyed equality before the law, is a prime example of the fact that community concerns overrode any strict application of the letter of the law.

This paper examines the way in which 'community' influenced the operation of the law in a changing legal system. It will become clear that De Villiers, in 1830, could appeal to his reputation because reputations of individuals were prime considerations in cases involving masters and slaves. The fact that slaveowners sought to emphasize their reputations, however, is unimaginable without the prior existence of a slaveholding community. The contours of the settler community, in many cases, influenced every aspect of the legal process in cases involving slaves and masters. It determined access to court for slaves, influenced events in court and, ultimately, influenced the eventual outcome of cases. Slaveowners known to treat their slaves with excessive brutality were condemned in public opinion. Slaves thus stood the biggest chance of success in the courtrooms where their masters had tainted reputations. It was probably this social sanction that prevented most slaveholders from engaging in *excessive* brutality towards their slaves.

5   Letter from the Cape Court of Justice to Major-General Craig, 14 Jan. 1796, in Du Toit and Giliomee, *Afrikaner Political Thought*, p. 91.

6   M. Rayner, 'Wine and Slaves: The Failure of an Export Economy and the Ending of Slavery in the Cape Colony, South Africa, 1806–34' (Ph.D. thesis, Duke University, 1986); Mason, 'The Slaves and their Protectors'; Mason, 'Hendrik Albertus and his Ex-Slave Mey: A Drama in Three Acts', *Journal of African History*, 31 (1990); C. Crais, *The Making of the Colonial Order: White Supremacy and Black Resistance in the Eastern Cape, 1770–1865* (Johannesburg, 1992), esp. pp. 55–63; Dooling, 'Slavery and Amelioration'; A. Bank, The *Decline of Urban Slavery at the Cape, 1806–34*, Centre for African Studies, University of Cape Town, Communications, no. 22 (1991).

7   I have not been able to locate these testimonies.

Without doubt, the relations between masters and slaves, masters and the colonial state, and slaves and the state were radically altered in the early decades of the nineteenth century. But the historiography of Cape slavery is as chronologically divided as it is divided along regional lines. In other words, these studies deal with either the eighteenth or early nineteenth centuries, with little attempt to straddle the different periods in a single study.[8] Furthermore, there is a preoccupation with what Orlando Patterson, in his monumental comparative study of slavery, has called the 'private determinants' of slave society, that is, the nature of relations between master and slave, independent of the master's place in society.[9] As important in the 'condition of slavery', Patterson argues, were the 'public determinants' of the master-slave relationship:

> the master, however independent he may have wished to be in his slave, needed his community to both confirm and support his power. The community, through its agents, wanted this support reciprocated if only to safeguard the interests of its members…the relationship between the master and his community was never a static one. The master wanted to influence public attitudes and deflect attempts to interfere with his proprietary claims on his slaves.[10]

Although no attempt will be made to give primacy to either the 'private' or 'public' determinants, this paper seeks to demonstrate that without due attention to the latter, the impact of a new 'hegemonic notion of the "rule of law"' can be overstated.[11] For 'community' permeated the workings of the law throughout the history of slavery at the Cape. It is within this context that change took place and by placing community on the agenda in the nineteenth-century court-rooms, as De Villiers had done, slaveholders were, to some extent, able to offset the revolutionary impulses of the period. Moreover, the slaveholders' ability to impose 'community' upon the court-room was just one aspect of their continued domination of settler society and a reflection of the failure of the British government to mould society completely in its own image. After giving a brief outline of the Cape legal system and the position of slaves within it, this paper will examine the way in which the shape of settler society influenced the functioning of the law.

---

8 Steven Hahn's study is an excellent example of the utility of bridging the gap between what has come to be seen as fundamental social divides; S. Hahn, *The Roots of Southern Populism: Yeoman Farmers and the Transformation of the Georgia Upcountry, 1850–90* (New York and Oxford, 1983). In the Cape context, the one exception is Crais, but his reading of the eighteenth century, at least as far as the operation of the law is concerned, is based on secondary readings of the period; Crais, *Making*, esp. pp. 58–60.

9 O. Patterson, *Slavery and Social Death: A Comparative Study* (Cambridge, Mass., 1982), pp. 172–3.

10 *Ibid.*, pp. 172–3.

11 Crais, *Colonial Order*, p. 58.

12 For a more detailed discussion of the Cape legal system, see G.G. Visagie, *Regspleging en Reg van die Kaap, 1652–1806: Met 'n Bespreeking van die Historiese Agtergrond* (Cape Town, 1969); G.G. Visagie, 'Regsveranderinge aan die Kaap Tussen 1823 en 1838' (MA thesis, University of Cape Town, 1954).

THE CAPE LEGAL SYSTEM[12]

Until 1817 the Court of Justice in Cape Town (established in 1685) was the only criminal court in the colony. In the country districts, the administration of the law was in the hands of boards of Landdrosts and Heemraden. Each district had a Landdrost, who was a Company official. He was assisted by several Heemraden who were chosen from the most notable of settlers. These boards could deal with petty civil disputes (for example, over water rights and land boundaries) which arose between settlers in the various districts. Criminal cases, however, had to be dealt with by the Court of Justice and in such cases the Landdrost and Heemraden could collect evidence which was to be presented before the Court of Justice, with the Landdrost acting as public prosecutor. Although the boards had no jurisdiction in criminal cases, in practice only the most severe of these were sent to the Court of Justice and the local boards dealt with the petty criminal cases.[13] These boards also had considerable powers in cases dealing with slaves.[14]

This system remained unchanged throughout the eighteenth century. Gradually, the British made alterations to the administration of justice in the colony. In 1811, in an attempt to make the administration of justice more efficient, circuit courts were established for the country districts. In 1817 the jurisdiction of the boards of Landdrosts and Heemraden was extended and the boards could deal with all but the most severe cases.[15] Acting upon the recommendations of a Commission of Inquiry, a royal charter was issued in 1827 which did away with the Court of Justice and established a Supreme Court, which sat in Cape Town and consisted of a Chief Justice and three Puisne judges.[16] Barristers from England and Ireland filled these posts.[17] The office of the Fiscal (the chief legal officer in the colony) was replaced by that of the Attorney General. The boards of Landdrosts and Heemraden were replaced by resident magistrates and civil commissioners. The charter also stipulated that criminal sessions before the Supreme and circuit courts were to be held before a jury of nine men.

13   P.J. Venter, 'Landdros en Heemrade', *Archives Yearbook for South African History*, vol. 3 (Cape Town, 1940), pp. 34–5.

14   *Ibid.*, p. 37.

15   Proclamation of 18 July 1817, in *Proclamations, Advertisements, and Other Official Notices Published by the Government of the Cape of Good Hope from the 10th January, 1806, to the 2nd May, 1825* (Cape Town, 1827), p. 394.

16   For an outline of changes in the administration of the law, see CA, GH 26/57, Bourke to Huskisson, 19 May 1828; J.W. Wessels, *History of the Roman-Dutch Law* (Grahamstown, 1908), pp. 355–85.

17   H.B. Fine, 'The History of the Cape Supreme Court and its Role in the Development of Judicial Precedent for the Period 1827–1910' (LLM thesis, University of Cape Town, 1986), p. 33.

18   Evidence of Daniel Denyssen, Esq., His Majesty's Fiscal, upon the Criminal Law and Practice of the Cape of Good Hope, 15 Aug. 1825, in G.M. Theal (ed.), *Records of the Cape Colony*, (hereafter *RCC*),

THE CHANGING LEGAL POSITION OF SLAVES

By the time of the Dutch conquest of the Cape, slavery had long ceased to exist in the Netherlands. The laws governing slavery at the Cape were those of the Dutch possession at Batavia, which in turn were derived from Roman-Dutch law.[18] These were brought together in the *Statuten van India*.[19] At the Cape, slave law found its most codified expression in a *placaat* (statute) issued in 1754.[20] These laws, for the most part, were designed to keep the slave population in check.

There was an inherent contradiction in the legal position of slaves. Juristically they were non-persons: slaves were 'considered in civil law as not existing'.[21] Thus, slaves were not permitted to marry or own property.[22] On the other hand, Roman law stipulated that the slave was not only property, but also *persona*.[23] In 1813 it was declared that the laws 'which allow slavery do not…allow that we are to discontinue to consider slaves as our fellow creatures or as the common subjects of the sovereign.'[24] Moreover, slaves 'had a share in the laws of nature'.[25] Thus, although they were not permitted to marry, slave men and women were allowed to cohabit.[26] The recognition of the slave as person was not unique to Roman law. As Orlando Patterson noted, 'there has never existed a slaveholding society, ancient or modern that did not recognize the slave as a person in law'.[27]

Throughout the history of slavery at the Cape, the treatment of slaves by their owners was nominally under the supervision of the state. Slaveowners were allowed to punish slaves for 'domestic offences' without the knowledge or consent of the authorities. Slaves, on the other hand, had the right to lodge complaints of ill-treatment against masters with the nearest authorities. However, the slaves were to be punished if their complaints were deemed unfounded.[28] Most importantly, masters did not have the right of life or death

---

(London, 1897–1905), vol. 33, p. 238.

19 J.A. van der Chijs, *Nederlandsch Indisch Plakaatboek, 1602–1811*, 17 vols. ('s-Gravenhage, 1885–1900).

20 K.M. Jeffreys (ed.), *Kaapse Plakaatboek*, 6 vols. (Cape Town, 1944–9), vol. 3, pp. 1–6.

21 D. Denyssen, Statement of the Laws of the Colony of the Cape of Good Hope Regarding Slavery, *RCC*, vol. 9, p. 150.

22 *Ibid.*

23 W.W. Buckland, *The Roman Law of Slavery: The Condition of the Slave in Private Law from Augustus to Justinian* (Cambridge, 1908), p. 4.

24 Statement of the Laws, *RCC*, vol. 9, p. 147.

25 *Ibid.*, p. 150.

26 *Ibid.*

27 Patterson, *Slavery and Social Death*, p. 22.

28 Van der Chijs, *Nederlandsch Indisch Plakaatboek*, vol. 9, p. 576; Statement of the Laws, *RCC*, vol 9, p. 151–2.

over their slaves. The law stipulated that 'he who deprives another of his life must be punished as a murderer, without making any distinction of the state or condition of the deceased, even if he be a slave.'[29]

Both the Batavian and the British governments passed several measures aimed at improving the condition of the slave in law. During the Batavian administration of the Cape (1803–6), a conscious attempt was made to bring slaves and Khoi more under the ambit of the law,[30] and during the second British Occupation of the colony the most significant changes in the legal position of the slaves were introduced.

In 1823, the British government launched a policy to 'ameliorate' the conditions of slaves in the colonies. In the course of the 1820s and 1830s a series of amelioratory measures were passed which gave slaves increasing protection under the law. These measures, Mary Rayner has argued, had two broad strategies: to promote the physical well-being of the slaves and to 'effect an educational and moral transformation of enslaved workers in the colonies'. Through this, it was hoped, a transformation of 'colonial slavery into some approximation of a free market in labour' could be effected.[31] One of the most important elements of the new legislation, therefore, was the promotion of stable family units by allowing slaves to marry[32] and by forbidding the sale in separate lots of husbands, wives and children under the age of ten years. Slaveowners were also obliged to provide their slaves with a minimum of food and clothing, described in laws passed in 1823 and 1826 as 'sufficient and wholesome food' and 'good and sufficient clothing'. In order to approach the ideal of a free market in labour, slaveowners were restricted in the extent to which they could extract labour from their slaves. Slaves were not to be employed in 'garden or field labour' for more than ten hours per day during winter, nor more than twelve hours during the summer months 'except during the ploughing or harvest seasons, or on other extraordinary occasions of unavoidable necessity'. Slaves could not be compelled to work on Sundays except for domestic work and 'work of necessity'. In 1830, such work (for which slaves were to received monetary remuneration) was defined as sowing, reaping, pruning, gathering, wine-making, irrigating, cattle-tending and other farm work.

Slaveowners were also restricted in their freedom to inflict punishment

---

29   Statement of the Laws, *RCC*, vol. 9, p. 151.

30   See, for example, the Ordinance for the Administration of the Country Districts, 23 Oct. 1805, in *Proclamations, Advertisements*, pp. 733–71. Also cited in Wessels, *History of the Roman-Dutch Law*, p. 413.

31   M. Rayner, 'Slaves, Slave-Owners and the British State, 1806–34', Institute of Commonwealth Studies, University of London, *Societies of Southern Africa*, vol. 12 (1981) p. 17; Rayner 'Wine and Slaves', p. 3; For a slightly different approach, see Mason, 'The Slaves', pp. 106–9.

32   Governor Somerset's 1823 measure conferred this right upon baptized slaves only.

upon their slaves. In terms of the 1823 and 1826 measures, punishment was not to exceed 25 stripes. Masters were not allowed to repeat such punishments within 24 hours. The punishment of female slaves especially was restricted. They were exempted from public flogging (this was not included in the 1823 proclamation) and punishment could be in the form of solitary confinement 'in any dry and proper place' for no more than three days, or by whipping 'privately on the shoulders'.

Ordinance 19 of 1826 made provision for the appointment of a Guardian of Slaves, with Assistant Guardians in the country districts. Slaves could lodge complaints with these functionaries who were obliged to investigate them and represent the slaves in criminal actions against their masters. From 1831 slaveowners were required to keep record books of punishments inflicted and these were to be submitted to the Slave Protectors biannually.

THE SETTLER COMMUNITY

'Community' is a slippery concept.[33] But there can be no doubting its utility in understanding human action in different historical periods, as the host of studies on eighteenth and nineteenth America, for example, testify. In both the North and the South, social life was centred around a series of discrete communities.[34] Moreover, communities showed remarkable resilience. Despite the severe social and economic dislocation unleashed by the Civil War, American Southern communities persisted into the postbellum era.[35]

A number of variants make up community. Although it is most common to see it defined in spatial terms, Bender argues that community can be better understood as 'an experience than as a place'.[36] This is not to suggest that community can be divorced from locality, but the emphasis on the experiential over the spatial underscores the fact that, above all else, community has to do with human *interaction*. Thus, community involves 'a network of social relations marked by mutuality and emotional bonds'.[37] It follows,

---

33 For a theoretical discussion about the difficulties of the use of the term, see T. Bender, *Community and Social Change in America* (New Brunswick, 1978).

34 On the North, see B.H. Mann, *Neighbors and Strangers: Law and Community in Early Connecticut* (Chapel Hill and London, 1987). For the application of the term to the South, see O.V. Burton and R.C. McMath Jr. (eds.), *Toward a New South? Studies in Post-Civil War Southern Communities* (Connecticut, 1982); B. Wyatt-Brown, *Southern Honor: Ethics and Behavior in the Old South* (New York and Oxford, 1982); Hahn, *The Roots of Southern Populism;* H.L. Watson, 'Conflict and Collaboration: Yeomen, Slaveholders and Politics in the Antebellum South', *Social History*, 10, 3 (1985). For the application of the term in a South African context, see B. Bozzoli (ed.), *Class, Community and Conflict* (Johannesburg, 1987).

35 Burton and McMath Jr., *Toward a New South?*

36 Bender, *Community*, p. 6.

37 *Ibid.*

then, that individuals are bound by close, emotional and face-to-face contact.[38]

In slave societies, communities acquired a particular shape. American Southern communities have been described as most striking in 'the paradoxical combination of stark domination of some human beings over others with a pervasive sense of reciprocity and even communal solidarity, grounded in...the "familiar and familial" circumstances of ordinary life.'[39] In this regard, Cape slave society displayed remarkable similarities. Most settlers were slaveholders. In 1782, for example, 74.5 per cent of Stellenbosch district farmers owned at least one slave.[40] As American Southern society manifested distinctions of wealth, so too did the Cape. The eighteenth century saw the emergence of a 'Cape gentry'.[41] These distinctions merely served to give the settler community a particular structure.

Foremost, perhaps, in the 'bonds of mutuality' were the ties of kinship. Cape settler society, according to Robert Shell, was a 'tangled cousinry'. Almost every settler family was related to every other.[42] J.W.D. Moodie, who visited the colony in the early nineteenth century, noted that the colonists were 'all intimately connected by intermarriage, and keep up a constant intercourse, employing much of their leisure time in riding out, and visiting each other.'[43]

Perhaps more important were the ties of patronage.[44] The extension of credit was one of the chief means through which patronage could be dispensed. The archival records point to the existence of an extensive network of credit relationships. For example, the former Heemraad of Stellenbosch,

38   *Ibid.*, p. 7.

39   R.C. McMath, 'Community, Region and Hegemony in the Nineteenth-Century South', in Burton and McMath, *New South*, p. 283–4.

40   N. Worden, *Slavery in Dutch South Africa* (Cambridge, 1985), p. 13.

41   R. Ross, 'The Rise of the Cape Gentry', *Journal of Southern African Studies*, 9, 2 (1983), pp. 193–217; L. Guelke and R.C-H. Shell, 'An Early Colonial Landed Gentry: Land and Wealth in the Cape Colony (1652–1731)', *Journal of Historical Geography*, vol. 9 (1983). The use of the term 'gentry' in the context of the colonial Cape can be questioned. For example, men of affluence in the Cape did not occupy positions of political power as their Southern counterparts did. On balance, however, the similarities are significant enough to give the term validity. Although big Cape slaveholders did not occupy positions of power in the cental political and judicial bodies, their dominance of local structures gave them the influence that they sought. Like their Southern counterparts, wealthy slaveowners sought to set themselves apart by ostentatious displays of wealth.

42   R. Shell, 'Slavery at the Cape of Good Hope, 1680–1731' (Ph.D thesis, Yale University, 1986), vol. 1, p. 247. The phrase is borrowed from Bernard Bailyn.

43   J.W.D. Moodie, *Ten Years in South Africa* (London, 1835), p. 146.

44   Definitions of patronage abound, but all emphasize that it involves relations between persons of unequal wealth and power through which the wealthy seek to legitimate their status by the distribution of resources through personal, non-market contact. Thus, patron-client ties in stratified agrarian communities, generally act to limit or preclude class conflict. See, for example, J.C. Scott, *Weapons of the Weak: Everyday Forms of Peasant Resistance* (New Haven and London, 1985); S. Silverman, 'Patronage and Community-Nation Relationships in Central Italy', *Ethnology*, 4, 2 (1965), p. 176.

Johannes Albertus Meyburgh, had no less than 48 debtors at the time of his death in 1790.[45] Furthermore, some of the credit agreements were exceptionally long-standing. Meyburgh had a number of outstanding monetary debts which had been contracted ten years earlier.[46] Had market forces prevailed over those of community, this situation would not have existed. Although in many cases the people who lent money were relatively wealthy while those who borrowed were relatively poor, ties of credit were not always between rich and poor. Often credit operated horizontally, or between individuals who were more or less equals.[47] Thus the extension of credit in this context was not primarily a form of capital accumulation. It was the means by which individuals were drawn into the boundaries of community.[48]

It is important to consider the role played by local authorities in the slaveholder community and the extent to which they formed part of it. The Heemraden were almost inevitably large slaveholders and thus members of the 'Cape gentry'. Indeed, it was through their wealth that they had come to dominate the offices in military, civil and ecclesiastical administration.[49] This is quite obvious in the magistracy of Stellenbosch, where the Heemraden came from the most notable of families—the Van der Byls, Cloetes, Meyburghs, De Villiers, Hoffmans, Faures, Morkels and Wiums.[50]

The position of the Landdrosts was less clear-cut. They were, after all, officials of the VOC. The theme of conflict between the Company and colonists is a persistent one in the history of the eighteenth-century Cape.[51] There are indications, however, that the Landdrosts had very distinct ties with the freeburgher population. For example, they too were linked to the colonists through credit. In the period 1773 to 1775, the Landdrost Marthinus Adriaan Berg had lent money to at least five individuals.[52] One contemporary noted that the Landdrost regularly socialized with members of the élite—the pastor, Heemraden, and village physician.[53]

---

45 CA, 1/STB 18/34, Inventory of J.A. Meyburgh, 9 Apr. 1790.

46 *Ibid.*

47 W. Dooling, *Law and Community in a Slave Society: Stellenbosch District, South Africa, c.1760–1820*, Centre for African Studies, University of Cape Town, Communications, no. 23 (1992), p. 11.

48 For American parallels on the way in which local exchange forged community bonds, see Hahn, *Roots*, esp. pp. 53–77; Mann, *Neighbors*, pp. 11–46; C. Clark, *The Roots of Rural Capitalism: Western Massachusetts, 1780–1860* (Ithaca and London, 1990), esp. pp. 28–38.

49 Ross, 'Cape Gentry', p. 208.

50 P.B. Borcherds, *An Autobiographical Memoir* (Cape Town, 1963), p. 190.

51 See, for example, G. Schutte, 'Company and Colonists at the Cape, 1652–1795', in R. Elphick and H. Giliomee (eds.), *The Shaping of South African Society, 1652–1840* (Cape Town, 1989), pp. 283–323.

52 CA, 1/STB 18/68, Obligaties of Christiaan Crynauw, 16 Mar. 1773, no. 112; Johannes Jurgen de Beer, 10 Mar. 1774, no. 94; Johan George Breedeham, 19 Oct. 1774, no. 99; Hermanus Combrink, 22 Mar. 1775, no. 108; Paulus Johannes Fick, 23 Mar. 1775.

53 Borcherds, *Autobiographical Memoir*, p. 28.

Still, it is particularly difficult to establish the place of the Landdrost in the community. There is some indication that the identity of interests between Landdrosts and Heemraden varied from one individual to the next. Freund notes that the 'Landdrost administered from a weak position, and the most successful Landdrosten such as Faure and Van der Riet, although sometimes able to maintain an independent point of view, had to know very well how to accommodate local interests'.[54] Perhaps the best way to explore the position of the Landdrost is to turn to the criminal records. It is worth exploring one case in detail.

In 1814, the Fiscal instituted charges of corruption and neglect of duty against the Landdrost of Tulbagh,[55] H. van de Graaff.[56] This case had its origins in February 1810, when Jacobus Johannes Burger fatally wounded the slave Galant. Galant's owner, G.B. Liebenberg, subsequently instituted a civil case against Burger for the loss of his slave. But the case failed to reach the attention of the Court of Justice. The Fiscal concluded that the Landdrost intended to leave the case unprosecuted.

The Fiscal also found that it appeared as if the Landdrost wanted to smother a case against another colonist, Gerrit Visser, for killing the 'bastard Hottentot', Marsitrie. The Landdrost received 125 sheep from Visser. In not prosecuting Jacobus Johan Burger and Gerrit Visser, it was found, he had deliberately made himself guilty of contravening the *Crimineele Ordonnantie* of 5 July 1570 (the Dutch ordinance guiding criminal procedure) and the oath that he had taken on the acceptance of his post.

Clearly, the Landdrost was guilty of corruption. Had the Secretary of the district not informed the Fiscal of these transgressions these details would never have become known.[57] Undoubtedly, many more like these exist. The case, however, clearly demonstrates the ties which existed between a Landdrost and the settler community. Gerrit Visser, the man against whom the Landdrost had failed to institute proceedings, came from an influential family. He was the son of the Veldcornet[58] of the Middel Roggeveld, Floris Visser.[59]

The identity of interests between resident magistrate and 'community' is exemplified by the actions of Faure, Landdrost of Stellenbosch, in 1831. On

---

54   W.M. Freund, 'Society and Government in Dutch South Africa, the Cape and the Batavians, 1803–6' (Ph.D. thesis, Yale University, 1972), p. 91.

55   This district originally formed part of the district of Stellenbosch and was only declared a separate district in 1804. Its first Landdrost was the retired Landdrost of Stellenbosch, H.L. Bletterman.

56   CA, CJ 560, Fiscal contra Landdrost van Tulbagh, 29 Dec. 1814, 2ff.

57   It is not clear from the case details why he had done this.

58   The Veldcornets served as local militia officers. They, too, were chosen from the settler population. The Veldcornet was a 'farmer among farmers'; G. Schutte, 'Company and Colonists', p. 291.

59   On one occasion Floris Visser returned unopened letters which the Landdrost of Stellenbosch had sent him. CA, 1/STB 20/30, Landdrost of Stellenbosch to Floris Visser, 10 Jan. 1799, no. 110.

11 April 1831, a 'mob' of Stellenbosch farmers had prevented others from returning their punishment record books, as stipulated by the amelioratory legislation.[60] On two occasions that day, Faure had refused to see the Assistant Protector of Slaves. The rioting continued in Stellenbosch for four successive days.

In the end the Governor found that Faure 'did not think proper to use any means himself, either by personal influence, (which from his numerous connections in the place ought to be considerable) or otherwise, for the preservation of the peace' until after the time for the return of the record books had expired. Faure was dismissed from his post, primarily because the Governor felt that he was 'actuated partly perhaps by timidity, but in a great measure by a similarity of sentiment with those who were hostile to compliance with the law'. The Governor noted that it was desirable that the post be filled by an Englishman, 'if possible unconnected in any way with the inhabitants, and free from local prejudices, at the same time, one acquainted with the character and language of the colonists'.

This situation might have been avoided had the government paid any attention to a Cape Town newspaper at the time of Faure's nomination for the post of Resident Magistrate. Then, *The Colonist*[61] noted that the district of Stellenbosch was 'the very seat of Mr. Faure's family, his friends and connections.'[62]

From the preceding it should be clear that conflict is central to any definition of community. Indeed, conflict was one of the binding forces of community. Bender puts the point succinctly:

> The solidarity that characterizes communities does not mean, however, that all is unity and harmony within. Many commentators err…by insisting that absence of conflict be part of the definition of community. Communal conflict…is real, though it differs from, say, market competition, in being mediated by emotional bonds.[63]

The reality of conflict was not lost on contemporary observers either. Lichtenstein, who travelled in the interior of the colony in the early nineteenth century, found that the 'colonists in general are too much disposed to quarrelling among themselves, principally with respect to the boundaries of their several estates; and perhaps among ten neighbours nine will be at variance.'[64] The civil records are replete with instances of disputes (mostly over

---

60   CA, GH 26/65, Governor Cole to Goderich, 3 July 1831; J. Mason, 'Slaveholder Resistance to the Amelioration of Slavery at the Cape', 'Western Cape—Roots and Realities' Conference paper, Centre for African Studies, University of Cape Town, July 1986.

61   The *South African Commercial Advertiser* was suspended after 10 Mar. 1827. Between 22 Nov. 1827 and 30 Sept. 1828 it was replaced by *The Colonist*. The *SACA* resumed publication on 3 Oct. 1828.

62   *The Colonist*, 3 Jan. 1828.

63   Bender, *Community*, p. 8.

64   H. Lichtenstein, *Travels in Southern Africa in the Years 1803, 1804, 1805 and 1806* (Cape Town, 1928), p. 117.

water and land) between settlers.[65] Moodie found that 'Notwithstanding the intimate familiarity which subsisted among [the settlers], they were afraid to open their mouths on any subject connected in the most distant way with local politics, in the fear of their remarks being carried to the "Landdrost".'[66] Not only does this comment highlight the existence of conflict in settler society, but it also draws attention to the intermeshing of law and community.

LAW AND COMMUNITY

Community influenced every aspect of the slaves' and masters' contact with the law at the Cape. For in small-scale personal communities the working of the law takes a particular form: 'the more personal, oral, and small-scale the community in which it is administered, the more certain it is that the law will reflect the neighbourhood will.'[67]

The fact that slaves had access to the courts has, on occasion, been written off as a dead letter.[68] It will become clear, however, that slaves gained access to court by way of the positions their masters occupied within the slaveholder community.[69] There are indications that the risk of punishment for bringing in 'unfounded' complaints weighed heavily upon the decisions of slaves in contemplating whether or not to proceed to the courts. In 1820, the slave woman Francina claimed that she was afraid to complain to the court because on a previous occasion the Landdrost had ordered her to be flogged.[70]

Instead, the slaves turned to their masters' neighbours. For example, in 1764 the slave Tas, who had deserted his master's farm, approached Jan Lodewyk Pretorius asking him to speak to his master, Jan Gysbert Olivier, on his behalf so that he would not receive any punishment for having deserted.[71] The slaves under the control of Johannes Kuuhn occasionally appealed to the Heemraad, Josias de Kock, to act on their behalf.[72] Kuuhn

65   For example, CA, 1/STB 1/132.

66   Moodie, *Ten Years*, p. 147.

67   Wyatt-Brown, *Southern Honor*, p. 364; also K. Wrightson, 'Two Concepts of Order', in J. Brewer and J. Styles (eds.), *An Ungovernable People: The English and Their Law in the Seventeenth and Eighteenth Centuries* (London, 1980), p. 25, where he writes: 'What really mattered [in village life] was the maintenance of specific, local, personal relationships, not conformity to impersonal law.'

68   Le Vaillant, an eighteenth-century Cape traveller, noted that 'These wise laws [regarding slaves] certainly do great honour to the Dutch government; but how many means are there to elude them.' F. le Vaillant, *Travels into the Interior Parts of Africa by Way of the Cape of Good Hope in the Years 1780–1785* (London, 1790), p. 87.

69   This argument is at variance with that made by Robert Ross who sees the differences between Company and colonists as the crucial factor. R. Ross, 'The Rule of Law at the Cape of Good Hope in the Eighteenth Century', *Journal of Imperial and Commonwealth History*, vol. 9 (1980), esp. p. 6.

70   CA, 1/STB 2/2, The Secretary of Stellenbosch contra Isaac Cornelis de Villiers and his wife, Neeltjie Bresler, 20 May 1820.

was said to have been responsible for tying one of his slaves to a ladder and drawing a curry-comb over his naked body from neck to buttocks. De Kock claimed that Kuuhn's slaves, out of fear of punishment, requested him on more than one occasion to appeal to their master not to beat them.

In 1765, the slave Fortuyn van Bengalen approached the Veldcorporaal, Johannes van Aarden, to appeal to his mistress not to punish him.[73] This Van Aarden did, and Fortuyn's mistress promised not to punish him on that occasion. The slave August, belonging to Carel Fredrik Paret, was not so lucky. When August appealed to one of Paret's neighbours to put in a good word for him on his return after having deserted, Paret had August beaten on the back and buttocks with quince sticks.[74]

In some instances, neighbours directed slaves to the law. In 1790, after having been beaten on the orders of his mistress, the slave boy Lakey went to the burgher, Izaak Minnaar, to complain about the incident.[75] Izaak Minnaar sent him to Stellenbosch to lodge his complaint. Occasionally, slaves had kin of their masters on their side, or at least acting on their behalf. When Damon was beaten by Hendrik Gildenhuijsen in 1815, Gildenhuijsen's brother, Pieter Johannes Gildenhuijsen, sent him to the Landdrost to seek redress. In court, Pieter Gildenhuijsen further stated that his brother treated all the slaves of his mother 'very strictly' and that this instance of ill-treatment was not the first.[76] This case clearly shows the extent to which the servile population's access to the court was mediated by conflicts which existed within the settler community.

How, it may be asked, were slaves aware of these conflicts? Moodie, a nineteenth-century observer, provides an indication:

> In a Cape farmer's house there is no privacy. The family sit at one end of their long halls, while the other is a kind of thoroughfare for the slaves and house-servants pursuing their culinary options, who overhear the conversation and know all the most private affairs of their master and mistress nearly as well as they do themselves.[77]

To be sure, not all slave complaints came to court as a consequence of disputes within the 'community'. In 1775, for example, the slave woman Filida told her master: 'There are still Sirs to whom I can complain and I shall put the slaves up to it.'[78] In 1795, the slaves Eva van die Caab and Mourits van

---

71 CA, 1/STB 3/11, Testimony of Jan Lodewyk Pretorius, 25 Jan. 1764.

72 CA, 1/STB 3/11, Testimony of Josias de Kock, 15 May 1770.

73 CA, 1/STB 3/11, Testimony of Hendrik Gildenhuysen, 19 Dec. 1765.

74 CA, 1/STB 3/13, Testimony of Adonis van Mallebaar, 12 Mar. 1795, no. 92.

75 CA, 1/STB 3/12, Testimony of Lakey, 11 Jan. 1790.

76 CA, 1/STB 3/24, Testimony of Pieter Johannes Gildenhuysen, 8 July 1815, no. 102.

77 Moodie, Ten Years, p. 102.

78 'Daar zijn nog wel Heeren daar ik mijn beklag aan doen kan en zal de jongen daartoe opmaken.' CA, 1/STB 3/11, Testimony of Elsie Anna Meijburgh, 7 Feb. 1775.

Mauritius collectively complained to the Landdrost and Heemraden about the ill treatment that they suffered at the hands of their master, Jan Abraham Meyer of Roodezand.[79] Eva complained of her heavy work load which included cleaning the kitchen in the morning, fetching wood, cooking, and watering the 'garden' during summer. Furthermore, she had to cut wheat with the male slaves. It was not so much the heavy work burden which prompted her to complain, however, but the fact that she was beaten with a *sjambok* for not being able to comply with all these demands.

The complaints of slaves to local authorities in the nineteenth century differed markedly in volume and scope from those of the eighteenth. In reaction to amelioratory measures introduced by the British, slaves attempted to use the courts to obtain their freedom, relieve their heavy work burden, gain better living conditions, protect their property, maintain family ties, end sexual exploitation and, above all else, to end the punishments that they suffered.[80] These complaints were marked by an awareness that they had rights in law and that there were functionaries employed by the state to look after their specific needs. There is little indication in the records of the 1820s and 1830s that slaves needed to turn to their masters' neighbours to gain access to the courts. However, the legacy of the eighteenth century could not be wiped away at a stroke. In 1830, Michiel de Kock was tried by the circuit court at Stellenbosch for assaulting Cupido, a slave belonging to W. Esterhuizen. In De Kock's defence it was 'attempted to be shown that the case had been brought forward from a feeling of animosity existing between the owner of the slave and De Kock'.[81]

HONOUR, REPUTATION AND COMMUNITY

The previous section has argued that slaves' access to court was determined by fissures which existed in the settler community. But attention to community did not cease once cases got to court. These concerns impressed themselves on happenings in court as well. As already noted, one of the most important consequences to flow out of the existence of community was the fact that individuals had particular reputations. The reputation of individuals became an issue of crucial importance in cases where slaveowners had to face charges of violence against their slaves. Thus in 1793, the Landdrost showed marked reluctance to prosecute Dirk Gysbert Verwey on the sole grounds that Verwey was someone known to treat his slaves well.[82] In

79   CA, 1/STB 3/13, Testimony of Eva van de Caab, 11 Feb. 1705, no. 83.
80   Dooling, 'Slavery and Amelioration'; Mason, 'The Slaves and Their Protectors'; Mason, 'Hendrik Albertus and his Ex-Slave Mey'.
81   CA, 1/STB 2/31, Resident Magistrate contra Michiel de Kock, 1–4 Sept. 1830.
82   CA, CJ 75, Landdrost of Stellenbosch to Court of Justice in case of D.G. Verwey, 4 July 1793, p. 132ff.

another case involving the death of a slave, Pieter Roux claimed that he was known to the Court of Justice as well as to his neighbours as someone who was used to treating his slaves 'in conformity with the duties of a Christian'.[83] In another incident involving the ill-treatment of a slave, the Landdrost of Stellenbosch, although accepting that he could not rule out the possibility that Daniel Rossouw may have been lying, argued that his declaration was assisted by his 'good name and reputation'.[84]

By contrast, a slaveholder who was regarded as an ill-treater of slaves ran the risk of attracting a bad reputation.[85] In 1826 a number of Stellenbosch burghers, in a memorial objecting to Ordinance 19, one of the major pieces of ameliorative legislation, wrote that a master who was condemned as an ill-treater of slaves stood 'to lose his whole credit and reputation'.[86] Clearly, their standing in the community was of paramount importance to Cape slave-holders. In 1794, the lawyer acting in Rudolph Cloete's defence, claimed that the Landdrost's insistence on prosecuting Rudolph Cloete would have the effect of making his 'good name and reputation subject to public suspicion…and this would be highly damaging to the accused and his family'.[87] The centrality of reputation and community concerns in the courts survived well into the nineteenth century. In 1832, W. de Vos of Worcester, writing on behalf of his sister-in-law, who was charged with murdering her slave, noted that the accusation, 'whether founded in truth or not, has destroyed…and blasted the reputation of her whole family.'[88]

It follows that the emphasis on reputation influenced the quality of justice that the slaves received. This becomes abundantly apparent when the question of slave testimony is examined. In many cases the slaves on the farms were the only ones who could give decisive evidence and the admissibility of their testimony came to be of crucial importance. Considerable confusion reigned in the Cape law courts about the validity of slave testimony and it is not at all clear that 'the Court of Justice treated the evidence of a slave as any more or less trustworthy than that of a white person, even including his master'.[89] In 1793, for example, the Landdrost of Stellenbosch could provide three laws, all of which, to a greater or lesser extent, rejected the validity of

---

83   CA, CJ 78, Pieter Roux to Court of Justice, 22 Sept. 1796, p. 192ff.

84   CA, CJ 74, Landdrost of Stellenbosch to Court of Justice in case of Daniel Rossouw, 5 July 1792, p. 193ff.

85   Robert Shell has picked up on this, but relates this to what he perceives to be the overarching importance of 'the family' in settler society; Shell, 'Slavery at the Cape', vol 1, p. 230.

86   Memorial from Stellenbosch burghers to the Burgher Senate against the provisions of Ordinance 19, 10 July 1886, in Du Toit and Giliomee, *Afrikaner Political Thought*, p. 103.

87   CA, CJ 76, B. de Waal to Court of Justice, 8/9 May 1794, 227ff.

88   CA, AG 80 Part II, W. de Vos to Attorney General, 31 July 1832.

89   Ross, 'Rule of Law', p. 7.

slave evidence.[90] But there is clear evidence that the willingness of local authorities to accept or reject slave testimony depended upon the reputation of their individual masters.[91]

Community pervaded the legal system to the very end. In most cases, masters guilty of violence against their slaves were let off with light fines.[92] Occasionally, those guilty of killing their slaves were banished from the colony. Banishment was considered a severe sentence and represented 'the limit beyond which the Court of Justice would not go in disciplining the more unruly members of the white population'.[93] But even here the influence of considerations of community and reputation are clear. A Commission of Inquiry found, in 1827, that banishment seemed to be

> peculiarly applicable to those who may have contributed by the notoriety or the nature of their offenses to awaken the animosity or hatred of the members of a small community, and to whom the presence of an obnoxious individual even in state of confinement or condemned to a pecuniary penalty serves only to furnish fresh causes of irritation and perhaps of vengeance.[94]

Furthermore, some punishments were intended specifically to defame individuals and this 'presupposed that the accused had a reputation in the community'.[95]

How were the outcomes of cases affected in a changing legal structure? If 'community' is to be a useful tool of analysis at all, it must be able to take account of historical change. Community concerns limited the effective operation of 'amelioration' as well. In 1830, the Assistant Guardian of Stellenbosch complained that his office was

> becoming every day more responsible, and very invidious to the slave proprietors, for whenever a case of ill-treatment or otherwise is presented by me, and the master condemned, I am not only to draw upon myself the ill will of such a master, but sometimes that of his whole family connexions and which renders any attempt of mine on private business fruitless.[96]

Again, as in the eighteenth century, the concern with community was not necessarily to the disadvantage of the slaves. In 1826, for example, one Graaff-Reinet burgher, B.G. Liebenberg, readily agreed to manumit his female slave, Eva, after she sought the court's assistance in obtaining her

---

90   CA, CJ 75, Landdrost of Stellenbosch to Court of Justice in case of D.G. Verwey, 18 July 1793, p. 150ff.

91   For an elaboration of this point, see Dooling, *Law and Community in a Slave Society*, pp. 47–9.

92   Worden, *Slavery*, p. 113.

93   Ross, 'Rule of Law', p. 8.

94   Report of Commissioners of Inquiry upon Criminal Law and Jurisprudence, 18 Aug. 1827, *RCC*, vol. 33, p. 101.

95   A. Sachs, *Justice in South Africa* (London, 1973), p. 25.

96   CA, GH 26/60, Assistant Guardian, Stellenbosch, to Secretary of Government, 23 July 1830.

freedom, claiming that her master had promised to manumit her if she agreed to have 'carnal connection' with him. Although Eva had no witnesses to prove her claim that the promise had actually been made, Liebenberg stated that he would manumit her 'to prevent an action of such a nature against him to the dishonour of himself and his family'.[97] Liebenberg's fear of 'dishonour' turns attention to 'honour', a concept of central importance in slave-holding societies.

In examining the responses of slaves to a changing world, John Mason has chronicled the case of the slave Mey who, in 1832, lodged a complaint against his master, Hendrik Albertus van Niekerk of Koeberg, for beating him with a cat o' nine tails.[98] In the end Mey was freed because 'Hendrik Albertus valued his honor more highly than one slave and a few pounds sterling'.[99] This analysis draws on Patterson's concept of honour: a '"strong sense of honor" is "universal" in the "experience of mastership".'[100] Hendrik Albertus 'sought to square himself with his slaves, the law and...with his God'.[101] Patterson, however, is drawing on the work of Julian Pitt-Rivers. To him, honour 'is a sentiment, a manifestation of this sentiment in conduct, and the *evaluation of this conduct by others*, that is to say, reputation.' [My emphasis.] It 'stands as a mediator between the individual aspirations and the judgement of society'.[102]

Clearly, to Pitt-Rivers and Patterson, honour and reputation are intimately linked. In a sense, honour *is* reputation.[103] Roman-Dutch law, too, established the connection. Simon van Leeuwen, second only to Hugo de Groot in the history of Roman-Dutch jurisprudence, wrote in 1678 that 'Next to life nothing is more precious than one's honour and *the good opinion which others have of us*.' [My emphasis.][104] Establishing the connection between honour and reputation is important, because it has implications for law, community and a changing legal system. Mason's failure to do this leads him to declare that Van Niekerk had little to fear from a trial by jury.[105] On the contrary, this is probably what Van Niekerk feared most, because a trial by jury

97   Cited in Dooling, 'Slavery and Amelioration', p. 92.

98   Mason, 'Hendrik Albertus and his Ex-Slave Mey'.

99   *Ibid.*, p. 445.

100 O. Patterson cited in Mason, *ibid.*, p. 442.

101 Mason, *ibid.*, p. 441.

102 J. Pitt-Rivers, 'Honor', *International Encyclopedia of the Social Sciences*, vol. 6 (New York, 1968), p. 503.

103 This point is also made by J. Oakes, *Slavery and Freedom: An Interpretation of the Old South* (New York, 1990), p. 15.

104 S. van Leeuwen, *Commentaries on Roman-Dutch Law*, translated by J.G. Kotze, vol. 2 (London, 1881), p. 299.

105 Mason, 'Hendrik Albertus and his Ex-Slave Mey', p. 444.

would have exposed him as an ill-treater of slaves *in the presence of his peers*, which would have been so much more damaging to a man of local standing, as Van Niekerk was. Moreover, the failure of juries to convict was only partial acquittal. Instead, slaveowners were delivered to the 'court of reputation'. 'Public opinion forms…a tribunal before which the claims to honour are brought, "the court of reputation"…and against the judgements there is no redress.'[106]

There can be no doubt that the introduction of the jury system in 1827 gave slaveholders more power in the court-rooms.[107] But it did not do this in any simplistic way. Community remained paramount. In the De Villiers case, with which this paper opened, the jury returned a verdict of guilty.[108] They pleaded, however, that the testimonies delivered in favour of his character be taken into consideration. De Villiers was sentenced to a fine of £10. Far more interesting, though, is the fact that De Villiers's case is a clear manifestation of the desire of a slaveholding community to come to terms with the inherent contradictions, exacerbated by a changing legal structure, between concerns over honour and reputation and the 'rule of law'. Upon dismissing him, the judge told De Villiers that he would return home 'without the slightest stain or mark of disgrace, attaching his character from the result of the day's trial'. But this attempt at overcoming the contradictions could, at best, meet with only partial success, because where law and honour coexist, they are always liable to clash: 'one relates to persons and is centred in the will; the other aspires to reduce persons to legal categories, which involves attacking the fundamental principle of personal autonomy.'[109]

CONCLUSION

Community was a prime factor in shaping the operation of the law in Cape slave society. It controlled the access of slaves to court, influenced happenings in court, and decided eventual outcomes of cases. Community straddled the changes in the law between the eighteenth and nineteenth centuries, and exposed the contradictions inherent in slave societies. Reputation, which grew out of community and one of its chief concerns, was defined by the

---

106 J. Pitt-Rivers, 'Honour and Social Status', in J.G. Peristiany (ed.), *Honour and Shame: The Values of Mediterranean Society* (Chicago, 1966), p. 27.

107 In 1828 a number of Graaff-Reinet public functionaries acknowledged that they considered trial by jury a 'generous boon'; *The Colonist*, 24 June 1828. In 1831, the Governor of the colony wrote that 'it is very questionable if the trial by jury in criminal cases has been a benefit to the colony' because in 'some recent cases of maltreatment of slaves…prisoners were acquitted in the teeth of the clearest evidence against them.'; CA, GH 26/64, Governor to Secretary of State, 18 Apr. 1831, also cited by Mason, 'The Slaves and Their Protectors', p. 115.

108 CA, 1/STB 2/31, Circuit Court Cases, 2 Sept. 1830, no. 14.

109 Pitt-Rivers, 'Honor', *International Encyclopedia of the Social Sciences*, pp. 509–10.

slaveholding class itself. To be condemned as an ill-treater of slaves was to
have a bad reputation. And it is probably this social sanction that served to
restrain most slaveholders from *excessive* violence against their slaves. This
is not to deny the *routine* violence in the lives of slaves. Orlando Patterson,
in his survey of 186 slave societies, has not found a single such society
'where the whip was not considered an indispensable instrument'.[110]

---

110 Patterson, *Slavery and Social Death*, p. 4.

Plate 3 The Boer's Voorhuis, 1850, by Charles Bell. *Library of Parliament.*

2

PATERNALISM UNDER SIEGE
SLAVERY IN THEORY & PRACTICE DURING THE ERA OF REFORM c1825 THROUGH EMANCIPATION[1]

— JOHN EDWIN MASON —

'I have found that, to make a contented slave, it is necessary to make a thought-less one. It is necessary to darken his moral and mental vision... He must be able to detect no inconsistencies in slavery; he must be made to feel that slavery is right.'

Frederick Douglass, American fugitive slave, autobiographer, and abolitionist leader, 1845

'...the Laws enacted during the last few years have...produced in the conduct and demeanour of the slave[s] a change which could scarcely fail to be construed into, and indeed, to partake of an insubordinate character.'

Lt. Col. T.F. Wade, Acting Governor of the Cape Colony, 1833

Let me begin with a story about a beating. Rather, I would like to open with a *series* of stories that the perpetrator, the victim, and a witness told about a furious whipping that a master gave a slave. It is not the assault itself that captures my attention; it was, at once, awful and ordinary. My concern is with what the beating meant to those involved. The tales told by the master, the slave, and the witness reveal much about the ways in which they under-stood their lives and made sense of the world around them. It is a record of shared assumptions and incompatible perceptions.

The bare facts of the beating were never contested. In October 1837, Roeloff Petrus Johannes Campher, a cattle farmer in the district of George,

---

1   Many thanks to Robert Harms, Leonard Thompson, Chris Lowe, Susan Newton-King, Robert Ross, and the editors of this volume for their comments on earlier drafts of this essay. I am especially indebted to Robert Shell, whose insistent questioning of my assumptions and assertions about Cape slavery has, over the years, forced me into what he may finally agree is a more nuanced analysis.

2   Like others of her class, Dina had been freed and effectively re-enslaved as an 'apprentice' by the Abolition Act of 1833, 3 and 4 Wm. IV, cap. LXXII. The Act took effect on 1 Dec. 1834; apprenticeship ended on 1 Dec. 1838.

beat Dina, his 'apprentice',[2] severely lacerating her back and drawing blood. What master, slave, and witness disputed was not action but meaning—the meaning of the whipping and of the events that preceded it. Things could hardly have been otherwise.

The meanings that masters and slaves found (and that I shall find) in the incidents of daily life in the slaveowning households of the Cape Colony were not inherent in the events themselves. People created meaning out of the beliefs, values, common sense, and the often half-learned and semi-articulate ideologies that they carried around with them. Conditioned by an individual's training, experience, and political and economic interests, these beliefs, values, and ideologies constituted a 'world-view'. Meaning, then, was the product of the application of a world-view to the interpretation of events.

There was, of course, no single world-view to be found at the Cape, especially in the 1820s and 1830s, an age of reform. The thinking of every individual—whether master, mistress, slave, free servant, or colonial official—was unique. Yet slaveowners, slaves, and officials tended to think in ways which were variations on themes specific to their class. A species of paternalism guided the Afrikaner[3] slaveowners' thinking and directed their deeds, especially in their efforts to create and sustain a patriarchal social structure. Colonial officials acted under the imperatives of a liberal ideology imported from Great Britain. This emergent liberalism celebrated individual rights and challenged the slaveowners' paternalism on both the ideological and practical planes.[4] Ironically, this liberalism manifested itself most notably as the liberal paternalism of the Protectors of Slaves, the officials who enforced the slavery reform laws of the 1820s and 1830s.[5] The world-view of the slaves is more difficult to characterize. Even more than the others, it was a world-view in flux.

Prior to the temporary occupation of the Cape by the British in 1795 and

---

3   There are many names by which the Dutch-speaking settlers were called at the time and might be called today—Boers, colonists, settlers, inhabitants, Christians, whites, Afrikanders. Today, their descendants are 'Afrikaners', a term which first appeared in the early eighteenth century and has been in constant, if not always predominant, use ever since.

4   The most effective discussions of the impact of liberalism on the slaveowning Cape are to be found in R.L. Watson's superb study, *The Slave Question: Liberty and Property in South Africa* (Hanover and London, 1990), and M. I. Rayner's 'Wine and Slaves: The Failure of an Export Economy and the Ending of Slavery in the Cape Colony, South Africa, 1806–34' (Ph.D. thesis, Duke University, 1986). In *White Supremacy and Black Resistance in Pre-Industrial South Africa: The Making of the Colonial Order in the Eastern Cape, 1770–1865* (Cambridge, 1992), C. Crais looks at the ideological struggles of the period from the perspective of the eastern Cape, where slavery was a less central element of the political economy. An excellent overview is J.B. Peires, 'The British and the Cape, 1814–34', in R. Elphick and H. Giliomee (eds.), *The Shaping of South African Society, 1652–1840*, 2nd edn. (Cape Town, 1989), pp. 472–518.

5   See below and J. E. Mason, 'Hendrik Albertus and His Ex-Slave Mey: A Drama in Three Acts', *Journal of African History*, 31 (1990), pp. 423–45.

its final conquest in 1806, the world-views of masters and servants alike had been subsumed within the slaveowners' hegemonic, though contested, paternalism. To say that this world-view—the content of which I discuss below— was hegemonic, is not to say that it precisely dictated the thinking of each master and every slave. It certainly did not create docile slaves. But paternalism did define the natural order of things, the taken-for-granted. It imposed limits on what could be thought of as reasonable and seen as possible. The coming of British liberalism, with its increasingly explicit rejection of slavery, fractured the hegemony of slaveowner paternalism and gave the slaves the psychological and intellectual freedom to begin more openly to affirm a new sense of what was and what might be.[6]

World-views were the theories that guided slaves, slaveowners, and colonial officials in their actions. Their actions, in turn, reinforced and sometimes refashioned their theories. The nature of the relationship between thought and deed, between the theories and the practices of slavery, is the elusive subject of this essay. The way to begin, perhaps, is to recount the ways in which those involved made sense of Dina's whipping.[7]

Without Dina, these stories would never have been preserved and could not be retold here. She complained to the Special Justice[8] in George Town[9] about the whipping, and he recorded her tale and those of the others to whom he later spoke. The Justice was one of the several magistrates charged with overseeing 'apprenticeship', the four-year purgatory between slavery and freedom. In many ways, a Special Justice's responsibilities were similar to those of the Protectors of Slaves. The law allowed both sets of officials to intervene directly in the master-servant relationship when enforcing statutes governing the masters' and mistresses' treatment of their servants and the servants' obligations to their masters. What the law allowed, the slaves and apprentices required. Thousands of them took their grievances to the

---

6   There is an interesting resonance between my analysis of the ideological turmoil of the 1820s and 1830s and A. du Toit's suggestion that there is, in the 1990s, 'a three-cornered hegemonic contest' in the western Cape 'between traditional paternalist farmers, the new proponents of "human resources management" and the beginnings of a militant farm workers' union.' See A. du Toit, 'The Micro Politics of Paternalism: The Discourses of Management and Resistance on South African Fruit and Wine Farms', *Journal of Southern African Studies*, 19, 2 (1993), p. 317.

7   Readers will recognize that many writers have influenced my discussion of world-views and hegemony. Most notable, during the writing of this essay, have been A. Gramsci, *Selections from the Prison Notebooks* (New York, 1971); Jean and John Comaroff, *Of Revelation and Revolution: Christianity, Colonialism, and Consciousness in South Africa*, vol. 1 (Chicago and London, 1991); E. D. Genovese, *Roll, Jordan, Roll: The World the Slaves Made* (New York, 1972, 1974); C. van Onselen, 'The Social and Economic Underpinnings of Paternalism and Violence on the Maize Farms of the South-Western Transvaal, 1900–50', African Studies Seminar Paper, University of the Witwatersrand, 13 May 1991; and E.P. Thompson, *Customs in Common: Studies in Traditional Popular Culture* (New York, 1993).

8   There were 22 Special Justices in the various towns and villages of the Cape, created under terms of the Abolition Act of 1833 and a local ordinance, Cape Colony Ordinance 1 of 1835.

9   At the time, this was the principal town in the district of George; it is now known simply as George.

Protectors of Slaves and the Special Justices, forcing them to act as 'protectors', indeed as alternative sources of quasi-paternal authority. The hearings and the trials which followed generated voluminous records in which the voices of the masters, mistresses, slaves, apprentices, and other denizens of the Cape Colony can be heard, though often muffled by paraphrase, translation, and the uneven power relationships within the Protectors' and Justices' chambers.[10]

Dina began her story by telling the Justice that on a Tuesday morning in mid October 1837 she had been 'occupied in digging the dung out of the kraal'. She was loading a wagon, which would later take the dung to the farm's garden.[11] About noon, her master, Roeloff Campher, appeared at the kraal and noticed that she was no longer throwing the dung into the wagon, but was instead building a pile on the ground. Dina said that Campher asked her why she was doing this. She replied that the wagon was full and told him that she would put the freshly dug dung into a second wagon. She then returned to her work. Campher, unsatisfied with her explanation, repeated his question, and Dina again told him that the wagon could hold no more dung. Annoyed, Campher told her that when the second wagon arrived he would 'see' just how well she loaded it.

Dina said that as her master spoke, she stopped her work and leaned against her spade to rest. Campher exclaimed, 'By heavens if I get hold of you, the skin which you have been born with you will not retain.' Dina asked him what she had done to provoke this threat. Rather than answer, Campher reached for an ox-strap and gave her two blows across the shoulders. Dina took off, running.

She flew to the side of old Mrs Campher, Roeloff's widowed mother, who was standing in the flower garden. Dina told her that Campher wanted to beat her because she was unwilling to overload the wagon. Philip, another apprentice, had followed Dina to the garden and, acting on his master's orders, seized her and began to drag her towards the big house. Dina said that she, in turn, had grabbed old Mrs Campher by the hand and that the three of them, 'in this way', went towards her master's house.

As she approached the house, Dina saw Campher standing next to a ladder which was propped against the front wall. She told the Justice that she 'immediately formed a conclusion that [she] was to be tied to the ladder' and whipped. Old Mrs Campher must have thought much the same thing; she appealed to her son not to beat Dina, 'repeatedly saying "Petrus Petrus"'. But Roeloff Petrus Johannes Campher was 'in a great passion', according to

---

10 See J. E. Mason, 'The Slaves and Their Protectors: Reforming Resistance in a Slave Society, the Cape Colony, 1826–34', *Journal of Southern African Studies*, 17, 1 (1991), pp. 103–28.

11 All information about this case is drawn from a letter and enclosures, Special Justice, George Town, to Secretary to Government, 13 Oct. 1837, Cape Archives (CA), CO 465.

Dina, and he exclaimed, 'By God I shall now punish her, and she may complain.' By this, he seems to have meant that he would punish her until he was
satisfied, the legal consequences be damned.[12]

Dina said that at this point she 'creeped [sic] under Mrs Campher' and
begged Campher not to tie her to the ladder, 'but to beat [her] loose'. Her
pleas were useless. Campher ordered Philip to help him tie her to the ladder
and 'to pull off all [her] clothes'. Dina said that Philip 'pulled off [her]
gown, and shift, so that [her] whole back was bare', and Campher laid 'a
great many blows on [her] bare back'. After Campher put his *sjambok* down,
he ordered Dina back to her work. She said that she 'went to the kraal, and
dug the dung as before'. Late in the evening of the same day, after her master
had gone to bed, she left the farm to lodge her complaint with the Special
Justice.

As she ended her tale, Dina insisted that she had given her master no
provocation on the day of the whipping: not 'by looks[,] sighs, or shrugs'
had she done anything that ought to have enraged him. She said that she had
never before had reason to complain about her master and that she was 'very
well treated in general'. Though she admitted that she had been wrong not to
throw more dung into the wagon when ordered to do so, she could not
account for her master's 'outrageous conduct'.

Of the three witnesses who testified at the Special Justice's hearing,
Sina's testimony was the most complete. Sina, a 'Hottentot'[13] servant on the
Campher farm, was in the kraal with Dina on the day of the beating. Her
testimony accorded with Dina's up to the point at which Dina told Campher
that the pile of dung she was building was for a second wagon. According to
Sina, Campher told Dina that this wagon was too big to enter the kraal; it
could come no further than the gate. He said that he would make her carry
the dung to the wagon and load it by herself. Dina told him that there 'was
no harm' in doing as she had done and that the dung could easily be thrown
from where it was onto the second wagon. The exchange probably became
heated at that point since Sina was able to quote it directly in her testimony.

Sina reported that Campher had said, 'Dina, my book is full, if I do take
hold of you, you will not retain the skin with which you were born.' Dina
had replied, 'Master it is no harm that I have thrown the dung together
there.' Campher then said, 'Do you still speak?' Upon which Dina again said
'Indeed it is no harm.' Sina indicated that it was then that Campher had
grabbed an ox-strap and given Dina two blows. Dina had bolted off toward
the flower garden and old Mrs Campher. Sina said that Campher had had his
son—not the apprentice, Philip—fetch her and that she had seen young

---

12   The private whipping of an apprentice was an illegal act; physical discipline had become the prerogative
     of the state. Ordinance 1 of 1835, cap. VI, para. 13.

13   'Hottentot' was ordinarily used to signify a person historians would identify as 'Khoikhoi' or 'Khoisan'.

Roeloff Campher heading toward the house with Dina and the old woman in tow.

'On seeing this,' Sina said, 'I went and set [sic] behind the house—from there I could not see what took place with Dina.' She had heard, but had not seen, Dina begging Campher not to tie her to the ladder; she had heard the blows strike Dina and had counted 21 lashes; and she had heard Dina crying. She added that she did not believe that the wagon Dina had been loading had been quite full. When Campher had pointed this out to Dina, she had argued that it was so full that any additional dung would certainly fall off.

In his declaration, Campher admitted that he had ordered Dina to be tied to ladder and that he had beaten her with a *sjambok*, though he said he had applied only six or eight stripes. He was 'extremely sorry for it,' but he explained that his 'feelings were irritated' by Dina's 'habitual insolent conduct...and her having obstinately refused to obey orders.' Without accepting the law's claim that he had had no right to beat Dina, he proposed a deal to end the legal proceedings. He would forego his rights to the last 13 months of Dina's apprenticeship, 'Provided', he said, 'that the case is finally settled, so that [he would have] nothing more to do with it.' He agreed, that is, to free Dina early in order to avoid prosecution. Dina, according to the Special Justice, 'voluntarily declared' that she was 'fully satisfied' with this proposal. The Justice immediately dropped the charges and closed the book on the case of Dina and her ex-master, Roeloff.

Something that happened while Dina was shovelling dung had brought on the beating; on that everyone agreed. The accounts differed on much else, however, and the differences revolved around a series of related questions: Had Dina given Campher sufficient reason to beat her? Had Campher acted as a master should? Had the whipping been an inexplicable outburst of needless violence, or had he been within his rights to employ violent punishment? The world-views that the tellers brought to the tale determined the answers they gave and the shape of the stories they told.

Dina's world-view incorporated elements of the paternalism of her master, the liberalism of the law, and the experience of enslavement. Her narrative consistently underplayed the intensity of the verbal clash between her and her master. She insisted that she had played by the rules of the patriarchal household. She claimed that she had answered her master's questions mildly and continued with her labours. When Campher threatened her with violence, she merely asked him what she had done to anger him. Her behaviour should not have provoked him. She had been a dutiful servant. Dina even provided a short list of insolent gestures which she had *not* made, in an effort to strengthen the case for her innocence. She had shown no disrespect by 'look[,] sigh, or shrug'. She admitted that she ought to have obeyed her master's order to fill the wagon, but she could not agree that such a minor offence should have resulted in a beating. She could not explain Campher's rage. Until that day, she said, he had always been a good master.

There was a subplot to Dina's narrative, involving not master and servant, but servant and mistress. Dina recognized the special place that the patriarchal household reserved for the women of the master class. When her master threatened her with violence, she fled, as if by habit or reflex, to old Mrs Campher. And, as Dina anticipated, her mistress attempted to persuade her son to set his *sjambok* aside. Nor did this turn of events surprise Roeloff Campher; he simply ignored his mother and went on with the whipping. As we shall see below, mistresses often played a role that tended to smooth the rough edges of slavery and temper the violence inherent in the master-servant relationship.

If Dina's world-view was partially paternalist, she was also something of a liberal. The very act of seeking a redress of her grievances through the Special Justice's office was an expression of her belief that she, as an individual, had rights which her master could not deny and which the law would vindicate. When speaking to the Justice, Dina demonstrated some understanding of British liberalism. She knew, perhaps from the experiences of fellow apprentices or from the periodic visits that the Justices made to the farms to speak to the apprentices, that while the law did attempt to restrain the violence and capriciousness inherent in master-servant relationships, it also sought to ensure the subordination of servants to their masters by other means. Her awareness of what was expected of a servant may account for some, though not all, of what seems to be her acceptance of an obligation to obey her master's reasonable demands.

Yet paternalism and liberalism do not in themselves describe Dina's world-view. Despite her posturing, she was not a well-disciplined servant. She was troublesome; habitually so, it seems. Before beating her, Campher had cried out, 'Dina, my book is full'. Though she had mastered paternalism and liberalism—two sets of rules which governed the relationship between herself and her master—she did not always follow the dictates of either. We do not know much about her life prior to the day of her beating, but we do know that she claimed never before to have had reason to complain about her treatment. We might suppose that there ordinarily had been limits below which her performance as a servant did not fall, and above which the intensity of her resistance did not rise. Dina's world-view required that she perform labour for her master, though not as much or as willingly as either Campher or the law saw fit, and it allowed her to cause her master some, but not unlimited, trouble.

The assumptions of a paternalist world-view structured Sina's narrative.

In her testimony, she reconstructed the events surrounding Dina's whipping in considerable detail. It was a moment of extraordinary tension, and she understood how provocative Dina's words must have been. Though she did not use the word 'insolence' in discussing the day's events, she had not been surprised that the day had ended in violence. Sina understood that within the paternalist world-view there was such a thing as insolence and that Dina had been guilty of it. That Sina accepted this ideology as a proper ordering of the world cannot be known. The fact that she had ducked behind the house, rather than witness the blows which fell on Dina's back, might be seen as a silent protest.

Roeloff Campher was a committed paternalist—admittedly a rather broad description. He presented himself as a good master who had finally been pushed too far by an obstinate and habitually impudent servant. He was sorry and perhaps ashamed to have been goaded into violence, but Dina's conduct had incited his justifiable anger. While Campher had long found Dina's behaviour annoying, he had probably accepted it as the unavoidable price of drawing his wealth from the labour of unfree servants. But Dina had finally done the intolerable and provoked a violent assertion of patriarchal authority. Old Mrs Campher's pleas on Dina's behalf were to no avail; she did not head this household. Dina had appealed to another authority, one that had no rightful place, as Campher saw it, in the patriarchal structure of slavery. The Special Justices, like the Protectors of Slaves, were representatives of a deeply-resented British imperialism[14] and the imperfect, yet effective, agents of the liberal policies which granted slaves certain rights and compelled slaveowners to respect them. Finding himself caught in galling circumstances, spinning ever further out of his control, Campher chose to have 'nothing more to do' with Dina and the law. The price was high. To free himself, he had to rid himself of his apprentice, losing 13 months of unpaid labour in the process.[15]

The narratives of the participants in this domestic drama were shaped by an interpretation of the events specific to the tellers. The tales necessarily contain assumptions about the way the world was and the way it ought to have been. A look at other such tales will tell us more about what the masters and slaves of the Cape thought of the world they had made. Violence and benevolence, insolence and deference, and defiance, despair, and pride will reappear, almost always in shades of grey.

---

14   See n. 4 and J. E. Mason, '"Fit for Freedom": The Slaves, Slavery, and Emancipation in the Cape Colony, South Africa, 1806 to 1842' (Ph.D. thesis, Yale University, 1992), pp. 76–144.

15   Campher had come by his paternalism naturally. While he had himself never owned more than two slaves, he had grown up in a large slaveowning household. His father had, at times, owned more than 30 slaves, making him one of the larger slaveowners in the colony. (The average size of a Cape slaveholding in the 1830s was less than six.) The ages of the Campher slaves would have reinforced the seeming

THE SETTING

A half-century ago, C.W. de Kiewiet remarked that in the Cape Colony '[h]ard times came in 1820 and stubbornly stayed.'[16] The onset of the decline was less abrupt and its trough came later than De Kiewiet indicated, but the general point remains: the 1820s and 1830s were a time of considerable social and economic tumult. The economy, which had been riding high on the false buoyancy of an inflated currency and a booming wine trade, hit a reef in 1825. In that year, the rixdollar was fixed against the pound sterling at a considerable discount, and the duties on French wines entering the United Kingdom were markedly reduced, all but eliminating the competitive advantage of the inferior Cape vintages.[17] For the next several years, farmers, merchants, and officials at the Cape complained loudly of 'the dismal state of the colony's wine industry and the generally poor state of the colonial economy'.[18]

Politics at the Cape were also in disarray during the 1820s and 1830s and, since so many of the problems revolved around questions of labour control, political untidiness and economic stagnation were snugly intertwined. The Cape's chronic labour shortage continued despite the depressed economy. At the same time, Parliament pressed the colony to enact a series of measures limiting the masters' ability to exploit their servants and slaves. In 1828, the laws that had bound the colonial Khoisan ('Hottentots' and 'Bushmen') to their masters—a class second only to the slaves as a source of labour—were largely swept away by Ordinance 50. Beginning in earnest in 1826, a series of statues limiting the ability of masters to coerce the labour of their slaves, and establishing the office of Protector of Slaves to enforce the new laws, kept the slaveowners off balance and angry.[19]

The frankly stated purpose of the slavery reform laws was to prepare the slaves for eventual emancipation. To this end, masters were to be weaned away from their reliance on the whip as the principal means of disciplining their slaves. Slaves were granted the right to marry and create families, and to earn money to purchase their freedom, among other provisions designed to foster self-discipline and initiative in a class of soon-to-be-free workers.

---

naturalness of patriarchal arrangements. Between 1816 and 1834, when Campher was in his youth and early adulthood, 14 slave children were born into his father's household. Register of Slaves, George, CA, SO 6/50. Average slaveholdings derived from Returns of the Total Number of Slaves in the Various Districts According to the Several Classes and Values, CA, SO 20/61.

16   C.W. de Kiewiet, *A History of South Africa: Social and Economic* (London, 1941), p. 38.

17   Rayner, 'Wine and Slaves', pp. 190–3; Peires, 'The British and the Cape', p. 494.

18   Rayner, 'Wine and Slaves,' p. 193.

19   See, R.L. Watson's thorough discussion in *The Slave Question, passim*. Also, see Rayner, 'Wine and Slaves', pp. 246–306; Mason, '"Fit for Freedom"', pp. 76–144.

Liberalism and slavery were ultimately incompatible and, in 1833, Parliament decided that slavery must end. Formal emancipation came in 1834, though slavery lived on as apprenticeship until 1838.[20] (The end of slavery was by no means an unambiguous triumph for liberalism. Liberal social practices could not survive in the pre-industrial, colonial economy of the Cape. Paternalism endured well into the twentieth century, perhaps up to the present day.)[21]

Slaveowners hotly opposed the reforms. In 1826, two things were especially on their minds. First, they thought that a misunderstanding of the law's provisions would incite the slaves to rebel. They argued that an earlier, ineffective reform law had sparked a minor, but bloody revolt in 1825. Second, it outraged the slaveowners that the law gave to 'a third person'—the Protector of Slaves—'without any right or reason, the odious power of interfering in the arrangement of private affairs'.[22]

Slaveowners were right to be concerned. Not about rebellion, but about the unsettling effects of the office of the Protector of Slaves. The law had created officials—the Principal Protector of Slaves in Cape Town and the Assistant Protectors in the countryside—whose job it was to attend trials, hearings, 'and all other proceedings' to which a slave was party, to prosecute masters for violations of the law, and, more generally, 'to act [in court] in such manner as may be most conducive to the benefit and advantage of [the] slave[s].'[23] Since these men[24] were independent of and superior to the slaveowners, the law struck at the heart of the master-slave relationship. It undercut the slaveowners' pretensions that they were the sole source of protection, discipline, and indulgence for their slaves. It unavoidably destabilized the patriarchal household and its paternalist world-view. Between 1834 and 1838, the Special Justices had the same effect. It would have been odd if these events had left the world-views of masters and slaves untouched, and according to many observers, events touched them deeply.

The man appointed to the position of Principal Protector of Slaves, Major George Jackman Rogers, believed that the laws he enforced had kept the slaveowners in a state of 'constant agitation' and had made them 'morose and certainly less kind to their slaves than formerly.' The bond of

---

20 See I. E. Edwards, *Towards Emancipation: A Study of South African Slavery* (Cardiff, 1942), pp. 177ff.; Mason, '"Fit for Freedom"', pp. 124–33.

21 See Du Toit, 'Micro Politics of Paternalism', *passim*.

22 Memorial of Burgher Senate to Lt. Governor Bourke, 30 June 1826, in G. McCall Theal, *Records of the Cape Colony (RCC)*, vols. 1–36 (London, 1897–1905), vol. 26, pp. 90–4; Memorial to the Burgher Senate, 3 July 1826, *ibid.*, vol. 26, pp. 98–100; Memorial to the Landdrost and Heemraden of the Stellenbosch District, 10 July 1826, *ibid.*, vol. 27, pp. 110ff.

23 Cape of Good Hope Ordinance 19 of 1826, paras. 7 and 17.

24 Ordinance 19 is quite specific about this. It denies to the Protector and 'his wife' the right to own slaves engaged in agricultural labour. *Ibid.*, para. 3.

paternalism had seemingly collapsed. 'The tie which formerly existed between the master and the slave seems thereby completed [sic] severed, the master does little now for his slave from real regard, and the slave nothing for his master from affection.'[25] Toward the end of the slave era, another of the Protectors of Slaves agreed that the 'more intelligent' masters (presumably the more wealthy) had become less indulgent and more severe.[26] The Protectors were almost certainly too quick to descry the death of paternalism. Slaveowners waged a determined campaign against the reforms, defending their patriarchal world, defying the laws, and sometimes speaking fiercely of 'the rights of Dutch burghers and the length of Boer rifles'.[27] But the Protectors rightly understood that the slaveowners felt besieged.

The restless times also affected the slaves. Mary Rayner, an historian of Cape slavery, writes of 'new patterns' of slave resistance set in motion by the reforms. Though the slaves may not have understood the precise implications of the laws, they did realize that the reforms had done more than weaken their owners' legal hold over them; they had eroded both the theoretical foundations and practical underpinnings of paternalism. The result was a less tractable slave community.[28]

Major Rogers felt that by sipping at the cup of reform the slaves had 'imbibed the idea that they must soon be free... [and] are constantly guilty of those petty neglects and annoyances which irritate their owners'.[29] Another Protector claimed that a slaveowner had told him that the slaves in his neighbourhood had been '*spoiled*...by the mistaken interference of government'.[30] Against this, it must be said that even Major Rogers was not convinced that the slaves' behaviour had changed as markedly as some claimed. He acknowledged that 'the owners complain, and with reason, that their slaves are becoming very insubordinate, and they do make very frivilous [sic] pretenses for resorting to the Protector.' 'Yet,' he added, it was doubtful whether 'these do not...amount to very much more [than] the same sort of plague always heretofore in practice about Christmas and harvest,' a time of heavy labour during which slaves always tended to be unruly.[31] Similarly, one of the Special Justices wrote in 1837 that 'it afforded [him] pleasure to

---

25 General Observations, Report of the Protector of Slaves, 25 Dec. 1830, Public Record Office (PRO), London, CO 53/51.

26 Report of the Protector of Slaves, Eastern Division, 24 Dec. 1834, PRO, CO 53/57.

27 Quoted in A. du Toit and H. Giliomee (eds.), *Afrikaner Political Thought: Analysis and Documents, 1780–1850*, vol. 1 (Berkeley, 1983), p. 279.

28 Rayner, 'Wine and Slaves', pp. 151–89.

29 Observations of the Protector, June 1831, in Confidential Reports, Protector of Slaves, CA, SO 3/20a.

30 General Observations, Report of the Protector of Slaves, Eastern Division, 24 Dec. 1833, PRO, CO 53/57. Emphasis in original.

31 Report of the Protector of Slaves, Western Division, 20 Jan. 1834, PRO, CO 53/57.

find [on a tour of his district] the most satisfactory proofs of mutual good-will prevailing between the employers and apprentices'.[32]

Reports of an upsurge of insolence among the slaves and disquiet among the masters were probably correct, but overstated. The slaves' and apprentices' ability to press complaints against their masters through the offices of the Protectors and Special Justices—those 'new patterns' of resistance—exaggerated the apparent effects of the reforms. The behaviour of slaveowners, as well, was transformed less than the rhetoric of the day suggested. While the tremors which shook politics and economics at the Cape during the age of emancipation certainly affected the social landscape, they did not cause a fundamental upheaval. Slaves and apprentices continued to labour unpaid and under duress. The world-views which guided master-slave relationships were shifting, but that of the slaveowners was still recognizably paternalist and that of the slaves was by no means fully divorced from paternalism. A novel world-view might incorporate the old, along with the new. It was not, for instance, that the slaves suddenly wished for the first time to be insolent, but that they felt both encouraged and protected in doing so.

THE PATRIARCH IN HIS HOUSEHOLD

Few travellers wrote about the Cape in the late eighteenth and early nineteenth centuries without mentioning the graciousness of Afrikaner hosts and hostesses. John Barrow, no friend of the settlers, admitted that '[r]ude and uncultivated as are their minds, there is one virtue in which they eminently excel—hospitality to strangers. A countryman, a foreigner, a relation, a friend, are all equally welcome to whatsoever the house will afford.'[33] This was an important virtue. Inns and boarding-houses were found only in Cape Town; in the hinterlands travellers either slept in a farmer's home or in the open. A Mr du Toit, whose home lay on the main road to the interior, once told an English visitor that he had received over 360 'strangers' in a single year. Despite his 'very numerous' family and his being 'not over wealthy', he was, said the traveller, 'like most of the Cape farmers...very hospitable.'[34] Few of the farmers accepted payment.[35] As with fabled hospitality of whites in the American South, this courtesy extended only to those of a similar hue; slaves and free non-whites shifted for themselves.[36] In societies

---

32   Letter, Special Justice, George Town, to Secretary to Government, 16 Sept. 1837, CA, CO 465.

33   J. Barrow, *An Account of Travels into the Interior of Southern Africa, in the Years 1797 and 1798* (London, 1801), vol. 1, pp. 83–4.

34   [Samuel?] Sinclair, 'Descriptive Account of the Voyages...', (MS, Archives and Papers, University of the Witwatersrand, A 98), p. 125.

35   Anonymous, *Gleanings in Africa...the Cape of Good Hope and Surrounding Country* (London, 1806), p. 267.

stratified more by colour than by class, discrimination of this sort both signaled and reinforced the boundary between those within the charmed circle and those without.

The hospitality of the Boers meant access to their homes. White travellers freely entered colonial homes and retailed their impressions of life at the Cape to eager audiences in Britain and on the Continent. The households, as the visitors described them, were marked by intimacy between the slaveowners and their servants. The complement of this intimacy, it seemed to the travellers, was social anarchy. An Englishman, who visited a Franschhoek wine farm, contrasted what he found there with the 'comforts' of rural life in England and southern France. Though the master's house was large and the wine-stores and slave lodges extensive, the atmosphere was one of squalor. He described the front room—the *voorhuis*—of the main house where 'all the members of the family congregate':

> ...here sits the Vrouw, issuing her commands from an easy chair; here the meals are eaten, the clothes ironed, the psalms sung; here the Dutch-children and those of the slaves, equally dirty, and distinguished only by colour, sprawl together on the mud floor.[37]

Such intimacy was the norm. Few masters were wealthy enough to maintain separate slave quarters, and the households themselves were small. In 1834, the average slaveowner kept fewer than six slaves. Only 5 per cent of the masters possessed 20 or more slaves (though these slaves did account for 25 per cent of the total).[38]

Not all Britons were offended by such promiscuous mingling of black and white. Lady Anne Barnard, who spent several years at the Cape, wrote of her stay at a 'very respectable looking farm house'. In the evening,

> the room filled with slaves—a dozen at least—here they were particularly clean and neat, [the mistress] sat like charity tormented by a legion of devils, with a black baby in her arms, one on each knee and three or four larger ones round her, smiling benign on the little mortals.[39]

Yet the slave household shocked more often than it amused. Another Briton described another household:

> The master and mistress, the children without number, slave boys, slave girls, and Hottentots, are seen running, higgledy piggledy, in all directions: the master

---

36 W. Burchell, *Travels in the Interior of Southern Africa* (London, 1822, 1824; reprint edn., Cape Town, 1967), vol. 1, p. 190.

37 C. Rose, *Four Years in Southern Africa* (London, 1829), pp. 23–5.

38 Derived from Returns of the Total Number of Slaves in the Various Districts According to the Several Classes and Values, CA, SO 20/61, and R. Ross, *Cape of Torments: Slavery and Resistance in South Africa* (London, 1983), p. 25.

39 Lady A. Barnard, *The Letters of Lady Anne Barnard to Henry Dundas from the Cape and Elsewhere, 1793–1803*, A.M. Robinson (ed.) (Cape Town, 1973), pp. 85–6.

holloas, the wife scolds in her shrill screaming voice, and slaves and children run through all the discordant notes of confusion, all apparently without meaning, and all for the want of a little arrangement.[40]

Travellers to an exotic land may well be blind to many things, but it seems unlikely that anyone could seriously have believed that masters and slaves lived so intimately in 'confusion', without 'meaning' and 'arrangement'. In fact, the requirements of slaveowning called forth highly-structured arrangements, with quite precise meanings.

Nearly constant physical proximity, frequent and familiar personal interaction, and only modestly unequal living conditions (in all but the most prosperous town and country households) tended to subvert the hierarchy of master and slave. Since the integrity of the Cape's social structure and the efficient exploitation of the servile work force required the due subordination of slave to master, the slaveowners developed a theory and a set of practices designed to counteract the potentially levelling influences of life within the household.

Slaveowners organized their social and economic lives around the household. In it and through it the slaveowners arranged production and subordinated their slaves and servants. It was the institution within which the master's family of wife, children, slaves, and servants pooled income and resources—both voluntarily and under duress—while the master unequally distributed the rewards. Robert Shell argues that masters had begun to define their households in patriarchal terms by the late seventeenth century.[41] By the end of the eighteenth century, their ideological commitment to paternalism was clear.

It is true that the term 'paternalism' can be something of a blunt instrument, too large, the late E.P. Thompson has cautioned, for 'discriminating analysis'. It is a 'description of social relations as they may be seen from above', from the perspective of powerful men. In itself, it has little to say about 'forms of property ownership' or the distinction between slavery and free labour. It can confuse the real and the ideal, and it cannot be divorced from its suggestion of 'human warmth', of a consensual relationship. The term is problematic. And yet, Thompson concedes that paternalism can 'be a profoundly important component not only of ideology but of the actual institutional mediation of social relations' in societies as diverse as Meiji Japan and the antebellum American South.[42]

Paternalism has, in fact, proven to be a useful framework within which to

---

40   E. Blount, *Notes on the Cape of Good Hope* (London, 1821), p. 28.

41   R. Shell, 'The Family and Slavery at the Cape, 1680–1808', in W. G. James and M. Simons (eds.), *The Angry Divide: Social and Economic History of the Western Cape* (Cape Town, 1989), p. 23. See also, R. C. H. Shell, 'Slavery at the Cape of Good Hope, 1680–1731' (Ph.D. thesis, Yale University, 1986), pp. 226–75.

analyse 'a set of social practices' which took root most easily 'in the pre-capitalist countryside'.[43] Though it can be defined in various ways, it must at least bring master and servants together in some sort of quasi-familial relationship which 'transcend[s] barriers of caste or class'.[44] This relationship has little to do with 'human warmth'. As Eugene Genovese has remarked, 'Ole Massa's...benevolence, kindness, and good cheer' are secondary concerns. Paternalism grows out of a need 'to discipline and morally justify a system of exploitation'.[45] Charles van Onselen points out that because paternalism is 'predicated on the notion of a *male* of legal standing who enjoys the right...of exercising traditionally sanctioned authority over... his "family"', it is also inescapably gendered. All women in the household—slave and free—are subordinated to the patriarch, the 'father'. Age, too, is an element of paternalism. It is assumed that the patriarch is 'old enough to command the respect and deference of his "children".'[46]

Though the slaveowners of the Cape Colony never created the sort of sophisticated ideological discourse found in the antebellum American South or the works of modern historians, they could, when circumstances warranted, defend their interests in terms of a clearly-articulated paternalist world-view. In 1796, for instance, members of the Court of Justice, all of whom were slaveholders, responded to the British governor's request to comment on his plan to abandon the use of torture in the execution of 'blacks', most of whom were slaves. The court opposed the idea. Attempts to protect the slaves from violent punishment and torture, the court contended, were necessarily misguided. The proposal would compromise the patriarchal order to which the members of the court were tied. Slaves were naturally barbarous and had to be kept under strict, though just control. The law ought therefore to 'leave in the hands of the master such power as is necessary for him to exercise in the direction of his family', in which they included slaves as well as kin. The court then issued a paean to the patriarchal world, unhesitatingly coupling the relationship between a father and his family to that of a master and his slaves. 'Masters', the court wrote,

---

42   Thompson, *Customs in Common*, pp. 21–4.

43   Van Onselen, 'Paternalism and Violence', p. 38. The most influential recent analysis of paternalism is undoubtedly Eugene Genovese's *Roll, Jordan, Roll*. For South Africa in the later nineteenth and early twentieth centuries, see, for instance, C. van Onselen, 'Race and Class in the South African Countryside: Cultural Osmosis and Social Relations in the Sharecropping Economy of the South-Western Transvaal, 1900–50', *American Historical Review*, 95, 1 (1990), pp. 99–123, and T. Keegan, *Rural Transformation in Industrializing South Africa: The Southern Highveld to 1914* (Johannesburg, 1986).

44   G. M. Frederickson, quoted in Van Onselen, 'Paternalism and Violence', p. 9.

45   Genovese, *Roll, Jordan, Roll*, p. 4.

46   Van Onselen, 'Paternalism and Violence', pp. 9–10.

47   Court of Justice to Governor of the Cape Colony, 14 Jan. 1796, in Du Toit and Giliomee, *Afrikaner Political Thought*, pp. 91–3.

should zealously endeavour to conduct themselves as fathers rather than judges in their families, and act according to the strictest rules of virtue and humanity, not only in punishing but in rewarding... Upon these principles we...[hope] that it is not impossible to inspire the slaves with affection for their masters, for it is indisputably true that affection is a reciprocal sentiment.[47]

Thirty years later, paternalism guided slaveowners in their protests against the slavery reform laws. The Burgher Senate echoed the sentiments of the majority of the Cape's slaveowners when it condemned the laws because they gave the Protectors of Slaves, 'without any right...[,] the...power of interfering in the arrangement of private affairs...' If common sense denied outsiders the right to come between a father and his children, neither should the law create an official whose power over the slaves was superior to that of their masters.[48] At about the same time, an eastern Cape slaveowner spoke of patriarchal arrangements in terms which stripped paternalism to its essence: a master's slaves were his children. But this, he seems to have understood, was ideology, not nature; the master-slave relationship was fundamentally coercive. He said:

I could not rule [my slaves], unless...I had the power of exacting prompt obedience and repressing insolence with an occasional correction with my hand or whatever I chanced to have in it, *they are children and must be treated as such or spoiled*. [My emphasis.][49]

The language of everyday life reinforced this paternalist world-view. For example, slaveowning society referred to a slave man as a *jong* ('boy') and a woman as a *meid* ('girl').[50]

Slaveowners schooled their sons and daughters in the theory and practice of paternalism. Children of the master class learned at an early age that their relationship to physical labour and capricious violence was very different from that of the slaves. Slave children learned the same lesson. John Barrow wrote of the baneful effects

that a state of slavery invariably produces on the minds and habits of a people, born and educated in the midst of it... Among the upper ranks it is the custom for every child to have its slave, whose sole employment is to humour its caprices, and to drag it about from place to place less it should too soon discover for what purposes nature had bestowed on it legs and arms.[51]

William Burchell, another Englishman who travelled the colony extensively, thought that the children of masters and those of the slaves were more

---

48   Memorial of the Burgher Senate to Governor of the Cape Colony, 30 June 1826, *RCC*, vol. 27, p. 92.

49   Quoted in Report of the Protector of Slaves, Eastern Division, 14 Aug. 1833, PRO, CO 53/56.

50   J.S. Marais, *The Cape Coloured People, 1652–1937* (London, 1939), p. 5; Shell, 'Slavery at the Cape of Good Hope', pp. 269–73.

51   Barrow, *Travels*, vol. 1, p. 47.

'playmates' than anything else and that, in later years, they became what he oddly termed 'associates'.[52] A third Englishman, Robert Percival, probably struck the right balance between playfulness and severity when he noted that one of the first lessons slaveowners' children learn

> is to domineer over, and insult the slaves, who are subject to all their whims and caprices. Observe the Dutch children, and those of the slaves playing and mixing together, you will see the former at one moment beating and tyrannizing over the latter, and at the next caressing and encouraging them; so that from an early period they acquire an arbitrary and capricious habit of mind.[53]

Many rituals reinforced the lessons about the proper relationship between master and servant that slaveowners and slaves learned as children. An episode involving the slave, Floris, and his master, Francois Jacobus Roos, will illustrate several of them.

As Floris told the story, he had been sick for several days when, on a Saturday morning, his master asked him if he were well.[54] He answered, 'not quite', but said that he could 'work a little'. His master sent him to a neighbouring farm, where he did a light day's labour and returned home after dark. Floris said that when he arrived back on the farm he went to the kitchen and took a seat near the hearth to rest. Presently, Abraham, another of Roos's slaves, came into the room and told him that his master was calling. Floris entered the *voorhuis* and, he said, 'saluted' his master. Roos asked him whether he had remembered that it was his job to wash his master's feet. Floris replied that he knew it was his duty, but that he had only just realized that Abraham had brought a bucket of water to the room. 'On this,' he said, his master beat him with a walking stick 'until it broke to pieces'. Floris said that he had not resisted, but had asked his master why he was beating him. He had received no answer. After Roos had vented his anger, Floris washed his feet and again asked him why he had been beaten. His master, he claimed, still did not answer, but called out to Abraham to find another stick. Abraham did as he was told, and Roos gave Floris several more strokes. Floris added that washing his master's feet was his daily chore, though Abraham had done the job during his recent illness.

Roos's version of events must be inferred from the answers Floris gave to the unrecorded questions that his master put to him on cross-examination. Roos hoped to establish that he had not hit Floris more than a very few times. Floris said, however, 'I am certain you gave me more than two strokes—the stick would not have broken to pieces with two strokes.' Roos

52 Burchell, *Travels*, vol. 1, p. 34.

53 Percival, *Account*, p. 280.

54 This tale is drawn from, Dagvarings en Verklarings, 1832–4, Assistant Protector of Slaves, Stellenbosch, CA, STB 22/165.

also tried to demonstrate that the slave had been insolent. In answer to one of his questions, Floris replied, 'I did not...say "You must account to God for having beaten me in this manner".' Rather, Floris insisted that he had said, 'if you were a sensible man you would listen to what I have to say.' Finally, Roos attempted to prove that his slave rarely accorded him the expected deference. Floris maintained that he did: 'On Sunday morning I was standing in the kitchen before the fire and did not see you come in, you said Good morning [and] I immediately turned round and saluted you—You only said Good morning to me once.'

Two witnesses contributed to the story. The first, Dr Daniel O'Flinn, a surgeon, testified that he had 'inspected' Floris and found 'severe livid contusions on the left shoulder and arm, across both shoulder-blades, and the left shoulder and arm very much swollen down to the elbow.' He believed that ten blows with a walking stick, if 'given with force by a strong man,' would have caused the wounds.

Abraham, the second slave, contradicted much of what Floris had said about the nature of the encounter. He thought that Floris had indeed spoken 'in an insolent manner'. Abraham said that when Roos asked Floris whether he had understood that he was to wash his master's feet, he had answered, 'Yes,' but had asked why Abraham could not do it since he had brought the water. Roos dared him to repeat what he had said, and Floris again asked why Abraham could not do the foot washing for the night. It was then that Roos had beaten his slave. Abraham added that, on that Saturday evening, Floris had not addressed Roos as 'Sir, or Master, or...any other form of respect'.

Several rituals of subordination are apparent in this passage—the foot washing, the salute, the deferential form of address, the beating. The most striking is the washing of the master's feet. John Barrow was one of a number of travellers who witnessed similar scenes, and he had no doubt that hygiene was not the point of the exercise. He described an Afrikaner farm woman, 'born in the wilds of Africa, and educated among slaves and Hottentots,' who made no

> scruple of having her legs and feet washed in warm water by a slave before strangers; an operation that is regularly performed every evening. If the motive of such a custom were that of cleanliness, the practice of it would deserve praise; but to see the tub with the same water passed round through all the branches of the family, according to seniority, is apt to create ideas of a very different nature.[55]

Washing the feet of another was, and is, a ritual familiar to anyone acquainted with John 13:1–20. In that passage, Jesus washes His disciples' feet, a demonstration of His humility. It was a sign as well that though He was their Lord

---

55   Barrow, *Travels*, vol. 1, p. 80–1. See also, Sir J. E. Alexander, *An Expedition of Discovery into the*

and Teacher (sometimes rendered 'Master'), He was also their Servant (sometimes rendered 'Slave'), who would die for them and for all people. Floris seems to have understood that the object of this daily rite was humiliation. The act of stooping at his master's feet to wash the lowest parts of his body emphasized the degradation of enslavement. It forced him to acknowledge and enact his subordination. It was shameful work which he had avoided while he was ill, and that he tried, unsuccessfully, to continue to evade.

There are less onerous rituals of deference contained in the story of Floris and Francois Roos. Like Floris, Cape slaves were to 'salute' their master; they were to speak before being spoken to. They were to address their masters with terms of respect: 'sir' and 'master', (English for *seur* and *baas*, both common words in the early nineteenth-century Cape). Any failure on the slaves' part to salute their masters and use the proper forms of address constituted disrespect, insubordination, insolence. Such omissions were signs of fissures in the structure of domination. Floris, despite his protests to the Protector, had not offered his master the deference and obedience that he expected, and he was punished for it. A beating was the ritual of last resort.

Floris's tale illustrates (in a negative way) the general demeanour that slaveowners expected of their slaves and the consequences of failing to meet those expectations. But the rituals of deference and discipline are not in themselves enough to explain the behaviour of either slaves or slaveowners. Some slaves and slaveowners most of the time, and most of them some of the time, accepted the terms of what was essentially a paternalist compromise: slaves gave their owners much of what they wanted in terms of work and respect and, in exchange, owners granted their slaves the indulgence that a parent might accord a troublesome child. While it is true that the physical and psychological restraints of slavery rubbed many slaves raw, and that slave resistance was persistent and inventive, slaves and their owners did not spend their lives constantly at each others' throats. Paternalism's humane aspects complemented and often masked elements that degraded, oppressed, and exploited. Paternalism was a compromise, but it was one that was continually renegotiated. Slaves alternately resisted and acquiesced to their owners' demands; slaveowners coerced and indulged.

Barend Swartz, for instance, was a master torn by the contradictory impulses that slaveowning generated. He was a Graaff-Reinet cattle dealer, who once ordered his apprentice, Dampie, to take 300 sheep to a military camp for sale. He so trusted Dampie that he gave him a rifle with which to protect the livestock from thieves and 'wolves'[56] and put him in charge of

---

Interior of Africa (London, 1838), p. 17.

56 Reports of slaves and apprentices carrying firearms are rare, but appear often enough to indicate that in the eastern Cape the practice was routine, as long as it was confined to known and trusted men. By 'wolves', colonists meant hyenas.

several Khoisan assistants. Dampie disappointed his master. He lost 24 sheep on his way to the soldiers' encampment and, on the trip home, assaulted Peet [sic], one of his assistants, with the butt of the rifle while in a drunken fury. Swartz took Dampie to the Special Justice in Graaff-Reinet, and the apprentice was condemned to receive 15 lashes. But Dampie never felt the lash. Swartz asked that the punishment be 'forgiven', since Dampie had always had 'a general good character' prior to this incident.[57] Dampie was not a perfect servant, but he was more than good enough. His record had been so free of trouble that his master had trusted him to guarantee the safe arrival and sale of valuable property and to return home with the profits, despite being equipped with a gun, a tool which would have greatly increased the odds of a successful escape. He was a servant worth indulging.

Many other masters and mistresses were quick to anger and quick to forgive. A Stellenbosch wine farmer first whipped his slave, August, for having been 'very improper and insolent' and immediately afterward 'caused a glass of wine to be given him,' when he 'begged his master's pardon.'[58] Moses, an apprentice on the farm of Roeloff van der Merwe of the Worcester district, narrowly avoided the sort of beating that August had received. In front of several other apprentices, he had accused his master of having stolen some cattle. He compounded his crime by repeating the charge to Van der Merwe's face. Moses then dared his master to strike him, knowing perhaps that physical punishment was illegal under apprenticeship. Instead, Van der Merwe took him to the Special Justice for punishment. He told the Justice that he had been so incensed by his apprentice's gross insolence that, as he put it, 'I was afraid of forgetting myself so I ran away.' The Justice ordered 15 lashes to be laid on the apprentice's back. Before the sentence could be executed, Moses was 'forgiven at the earnest request of his mistress'.[59]

Moses, like Dampie, escaped punishment and, like August as well, was forgiven. The absolution the three received was almost certainly sincere, yet it came only after the hierarchy of master and slave had been reasserted through violence or the threat of violence. In Moses's case, his mistress, not his master, had forgiven him. This was not uncommon. Mistresses shared much of the authority over subordinates that the paternalism conferred on the master, but they seem often to have used it in less violent ways.

THE MISTRESS AND HER SLAVES

Paternalism legitimated the subordination of slaves and women by infantilizing them; they were permanent minors in the 'father's' household. But

---

57   Minutes of the Special Justice, Graaff-Reinet, 1835–8, CA, GR 17/45.

58   Report of the Protector of Slaves, Assistant Protector, Stellenbosch, 24 June 1831, PRO, CO 53/52.

59   Criminal Record Book, Special Magistrate, Worcester, 1835–6, CA, WOC 19/26.

paternalism did not reduce women of the slaveowning class to the level of slaves. Their privileges derived from the exploitation of the slave labour, and they possessed power over the slaves which flowed to them through their relationship with their husbands. Paternalism, on the other hand, twice burdened female slaves: they were subordinated by virtue of their status as slaves and as women. Between them and their mistresses there could be only an attenuated sisterhood of the oppressed.[60] The mistresses and their female slaves and apprentices did, however, share the intimate world of the home in ways that masters and their male and female slaves did not.[61]

Mistresses rarely worked outside of the household, nor did they labour in the fields. They supervised slave servants in the performance of domestic chores in the home and garden, and the poorer mistresses performed some of the household labour themselves. The rhythms of their lives determined that they would spend most of their time in close physical and emotional proximity to some of their slaves, coping with the problems inherent in the enslavement of willful, self-conscious human beings.

Mistresses sometimes turned to violence when they could not control their slaves by other means, and they justified their actions in terms similar to those the masters used. Hester van Rooyen, the wife of a small farmer in the Albany district, was such a woman. For reasons which cannot be known, Van Rooyen assaulted her slave housemaid, Candase. As Candase told it, Van Rooyen beat her with her fists, slammed her head against the ground, and lashed her with a whip. A white visitor, Lena Osthuisen, tried to pull Van Rooyen off her slave, knowing that it was illegal under the terms of the reform laws to beat a female slave and that Van Rooyen might be fined. But Van Rooyen had shouted, 'it's my money, my slave and if I beat her dead it is no ones [sic] business.' In court, Van Rooyen, whose husband was bedridden and who was herself 'within a short time of her confinement',[62] admitted her guilt.[63] Her husband's illness had, perhaps, forced her to assume the role of head of household. If so, she was well prepared. Her words and deeds indicated that she shared much of the paternalist ethos of the men of her class and race. And she reaffirmed her allegiance to that ethos when it was challenged by an appeal to the liberalism of the reform laws.

---

60   This discussion draws on D. G. White, *Ar'n't I a Woman?: Female Slaves in the Plantation South* (New York, 1985); J. Jones, *Labor of Love, Labor of Sorrow: Black Women, Work, and the Family from Slavery to the Present* (New York, 1985), pp. 11–13, 24–9; and E. Fox-Genovese, *Within the Plantation Household: Black and White Women of the Old South* (Chapel Hill, 1988), pp. 34–5 and chs. 2 and 3, *passim*.

61   The sexual exploitation of slave women by their masters, which will not be discussed in this essay, was a severe and persistent problem. See Mason, '"Fit for Freedom"', pp. 202–25.

62   She had recently given birth.

63   Day Book, Assistant Guardian of Slaves, Graham's Town, *c*.1826, CA, GR 17/17.

There was, of course, more to the mistress-slave relationship than violence and resistance. A story told by the slave housemaid, Regina, captures some of the complexities criss-crossing the relationships between women in the slaveowning household.[64] Regina's mistress was Bella de Jong, the wife of Francis de Jong, a small farmer. Regina was the family's only slave. She had been with them since her early teenage years, and she was now 23 years old.[65] According to Regina, the trouble began when she and her mistress exchanged harsh words about Regina's children. Both were boys and had died as infants. Bella de Jong accused Regina of having been a careless mother and said that she had been to blame for her babies' deaths. Regina's retort was equally cutting. She told her mistress that the boys had died because she and her husband had not allowed her enough time to care for them and 'that if she had another mistress she could have brought her children up.'

The matter smouldered until the following day. In the morning, Regina, her mistress, and the two De Jong daughters were 'picking and cleaning corn for the mill'. De Jong began to scold Regina about her alleged maternal negligence, and she had mocked her slave, 'calling her "big belly"'. (Regina was pregnant at the time.) At this, Regina said, the girls had left the house and gone out into the yard; the atmosphere, apparently, had become noticeably threatening. Regina told her mistress 'that she should not say such things before the children as it would make them wicked'. De Jong then shut the door, hustled Regina into the bedroom, and beat her.

The intimacy of the relationship between Regina and De Jong is apparent, as is intimacy's price. De Jong had been present at some of the most private and painful moments of Regina's life, having watched her grow from adolescence into adulthood, give birth, and lose her children in infancy. She drew on that knowledge when subjecting her slave to scornful teasing. Regina's willingness to rebuke her mistress for the indelicacy of the words she used in front of the children suggests that there had been moments in which she was able to transcend her role as a slave. Her impertinence was born of familiarity and perhaps friendship. But De Jong allowed none of this to undermine the hierarchy that defined the mistress-slave relationship. When Regina presumed to speak to her mistress as an equal, her mistress shamed her in a effort to put her back in her place. Later she turned to violence, the foundation on which the subordination of the slave ultimately rested. Familiarity was possible, but its terms were decidedly unequal.

As the story of Regina and Bella illustrates, there could be a suppleness to mistress-slave relations. Slaves, for instance, sometimes ran to mistresses for

64 The following relies on Day Book, Assistant Protector of Slaves, Graham's Town, c.1832, CA, GR 17/17.

65 Register of Slaves, Albany, CA, SO 6/2.

protection when threatened with physical punishment. Dina, seen at length above, sought out old Mrs Campher, her master's widowed mother, when Roeloff Campher began to beat her. The old woman implored her son to stop, repeatedly calling his name, but to no avail. Her son was 'in a great passion', and he wielded the authority of a patriarch.[66]

Slave children sometimes tried to escape parental wrath by seeking a mistress's protection. When Grietje, a slave housemaid, tried to punish her child, it ran to its mistress for protection. Grietje followed, a witness reported, and accidentally hit her mistress with a switch while striking at her child, who had hidden behind its mistress. Grietje got the worst of what followed; her master and mistress retaliated, covering her arms and shoulders with 'livid contusions'.[67] Grietje's mistress played the roles that paternalism assigned her, at once protector and disciplinarian.

If there was bitterness between mistress and slave, there was also humour. Undoubtedly, masters and slaves laughed at and with each other, told jokes, and engaged in horseplay. But most of the evidence of lightheartedness which has survived involves banter between the women of the household. (Is this just a quirk of the records?) For instance, the Assistant Protector of Slaves in Stellenbosch once heard about what had passed between the slave woman, Claartje, and her mistress. As Claartje's mistress told the story, she had been

> in her garden eating an apple with a dessert knife in her hand, [when Claartje] who was working with the other slaves, laughed at, and mimicked her—she called [Claartje], and asked her how she darest do so—[Claartje] denied it[,] on which with the flat of the knife, she tapped [Claartje] on the arm, and told her to go about her business; [Claartje] acknowledged this statement to be true.[68]

It is clear that disrespect did not always bring on violence. The playfulness in Claartje's teasing and in her mistress's response, coexists with the inherent seriousness the slave's subordination. This element of play, which was never without its cutting edge, is also evident in Romana's case.

Romana, a slave woman, charged her mistress with hitting and kicking her seven-year-old daughter, Marie. Witnesses told a different story. Marie said that her mistress had not kicked her, but had slapped her once. Truy and Roslyn, two slave women, said that Romana had argued with her mistress after had she slapped Marie. Truy said that her mistress's response was to make Romana sit on a stool 'to make her ashamed'. Roslyn explained that when Romana 'spoke loud...[,] her mistress told her that if she spoke so much to sit in that chair and be mistress and she would be the servant.' When

---

66 Letter and enclosures, Special Justice, George Town, to Secretary to Government, 13 Oct. 1837, CA, CO 465.

67 Report of the Protector of Slaves, Assistant Protector, Stellenbosch, 24 June 1831, PRO, CO 53/52.

68 Report of the Protector of Slaves, Western Division, Stellenbosch, 28 May 1833, PRO, CO 53/55.

Romana refused to sit, 'her mistress forced her to do so'.[69]

Romana's mistress punished her by shaming her, by forcing her to assume the farcical position of the mistress. Though the reversal of power relationships is often an element of the carnivals of the lower classes, here the inversion was coerced and chastening. The element of teasing is readily apparent, however, and demonstrates one of the ways in which humour might ease the tensions inherent in slavery.

THE SLAVES RESPOND

How did the slaves respond to paternalism and the patriarchal world it shaped? They responded in as many ways as there were slaves. They might display self-respect and generosity at one moment, and avarice and opportunism the next. They possessed the complexity of all human beings; in this, of course, they were no different from their owners. Some slaves nobly resisted enslavement and struggled to topple the material and ideological structures of domination. Others withered under the physical and psychological onslaught. Most slaves moved between these poles, tending to neither extreme, as Fortuin's tale will show.

Fortuin, who was 18 years old, was one of 11 slaves belonging to Jacob Eksteen, a farmer in the Stellenbosch district.[70] One day in October 1832, he appeared at the office of the Assistant Protector of Slaves in Stellenbosch to register a complaint.[71] Eksteen had beaten him, he said, because of a remark Eksteen's daughter had allegedly overheard him make. The incident began, he continued, on a Sunday morning, the slaves' customary day off, when his master had sent another slave to summon him to the house. Eksteen had wanted him to tend the horses while Phoebus, the wagon driver, planted melons in his mistress's garden. Fortuin said that he had made no move to answer his master's call. Soon afterwards, his master summoned him again, and this time he did appear. Fortuin said that Eksteen confronted him about the remark his daughter had overheard. The girl told her father that Fortuin had 'grumbled at having to take care of the horses', saying that he wished instead to mend his clothes. This, Eksteen felt, constituted insolence. Fortuin told his master that he would indeed have preferred to patch his clothing, but he insisted that he had not been disrespectful. At that, his master beat him with a piece of wood.

Fortuin left the farm the next morning, ostensibly on his way to the Protector's office in Stellenbosch. He went first to the village of Paarl, where

---

69   Report of the Protector of Slaves, Eastern Division, Graaff-Reinet, 23 Jan. 1834, PRO, CO 53/57.

70   Register of Slaves, Stellenbosch, CA, SO 6/50.

71   What follows is drawn from Dagvarings en Verklarings, 1832–4, Assistant Protector of Slaves, Stellenbosch, CA, STB 22/165.

he spent the night. The next day, he travelled to the Clapmuts River where he found Piet, a runaway slave. Piet asked him to stay, but Fortuin instead went on to Kuils River and the farm of a Mr Wolff. He told Wolff about his encounter with Piet. Wolff assembled a party of armed riders and, with Fortuin leading the way, went back to the place Piet had last been seen. Though Piet had disappeared by the time the party arrived, another runaway, Maart, and 'a girl' were found in the vicinity and captured. Fortuin said that he then left the riders and went on to the Protector's office.

Under cross-examination at the Protector's hearing, Fortuin denied his master's claim that he had called Eksteen's daughter a liar. He also said that he could not recollect having grumbled about the extra work. He mentioned that, 'until about two days' before the Sunday in question, the job of tending the horses had been his. His master had removed him from the job, telling him that he had not taken 'proper care' of the animals.

Witnesses added little to the story. Flora, the cook, said that her master had indeed beaten Fortuin, but that he had given him only two strokes with a thin stick. She added that by the time Fortuin and Eksteen had finished their argument, Phoebus had long since planted the melons and was ready to return to the horses. Phoebus confirmed the gist of Flora's testimony and said of Fortuin, he 'is not a good slave, he is a great rascal.'

Phoebus's typology is as ambiguous as it is pithy. What qualities constituted 'goodness' in a slave? Did Phoebus, for instance, consider himself to be 'good'? His master had, after all, given him the job of tending the horses after Fortuin had proved to be unsatisfactory, and, on the day in question, he quickly had set about the work of planting the melons. He seems to have been a slave who knew how to avoid friction and earn rewards. Did this make him clever or cowardly? As for Fortuin, did Phoebus believe that he was a 'great rascal' because he was careless about his work, because he shirked extra duties, or because his insolence had provoked a mild beating? We do not know enough about Phoebus to answer these questions. But Phoebus's world-view did (for whatever reasons) define Fortuin as 'not good'. Flora seems to have shared his assessment.

It is possible to see Fortuin in another light. He may have been a young man engaged in spirited resistance, at one point defending his right to a day off, at another contemplating escape, at yet another seeking legal redress. Surely any slave was right to resist a master's demands. Would Phoebus have said that it was bad for a slave to be unable to swallow his pride and do the master's bidding? It is equally possible, however, that Fortuin was driven by impulse, not principle. By no means did he leave the farm and go directly to the Protector's office. He meandered about the countryside, spending some of the time with Piet, the runaway. In the end, he did not join him; he betrayed him. It is likely that Fortuin calculated that the miseries of life on his master's farm were less onerous than the difficulties of life on the run. He probably hoped, as well, to curry favour with his master and the Protector by turning in a runaway. From the perspective of fugitive slaves—say, Maart and 'the girl'—such opportunism would certainly have made Fortuin 'a great rascal'.

Still we should not discount the authenticity of his acts of resistance. We should not expect anyone's personality, certainly not a slave's and especially not a teenage slave's, to be perfectly consistent. Fortuin was a youth on the verge of manhood, trapped in a system which defined 'manhood' as the prerogative of masters, not slaves. Slavery wore away at the souls of all slaves, men and women, even as they struggled to preserve a measure of dignity. Some slaves, of course, lost the battle.

One response to enslavement was to accept one's role as paternalism defined it and sink into despair and self-hatred. Blom, one of many slaves who drank to excess, once charged his master with having beaten him without due cause. At the Protector's hearing, however, he admitted that he had been insolent when answering his master and that he 'frequently gets drunk and merits punishment'. He withdrew his complaint, acknowledging that 'his master could daily find sufficient grounds for punishing him if so disposed.'[72] Blom seems to have been doing more than merely mouthing the expected lines in the hope of avoiding punishment. He seems to have internalized the degraded role paternalism had prepared for him. If so, he was not alone.

One or two examples of degradation will stand for many. There was the apprentice, Lydia, of Graaff-Reinet village, who used 'horrid and indecent' language, while making 'a noise in the street', who stood in the street before the door of a 'Hottentot' woman 'for a considerable time and indecently exposed her person', who refused to work as ordered, who was repeatedly hauled before the Special Justice and punished, and who still did not mend her ways. There was the more ambiguous case of the apprentice, Eva, also of Graaff-Reinet. She was very often drunk; she once 'purposely' broke two basins and threw bread about the house; she used indecent language in front of her master's children; she 'contumaciously' refused to work; she twice ran away in the company of Khoikhoi; she was repeatedly incarcerated in the jail on bread and water, and, consequently, she was sent back and forth between masters, never pleasing one.[73]

Lydia's behaviour appears irrational and self-destructive. While she caused her master a considerable amount of trouble, it was not counter-balanced by any good she did herself. Even her refusal to work was a dead end, a blind lashing out that brought only more grief. Eva also engaged in

72   Report of the Protector of Slaves, Eastern Division, Graaff-Reinet, 23 Jan. 1834, PRO, CO 53/57.

73   Both cases in, Minutes of the Special Justice, 1835–8, Graaff-Reinet, CA, GR 17/45.

self-destructive behaviour, but that was not all: she ran away, an act of resistance. Despite her drinking, the Eva we see in the records was not so broken by slavery that she did not attempt to escape the institution which produced her unhappiness.

Most slaves found ways to avoid the cycles of despair and degradation that trapped Blom, Lydia, and even Eva. These slaves engaged in resistance. The slaves' open and determined physical resistance to slavery has been amply documented elsewhere.[74] But ideological resistance was just as important. Many slaves refused to accept passively the roles paternalism established for them. Instead, they created alternative world-views—appropriating elements of religious teachings and liberalism, reinterpreting paternalism, drawing on the pride they took in their work and the love they felt for their families, and improvising other elements from whatever materials fell to hand.

Paternalism promised a world of reciprocal rights and obligations on which it was hard to deliver. The realities of oppression and exploitation were always close to the surface, making it inevitable that slaves would often see through their owners' pretensions. The slaves' refusal to accept their masters' reading of paternalism is readily apparent in the records of the Protectors and Special Justices. The reports contain numerous incidents illustrating physical and ideological confrontations between slaveowners and slaves. Valentyn Snitler[75] and his master, Jacobus Vermaak, engaged in one such skirmish.

Snitler told the Assistant Protector of Slaves in Uitenhage that his master had beaten him because he could not work due to an illness. Vermaak saw it differently. Snitler had done his chores, but poorly, and Vermaak had asked him why this was the case. A witness testified that Snitler had answered, 'in a very impertinent manner', that he was not well. Vermaak ordered him to take medicine or continue working. Snitler had refused to do either and, according to the witness,

> thereupon commenced to cursing and swearing, and holding his finger in his master's face said 'We have been created by one God and I am as good as you.'

Vermaak whipped the insolent slave.[76] Snitler's God, whether the God of Moses or Muhammad,[77] had shaped his consciousness and sanctioned his

---

74 See Rayner, 'Wine and Slaves', pp. 130–89; Ross, *Cape of Torments, passim*; N. Worden, *Slavery in Dutch South Africa* (Cambridge, 1985), pp. 119–37; Mason, '"Fit for Freedom"', pp. 110–44, 372–424.

75 Though it was the custom in legal records to identify a slave or apprentice by a single given name—a custom which for freed people, Khoisan, Bastaards, and other blacks continued deep into the nineteenth century—slave and apprentice surnames did occasionally enter the records. The slaves did, indeed, possess family names by which they called themselves, and they passed these names on through the generations.

76 Report of the Protector of Slaves, Eastern Division, Uitenhage, 11 Jan. 1833, PRO, CO 53/55.

77 For a brief, effective passage on Islam as an ideology of resistance among Cape slaves, see Watson, *The*

resistance. Drawing on religious teachings, he rejected the paternalist assumption that he was by colour and class innately inferior to his master.

The resistance of skilled slaves sometimes testified to the self-esteem they had developed or preserved, a pride that they derived from their work. For instance, Maart, a slave cooper, brought a complaint about his master to the Assistant Protector in Graham's Town. The Protector recorded that Maart said

> he is a cooper but his master made him feed the pigs, saying that he was not fit to work at his trade—his master then employed one Coetzee as a cooper but has now turned away said Coetzee and wants [Maart] to work at his trade which he is not inclined to do.

The law gave the Protector no room to assuage Maart's bruised honour.[78] Maart's pride, which might have made him an exemplary free craftsman, ill-suited him for life as a slave. Frederick, an apprentice, was more concerned with developing his skills than with preserving the dignity of his craft. He told the Special Justice in Worcester that he had left his master because, as he put it, 'I did not improve in the trade as blacksmith.' He explained, 'It was the fault of my master that I did not improve in my trade... Because my master had not custom enough.'[79] Frederick did not believe that his status as an apprentice ought to limit his aspirations or that he should be the victim of his master's incompetence.

Slave resistance could be motivated by much else besides pride. Anger and bitterness, weariness and resignation, are all evident in Amilia's account of a run-in with her mistress. One day, while the 55-year-old slave was washing clothes in a brook, her mistress scolded her and ordered her to take the clothes further up stream, saying that the water she was using was dirty. Amilia told the Protector of Slaves that she replied

> that her body was too full of pain to go further, and that her mistress had better go home, as she had already destroyed all the strength of [her] body, and that she was now no more able to do anything.[80]

Resistance to forced labour took many forms, and Amilia's was among the most direct. Bodily pain forced her to refuse to acknowledge the legitimacy of her mistress's authority.

Nowhere is the slaves' repudiation of paternalism more explicit and their creation of an alternative world-view more apparent than in their family relationships. In slavery and apprenticeship, slave men and slave women

---

Slave Question, pp. 172–6. Easily the most insightful writing on slavery and Islam in the Cape Colony is A. Davids's, 'The Afrikaans of the Cape Muslims, from 1815 to 1915: A Socio-Linguistic Study' (MA thesis, University of Natal, Durban, 1991), esp. pp. 23–85.

78   Day Book, Assistant Protector of Slaves, Graham's Town, CA, GR 17/17, c.1826.

79   Criminal Record Book, 1835–8, Special Justice, Worcester, CA, WOC 19/26.

80   Report of the Protector of Slaves, Eastern Division, Graaff-Reinet, 23 Jan. 1834, PRO, CO 53/57.

married and created families.[81] Those who did not find partners within the slave community married Khoisan, Free Blacks, and even whites.[82] Most slaves refused to concede that their masters and mistresses rightfully wielded more authority over their families than they did. These families and marriages were always fragile, however. Prior to the reforms of the 1820s, the laws of the Cape offered slave marriages and slave families no protection. Slaves were property first and people second; an owner's property rights superseded whatever human rights the law was willing to concede. Consequently, slaves could not legally marry, and they had no rights over their children.[83]

The reform laws of the 1820s and 1830s gave the slave family a legal existence. Believing that slavery ought someday to be abolished, yet certain that the slaves were not fit for freedom, the British initiated the reforms in an effort to civilize and Christianize the slaves. Stable slave families were to be both instruments and results of this process. The ordinance of 1826 granted slaves the right to marry. At the same time, it prohibited the separate sale of husbands and wives belonging to the same owner and of children under the age of ten years from their mothers.[84] A later ordinance strengthened these protections. Husbands and wives owned by the same master, whether formally married or 'reputed' to be husband and wife, were not to be separated by sale, and children were not to be sold away from either parent.[85] Though

---

81 I use 'marriage' to designate a solid and loving, if not stable, sexual and emotional partnership between a man and a woman. No marriage ritual was necessarily involved. (While I admit that homosexual couplings can conform to a slight modification of this rule, I have found no evidence of homosexual slave marriages.) By 'family', I mean a solid and loving partnership among persons who are bound by the rights and duties accruing to kin. Slave families at the Cape have recently begun to receive the attention that they deserve. It is now clear that, by the turn of the nineteenth century at the latest, slave families and families composed of slaves and other servants were common features of the colonial landscape. See, for instance, Mason, '"Fit for Freedom"', pp. 425–526; R. Shell, 'Tender Ties: Women and the Slave Household, 1652–1834', *The Societies of Southern Africa in the 19th and 20th Centuries*, vol. 17, Collected Seminar Papers no. 42 (University of London, Institute of Commonwealth Studies, 1992); P. van der Spuy, 'Slave Women and the Family in Nineteenth-Century Cape Town', *South African Historical Journal*, 27 (1992), pp. 50–74; and Scully, ch. 8 in this volume.

82 Slave families took on a variety of forms. Most slave families were single-parent families; most of these were matrifocal. Married couples and families composed of two parents and their children do appear frequently in the records. Some of these families fit the Western norm: two parents and their children, sharing a residence. Others deviated from the norm. Husband and wife often belonged to different masters and lived within the separate slaveowning households. Almost invariably, the mother cared for the couple's children, the property of her master. Slaves sometimes married free people; the children of these marriages were free if their mothers were free, slaves if they were enslaved. Slave men and women also married both Khoikhoi and Free Blacks. More often in Cape Town than in the countryside, lower-class white men married slave women. Any of these core families might be extended vertically through generations or horizontally to incorporate kin by blood and marriage. For more on the slave family, see Mason, '"Fit for Freedom"', pp. 425–526.

83 Statement of the Laws of the Colony of the Cape of Good Hope Regarding Slavery, *RCC*, vol. 9, p. 150.

84 Cape of Good Hope Ordinance 19 of 1826, paras. 18, 22, 23.

85 Order of the King in Council, 2 Feb. 1830, para. XLVI.

the laws could not fully shelter them from the overwhelming power of their owners, slaves seized upon them in their efforts to protect their families.

An incident in which a slave turned to the law in a effort to preserve his marriage, illustrates the clashes that ensued when world-views came into conflict. Jacob, a slave in the Worcester district, visited the office of a Protector of Slaves and told him that his master, Frans Johannes Marais, had 'banished' his wife from his farm, telling her never to return. (Why Marais chose to rid himself of a woman who was his slave and presumably a valuable financial asset cannot be known.) The Protector determined that Marais had acted illegally in separating husband and wife. He sensed the depth of Jacob's loss and addressed a letter to Marais in which he 'exhorted him to appease [Jacob's] feelings, in having his wife returned home.'[86]

When Jacob arrived back at his master's farm, he discovered that Marais had left for Cape Town. He gave the letter instead to his mistress, who read it and immediately set a messenger off on horseback to intercept her husband and ask him to return. Marais turned back and, on reading the Protector's letter, asked Jacob how he dared to leave the farm without his permission. Jacob told his master that he had visited the Protector to learn whether or not it was legal to 'separate man and wife'. Perhaps because he had been insolent, perhaps simply for initiating a course of action which threatened the hierarchy of master and slave, Marais gave Jacob 18 lashes. After the beating, Jacob returned to the Protector's office, this time to press charges of 'ill-treatment'. The Protector opened legal proceedings, but the case was settled before the issue could come to trial. Marais agreed to allow Jacob's wife 'to return home', and Jacob dropped the charges.[87]

Jacob's case illustrates the collision of world-views; Jacob rejected the patriarchal notion that his family was merely a subordinate part of his master's 'family'. The liberalism of the reform laws helped him to rebuff Marais's efforts to assert his patriarchal rights. This had not come easily or without the master's violent resistance. It was possible only because of the actions of a determined slave, who was armed with a sense of the rights inhering in him and his wife as individuals, and the knowledge that these could be enforced.

Sometimes the slaves' rejection of paternalism was quite explicit. Slave parents who disciplined their children unavoidably asserted rights which were inconsistent with the patriarchal ideology of slavery, and they occasionally gave voice to their alternative views of the world. This can be seen in the record of the complaint that the slave, Cupido, pressed against his master, Andries Petrus Lubbe, a wheat farmer in the Clanwilliam district.

86   Report of the Protector of Slaves, Western Division, Worcester, 13 Aug. 1833, PRO, CO 53/55.
87   *Ibid.*

Cupido told an Assistant Protector of Slaves that his master had given him 13 strokes with a cat o' nine tails, over his 'bare buttocks', because he had 'chastized his [own] child Davis...for disobedience'.[88] Later the same day, while he was at work in the fields, Lubbe had given him 15 additional stripes because he was 'in the rear of the [other] reapers'. The trouble had begun, Cupido said, when his master asked him why he had punished his son on the previous evening. He told Lubbe that Davis had disobeyed him. According to Cupido, Lubbe was not satisfied with his answer. His master ordered two other slaves, April and Pero, and the 'free person of color', Danzer, to stretch him out on the ground and hold him, while he, Lubbe, wielded the whip. Later, when Cupido fell behind the other workers, Lubbe had noticed and had again given him a beating.

April, Pero, and Danzer told the tale differently. They testified that Lubbe had initially whipped Cupido for having 'ill treated' Davis. His master had beaten him a second time not only because he had fallen behind in his work, 'for which he stated to be unwell and could not keep up', but because he had provoked Lubbe 'by his improper language'. The three said that Cupido had declared 'that their master could do with him what he pleased that day, even if he should like to hang him...[,]' but 'he should [continue to] do with his wife and child, what he pleases, as they were free persons.' Speaking in his own defence, Lubbe admitted that he had beaten his slave on the two separate occasions. The first time, he said, 'was to prevent him from committing a murder on his child Davis, as he frequently committs crueltyes [sic] on that child'. The second whipping was due to Cupido's 'improper conduct in presence [sic] of my other slaves'.

If we accept the testimony of Lubbe and the witnesses, Cupido had displayed conduct unbecoming a slave in several ways. Most importantly, he had asserted that he, not his master, possessed patriarchal rights over his wife and son, including the unrestricted right to inflict violent punishment. His claim ironically mirrored the slaveowners' assertion of the patriarchal right to discipline all of the members of their households, slave and free. He insisted that Lubbe had no right to interfere in the private affairs of his family, an argument similar to the slaveowners' objections to the powers of the Protectors of Slaves.

Cupido had internalized important aspects of paternalism, but this very act of internalization had intensified his antagonism towards his master, rather than lessened it. Acting on the assumptions of his world-view, Cupido had defied his master in the presence of other subordinate members of the household. Since the maintenance of Lubbe's patriarchal authority required that challenges be quickly suppressed, he had duly punished his slave for

---

88   The following narrative draws on the report of the Protector of Slaves, Western Division, Clanwilliam, 20 Jan. 1833, PRO, CO 53/55.

insubordination. Cupido found no relief in the Protector's office. Lubbe was vindicated in his conviction that this particular exercise of his patriarchal authority was right and proper.

As Cupido's case suggests, violence underpinned many personal relationships at the Cape, not merely those between slaves and slaveowners. It was a language, a discourse, a way of thinking about and behaving towards others which slaves could not entirely escape. Through violence, some slaves defined and structured many of the relationships of which they were a part; some slaves, many relationships, but not all. Most slave parents, for instance, assumed the responsibilities of parenthood in a more benign manner, making the slave family a means of coping with the stresses of slavery, rather than adding to them. Cupido was also in the minority as a male head of his family. Slave matriarchs[89] were more common than slave patriarchs. Families headed by the slaves, Marie and Rosetta, might serve as examples.

Marie was a housemaid whose impoverished master had turned her and her two children out of his home because he could no longer afford to feed, clothe, and shelter them. He ordered Marie to find work to support herself and her family. She located employment in the village of Somerset and managed to keep her children from going hungry. Marie's diligence ensured the survival of her children, but because she received no wages, only food and shelter in exchange for her labours, she and the children wore clothes which were described as 'old and nearly worn out'.[90]

Rosetta, another slave housemaid and mother, found herself in similar straits. She had once filed charges of mistreatment against her master, Johannes Hubertus Theunissen, only to see the Protector reject them. In retaliation for what he called her 'unfounded complaint', Rosetta's master had ordered her out of his house. Rosetta took her youngest daughter, Clara, with her when she left. During the following 14 months, Rosetta had hired herself out as a maid in Cape Town and, she said, 'faithfully paid her wages'—that is, her hire-money[91]—to her master. She had managed at the same time to care for her daughter. But now Theunissen wanted to take 'Clara from Cape Town into the country', and Rosetta turned to the Protector for help. Though the law did not protect Rosetta's family in these circumstances, the Protector arranged a settlement. Theunissen would return Clara to his farm, because she was now old enough to be 'useful' and 'to take care of his children', but he agreed to allow her to visit her mother 'whenever Mrs Theunissen came to [Cape] Town (which is very often)'. If Rosetta 'behaved herself better for the future', he would permit her 'to come to his place now

---

89   I use the term loosely and assign it no analytical weight. See n. 82.

90   Report of the Protector of Slaves, Assistant Protector, Somerset, 28 May 1833, PRO, CO 53/55.

91   Slaves commonly hired themselves out to employers—especially in the towns and villages—paying their master an agreed upon monthly or weekly sum out of their earnings.

and then to visit her children'. Rosetta accepted these terms both because she 'wished to remain in town and her owner [lived] only two hours from it' and because she had little choice. In this case, the reform laws supported Theunissen's patriarchal prerogatives, not Rosetta's parental rights.[92]

Marie and Rosetta were representative of the many slave parents who acted not as eternal children, but as responsible adults, fully capable of taking care of themselves and their families. They joined with thousands of other slaves in formulating a world-view that rejected the legitimacy of slaveowner paternalism, and instead stressed individual rights and familial autonomy. In creating this alternative, slaves drew on paternalism, liberalism, religion, and their experiences as workers, parents, and lovers, to mention the most notable elements. To speak of a single world-view, however, is misleading. The slaves' world-views did not cohere into one, and they could not have in a period of such fundamental social change. But the slaves had clearly differentiated their views of themselves and the world in which they lived from those of both their masters and their Protectors. The world-views the slaves made were more alike than not.

CONCLUSION

The Cape Colony of the early nineteenth century was a society undergoing a profound social transformation. Ideological confusion mirrored disruptions in politics and economics. It cannot be said that any of the world-views to be found in and around the slaveowning households had established the framework within which people understood their lives. No world-view was hegemonic—not the slaveowners' paternalism, the liberalism of the British, nor the slaves' oppositional world-views. Meaning was contested; ways of knowing were unreconciled.

In an earlier period, perhaps, paternalism and its associated patriarchal practices did frame the world in which slaves and slaveowners lived. But by the 1820s and 1830s, that world-view and those practices had been splintered by the liberalism of the British colonial state and by the actions of the slaves, who had been quick to seize the opening. When contemporaries complained of unruly slaves and angry masters, this is what worried them: the material and ideological foundations which Cape society had been opened to challenge, debate, and struggle. The fight was no longer over the rules, but over whether the game was to be played at all.

---

92   Report of the Protector of Slaves, Western Division, 26 July 1833, PRO, CO 53/56.

Plate 4 Greenmarket Square, 1833, by Charles D'Oyly. *Cape Archives.*

3

THE EROSION OF URBAN SLAVERY
AT THE CAPE, 1806 TO 1834

– ANDREW BANK –

As the Cape Colony's only major port, Cape Town was the point of contact between the domestic and the world economy from the birth of colonial slavery at the Cape in the 1650s until its formal extinction in the 1830s. The importation of human cargo in the form of slaves from the first decades of European settlement, and the exportation of grain and later wine in the eighteenth century, enmeshed the Cape in wider economic networks. These ties were vastly extended in the early nineteenth century when the colonial economy became harnessed to one of the world's most advanced industrial powers with a pre-eminent share of international commerce.[1] The value of Cape exports multiplied over tenfold in the years 1807 to 1817, while the increase in the scale of imports, largely European manufactured goods, was scarcely less spectacular over the corresponding decade.[2]

Cape Town's role as the locus of the colony's domestic market was inextricably linked to her function as a pivot between the colonial and metropolitan economies. The port city acted as the centre for the buying, selling and consumption of arable and pastoral produce, farmed in the south-western districts and beyond. Economic bonds between city and countryside were particularly strong at a time when the urban economy was gearing itself towards the increased exportation of the produce of a booming wine industry.[3] Cape Town was further bonded to her hinterland through the extensive hiring out and sale of urban slaves to rural farmers.

Within the structural context of tighter global and regional economic

1   According to Bayly, Britain commanded no less than one-third of world trade by the 1830s; C. Bayly, *Imperial Meridian* (London and New York, 1989), p. 5.

2   W. Freund, 'The Cape Under the Transitional Governments, 1795–1814', in R. Elphick and H. Giliomee (eds.), *The Shaping of South African Society, 1652–1840,* 2nd. edn. (Cape Town, 1989), pp. 329, 354.

3   M. Rayner, 'Wine and Slaves: The Failure of an Export Economy and the Ending of Slavery in the Cape Colony, South Africa, 1806–34' (Ph.D. thesis, Duke University, 1986), ch. 1.

networks, the early nineteenth century saw the emergence of an increasingly diversified urban economy. Alongside the expansion of mercantile activity and the associated rise of an indigenous urban merchant strata went changes at the lower and middle ranges of the economy. For the Dutch colonial period the urban economy was firmly service-based and, as the city's primary work force, slave labourers were overwhelmingly engaged in service capacities. Slave artisans may have come to dominate craft production in eighteenth-century Cape Town, as Ross suggests,[4] but there is little reason to suspect that they emerged in any numerically substantial form in this era. In the early nineteenth century, however, under the dual impact of population growth and economic expansion, craft production was transformed into a numerically, as well as functionally, significant sector of the urban economy. Computations based on the Slave Office registers indicate that, over the period 1816 to 1834, perhaps as many as a quarter of urban slaves worked primarily as artisans.[5] Many of the listed occupations in the expanding craft sector—from sailmakers to silversmiths, from habitmakers to hatters, from watchmakers to wagonmakers—described specialized and highly-skilled economic functions.[6]

A TRANSITION TOWARDS WAGE LABOUR

The diversification and specialization of slave labour reflected deeper structural shifts in the economy of Cape Town. The city's century-and-a-half-old reliance on slaves as direct producers, and slavery as the dominant system of production, eroded long before the passing of metropolitan acts to outlaw chattel status. The early decades of the nineteenth century witnessed a steady economic trend away from slavery, as wage labour increasingly characterized relations of production in the port city.

The most obvious and immediate measure of the economic decline of slavery in pre-emancipation Cape Town was the steady plummeting in the size of the city's slave population. The number of urban slaves shrunk noticeably and fairly rapidly from 9,367 in 1806 to 8,451 in 1812; 7,498 in 1817; 7,160 in 1822; 6,222 in 1827; to only 5,583 by 1834.[7] At the colony-wide level, the proportion of slaves to the total dropped from around 33 per

---

4   R. Ross, 'The Occupations of Slaves in Eighteenth Century Cape Town', *Studies in the History of Cape Town*, vol. 2 (1984), pp. 9–10.

5   This is not to deny the diverse nature of tasks performed by single slaves, but in the vast majority of cases the registers recorded one, and therefore it seems fair to assume, primary slave occupation.

6   For a discussion of the specific nature of the urban economy, see A. Bank, *The Decline of Urban Slavery at the Cape, 1806 to 1834*, Centre for African Studies, University of Cape Town, Communications, no. 22 (1991), pp. 26–38.

7   G.M. Theal, *Records of the Cape Colony (RCC)*, vol. 6 (London, 1897–1905), p. 75; vol. 9, p. 40; vol. 11, p. 438; vol. 15, p. 198; vol. 35, p. 81.

cent at the time of the abolition of the slave trade to under 15 per cent at the time of emancipation. Within the city itself, slaves had represented over half of the total number of resident urban dwellers listed in 1806 (excluding troops) and probably well over 80 per cent of the city's total work force. By the time of emancipation, however, slaves accounted for little more than a quarter of the number of resident urban dwellers (again excluding troops) and well under half of the city's total work force. As a ratio of the city's population to that of the colony, and as a ratio of the overall urban population and labour force, the percentage of slaves had thus halved between 1806 and 1834.

The impact of demography on urban slave productivity was even more pronounced in view of changes in the age structure of the slave population. At the Cape, as in the Americas, the slave trade was heavily weighted in favour of able-bodied adults. This was directly reflected in the composition of the local slave population. According to computations based on tax returns, at the turn of the century over three-quarters of Cape Town's slaves were adult.[8] In the decades following the abolition of the slave trade (1808), however, the proportion of slave adults declined and that of aged slaves and slave children rose accordingly. Thus, by the early 1830s, over 35 per cent of the slave population of Cape Town and the Cape district were under the age of 18 years, and 20 per cent of slaves listed were 50 years and older.[9]

The decline in the size of the productive urban slave population was offset by a massive increase in the size of the non-slave labour force in Cape Town between 1806 and 1834. In direct response to the acute post-abolition labour shortage, the British colonial state initiated a series of schemes for the importation of 'free' labour to the colony. Between 1808 and 1816 the crusade against foreign slavers, waged by the British naval patrol, boosted the urban labour force by almost a thousand.[10] This 'Prize Negro' scheme was followed, in 1817 and 1823, by the immigration of hundreds of European indentured labourers to the Cape, most of whom worked as skilled artisans in the port city. And then, from 1833 onwards, several hundred British children, primarily juvenile delinquents of 14 years and younger, were apprenticed in the colony under the so-called 'Children's Friend Scheme'.[11]

---

8   In the 1800 tax returns for Cape Town, there were 5,228 slave men listed; 1,958 slave women; 1,214 slave boys; and 1,076 slave girls. (Figures computed from Cape Archives (CA), J 37, Cape Town, List of Permanent Residents, 1800.) The total of 9,476 is seemingly fairly accurate given that the urban slave population numbered 9,367 according to the 1806 census.

9   Computed from a Slave Office census in CA, SO 3/12, Report of the Guardian of the Slaves for the Half-Year, June to Dec. 1833.

10   The 1822 census records that there were 833 'Prize Negroes' domiciled in Cape Town. These captives were contractually bound to private individuals for periods of 14 years.

11   E. Bradlow, 'The Children's Friend Society at the Cape of Good Hope', *Victorian Studies*, 27 (1984), p. 165.

In terms of indigenous (as opposed to immigrant) population growth, the 'free' labour force of Cape Town also registered a vast increase in the decades preceding emancipation. As a combined result of high manumission rates (see later discussion) and the ending of 'Prize Negro' apprenticeships, the number of Free Blacks in Cape Town grew from little over 1,000 in 1806 to perhaps four times that number by 1834.[12]

The transition from slavery to wage labour was reflected not only in the composition of the labour force, but in the nature of the urban labour market in the early nineteenth century. It was not just that slave and 'free' labour coexisted (with a marked decline in the number of slaves and an equally marked growth in the size of the 'free' labour force), but that urban slaves were increasingly working alongside and competing with 'free' labourers as hirelings, earning comparable wages at comparable rates of productivity. In an interview by the Council for Slave Tax during the mid 1820s, master-builder John Cannon maintained that 'common European labourers, if hired as such, get no more than a slave; nor mechanics if the two are equally good.'[13] Indeed, advertisements in contemporary newspapers suggest that slave and 'free' labour in the city were often interchangeable, at least by the 1820s and early 1830s. The following advertisements were typical: 'Wanted. Six or eight tailor-boys, slave or free, to whom will be given 30 rixdollars per month each. Apply to J.M.T. Brown, No. 2 Short-Market Street.'[14] or 'Wanted, four or five good shoemakers, to whom liberal wages will be given. No objection to slaves, if of good character.'[15]

In the context of an increasingly diverse and flexible urban economy in the throes of a severe labour shortage, the system of hiring out served as a convenient mechanism whereby the existing labour supply could be more widely distributed. Newspaper sources suggest that the hiring out of urban slaves, over the decades between 1806 and 1834, was almost as common-place as the buying and selling of human property in the city. A letter written by Major General Bourke to the Commissioners of Inquiry into a proposed slave tax gives a concrete indication as to the extent of this economic system in the mid 1820s. Bourke estimated that no fewer than 2,000 slaves were 'let out by their owners either to work for hire with others, or permitted to work for themselves on paying a proportion of their gains to the owners'.[16] The

---

12   Between 1827 and 1830 the number of 'whites' and 'Free Blacks' combined, increased by over 1,000 and, since the 'white' population was only expanding gradually, it seems fair to assume that the 3,267 'Free Blacks' recorded in the April 1827 census had grown to around 4,000 by 1830. Figures taken from Cape Blue Books, CA, CO 5971 and CO 5974.

13   Theal, *RCC*, vol. 29, p. 460.

14   *De Zuid-Afrikaan*, 2 July 1830.

15   *South African Commercial Advertiser*, 26 Feb. 1826.

16   Cited in Theal, *RCC*, vol. 29, p. 81.

latter 'freer' system of hiring out (whereby the slaves chose their own employers and reaped part of the fruits of their labour) was becoming increasingly prominent, perhaps typical, in Cape Town by the late slave period.

THE PROBLEMS OF URBAN SLAVE DISCIPLINE

The very nature of urban life generated acute problems of social control for slaveowners, to the extent that the pioneering historian of urban slavery in the United States posited a fundamental contradiction between slavery and the city.[17] Returns for population registration record that there were, on average, 2,000 or more inhabitants per square mile in early nineteenth-century Cape Town (as opposed to a mere six in the Stellenbosch district; four in the Cape district; and less than one in both Worcester and Clanwilliam).[18] This demographic concentration facilitated extensive and inevitable contact between slaves and other inhabitants of the city. Cape Town slaves had far greater opportunity to interact outside of the slaveholding unit than did their rural counterparts, as the small average size of urban slaveholdings, probably only between six and seven slaves per unit,[19] was more than compensated for by the day-to-day 'rubbing of shoulders' in the work and leisure routine of city life.

Early nineteenth-century writings evoke a strong sense of the daily scenes of interaction that set urban slavery apart. One commentator suggested that 'the portico of the Stadthouse in [Green] Market Square may be called the slave's portico: for here when unemployed, especially in rainy weather, or towards the close of summer evenings, they assemble together in groups and talk over the hardships of a life in slavery.' He went on to describe Market Square as 'the place of resort for the slaves, who assemble sometimes in such numbers as to fill a great part of the Square'.[20] The works of local artists substantiate the impressions of contemporary authors. D'Oyly's lively sketches of the early 1830s bring to life the more sociable side of slavery in Cape Town. The city squares, particularly Greenmarket Square, the fish market, the Heerengracht and the Grand Parade are all depicted as hubs of human activity, with slaves mingling freely with other inhabitants of the city, both slave and free.[21]

Apart from their social interactions during their unemployed or leisure

17   R.C. Wade, *Slavery in the Cities: The South, 1820–1860* (New York, 1964).

18   CA, CCP, 9/1, Cape of Good Hope Population Return, 1838.

19   Computed from CA, SO 6/12–6/35, Slave Registers for Cape Town and the Cape District, 1816–34.

20   R. Semple, *Walks and Sketches at the Cape of Good Hope* (London, 1805), pp. 18, 21.

21   See plates in C. Pama, *Regency Cape Town* (Cape Town, 1975), pp. 21, 24, 46, 55.

hours, the working lives of many city slaves drew them beyond the perimeters of the household unit and into direct contact with other slaves. The occupations of slaves, in both service and productive sectors of the urban economy, took them off their owner's property into the streets of the city or even onto the slopes of Table Mountain. The outdoor occupations of service slaves involved in transportation (coachmen, watercarriers, woodcutters, boatmen or hawkers), as well as those involved in production in the building line (masons, brickmakers, miners, thatchers or painters), allowed for an enhanced degree of physical mobility and social space, free from owner surveillance. Even domestic slaves, conventionally seen by historians of slavery as fettered to the household unit,[22] had frequent opportunities to socialize outside of the master-slave relationship.

The economic practice of hiring out further undermined social control in pre-emancipation Cape Town. As a system of labour mobilization which took slaves away from their owner's property, hiring out entailed a diffusion of owner authority and allowed slaves a greater degree of social and economic independence. Moreover, in a context in which slaves were employed alongside Free Blacks, 'Prize Negroes', Khoi and European apprentices, the hiring out system facilitated extensive contact between slave and free. The scale of such contact was sometimes fairly extensive: for example, a large-scale employer like John Cannon could claim to employ as many as 70 slaves and free people at one time.[23]

The effects of hiring out in eroding social control were compounded by the regular practice of living out. The connection between hiring out and living out was often quite direct, since many slave hirelings were permitted to rent their own accommodation by the late slave period. According to John Cannon, 'it was common practice [in the mid 1820s] to let slaves dispose of their own labour provided they pay a certain sum to their owners. These men are generally married, and live in houses hired by themselves, sometimes at the house where the wives reside.'[24] The numerous references to urban slave hirelings living apart from their masters, both in the court and Slave Office records, support this impression. That most notable of all Cape Town slave 'criminals', Louis of Mauritius, the instigator and major moving force behind the 1808 rebellion, worked as a tailor on his own account and lived apart from his owner.[25]

Many slaves slept outside the bounds of their owner's property on a more

---

22   In the colonial and antebellum plantation contexts, see respectively G.W. Mullin, *Flight and Rebellion* (New York, 1972); E.D. Genovese, *Roll, Jordan, Roll* (New York, 1974), pp. 325–63; in the urban context, see M. Karasch, *Slave Life in Rio de Janeiro* (Princeton, 1987), pp. 59–60.

23   Theal, *RCC*, vol. 29, p. 459.

24   *Ibid.*, p. 463.

25   CA, CJ 802, Court of Justice, Criminal Sentences, 1807–8.

temporary basis, usually at the houses or in the rooms of their common-law wives (or 'concubines' as the court clerks customarily referred to them). Sometimes these practices had the consent of owners, like Jacob van Reenen, living in Green Point, who 'had been in the habit of allowing November [his slave] to go and sleep in town with his wife, who is a free woman'.[26] On other occasions, slaves took matters into their own hands. In a complaint brought before the Slave Office in the early 1830s, the master of Adonis, an urban domestic slave, testified that the complainant 'continually entered the house of his concubine's owner and remained there at night without a pass or permission'.[27]

FRAGMENTING STRUCTURES OF URBAN CONTROL

In attempting to combat the general and structural problems of urban slave discipline, Cape Town slaveowners relied predominantly on violence and threat in the private and public domain.[28] There is no doubt, however, that levels of violence in Cape Town were far lower than in the rural Cape. The less intensive nature of production, the smaller size of slaveholding units and the closer proximity to official authority structures in the city, ensured that Cape slaveowner brutality assumed a firm regional dimension.

Slavery in early nineteenth-century Cape Town was not only less brutal than that in the Cape countryside, but it was also less brutal than its seventeenth- and eighteenth-century precursor. A series of legal changes, implemented by the British, progressively served to erode the coercive powers of the dominant class over the underclass and, more specifically, of slaveowners over slaves. The general easing up of the Cape legal system began during the First British Occupation, with the outlawing of the barbaric eighteenth-century punishments of impalement up the anus and breaking alive on the wheel, along with the practice of extracting confessions through torture.[29] More changes followed during the Second British Occupation: in 1808 rights of appeal were permitted; in 1811 a circuit court was established to extend powers of legal jurisdiction; in 1813 court proceedings were opened to the public and, most fundamentally, the colony's legal structure was totally overhauled in the late 1820s. The professional and anglicized Supreme Court system, created in 1828, was firmly based on legal equality and marked a decisive institutional break from the Roman-Dutch system where 'status

26   CA, SO 3/5, Report of the Guardian of the Slaves, Dec. 1829 to June 1830.

27   CA, S.O. 3/10, Report of the Guardian of the Slaves, June to Dec. 1832.

28   For an extended account of coercive mechanisms of control in early nineteenth-century Cape Town, see Bank, *The Decline of Urban Slavery at the Cape*, pp. 63–76.

29   Ross, 'The Rule of Law at the Cape of Good Hope in the Eighteenth Century', *Journal of Imperial and Commonwealth History*, 9 (1980), pp. 5–16.

determined the justice one got [and hence] inequality before the law was the guiding principle.'[30]

The abolition of the slave trade in 1808 also had a positive impact on 'slave treatment' in the narrower sense of the term. Once the supply of slaves had been cut off, slave prices rose markedly and owners were faced with a growing labour shortage in the colony. Henceforth slaves were no longer cheap and easily-replaceable commodities. As Chief Justice Truter explained in a letter to Sir John Cradock in September 1812: 'By the abolition of the slave trade...the value of a slave here has become so great that it is now an essential object to the master. This certainly is important for the state of the slaves, the master is thereby obliged to treat them well, to feed and clothe them properly, and to pay attention to them in sickness.'[31]

The effects of abolition in reducing levels of coercion in the owner-slave relationship were reinforced by ameliorative legislation, introduced in the 1820s and early 1830s. As has been well-documented elsewhere,[32] amelioration placed owners under legal obligation to ensure that their slaves were 'sufficiently' fed and clothed. It fixed the bounds of slave working hours and decreased the number of lashes slaveowners were empowered to administer; it also placed a Guardian and Protector in a mediating role between owner and slave. Even given a degree of disjuncture between the theoretical import of these measures and how they worked themselves out in practice, ameliorative legislation undoubtedly served to exercise a restraining influence on owners by diminishing their legal power over slaves.

In more general terms, amelioration expanded the rights of slaves as persons in preparing for the transition from chattel slavery to free labour. The contradiction in Roman Law between the 'laws of nature' and the 'laws of nations', the former contrary to slavery and the latter sanctioning slavery, was legally embodied in the contradiction between the sixth and seventh clauses of the statutes regarding slavery at the Cape of Good Hope, as they stood in 1813. The sixth clause stated that 'slaves are the property of their owners and consequently they stand under the voluntary command of their masters, can be alienated at pleasure, and on the death of the owner devolve to the legal successor',[33] while the seventh clause decreed that 'the laws which allow slavery do not however allow that we are to discontinue to

---

30   R.L. Watson, *The Slave Question* (Hanover and London, 1990), p. 14.

31   Theal, *RCC*, vol. 8, p. 491. As earlier discussion implies, the positive impact of abolition on the psyche of slaveowners was by no means universal.

32   W. Dooling, 'Slaves, Slaveowners and Amelioration in Graaff-Reinet, 1823–30', *South African Historical Journal*, 27 (1992), pp. 75–94; M. Rayner, 'Slaves, Slaveowners and the British State, 1806–34', Institute of Commonwealth Studies, University of London, *Societies of Southern Africa*, vol. 12, pp. 15–32; J.E. Mason, 'The Slaves and Their Protectors: Reforming Resistance in a Slave Society: The Cape Colony, 1826–34', *Journal of Southern African Studies*, 17 (1991), pp. 103–28.

33   Theal, *RCC*, vol. 9, p. 147.

consider slaves as our fellow creatures.'[34] As David Brion Davis has pointed out: 'The inherent contradiction of slavery lay not in its cruelty or economic exploitation, but in the underlying conception of man as a conveyable possession with no more autonomy of will and consciousness than a domestic animal.'[35] Ameliorative legislation at the Cape rendered this contradiction all the more acute by extending the rights of slaves as persons, thereby undermining their continued chattel status.[36]

If there was a relaxing of social control in its coercive aspect in early nineteenth-century Cape Town, then urban social control in its consensual aspect was almost totally eroded in this period. Cultural control was essential to ensure the continuity of domination, but at this all-important level the city's masters were unable to make slaves accomplices in their own subordination. The incorporation of slaves into the 'familia', which Shell has identified as a central mode of cultural control at the Cape, was undermined during the pre-emancipation decades by the emergence of a dynamic slave/underclass urban subculture and, in particular, the strengthening of slave family ties. Furthermore, the spatial expansion of Cape households and frequent separation of slave quarters from the main house ensured that slaves were no longer forced 'by reason of space, to be under the broad thumbs of the master and his family'.[37] Paternalism as a potential mechanism of 'hegemonic' control in Genovese's sense[38] was undercut by the economic flexibility of the urban labour market and came into competition with an emergent liberal, *laissez-faire* ideology transplanted from Britain into the Cape Colony via the urban-based merchant grouping. Likewise, Christianity failed as a tool with which to reshape the perceptions and values of Cape Town slaves and, increasingly, was eclipsed by Islam as the religion of the urban underclass. There were a mere six slave baptisms per annum throughout the Cape Colony between 1810 and 1824; by contrast, Islam could boast well over 1,000 urban slave converts by 1831.

The weakness of cultural/collective mechanisms of control in the city was a direct function of the fragmentation of the urban dominant class in the early nineteenth century. The increasing specialization and diversification in

---

34   *Ibid.*, p. 147.

35   D.B. Davis, *The Problem of Slavery in Western Culture* (New York, 1966), p. 62.

36   As Dooling demonstrates, this legal tension between slaves as property and slaves as persons was by no means unique to the early nineteenth century. In passing court sentences, judges and local magistrates in the Dutch colonial period made constant reference to the importance of 'continuing to treat slaves as persons'. W. Dooling, *Law and Community in a Slave Society: Stellenbosch District, c.1760–1820*, Centre for African Studies, University of Cape Town, Communications, no. 23 (1992).

37   R. Shell, 'The Family and Slavery at the Cape, 1680–1808', in W. James and M. Simons (eds.), *The Angry Divide: Social and Economic History of the Western Cape* (Cape Town, 1989), p. 21. For a more extended discussion on the 'familia', paternalism, Christianity and other elements of owner ideology, see Bank, *Decline of Urban Slavery*, pp. 76–81.

38   E.D. Genovese, *The World the Slaveholders Made* (New York, 1969); E.D. Genovese, *Roll, Jordan, Roll.*

the pre-emancipation urban economy was reflected in the composition of the city's upper strata. The urban dominant class comprised an ascendant merchant grouping with growing metropolitan links, smaller scale retailers, amongst whom there were a handful of Free Blacks, a limited number of professionals in the form of doctors, lawyers, teachers etc., and a social tail of independent craftsmen (as well as the military élite and other members of the apparatus of the colonial state). Superimposed and overlapping with these broad occupational divisions were economic differences between slaveowners and non-slaveowners, and ethnic rifts between the Dutch and the British.

Economic and ethnic heterogeneity gave rise to diverse group interests and a divided ideological standpoint. The varying and conflicting positions of members of the upper class towards slavery in the 1820s and early 1830s strikingly illustrate the fragmentation of their world-view. From Watson's analysis of the Cape anti-slavery movement, it is apparent that urban dominant class attitudes could be separated into no fewer than four camps. Firstly, rallying together under the banner of *De Zuid-Afrikaan* were a group of slaveowners 'grudgingly sympathetic regarding emancipation but who feared losing the stability of the social order based on slavery'.[39] Secondly, the middle ground was occupied by a strata of urbanized Dutch, mainly 'slaveowners but tied by occupation or a cosmopolitan culture to the British'.[40] Thirdly, clustered around John Fairbairn and the *South African Commercial Advertiser,* was the Cape Town merchant community, largely non-slaveholding English-speakers who viewed slavery as economically irrational. Finally, albeit as an isolated voice, there was the government employee, Thomas Miller's explicit moral and philosophical condemnation of slavery.

Yet the crisis of power faced by urban slaveholders went beyond their regional integration into a divided dominant class. It arose out of a fundamental problem they shared with rural slaveowners: they lacked direct political power. As Ross observed:

> [T]he main body of [Cape] slaveowners was remarkably powerless. In most European colonies which relied on slave labour, the great planters had, at the least, great influence over the conduct of government in all its actions. At the Cape their sway did not reach the main institution of legislation and justice. This meant that the position of the slave with regard to his master was stronger than in many other slave colonies.[41]

Problems of political control for Cape slaveowners came to a head in the early nineteenth century, as the British government intervened far more

---

39 Watson, *The Slave Question*, p. 129.

40 *Ibid.*, p. 130.

41 Ross, 'The Rule of Law', p. 7.

directly in colonial social relations than its predecessors had done. The introduction of ameliorative legislation from the mid 1820s represented the most
decisive act of interventionism by the British state and broke the already
fragile compact between the politically powerful and the economically
powerful. As Watson maintains, 'the amelioration ordinances imposed on the
colonies courted the disapproval of slaveholders, most of them Dutch, in a
colony already divided by Dutch resentment at British rule.'[42] The
Stellenbosch slaveowner riot of 1831 represented the physical and symbolic
rupture of relations between slaveowners and the colonial state.[43]

Political weakness at the level of central government was matched by
institutional inertia at the level of local government. The urban police force,
who bore public responsibility for the implementation of the law, were both
drastically understaffed and notoriously incompetent. Newspaper notices,
such as the following, were not infrequent and could have done little to instil
the urban dominant class with a sense of security: 'Two police officers,
named Coughlan and Digby, were brought up on a charge of absenting themselves from duty, and being drunk. Their offences were aggravated by
riotous conduct on the streets.'[44]

A CULTURAL WORLD IN THE MAKING

The erosion of urban dominant class control over the underclass and, in particular, the weakness of cultural mechanisms of domination, provides the
backdrop against which to view patterns of slave culture in the city. The
structure of the underclass itself was also fundamental in shaping the socio-
cultural experience of the enslaved. The introductory section of this chapter
documented the economic integration of slaves into a predominantly free
urban underclass. Cape Town slaves were not an economically self-contained class in the sense that Genovese has referred to slaves on antebellum
Southern plantations as a class, but were rather a legally-defined subset of an
urban underclass, which included Khoi, Free Blacks, 'Prize Negroes' and
European apprentices. This obviously had profound cultural implications.[45]

So too at the demographic level, the early nineteenth century saw
changes which greatly facilitated 'a cultural world in the making'. At the

---

42 Watson, *The Slave Question*, p. 14.

43 For a discussion of the 1831 riot, see J.E. Mason, 'Slaveholder Resistance to the Amelioration of Slavery
    at the Cape', Centre for African Studies, University of Cape Town, 'Western Cape—Roots and Realities'
    (unpub. conference paper, July 1986).

44 *South African Commercial Advertiser*, 15 July 1826.

45 The revisionist quest for 'norms and values' that were specific to slaves is misplaced; see esp. R. Ross,
    Cape of Torments (London, 1983); N. Worden, *Slavery in Dutch South Africa* (Cambridge, 1985). In a
    society where slaves (both urban and rural) worked alongside and interacted with non-slave labourers,
    the hunt for a 'slave bubble' was destined to prove elusive.

Cape, as in Jamaica, the abolition of the slave trade had important cultural consequences. The stabilizing post-abolition demographic trends towards more balanced gender ratios, higher fertility rates and, most significantly, a creolized slave population[46] underpinned a basic change in the nature of underclass culture. Locally-born slaves comprised over 70 per cent of the slave population of Cape Town and the Cape district between 1816 and 1834, as opposed to the hitherto predominantly foreign-born demographic composition. As a direct consequence of this demographic shift, the predominantly Eastern-based slave culture of late eighteenth-century Cape Town[47] was transformed into a creolized and far more vibrant slave/underclass culture in the early nineteenth century.

In the sphere of family life, there is firm evidence to suggest that more secure relations were beginning to emerge between male and female slaves at the Cape by the 1820s and early 1830s. Slave Office complaint cases document regular and lasting attachments between spouses in the final decade of slavery.[48] Dozens of slaves complained to the Guardian of being denied rights to visit their 'husbands' or 'wives', or expressed fears of sale on the grounds of separation from spouses. Material from other sources reinforces the impression of less unstable family structures in the late slave period: levels of sexual violence among the slave population were noticeably lower than in the Dutch colonial period, and rates of fertility among slave mothers rose steadily throughout the early nineteenth century.

While increasing numbers of slaves were able to set up and maintain ties of kinship with fellow slaves, others established temporary or more permanent bonds of intimacy with free inhabitants of the city. Social links between urban slaves and Free Blacks were especially close and relations of sexual intimacy frequently straddled the boundaries of legal status. One of many slave-Free Black attachments came to a tragic end in 1829, when a slave woman, Philida, was allegedly murdered by her spouse, Willem. The sentence was based purely on circumstantial evidence, in a trial that lasted 22 hours. Testimony revealed that the couple had cohabited for over ten years and reared three children.[49]

It was partly through Islam that the slave family (and slave-Free Black bonds) came together in the pre-emancipation decades. Slave converts were permitted to marry in the Islamic community and, according to a local ·

---

46   For an outline of the demographic impact of abolition, see Bank, *The Decline of Urban Slavery*, pp. 6–9.

47   N. Penn, 'Daily Life in Eighteenth Century Cape Town', *Cabo*, 4 (1986), p. 7.

48   See complaint cases brought before the Guardian in CA, SO 3/1–3/20. Unfortunately, there is no comparable source for the period 1806–25.

49   CA, SO 3/4, Appendix B, Report of the Guardian of the Slaves, June to Dec. 1829.

50   W. Wright, *Slavery at the Cape of Good Hope* (London, 1831), p. 16.

commentator, slave marriages were 'regularly performed by priests of the communion'.[50] As this implies, Muslim support networks extended beyond the various religious rituals, feasts and festivals throughout the year, which Cape Muslims increasingly insisted on attending 'by custom'.[51] Islam offered educational facilities which accommodated a prolific spread of literacy, health services administered by Muslim doctors, and economic aid for the indigent. These extensive secular support systems help to explain why at least one-fifth of the urban slave population, probably more, had converted to the religion of the underclass by the early 1830s.

Though the overlap between Islam and the urban canteen world was at most partial,[52] recreation, like religion, had a fairly rigid class dimension in early nineteenth-century Cape Town. The dividing line between popular and élite forms of leisure closely followed the economic contours of class. For the urban élite the seasonal rituals of fox-hunting and horse-racing complemented the regular cerebral indoor pursuits of theatre, concerts, ballets and home entertainment. The city's subordinate groupings, because of their relative lack of private space, were forced to rely far more heavily on public space. Their recreational activities revolved around the canteens, smuggling houses, pubs and streets of Cape Town. It was a culture of drinking, gambling, street-brawling and music-making that thrived on the weekends, outside the places of work. From the point of view of urban slaves, it was a part of life experience that was independent of the owner class and took place beyond the household or production unit.

Under the demographic impact of creolization and the economic impact of the trend towards free labour, slave recreational activities intersected more closely with those of Free Blacks, 'Negro apprentices', Khoi, sailors and soldiers. Contemporary court records document extensive leisure-time interaction between slaves and free inhabitants of Cape Town in the late slave period. To cite one of many examples, a trial brought before the Court of Justice recounts how two native-born slaves, Adam and Claas, went drinking on the Saturday night over the weekend of 11 to 12 December 1814 with their Khoi mates, Hendrik and Booy Alexander. On the way to a canteen in the seedy and overcrowded Kromme Elleboog Street, they met up with a sailor, Lawrence Highwell, who bought them a round of drinks. The hapless sailor was robbed of his remaining money, but his drinking companions paid dearly for their ingratitude—they were uniformly sentenced to a scourging and five years' hard labour in irons.[53]

The cultural world of slaves and the urban underclass was by no means

---

51 CA, SO 3/10, Report of the Guardian of Slaves, June to Dec. 1832.

52 As the commissioners into policing reported in the late 1820s, the tenets of Islam prohibited the 'use of spiritous liquors' and were responsible for greater sobriety among Muslims. Theal, *RCC*, vol. 35, p. 140.

53 CA, CJ 808, Court of Justice, Criminal Sentences, 1815.

confined to the family, Islam and popular forms of leisure. These were among the more overt and visible signs that surfaced readily in contemporary accounts and court records. Exactly what this culture meant to slaves, and how action affected consciousness, warrants far closer investigation. So too do the symbolic expressions of culture, which new resources like archaeology and underclass street songs (*ghoemaliedjies*) may begin to open up.[54]

THE CHALLENGE FROM BELOW

Embedded within the underclass cultural matrix, acts of resistance by slaves in early nineteenth-century Cape Town were expressed through increasingly active, overt (and sometimes collective) channels. Ameliorative legislation expanded the rights of slaves as witnesses and thereby opened up an institutionalized mode of slave resistance that was extensively exploited by urban slaves. Apart from their regular attempts to defend their new legal privileges, urban slaves used the courts in order to bargain for greater social and economic space. Thus, for example, hirelings solicited the Guardian's support in order to retrieve debts from employers or to negotiate the lowering of proportions of earnings payable to their owners.[55]

Desertion was a direct, overt slave challenge to bondage that remained widespread right up to emancipation. But it was in the period-specific and largely urban-specific form of burglary that slave/underclass resistance assumed its most collective expression, and cases of large-scale premeditated theft by Cape Town's underclass were uncovered annually. To cite one spectacular such instance: no fewer than 33 slaves, one Khoi and four Free Blacks stood accused before the higher court in 1813 of involvement, either as protagonists or as receivers of stolen goods, in break-ins on eight different occasions. The stores and packhouses of prominent Cape Town merchants were plundered and the value of goods stolen from one merchant alone was estimated at over 12,000 rixdollars![56]

Alongside changes in the *nature* of urban slave/underclass resistance went an acceleration in *rates* of resistance at the Cape. The reasons for heightened levels of protest in the late slave period related directly to the cumulative impact of wider political and socio-economic shifts on the collective consciousness of the enslaved.

The regular changes of government in the years leading up to 1806, and the abolition of the slave trade, gave rise to a dominant class crisis in the early years of the Second British Occupation. The slaves' perceptions of

---

54 C. Winberg, 'The Ghoemaliedjies: Remnants of a Slave Culture' (unpub. paper, 1990).

55 Cases from the Slave Office records, CA, SO 3/1 to 3/14.

56 CA, CJ 805, Court of Justice, Criminal Sentences, 1812–13.

changing structures of control and shifts in élite ideology sparked off the creole-led 1808 slave uprising. It appears that non-violent modes of protest also intensified in this period. In particular, the frequency of newspaper reports of runaways suggests that foreign-born slaves were deserting *en masse* while the external trade remained open. Indeed, official concern over desertion was such that the Colonial Governor promulgated legislation in June 1809 offering runaways reprieve if they would return to the owners:

> [I]t has been represented to me that there are at this time wandering about the country several runaway slaves, who might be induced to return to their duty upon a promise of pardon being held out to them... I do therefore hereby declare that all such runaway slaves who shall either surrender themselves to their respective masters, to his Majesty's Fiscal, or to the Landdrost of the district in which they may be, shall receive a full pardon, and not be liable to any punishment whatever, domestic or otherwise.[57]

It was particularly in the final decade of slavery at the Cape that levels of slave resistance (both urban and rural) soared. The late 1820s and early 1830s saw a challenge from below, far more threatening than the crisis of control around 1806. Against the hemispheric background of revolutionary uprisings in the Americas, the 1825 Galant revolt imprinted itself deeply on the psyche of slaves, slaveowners and colonial officials. In the aftermath of the uprising, the Chief of Justice warned Lord Charles Somerset that

> an idea and expectation of a general emancipation has spread itself... The slaves, misled by evil-designing persons, as if a general emancipation was intended by the government, consider themselves as having actually acquired a just claim thereto and look upon their masters as the obstacles in the way of their freedom. This naturally engenders animosity against them, whereof the consequences are incalculable, as leading to insubordination, dissoluteness and actual resistance.[58]

This rupture in owner-slave relations and transformation in slave consciousness was reinforced by amelioration. In his June to December 1830 report, the Guardian expressed concern that 'the constant legislative changes' made owners 'morose and less kind to their slaves than formerly, whilst the slaves themselves hearing so much discussion respecting them, believe their emancipation is near at hand, and...look upon their owners as their worst enemies and the only impediment to their liberation.'[59]

Slave perceptions of state support and general anticipations of freedom fuelled a more resistant attitude towards bondage. Court records point to a rise in slave criminality in the years immediately preceding emancipation,[60]

---

57   Theal, *RCC*, vol. 7, p. 8.

58   Theal, *RCC*, vol. 20, p. 286.

59   CA, SO 3/6, Report of the Guardian of the Slaves, June to Dec. 1831.

60   See esp. CA, Cape Supreme Court 1/1/1/6, 1/1/1/7.

while police lists document a marked growth in the rates of slave and under-class desertion. The number of underclass deserters apprehended in Cape Town and lodged in the town prison rose steadily from 232 in 1829 to 423 by 1834; the corresponding figures for slaves were 150 and 260.[61] The flood of complaint cases brought before the Guardian from the mid 1820s onwards suggests that slaves were making extensive use of new institutionalized channels of resistance, as well as the old, in order to challenge the authority of the dominant classes. As urban dominant-class ideology fragmented and structures of owner control buckled, so the challenge to the slave system from below became increasingly threatening, both in élite / official percep-tion and in reality.

ENHANCED ACCESS TO FREEDOM

The extent of accessibility of the unfree to freedom has generally been seen by historians of slavery as one of the key indices of the relative openness of a slave society.[62] It is thus particularly significant that rates of manumission at the Cape, and especially in Cape Town, showed a marked increase in the early nineteenth century. Whereas there were little over a thousand (1,075) manumissions in the last eight decades of Dutch slavery in South Africa,[63] there were well over two thousand (2,312) slaves freed in the Cape between 1808 and 1834 alone.[64] Or, considered on a yearly basis, the average number of slaves liberated rose from 13 per annum between 1715 and 1791, to almost 100 per annum in the decades between the ending of the slave trade and emancipation.

The reasons for the increase in the rate and number of manumissions at the Cape in the early nineteenth century related directly to period-specific legislation. On the one hand, the abolition of the slave trade and the con-sequent trend towards creolization and the equalization of sex ratios had a dual impact in facilitating higher rates of manumission, since there was a universal bias in slaveholding societies (and the Cape was no exception in this regard) towards the liberation of female and of native-born slaves.[65] On the other hand, and more significantly, the removal of a series of legislative

---

61   These figures are computed from police lists of desertion, CA, POC 14, Police Office, Cape Town, Register of Deserters, Jan. 1829 to Dec. 1836.

62   G. Freyre, *The Masters and the Slaves* (New York, 1946); S. Elkins, *Slavery* (Chicago, 1959), pp. 72–5; F. Tannenbaum, *Slave and Citizen* (New York, 1946), pp. 50–62; and in the Cape context, R. Elphick and R. Shell, 'Intergroup Relations: Khoikoi, Settlers, Slaves and Free Blacks, 1652–1795', in Elphick and Giliomee, *Shaping of South African Society*, pp. 184–239.

63   Elphick and Shell, *ibid.*, p. 203.

64   Computed from CA, SO 12/3–12/7, 12/11, Slave Office deeds of manumission and official figures for 1808–23.

65   O. Patterson, *Slavery and Social Death* (Cambridge, Mass., and London, 1982), pp. 263–4.

obstacles deterring owners from manumitting their slaves, and the opening up of a new escape hatch to freedom via Ordinance 19 of 1826, was responsible for a dramatic increase in the number of manumissions in the late 1820s.[66] There was an average of 150 manumissions per annum in the period between the passing of Ordinance 19 in 1826 and the implementation of the Abolition Act in December 1834.

The 'startling regional pattern [of manumissions]' that emerged at the Cape in the eighteenth century[67] was quite as startling in the early nineteenth century. In the two decades preceding emancipation, no fewer than 1,656 urban slaves were freed, representing nine-tenths of manumissions at the colony-wide level. And this despite the fact that the city's slave population represented a steadily declining proportion of the overall slave population at the Cape.[68]

The urban bias in manumission patterns related directly to regional socio-economic factors. Slaves in Cape Town had more abundant opportunity to acquire skills and to exercise control over their earnings. Moreover, in the wake of Ordinance 19 (which allowed slaves to have their freedom purchased by family), a growing number of urban slaves were able to use ties of kinship to procure their freedom. In this regard the cultural contacts of slaves with free inhabitants of the city acted as a crucial variable in determining the access of the unfree to freedom. In some cases, spouses or lovers bought the manumission of their partners. Thus the free man, Henry Akields, purchased the freedom of a 16-year-old slave girl, Hessa, in August 1832,[69] and Jan of Bengal put forward a £100 purchase price on behalf of a Creole women in her mid twenties.[70] In other instances, parents bought the freedom of their children. So, for example, shortly after the passing of Ordinance 19, the mother of an infant slave, Wilhelmina, paid local slaveowner and merchant, Hamilton Ross, £15 to ensure that her child did not grow up in bondage.[71] Less frequently, brothers or sisters would purchase the emancipation of their siblings. This was, perhaps, the connection between the adult male slave, Lodewyk, and the Free Black, Welkom of the Cape, who met his £22

---

66 To quote the respective clauses from Ordinance 19: '[N]o Duty Tax or Impost and no Fee of Office, shall be hereafter paid…in respect of the manumission of any Slaves' (clause 32 cited in Theal, *RCC*, vol. 28, p. 482); and more significantly 'in case any slave within the said colony shall be desirous to purchase the freedom of himself, or of his or her wife or husband, or child, or brother, or sister, it shall and may be lawful' (clause 33, *ibid.*).

67 Elphick and Shell indicate that of the 609 private owners manumitting slaves in their sample, only 29 lived outside the Cape district ('Intergroup Relations', p. 212).

68 The high rates of manumission for Cape Town slaves over this period, and in the 1820s in particular, is obviously among the major reasons for the rapid demographic decline of the urban slave population in these years.

69 CA, SO 12/7, deed 1479.

70 CA, SO 12/7, deed 1492.

71 CA, SO 12/4, deed 578.

purchase price in the late 1820s.[72]

For slaves in all slaveholding societies, the actual journey from slavery to freedom in the form of manumission meant more than just the possibility of enhanced economic opportunity and increased social mobility. It was an extended rite of passage in psychological terms as well. One of the three constituent elements in Patterson's definition of the institution of slavery is that slaves were generally dishonoured and degraded persons.[73] Seen from this point of view, it is evident that the attainment of freedom represented the decisive moment in the creation of a new social identity and the assertion of individual self-dignity.

In the specific context of the Cape Colony in the late slave period, the regular practice of elderly slaves buying up their freedom strongly suggests that, quite apart from the economic benefits of free status, liberation had a deep psychological dimension as well. Deeds of manumission indicate that in the period from August 1826 to December 1832, no fewer than 37 slaves of 60 years and older, that is, well beyond their economically-productive years, purchased their own freedom or had their freedom bought for them by their families. In one such manumission, in June 1829, an ageing male slave was willing to pay his master the tidy sum of £64 for his liberation.[74] It was the psychological importance of freedom, what it meant in terms of identity and self-dignity, that induced superannuated slaves to go to such lengths to achieve free status. In his June to December 1830 biannual report, Rogers recounted: 'I have known many instances of slaves on the verge of the grave praying to be emancipated that they may die free.'[75] Whether or not the desire to die free sprung from a perception that the enslaved had inferior chances of spiritual salvation is impossible to determine. What we can say with certainty is that slaves viewed death in bondage as a dishonourable fate.

Slave perceptions of freedom should not, of course, be treated as a constant. The momentous changes in the rate and nature of emancipation at the Cape in the late slave period could hardly have failed to impress itself on the minds of the enslaved. The manumission of fellow slaves owned by the same master, slaves with whom they worked, gambled, drank or worshipped, the manumission of family members, all contributed to a changing slave consciousness in the final decade of slavery. Freedom became so much more accessible at a time when ameliorative changes were enhancing the legal status of slaves in other spheres. When the Guardian commented in the early

---

72   CA, SO 12/4, deed 614. Unfortunately, the deeds do not usually state the kinship relations between the various parties in cases of manumission by purchase. However, inferences can often be made based on the age and sex of the slave and purchaser.

73   Patterson, *Slavery and Social Death*, p. 13.

74   CA, SO 12/6, deed 945.

75   CA, SO 3/6, Report of the Guardian of the Slaves, June to Dec. 1830.

1830s that 'the slave population have imbibed the idea that they must soon be free',[76] this transformation of consciousness probably had as much to do with the massive increase in urban rates of manumission as with news of pending emancipation. It was partly that amelioration made slaves alive to the prospect of universal emancipation, but also that their own chances of freedom (and this applies far more readily to urban slaves) were made so much more tangible by Ordinance 19.

CONCLUSION

The institution of slavery in Cape Town was eroding at every level by the late slave period. Demographically, the number of urban slaves fell at a steady rate from over 9,000 in 1806 to no more than 5,500 in 1834. The dwindling size of the productive, urban slave population, the marked increase in the size of the free labour force, and the spread of the hiring out system in an increasingly diversified urban labour market, were indices of the move from slave to wage labour—signposts on the road from slavery to capitalism.

The economic decline of urban slavery made the problem of slave discipline in the city all the more acute. The general problems of social control in the demographically dense urban environment were compounded in early nineteenth-century Cape Town by hiring out, the associated practice of living out, and the structural integration of slaves into an urban underclass. In its attempts to combat these problems, Cape Town's dominant class was unable to achieve effective 'hegemony' over the subordinate class. Coercive mechanisms of control operated on a regionally and temporally tempered scale, while cultural/consensual modes of control (the family, paternalism, and religion) had limited impact in remoulding the perceptions and values of urban slaves. The economic, ideological and ethnic fragmentation of the urban dominant class and their general political weakness ensured that the collective hold over labour remained tenuous.

The erosion of slavery in pre-emancipation Cape Town was further reflected in the changing nature of the slave experience and the transforming consciousness of slaves. This period saw the emergence of an increasingly vibrant slave/underclass culture in the city. Though primarily alternative rather than oppositional, the private, religious and popular cultural expressions may be interpreted as channels of slave resistance. At the very least, through their integration into an urban underclass subculture, slaves were resisting their legal definition as property and asserting their rights as persons. Cultural responses to slavery were, by definition, collective and served

76   CA, SO 3/8, Report of the Guardian of the Slaves, June to Dec. 1831.

primarily to separate the identity of slave and master, and to cement bonds between slaves and other members of the subordinate class.

Within this cultural network, underclass actions, directed at the avoidance or disruption of structures of domination, took on increasingly active and overt forms in this period. Urban slaves made extensive use of the enhanced legal space opened up by amelioration; they actively expressed their rejection of the institution of slavery through physical escape; and mobilized with other members of the underclass in collective attacks on the property of the city's élite. Rising rates of slave protest after 1806, and especially in the 1820s and early 1830s, likewise reflected a changing consciousness and a more oppositional attitude towards bondage.

The psychological journey from slavery to freedom converged with the actual journey to freedom in the form of manumission. Rates of manumission in Cape Town rose rapidly, with more urban slaves being liberated in the last eight years of slavery's formal existence than in the last eight decades of Dutch colonial rule at the Cape. The enhanced accessibility of rites of passage to freedom, both physically and symbolically embodied a broader demographic and socio-economic trend.

4

'FREE, YET SLAVES'
PRIZE NEGROES AT THE CAPE REVISITED[1]

— CHRISTOPHER SAUNDERS —

In an article on 'Liberated Africans in Cape Colony in the First Half of the Nineteenth Century', drafted in 1979 and published six years later,[2] I discussed how and in what numbers men, women and children were freed from slave ships at the Cape in the decades after the British ended their participation in the Atlantic slave trade in 1808.[3] I went on to offer some remarks about what happened to these people when they became 'apprentices', and I suggested both that they constituted an important labour source after the importation of slaves came to an end, and that, though technically they were freed from slavery, their status resembled that of the slaves at the Cape. This chapter carries further that earlier work, exploring in greater depth their ambiguous status and reflecting on how their position changed over time in the years before and after the emancipation of the Cape slave population in the 1830s.

In Freetown, Sierra Leone, those released from slave ships by the British navy after 1808 were known as 'Liberated Africans'.[4] In the British West

---

1   I would like to thank Robert Shell, Nigel Worden and Andrew Bank for comments on a draft of this chapter.

2   C. Saunders, '"Prize Negroes" at the Cape of Good Hope', (paper to History Workshop, University of Cape Town, 1979); C. Saunders, 'Between Slavery and Freedom', *Kronos*, 9 (1984), pp. 36–43; C. Saunders, 'Liberated Africans in Cape Colony in the First Half of the Nineteenth Century', *International Journal of African Historical Studies*, 18 (1985), pp. 223–39. Cf. also C. Saunders, 'A Nineteenth Century Farce: The Anglo-Portuguese Mixed Commission at the Cape', *Quarterly Bulletin of the South African Library*, 37 (1982), pp. 298–302; C. Saunders, 'Education and Liberation: The South African College and Prize Negroes', *Cabo*, 4 (1986), pp. 19–21.

3   In all, the British navy was responsible for the capture of over 116,000 slaves between 1810 and 1846, over half of whom were settled in Sierra Leone, over 20,000 in the British West Indies: A.O. Thompson, 'African "Recaptives" under Apprenticeship in the British West Indies 1807–28', *Immigrants and Minorities*, 9 (1990), p. 124. (I thank Nigel Worden for drawing my attention to this article.) At the Cape over 5,000 Prize Negroes were landed between 1808 and the early 1840s.

4   See, for example, J. Peterson, *Province of Freedom* (London, 1969); J.A. Asiegbu, *Slavery and the*

Indies case they are usually referred to as 'recaptives'.[5] At the Cape they were, with rare exceptions, not called 'Liberated Africans',[6] but either 'Prize Negroes' or, as they were as frequently termed in the official records of the 1820s, 'Prize Slaves'.[7] They had been seized as slaves, and they were declared 'prizes' when the Vice-Admiralty Court in Cape Town legalized their prior seizure by the British naval squadron operating from the Cape.

That they were so often called 'Prize Slaves' and not given a name which emphasized their release from enslavement was not so much a reflection of their slave status before 'liberation' as of their status afterwards. For in the pre-emancipation Cape these people occupied positions in society very similar to, or even the same as, members of the slave population. In the British West Indies, likewise, 'recaptives' were also often called 'slaves'.[8] In Sierra Leone, on the other hand, where there was no slave population, they were 'Liberated Africans' and not 'Prize Slaves'.

There is of course an irony in their being called 'Prize Slaves', and especially in the fact that the name 'Prize Slaves' should have been used so frequently in the court and other official records of the 1820s. The British government proclaimed both the ending of the slave trade and the activities of its anti-slavery squadrons to be acts of humanitarianism. Those seized as slaves from the ships of other nations were to be 'liberated' and then bound 'to prudent and humane masters and mistresses…to learn such trades, handicrafts, or employment as they may seem most fit for, or most likely to gain their livelihood by, when their apprenticeship shall expire'.[9] According to the indenture of a Prize Negro named Myndola, issued in June 1813, the master was to 'diligently and faithfully instruct [him] in the said trade of house servant, and…in the Christian religion, and shall have him baptized when sufficiently instructed…'[10] But the rhetoric was far removed from the reality. As

Politics of Liberation 1787–1861. A Study of Liberated African Emigration and the British Anti-Slavery Policy (London, 1969).

5   Thompson, 'African "Recaptives"', *passim.*

6   The main one being the naval records of Simonstown, e.g. Sexton's Register, St. Francis Church, Benjamin Mohanza, 31 Oct. 1854. (I thank Arthur Davey for this reference.) It is possible that Mohanza and others termed 'Liberated Africans' were from West Africa. I chose the title 'Liberated Africans' for my article because it was for an international Africanist journal and I wanted to make the connection with Sierra Leone.

7   The use of 'Prize Slave' for them in preference to 'Prize Negro' or 'apprentice' varied; in the lower court records of the 1820s it is routine. But while 'Prize Negro' was only used from 1808, 'Prize Slave' had long been used for slaves taken as 'prizes' when captured at sea: cf. e.g. R. Shell, 'Slavery at the Cape of Good Hope, 1680 to 1731' (Ph.D. thesis, Yale University, 1986), vol. 1, pp. 59–60. The largest number of such 'Prize Slaves' were introduced in the years 1795 to 1807 (R. Shell, personal communication). In this chapter I am not concerned with such 'Prize Slaves', and to avoid possible confusion I use 'Prize Negro' throughout.

8   Thompson, 'African "Recaptives"', pp. 126–7.

9   Quoted Asiegbu, *Slavery and the Politics of Liberation*, p. 27, n. 1.

10   *British Parliamentary Papers* (*BPP*), 1826–7, xxi (42), p. 125.

Plate 5   Jan Persent, brought to the Cape from Mozambique as a 'Prize Negro'.
Photograph taken in 1916. *South African Library*.

the amateur historian, George Cory, recognized early this century, the Prize Negroes were 'to all intents and purposes slaves'.[11] That the term 'Prize Slave' was so often used in official documents implies acceptance of the fact that, though technically no longer slaves, they belonged to the category of 'slave' rather than 'free'.

At least 2,000 Prize Negroes were introduced into the Cape Colony in the decade after British involvement in the slave trade ceased on the first day of 1808. Their arrival in the colony meant that the supply of African labour did not stop when British involvement in the slave trade was ended. There had been a sharp increase in the number of slaves brought into the colony just prior to the end of the legal trade and, if one considers the decades before and after abolition, it is clear that only because of the arrival of so many Prize Negroes was the supply of *de facto* slaves not disrupted seriously by the ending of the trade.[12]

That the lives of Prize Negroes at the Cape resembled those of slaves did not mean, of course, that their position did not change over time, or that all of them had similar experiences. Slavery itself, especially in Cape Town, underwent significant transformations in the early nineteenth century, and the position of the Prize Negroes, like that of the slaves proper, varied greatly, depending on when and where they lived.

Their social history, however, remains virtually unexplored. Admittedly, documentation on that history is extremely sparse: a search in the judicial records in the Cape Archives revealed relatively little of value.[13] The single most important source for the pre-emancipation period is *Papers Relating to Prize Slaves at the Cape of Good Hope*, the report and evidence of a commission of enquiry held in 1825 into the distribution of Prize Negroes at the Cape.[14] This document, printed as a British Parliamentary Paper in 1826, provides more detail than any other on the way in which 'apprentices'— another term frequently used for Prize Negroes at the Cape—lived in Cape Town and its environs in the two decades after the ending of the slave trade. The commission enquired only into cases relating to the allegations of corruption on the part of those responsible for distributing 'Prize Slaves', as the

---

11   G. Cory, *The Rise of South Africa*, vol. 2 (London, 1913), p. 256. Cory's is the fullest account of the 'Cooke affair' and was drawn upon by E. Roux in *Time Longer Than Rope* (London, 1948), pp. 21–2.

12   Cf. R. Ross, 'The Last Years of the Slave Trade to the Cape Colony', *Slavery and Abolition*, 9, 3 (1988), pp. 209–19. Some slaves had been declared prizes by the Admiralty Court at the Cape during the First British Occupation: e.g. G. Theal (ed.), *Records of the Cape Colony (RCC)*, vol. 3, p. 487. None of these, it seems, went to individuals: Theal, *RCC*, vol. 17, p. 166.

13   My thanks to Andrew Bank for undertaking this research on my behalf. As their position resembled that of slaves, it is not surprising to find that the nature of the crimes they committed were similar.

14   *BPP*, 1826–7, xxi (42). Theal printed the report of the Commissioners in *RCC*, vol. 22, but not the annexures, because they were so lengthy and on the grounds that the report gave the substance of the matter. It is the annexures, however, which contain the more interesting detail.

title of the report referred to them. The evidence assembled by the commission, therefore, is far from representative, let alone comprehensive. But when that evidence is set in the context of the work recently completed on slavery in this period, and is used together with information from the Cape Archives and the newspapers, interesting details emerge on aspects of the role the Prize Negroes occupied in colonial life.

The commissioners reported in 1825 that 'after the lapse of one year from the date of the abolition of the slave trade, the competition for the assignment of Prize Negroes at the Cape has been pressing and constant'.[15] Whereas masters had to buy slaves—and prices shot up after the ending of the slave trade—Prize Negroes were distributed by the state without cost to the employer. The obligation imposed in terms of the indenture to provide training and instruction was, as in the British West Indies,[16] ignored in almost all cases, and all the master provided was shelter and food. It is not surprising, therefore, that colonists were so keen to obtain Prize Negroes, especially as they could—as we shall see—hire them out for profit. Colonists wanted them despite the fact that they came from up the east African coast, whose slaves were regarded as 'the least valuable'.[17] In 1815, to take just one example, applications were received from colonists for three or four times the number of Prize Negroes available for distribution.[18]

In a few cases the captured slaves were condemned by the Court of Justice and distributed by the Fiscal, but the more common practice was for the Vice-Admiralty Court, which was independent of the colonial government, to condemn the captured slaves as 'prizes'. Then, in terms of instructions from London common for all the colonies, the Prize Negroes were distributed by the Collector of Customs. At the Cape, the Collector worked closely with the Comptroller of Customs.[19]

On receiving Prize Negroes, the Collector had to 'give notice to the Chief Officer of His Majesty's land forces in the colony...of the number of male negroes fit for military service so received, to the intent that such officer or commander-in-chief may take any number such negroes...' The naval officers, likewise, were to 'receive into His Majesty's naval service any number of such negroes that the service may want, and that may be fit for the same'.[20] After the military and navy had taken the strongest and fittest for

---

15   *BPP*, 1826–7, xxi (42), p. 19.

16   Thompson, 'African "Recaptives"', esp. p. 132.

17   W. Bird, *State of the Cape of Good Hope in 1822* (London, 1823), p. 73.

18   *BPP*, 1826–7, xxi (42), p. 146.

19   For the relationship between the two officials, see the book produced by the Comptroller: Bird, *State of the Cape*, p. 135. Though so involved with them, Bird said little about Prize Negroes in his book.

20   Quoted in Asiegbu, *Slavery and the Politics of Liberation*, p. 27, n. 1

their own use, some went into government employ, and the rest were distributed to colonists.

The way in which Prize Negroes were distributed at the Cape may be illustrated from the example of what happened when, in the early 1820s, 155 slaves from Madagascar were landed in Table Bay. The Vice-Admiralty Court in the city 'condemned' the vessel and its cargo, and the slaves were declared 'Prizes' of His Majesty. During the 23 days they were housed at the Custom House, a serjeant of the engineers selected 20 'of superior strength' for the army. Before the remainder were distributed to private individuals, they were housed in the new slave lodge at the northern end of the government gardens, today the site of the Hiddingh Hall campus of the University of Cape Town. They were listed by name, age and marks, and each person was given a ticket with a number on it, a jacket, a shirt and a pair of trousers. The cost of the clothing was recovered from the person to whom they were assigned. Colonists sent in applications, stating the sex and age of the Prize Negroes they required.[21] Most were apprenticed in Cape Town, but a few were apprenticed far away.[22]

From 1808 to 1826 the office of Collector of Customs was held by Charles Blair.[23] Like other officials at the Cape at the time, Blair used his office for his own personal advancement. The distribution of Prize Negroes to private individuals was fundamentally affected by the way the Collector controlled the process. He kept a considerable number of Prize Negroes for himself; the commissioners found out about 54, but there were probably others.[24] Yet others he assigned to friends or people from whom he obtained services.

For example, Blair assigned 22 Prize Negroes to Samuel Murray, a merchant who had fallen on hard times and who used them 'for the sole purpose of receiving their hire'. As Andrew Bank has shown,[25] masters in Cape Town commonly hired out their slaves in the 1820s, and this practice was followed with the Prize Negroes as well. Using one's Prize Negro solely for hire was said to be 'very general' in Cape Town in the early 1820s.[26] As with the slaves, some of those hired out also lived away from their master.[27] They performed a wide variety of mostly menial tasks; the acquisition of skills was rare. Most of what they earned went to their masters, but, as with the

---

21 *BPP*, 1826–7, xxi (42), pp. 152, 145, 129.

22 Cape Archives (CA), Court of Justice records: Anthony, apprenticed first at Uitenhage, then George.

23 Theal, *RCC*, vol. 35, p. 41.

24 *BPP*, 1826–7, xxi (42), p. 33.

25 A. Bank, *The Decline of Urban Slavery at the Cape, 1806–34*, Centre for African Studies, University of Cape Town, Communications, no. 22 (1991), pp. 38–43.

26 *BPP*, 1826–7, xxi (42), p. 130, evidence of J.B. Hoffman.

27 For instance, CA, Court of Justice records, 819 of 1825: Harry, in the service of R. Eaton.

slaves proper, Prize Negroes who were hired out sometimes were able, at the discretion of the master, to keep a fraction of their earnings for themselves. The commission was told, in 1825, that they were worth, on average, 20 rixdollars per month to their masters, and that the Prize Negroes themselves at best received perhaps six or seven rixdollars.[28] Had there been no Prize Negroes at the Cape, it is possible that the hiring-out system among slaves might have been even more extensive than it was. Prize Negroes who were hired out usually obtained less for their masters than did slaves, probably because they were regarded as less valuable, for many slaves had acquired skills as artisans. It must be remembered, however, that slaves had had to be purchased, whereas Prize Negroes were obtained by masters at no cost.[29] A Cape Town shipowner was willing to pay 330 rixdollars to obtain a Prize Negro whose indenture still had 11 years to run. He had been paying 30 rixdollars a month for the hire of the man. His application was not allowed, but in making it he claimed that transfers of Prize Negroes for money were frequent.[30]

When accused of corruption, Blair denied knowing that Murray had used Prize Negroes for hire, but he did add that he had 'been lately assured that it is legal so to do'.[31] Blair did not only assign Prize Negroes initially in a corrupt manner; he also reassigned them to new masters in a way in which his instructions had never intended. In both cases, he acted for personal gain. To say that the introduction of Prize Negroes benefited the colonists as a class is to obscure the fact that relatively few individuals—chief among them the Collector of Customs—gained quite disproportionately from what the British state had proclaimed to be a humanitarian venture.

In part as a result of the corrupt system of distribution at the Cape, many colonists who applied for Prize Negroes failed to obtain any. Some were so keen to obtain them that they, in effect, bid for them. In 1815, for example, J.B. Hoffman offered to manumit one of his young female slaves if he were given four Prize Negroes in her place. He pointed out to Blair that if all female children of slaves were freed, slavery would eventually disappear. He expressed the hope that others would follow his example in working towards that end by freeing the female children of their slaves. He offered to manumit all four of his female slave children if Blair assigned him three Prize Negroes for each of the slaves he freed. When this did not work, he chose another tack: he asked for eight or ten Prize Negroes and promised to place

---

28   *BPP*, 1826–7, xxi (42), p. 129, evidence of J.B. Hoffman.

29   See evidence of William Mackrill in Theal, *RCC*, vol. 30, p. 406, quoted in Bank, *Decline of Urban Slavery*, p. 42.

30   *BPP*, 1826–7, xxi (42), p. 136. A slave, by comparison, was worth on average 800 rixdollars: *ibid.*, p. 144.

31   *BPP*, 1826–7, xxi (42), p. 111.

the sum of 50 rixdollars dollars for each of them in the discount bank each year, the money to be divided among them, or their survivors, at the expiration of their 14 years of apprenticeship.[32] But he did not manage to persuade Blair to assign any to him, presumably because what he offered was of no personal advantage to the Collector of Customs. Hoffman's request was by no means the largest not to succeed; the Smit brothers also did not obtain any of the 20 Prize Negroes they had requested.[33]

Not surprisingly, those colonists who applied for Prize Negroes and received none resented the way in which they were distributed. In the repressive atmosphere of the Cape under the government of Lord Charles Somerset, it required courage to stand up and point to corruption. In this case, the man who showed that courage was Lancelot Cooke, a Cape Town merchant who had himself benefited from the use of Prize Negroes. At the end of 1823, he was led to take action when he fell victim to Blair's corrupt practices, this time involving the reassigning of a Prize Slave after the death of the master. When Cooke drew up a memorial charging Blair with corruption, other colonists came forward and testified against Blair. When the imperial Commissioners, J.T. Bigge and W.M.G. Colebrooke, reported on the matter, they bent over backwards to exonerate Blair of corruption, but in the face of the overwhelming evidence, they could do no other than find that 'the personal accommodation of the Collector and Comptroller of the Customs is now become a prevailing principle in the distribution of Prize Negroes who are in a situation to be reassigned to new masters.'[34] Despite the criticisms made against him, Blair remained in office.

The case which sparked off the enquiry of 1825 concerned Jean Elle, formerly known as Jean Marie. A man of mixed descent, he had been on board a French ship intercepted by a British naval vessel between Réunion and Mauritius in 1809.[35] The British vessel took the French ship to Cape Town, where Elle and others were 'liberated' and 'apprenticed'. Elle was later to claim that he had not been a slave on the French vessel, and that it was only because he had not been able to speak English or Dutch, and so had not been able to explain his circumstance, that he had been assumed to be a slave.

Whatever the truth of this claim, Blair placed Elle as an 'apprentice', first to a Dutch-speaking colonist, who so ill-treated him that he was taken away and given to an English civil servant. After serving a further two masters, and having become a competent cook, Elle was taken back by Blair and placed with Blair's friend, Samuel Murray. He in turn hired him out to a firm of merchants for 35 rixdollars a month, all of which went to Murray. Cooke

---

32   *Ibid.*, p. 34.

33   *Ibid.*, p. 152.

34   *Ibid.*, p. 20.

35   *Ibid.*, pp. 38–9.

became one of the partners of the firm hiring Elle, and found him to be a good worker. Elle, for his part, was, when working for Cooke, 'so well treated and happy as almost not to regret his slavery'.[36] In 1823, however, Murray died. For some months Elle continued to work for Cooke, who did not pay him anything for his services.[37] Then Blair again recalled Elle, ordering him to report to the Custom House, his intention being to place him with the son-in-law of his colleague, Wilberforce Bird, who required a cook. Elle did not wish to leave a master who treated him well; he also knew that within a few months he would have served his full 14 years' apprenticeship. Wanting to retain Elle's services, Cooke offered to pay Bird's son-in-law for Elle's services. This was refused, however, and Elle was forced to work for the new master, who gave him one rixdollar per week.[38] The British Order-in-Council of 16 March 1808, which provided for 'apprenticeship', had only intended reapprenticeship to take place if people were unable to stand on their own feet.[39] Elle, as a cook, quite clearly could, yet he was reassigned to a new master shortly before his period of 'apprenticeship' was up.

Furious at this, Cooke decided to expose Blair's favouritism and corruption, and prepared a memorial detailing not only the Elle case, but also other examples of corrupt practice, such as the distribution of Prize Negroes to people to whom he was indebted, in lieu of payment. There is no doubt that in assigning Prize Negroes, Blair looked after his own interests and did not consider what a master could offer the Prize Negro, or whether he was likely to look after his charge properly. Charles Dixon, keeper of a livery-stable in Cape Town, was assigned 15 Prize Negroes between 1810 and 1816, in return for overlooking a debt Blair owed him. Blair also gave a tradesman by the name of Durham, to whom he owed money for household furniture, 15 Prize Negroes. The Commissioners concluded that 'such great indulgence would not have been granted to Mr Blair if Mr Durham had not been accommodated with the services of so many Prize Negroes'.[40] Of the tradespeople who had received Prize Negroes, examined by the Commission, all but one had been owed money by Blair.[41] Samuel Murray, who had been assigned more than anyone else, had supplied Blair with wine on a regular basis. William Duckitt, who farmed at Klaver Valley in the Darling district north of Cape Town, obtained, so the Commission was told, 10 Prize Negroes, in

36 *Ibid.*, p. 30. On the Elle story, see esp. p. 127.

37 Somerset to Bathurst, 22 Feb. 1824, in Theal, *RCC*, vol. 17, p. 109.

38 *BPP*, 1826–7, xxi (42), p. 128.

39 *Ibid.*, p. 13 and cf. p. 42.

40 *Ibid.*, p. 18.

41 *Ibid.*, p. 19.

42 E.A. Host, 'Capitalization and Proletarianization on a Western Cape Farm: Klaver Valley 1812–98' (MA

return for which Blair got forage from Duckitt's farm. The records of the opgaaf suggest that the number allocated Duckitt was, in fact, larger.[42] Blair gave almost 40 Prize Negroes to a farmer at the Hottentots Holland whose hospitality he often enjoyed, two or three to a farmer who gave him barley, and many more to Thomas Dreyer of Wynberg, who supplied him with veal, fruit and game.[43]

From the evidence the Commissioners collected, it is clear that Blair used any opportunity to recall Prize Negroes for his own purposes. Consider the case of William Cobbitt, who got Blair's permission to take to England, for up to a year, a Prize Negro by the name of Malamo, known also as Jack. As Cobbitt wished to remain in England, he sent Malamo back to the Cape, where a friend gave him employment as a house servant and shop assistant, to help carry parcels and do errands. Claiming that Cobbitt had broken the agreement he had made to return with the Prize Negro, Blair removed him from his new master and took him into his own employment.[44] The authority given the Collector and Comptroller to reassign Prize Negroes had been intended to meet the case where a master could, for some reason, not provide them with adequate 'apprenticeship'. The Commissioners rejected the idea that they could legally be reassigned, as they found had been the case at the Cape, 'to the maintenance and augmentation of the Collector's and Comptroller's patronage'.[45]

In his memorial, Cooke made the point that had Elle been a slave, his master would have had to support him in his old age, whereas as a Prize Negro he could expect no such support. Instead, he would be 'cursed with liberty at the end of a cruel, abject and unprofitable slavery of fourteen years, left to starve in the decline of life, after having worn away his strength by the goadings of those who have no interest (like the real slave proprietor) in well treating these poor people...'[46] The 1825 Commission heard from a number of witnesses that Prize Negroes were, in certain respects, in a worse position than those actually in bondage. J.B. Hoffman pointed out that when their indentures ended they were worse off than slaves who had been manumitted: 'They have not the privilege of a manumitted slave', he explained, 'for they are obliged to find a master with whom they make a contract; they cannot take a house, as a manumitted slave may do.'[47]. Another witness before the

---

thesis, University of Cape Town, 1992), p. 74 and notes 7 and 10, citing CA, J46 and J48, Opgaaf records, 1815 and 1818. In 1815 there were 22 Prize Negroes on the farm, 15 men, 5 women and 2 children; in 1818, 27 adults and 12 children.

43   *BPP*, 1826–7, xxi (42), Report of July 1825, pp. 11ff. and Evidence, pp. 127ff.

44   *Ibid.*, p. 170.

45   *Ibid.*, p. 19.

46   *Ibid.*, p. 7.

47   *Ibid.*, p. 129.

Commission, when asked whether the Prize Negroes were treated as *de facto* slaves, replied: 'Precisely; if there is a difference between them, I think that it is in favour of the slaves, from the regard the masters feel for them, as their property.'[48]

Relations between Prize Negroes and slaves were complex and followed no one pattern. In the years following the end of the slave trade there was some confusion of the two categories. In a report prepared for the Cape Governor in 1824, the Fiscal investigated what had happened to the Prize Negroes from the Portuguese ship 'Constantia' who had been 'apprenticed' to Alexander Tennant, a prominent dealer in slaves, in March 1808. The Fiscal found it difficult to trace them, despite the fact that they had been 'marked on the right arm near the shoulder with two crosses'. He did, however, ascertain that some were sold as slaves despite their being what the Fiscal called 'free apprentices'.[49] The introduction of a slave register by the Governor, Lord Charles Somerset, in April 1816, was, in part, designed to ensure that this did not happen again. As late as 1831, however, Commissioner J.T. Bigge thought it possible that in 'remote districts' progeny of Prize Negroes had been entered onto the slave register as slaves.[50] We know that a number of Prize Negroes married slaves.[51] It was possible, too, for ex-slaves to obtain Prize Negroes. Wilhelmina Rosina Hendriksen, for example, who gave evidence before the 1825 Commission, had acquired Samina, a Prize Negro, not long after she herself had been manumitted from slavery.[52]

Both in Cape Town and on the farms, Prize Negroes and slaves, and Prize Negroes and Free Blacks lived and worked together.[53] On William Duckitt's Klaver Valley farm in the Darling district, Prize Negroes, together with a few slaves, played an important role in the change from stock farming to wine and grain production after 1815. By 1825 the Klaver Valley farm community was made up of Free Blacks and Prize Negroes, and once again all did similar work.[54]

Only a minority of the Prize Negroes distributed at the Cape settled permanently on farms in the rural areas, but others were sent out to the farms

---

48 *Ibid.*, p. 131, evidence of Thomas Thwaits.

49 *Ibid.*, p. 130; Denyssen to Somerset, 23 Mar. 1824, in Theal, *RCC*, vol. 17, pp. 157–67.

50 Theal, *RCC*, vol. 35, p. 359: Report upon the Slaves and the State of Slavery at the Cape of Good Hope by J.T. Bigge, Apr. 1831.

51 For instance, CA, SO 3/11.

52 *BPP* 1826–7, xxi (41), pp. 157–8, evidence of Mrs Hendriksen.

53 For Cape Town, see esp. *ibid.*, p. 150; for the farms, see the evidence from farmers in Theal, *RCC*, vol. 29, esp. William Duckitt of Klaver Valley, p. 450; W. Proctor of Drooge Valley in the Stellenbosch district, pp. 481, 491.

54 Host, 'Capitalization and Proletarianization', pp. 9, 10, 14–15, and esp. pp. 75–6, where Opgaaf Returns are cited.

during harvest time. One farmer in the Stellenbosch district hired more Prize Negroes than slaves during harvest-time in 1825, and paid each master 20 rixdollars per month for each one's services.[55] Conditions for the Prize Negroes on the farms were, as for the slaves proper, considerably worse than in Cape Town. Those Prize Negroes who worked on the wine estates—and in 1823, 54 Prize Negroes, 36 of whom were men, were employed on Stellenbosch wine farms, and 116 on wine farms in the Cape district[56]—suffered, along with the slaves proper, during the early 1820s as the demand for greater production, at a time of soaring prices for colonial wine, led to a greater coercion of workers.[57]

Stiff penalties were laid down in the indentures of Prize Negroes if they were sold as slaves: the seller would have to forfeit double the value of the sale price.[58] But that did not prevent them in effect being sold, their employers selling them along with other property to others. There are a number of cases in the records of Prize Negroes having been included in the sale price of a farm and sold along with the farm on which they lived. The 1825 Commission heard that when Blair's own estate, Stellenberg, had been sold in April 1820, the sale had included 10 Prize Negroes then working on it.[59] Blair had promised the new owner that they would not be withdrawn until their 14-year apprenticeships expired. The property was estimated to be worth 20 per cent more than would have been the case had there been no Prize Negroes on it.[60] Similarly, the Comptroller sold his Groene River estate with a promise that the new owner might continue to have the use of three Prize Negroes. In that case, the person who bought the farm had previously received an official reprove for the severe treatment he had meted out to Prize Negroes in his employ.[61]

Ill-treatment of Prize Negroes was common-place. Dixon, who was assigned a number by Blair, beat and flogged them 'most unmercifully' with a broomstick. Even after Dixon's cruel treatment had come to official attention, Blair continued to assign more Prize Negroes to him.[62] Blair, rather

---

55 M. Rayner, "'Laborers in the Vineyard": Work and Resistance to Servitude during the Years of the Wine-Farming Boom in the Cape Colony, 1806–24' (unpub. paper), p.14. Cf. also M. Rayner, 'Wine and Slaves: The Failure of an Export Economy and the Ending of Slavery in the Cape Colony, South Africa, 1806–34' (Ph.D. thesis, Duke University, 1986).

56 *Ibid.*

57 *Ibid.*

58 For instance, indenture of Myndola, in *BPP*, 1826–7, xxi (42), p. 125. The penalty was 'double the supposed value of the said Negro'. Cf. Theal, *RCC*, vol. 15, p. 228: 'A Copy of the Indenture by which Prize Negroes are Apprenticed According to the King's Order-in-Council'.

59 *Ibid.*, p. 15 (Report).

60 *Ibid.*

61 *Ibid.*, p.16. Cf. *ibid.*, p. 103.

62 *Ibid.*, pp. 17, 35, 103–4, 133.

than setting an example in such matters, himself gave, so the enquiry established, 'unauthorized punishments...in moments of irritation'.[63] A Prize Negro who worked for him told the Commission that he was 'so very passionate, that he whips and flogs all the Prize Negroes in his service in a most cruel manner...'[64] When one of his Prize Negroes attempted to run away from him, he shot him in the hand, and he had another severely flogged for a minor offence.[65]

At least in theory, masters were required to apply to the Collector of Customs whenever they wished to punish a Prize Slave, for the Fiscal refused to sanction punishment unless Blair or the Comptroller signed an application authorizing the punishment. But, the Commission was told, Blair did not ascertain whether punishment was justified. And when a Prize Negro complained to Blair about the way he had been punished, all Blair did was send for his master 'and inquired into it', without further result.[66] Given the harsh punishments so frequently meted out, it must have taken courage for the Prize Negro, William Cousins, to put his mark to a declaration laid before the Commission which described the way in which he had been treated by Blair, and for Samboo to tell the Commissioners that Blair had struck his fellow 'house-boy' Malamo 'with his fist, on his face'.[67] Malamo himself recounted how he had been 'flogged with a samtok [sic], because the candle was not fixed properly in the lamp'.[68] That such evidence was forthcoming is surely testimony to a deep sense of grievance.

Like slaves, Prize Negroes often ran away. Wynberg, outside Cape Town, was a favourite destination.[69] The crimes they committed tended to be petty ones, in most cases directed against their masters. The sentences they received were usually lesser ones than those imposed on the slaves, perhaps because they were seen as less of a threat, and masters were keen to have them back in service.[70]

Though treated as slaves, Prize Negroes were not slaves. Their 'apprenticeship' had a finite end to it. The Order-in-Council of 1808, which provided for their apprenticeship, stated that it was to be for such terms or periods 'only as may be sufficient for their acquiring the knowledge of their business as servants'.[71] But, as in the British West Indies,[72] the Collector of

---

63   Ibid., p. 20.

64   Ibid., p. 32, declaration of W. Cousins, 1824.

65   Ibid.

66   Ibid., p. 147.

67   Ibid., pp. 31, 169.

68   Ibid., p. 170.

69   For instance, Cape Town Gazette, 15 and 16 June 1822, 19 Mar. 1824.

70   Evidence from court records in the Cape Archives and personal communications from Andrew Bank.

71   Quoted in Thompson, 'African "Recaptives"', p. 129.

Customs indentured all Prize Negroes for the maximum term of 14 years. Many did not know when that period was up, and some masters deliberately kept them in the dark as to how long their 'apprenticeship' still had to run. Samboo asked the Commissioners to 'find out how long I have to serve, as I do not know'.[73] In the late 1820s the government did take steps to ensure that Prize Negroes were released from 'apprenticeship' at the due time: the names of those whose periods of apprenticeship had expired were listed in the official *Gazette*.

After 14 years as *de facto* slaves, Prize Negroes had to fend for themselves, if not re-employed by their former master. Had their 'apprenticeship' meant what that word had originally intended, they would have been better able to fend for themselves. But, as in the British West Indies,[74] 'apprenticeship' meant nothing in almost all cases. Even Malamo, who was taken to England, received no instruction or training and, on his return to Cape Town, he was sent to the free school, but only for one day, and that a holiday.[75] For most Prize Negroes there was not even a pretence of offering instruction. So this 'apprenticeship', which foreshadowed the larger scheme for the slaves themselves from 1834, was little more than a farce; the colonists ignored the intentions of those who conceived it in England, and did so with impunity. And what happened to the Prize Negroes after their indentures expired can be guessed from Bird's cynical comment in the book he wrote about the Cape for prospective English immigrants:

> A question, not devoid of interest, arises concerning the disposal of prize [negroes] on the expiration of their term (14 years) for which they are bound. They neither can be held in thraldom, with any semblance of justice, after that term expires, nor can they be with safety cast loose, and abandoned to their own sole guidance and discretion. Fancy may conjecture a middle course as likely to be pursued.[76]

Considering the way they were treated by masters who professed Christianity, it is not surprising that Islam spread rapidly among Prize Negroes, even among those who had been baptized Christians. On at least one occasion, 'apprentices' who had been indentured to Free Blacks who were Muslims were removed from them and re-assigned to Christians. A few years later, the Fiscal cited 'frequent intercourse with Mahomedan [sic] slaves' as the reason why Prize Negroes were becoming Muslim in large

---

72   *Ibid.*, p. 130.

73   *BPP*, 1826–7, xxi (42), p. 169. He did add that he had not asked Blair, presumably with good reason.

74   Thompson, 'African "Recaptives"', p. 132.

75   *BPP*, 1826–7, xxi (42), p. 170.

76   Bird, *State of the Cape*, p. 357. The colonists assumed as a matter of course that the Prize Negroes were not ready for full liberty, even after 14 years.

77   Theal, *RCC*, vol. 17, pp. 162, 166–7.

numbers.[77] In 1826 the Commissioners reported that the 'great majority' of Prize Negroes were Muslims.[78] As for slaves, Islam offered the Prize Negroes membership of new socio-economic networks and a belief-system which gave them a new sense of self-worth along with a new code of behaviour.

While in this respect, as in others, slaves and Prize Negroes often lived similar lives, colonists on occasion drew sharp distinctions between them. In the early 1830s, the *South African Commercial Advertiser* saw the stereotypical slave as 'a native of the colony…trained up in steady industrious habits', one who 'speaks the same language, and has nearly the same manners and religion as his master', one who 'has been accustomed from infancy to live in a house, to eat regular meals and to perform as it were instinctively all the evolutions of the well-ordered army of social life.' Unlike the slave, viewed here as 'domesticated other', the Prize Negro was seen as a person

> torn from his home, his family, and relations…brought to the Cape, and bound to serve fourteen years without wages, in a strange country, among people of a strange language, professing an unknown religion, and exhibiting customs and manners which to him are utterly unintelligible. At the end of this strange process he is told he is free. Free to do what?…He has no pride of nation or tribe…no family.'[79]

Though overdrawn, this picture of two quite distinct communities was valid in as much as the slave community was, by the early 1830s, reproducing itself, and acculturation and creolization had gone a long way. In most cases, however, it naturally took a long time for Prize Negroes, landed at the Cape in circumstances as alienating as had existed for the slaves who had come before 1807, to become part of that wider acculturated society.

The impact which the presence of the Prize Negroes had on slave consciousness at the Cape is difficult to gauge. Though they were treated as slaves, and worked alongside slaves on an equal footing, they were in that position for a limited period of time, for their 'apprenticeship' was for a finite period. Seeing what happened to them when they became 'free' cannot have encouraged the slaves to look forward to their own day of emancipation. By the early 1820s it was possible to foresee that a day would dawn on which all slaves would be freed. If they considered the lot of the Prize Negroes, already nominally free, the slaves must have realized that their own 'emancipation' was unlikely to bring them full freedom, at least initially. On the other hand, that Prize Negroes were continually, at the end of their periods of 'apprenticeship', becoming 'free' may have encouraged the slaves to think of a time when they too would be 'free'.

---

78   Theal, *RCC*, vol. 28, p. 36: report of 6 Sept. 1826. Cf. BPP, 1826–7, xxi (42), p. 129.

79   *South African Commercial Advertiser*, leader article, 2 Mar. 1831. I thank Andrew Bank for this reference.

Historians of slavery at the Cape may lay too great a stress on the great day of freedom, whether 1 December 1834 or the more important day four years later.[80] Freedom had come to many individuals long before either of those dates, both to those manumitted from slavery—and Bank has shown that there were large numbers of manumissions in Cape Town in the 1820s[81]—and to the Prize Negroes. Individually and collectively they moved from effective slavery to 'freedom' before emancipation day dawned for the slaves. The presence of so many Prize Negroes at the Cape in the pre-emancipation decades did not only bridge a gap in terms of the labour needs of the colonists; as important, it helped blur the distinction between slave and free at the Cape, promote the decline in slavery in Cape Town before 1834 and so prepare the way for the new era of general emancipation.

The evidence used in this chapter thus makes it even more difficult than before to advance generalizations about the position of the Prize Negroes at the Cape in the 1820s. Though treated, for the most part, as if they were slaves, their lot depended on many variables, perhaps most importantly who their master was, whether they were under the direct control of the master or were hired out, and whether they laboured in Cape Town or on a farm. In this, of course, the position of the Prize Negroes resembled that of the slaves themselves, for whom it is as difficult to generalize. For both Prize Negroes and slaves, conditions undoubtedly improved as the 1820s advanced, thanks largely to the amelioration legislation designed to improve the lot of the slaves. Prize Negroes began to use the colonial courts. In 1829, for example, Fahettee took the Rev. Fallows of the newly-established Royal Observatory to court, claiming that he had a right to a mattress, blanket, pair of trousers and waistcoat. He won his case and Fallows had to pay up.[82] By the early 1830s a Prize Negro, and a woman at that, could appeal to the Guardian of Slaves—it is a reflection of the status of Prize Negroes that the applicant both approached that official and he entertained the case—and gain what she asked for.[83]

Prize Negroes continued to be 'apprenticed' at the Cape into the late 1820s. However the majority, 'apprenticed' before the emancipation of the slaves in the 1830s, entered service during the European war which ended in 1815. Their periods of indenture, therefore, ended by the late 1820s at the latest. By the early 1830s there were relatively few Prize Negroes still under indenture, and by the time the day of emancipation dawned for the slaves there were none.[84]

---

80   Cf. J. Mason, '"Fit for Freedom" The Slaves, Slavery and Emancipation in the Cape Colony, South Africa, 1806 to 1842' (Ph.D. thesis, Yale University, 1992), ch. 8.

81   Bank, *Decline of Urban Slavery*, ch. 5.

82   *Cape Town Gazette and African Advertiser*, 24 June 1829. I thank Brian Warner for this reference.

83   CA, SO 3/11, case 434: appeal by Clare for medical attention to be given to the slave Rachel, 1833.

But this is not the end of the story of the Prize Negroes at the Cape. By the time there was another large-scale introduction of such people, at the end of the 1830s,[85] slavery was no longer legal and the acculturation of the now ex-slaves had proceeded even further. It is as difficult to generalize about the position of Prize Negroes in the post-slavery era as it is about their position in the 1820s. From 1839, the periods for which they were apprenticed were shorter—usually seven years, sometimes less[86]—but in most cases, it would seem that during their 'apprenticeship' they were still regarded by their masters as *de facto* slaves and were treated as such. However they were now no longer called 'Prize Slaves'.[87] A greater number of the later Prize Negroes seem to have practised Christianity and not become Muslims—even though Islam was on the increase in Cape Town at the time and there was more open competition between the two religions for converts than before.[88] What can be said is that the end of chattel slavery did not substantially alter the way in which the later Prize Negroes were treated. Then, as earlier, it was only when they had served their apprenticeship that their second, and effective 'liberation' took place, though for many, as for the emancipated slaves, that 'liberation' was of more psychological than material significance, for their socio-economic status changed little, if at all. On William Duckitt's Klaver Valley farm, where Prize Negroes had been an important source of labour from soon after the end of the slave trade, some stayed on the farm from the end of their indentures in the late 1820s into the early 1840s, by which time new ones had been obtained.[89] Those Duckitt obtained in Cape Town in the early 1840s served shorter periods of indenture and when the indentures expired some left the farm; but others remained, engaged themselves from year to year, and died on the farm decades later.[90] The Prize Negroes intermarried into the Free Black and ex-slave population of the colony and gradually lost their distinctiveness. In time they too would be labelled, and would call themselves, 'coloured'.[91]

---

84   Saunders, 'Liberated Africans', pp. 229–30. Similarly in the British West Indies, where by 1832 almost 2,000 had been liberated: Thompson, 'African "Recaptives"', p. 138.

85   For details, see Saunders, 'Liberated Africans', pp. 230ff.

86   There were exceptions: Kebooka was indentured for 11 years in 1842: Host, 'Capitalization and Proletarianization', pp. 77–8 and n. 26, citing Klaver Valley farm journal.

87   That they were often called 'apprentices' means that it is not always easy to distinguish them from the colonial slaves who became 'apprentices' in 1834.

88   For instance, after St. Stephen's opened as a place of worship in Riebeeck Square, Cape Town, in the 1840s, the congregants included 'negro slaves captured by men-of-war and liberated here': *Free Church Missionary Record* (1850), p. 81, quoted in G. Cuthbertson, 'The Impact of the Emancipation of Slaves on St. Andrew's Scottish Church, Cape Town, 1838–78', in *Studies in the History of Cape Town*, 3 (1984), p. 7.

89   Host, 'Capitalization and Proletarianization', p. 77, citing Klaver Valley journals. Alexander, for example, was an 'apprentice' until 1829, continued on the farm as a labourer, and died in 1843.

90   *Ibid.*, p. 77. November, for example, a Mozambican, died on the farm in 1861.

91   Cf, for a preliminary discussion, Saunders 'Liberated Africans', pp. 230ff.

ANNO **TERTIO** & **QUARTO**

GULIELMI IV. REGIS.

****

C A P. LXXIII.

An Act for the Abolition of Slavery throughout the *British* Colonies ; for promoting the Industry of the manumitted Slaves ; and for compensating the Persons hitherto entitled to the Services of such Slaves.   [28th *August* 1833.]

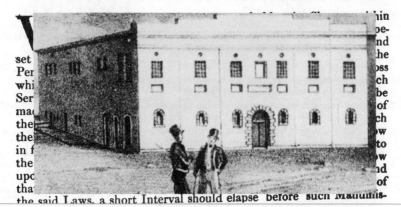

set
Per
whi
Ser
ma
the
the
in f
the
upo
tha
the said Laws, a short Interval should elapse before such manumis-

Plate 6   Slave Abolition Act; and the Cape Town Jail, 1832, by De Meillon. *Cape Archives.*

5

BETWEEN SLAVERY & FREEDOM
THE APPRENTICESHIP PERIOD, 1834 TO 1838

- NIGEL WORDEN -

On 1 December 1834, the day that Cape slaves stopped being slaves, they did not become free. As elsewhere in the British colonies, the Abolition Act tied them to their owners as 'apprentices' for a further four years, a period designed to prepare them for a future as wage labourers and to permit the colonists to adjust to a new type of work force. New laws and new means of imposing them attempted to bring both ex-slave and ex-owner under the control of the state. But in the process both apprentices and their owners sought to redefine the meaning of freedom in ways which differed markedly from the intentions of the framers of the apprenticeship system.

NOTIONS OF APPRENTICESHIP

The system of slave apprenticeship reveals much about the ideology and thinking that lay behind emancipation in the British colonies. Despite differences of emphasis, the rich historical literature on British slave abolition has shown that, by the late 1820s, both abolitionists and administrators, steeped in the ideology of a bourgeois and newly-industializing Britain, had a specific vision of the kind of colonial society they wished to see emerge after emancipation.[1] They believed that not only was slavery inhumane and gave dangerously unlimited powers to masters, but that it also limited worker incentive and productivity. It needed to be replaced with a labour system which avoided direct physical coercion, but which also ensured the

---

1 The classic texts on this are E. Williams, *Capitalism and Slavery* (London, 1964) and D.B. Davis, *The Problem of Slavery in the Age of Revolution, 1770–1823* (Ithaca, 1975). Debates around their arguments have been extensive, although the essential point of the link between capitalist ideology and anti-slavery remains unchallenged: see B. Solow and S. Engerman, *British Capitalism and Caribbean Slavery* (Cambridge, 1987) and T. Bender (ed.), *The Antislavery Debate: Capitalism and Abolitionism as a Problem in Historical Interpretation* (Berkeley, 1992).

dependence of workers on employers for income and subsistence. Slaves were to be freed from bondage but not from labour. In this way the flow of colonial produce would not be interrupted. A vital component of this vision was the belief that slaves had to be 'trained' towards the self-discipline and 'responsibility' deemed to be essential for 'free' labourers.[2] This was a concept equally apparent in reforms in the metropolis at the time. The new Poor Law placed the indigent in workhouses, Factory Acts limited unfettered employer controls over workers but also stressed the inculcation of a disciplined factory labour force for its 'own good', and educational provisions were being made to train a new working class in its dutiful role within an industrializing society.[3] Thus the Abolition Act stated in its title that it provided for 'promoting the industry of the manumitted slaves' and the dispatch sent by the Colonial Secretary to the colonies together with the copy of the Act stressed that its aim was to

> lay the foundation in our colonies of a social system absolved for ever from the reproach of slavery and in which voluntary and effective industry shall take the place of compulsory labour, to the mutual benefit of the owner and the cultivator of the soil.[4]

Abolitionism in the early 1830s was not only the ideology of the middle classes. Small-scale artisan and working-class radicalism also played an important part, and many supporters of slave emancipation did not necessarily favour wage labour over independent production. The language of 'self-improvement' often replaced a crude demand for a docile work force in abolitionist thinking.[5] But support for emancipation by the ruling oligarchy, both in Parliament and in the slave colonies, could only be forthcoming if it offered a vision of an ordered society in which social and economic control over a freed labour force would be maintained. And even more radical and humanitarian abolitionists believed that slaves, as much or more than their owners, had to be prepared for such 'responsibilities' after freedom.

---

2   The shift in thinking away from coerced to wage labour was also evident in the debates of the 1830s over the future of convict labour in the Australian colonies; see J.B. Hirst, *Convict Society and its Enemies* (Sydney, 1983); J. Ritchie, 'Towards Ending an Unclean Thing: The Molesworth Committee and the Abolition of Transportation to New South Wales, 1837–40', *Australian Historical Studies*, 17 (1976), pp. 144–64.

3   D. Turley, *The Culture of English Antislavery, 1780–1860* (London and New York, 1981), ch. 5; T. Holt, *The Problem of Freedom*, pp. 33–7; N. McKendrick, 'Josiah Wedgewood and Factory Discipline', *Historical Journal*, 4 (1961), pp. 30–55.

4   An Act for the Abolition of Slavery Throughout the British Colonies; For Promoting the Industry of the Manumitted Slaves; and For Compensating the Persons Hitherto Entitled to the Services of Such Slaves, 28 Aug. 1833. Stanley to Cole, 18 July 1833, Cape Archives (CA), GH 1/94, f.02.

5   R. Blackburn, *The Overthrow of Colonial Slavery, 1776–1848* (London, 1988), pp. 466–7; J. Walvin, 'The Impact of Slavery on British Radical Politics, 1787–1838', in V. Rubin and A. Tuden (eds.), *Comparative Perspectives on Slavery in New World Plantation Societies* (New York, 1977), pp. 351–2. J. and J. Comaroff, *Of Revelation and Revolution: Christianity, Colonialism and Consciousness in South Africa*, vol. I (Chicago, 1991), p. 63.

For these reasons few abolitionists supported unconditional slave emancipation.[6] In the 1820s, legislation to control the worst abuses of planter tyranny had been passed, with some, albeit limited, effects.[7] During the parliamentary debates of 1833, several schemes were presented which proposed an extension of this ameliorative approach through manumission of deserving slaves, freedom to children born of slave women, and special self-purchase schemes. These measures were intended to promote 'self-help' and incentive without throwing colonial society and production into turmoil.[8] In the Caribbean and Mauritius there was little support for such ideas. But at the Cape the gradualist approach to emancipation already had some advocates. In 1826, an unknown writer stressed in a classic statement of the thinking behind gradualism that immediate emancipation was undesirable since:

> unless we are infatuated by the mere sound of a word, we must acknowledge that the power of doing whatsoever a man pleases, if unaccompanied by some moral stimulus which shall ensure habitual industry and correct the profligate propensities of savage nature, is so far from being a step in advance that it is rather a stride backwards; instead of being a blessing it is plainly a curse. The body of the slave population do not at present possess this moral stimulus. Emancipation therefore would not put them on the road to become good citizens.[9]

The means to do this included not only education, but also encouragement of task work, self-purchase of freedom by slaves modelled on the Spanish American system, and encouragement of the notion that freedom had to be earned so that, 'the slave would only cease to labor by compulsion when he had become willing to labor for hire.'[10]

Such ideas reflected local circumstances. In 1826, Cape slaveholders held protest meetings against Ordinance 19 which had fixed limits to the amount of punishment owners could give their slaves, established the office of Guardian of Slaves, and given slaves the right to complain against their owners and to purchase their freedom. In its place they proposed limited measures of gradualist abolition, such as the freeing of new-born children, which would not threaten the control of owners over their slaves by outside officials.[11] Such schemes were not only developed by defenders of slavery.

6　D. Eltis, 'Abolitionist Perceptions of Society After Slavery', in J. Walvin (ed.), *Slavery and British Society, 1776–1846* (London, 1982), p. 200.

7　M. Rayner, 'Slaves, Slaveowners and the British State: The Cape Colony, 1806–34', *The Societies of Southern Africa in the 19th and 20th Centuries*, vol. 12 (Institute of Commonwealth Studies, University of London, Collected Seminar Papers, no. 28), pp. 15–32.

8　T. Holt, *The Problem of Freedom: Race, Labor and Politics in Jamaica and Britain, 1832–1938* (Baltimore and London, 1992), pp. 42–53.

9　CA, M 142 (3). Papers concerned with the laws affecting slaves and copies of documents transmitted to the Commission of Enquiry 1825/6, p. 1. The writer is unidentified, but may well have been associated with the schemes mooted in Cape Town and Graaff-Reinet for gradual emancipation.

10　*Ibid.*, p. 4.

In Cape Town, leading liberals subscribed to the Cape of Good Hope Philanthropic Society for Aiding Deserving Slaves to Purchase Their Freedom, founded in 1828. As historians have stressed, none of these initiatives aimed to disrupt the rights of slaveowners in their human property and the reformers were as much concerned with social stability and ordered control as with the personal liberty of the slaves.[12] By 1831, gradualist abolition was also being advocated in Cape Town as an alternative to more radical proposals for immediate slave freedom.[13]

Another event which persuaded Cape slaveowners that gradualist abolition might be necessary and even desirable, was the spectre of slave revolt evoked by the uprising of slave and Khoi workers against their owners on a remote Bokkeveld farm in 1825.[14] This, combined with the increasing assertiveness of slaves who were bringing complaints against their owners and demanding rights of liberty beyond those prescribed by the amelioration laws, demonstrates the role that slaves played in the move towards emancipation at the Cape.[15] The example of the successful slave revolt of St. Domingue in 1793 and of the less successful, but no less threatening, slave uprisings in the British sugar islands, certainly made slaveowners uneasy. The Jamaican slave revolt of 1831 brought matters to a head. But to the British authorities, the uprising seemed to indicate that gradualism and amelioration had only succeeded in raising and frustrating slave expectations, and that further resistance would occur if the move to freedom was not swifter, thus negating the aim of an ordered transition to a stable and diligent work force.

Holt has shown that in these circumstance the British authorities abandoned amelioration and gradualism in favour of more immediate emancipation.[16] But slaveowner opposition to such a move remained a force with which to contend. Abolitionists were calling for emancipation but many still

---

11   M. Rayner, 'Wine and Slaves: The Failure of an Export Economy and the Ending of Slavery in South Africa, 1806–34' (Ph.D. thesis, Duke University, 1986)', pp. 262–4; A. du Toit and H. Giliomee, *Afrikaner Political Thought: Analysis and Documents*, vol. I (Cape Town and Johannesburg, 1983), pp. 65–6.

12   R.L. Watson, *The Slave Question: Liberty and Property in South Africa* (Hanover, New England and Johannesburg, 1990); K. McKenzie, '*The South African Commercial Advertiser* and the Making of Middle-Class Identity in Early Nineteenth-Century Cape Town' (MA thesis, University of Cape Town, 1993), ch. 4; C. Iannini, 'Slavery, Philanthropy and Hegemony: A History of the Cape of Good Hope Philanthropic Society, 1828–33' (BA Hons. thesis, University of Cape Town, 1993).

13   For instance, J. Centlivres Chase, *Practical Considerations in the Exact Position of the Slave Question* (Cape Town, 1831).

14   R. Ross, *Cape of Torments: Slavery and Resistance in South Africa* (London, 1983), pp. 97–116; R. Watson, *Slave Question*, pp. 50–9.

15   J. Mason, 'The Slaves and Their Protectors: Reforming Resistance in a Slave Society: The Cape Colony, 1826–34', *Journal of Southern African Studies*, 17 (1991), pp. 103–28; W. Dooling, 'Slavery and Amelioration in the Graaff-Reinet District, 1823–30', *South African Historical Journal*, 27 (1992), pp. 75–94.

believed that the slaves required a period of preparation for freedom, if the 'barbarity' revealed by the revolts was to be tamed, a notion with which the government concurred. In the final debates leading to the Abolition Act of 1833, apprenticeship thus emerged as the system of transition from slavery to freedom. Slavery was abolished with immediate effect, but the ex-slaves had to continue working for their owners for a specified number of years as 'apprentices'. They were to be maintained by their employers, but with pay only for work which exceeded an allotted number of hours per week. Laws, to be administered by specially-appointed magistrates, both regulated their freedom and protected them from employer abuse. To pre-empt planter revolt, slaveowners were to be financially compensated for the loss of their slaves.[17] Apprenticeship thus emerged as a compromise between the demands of planters, abolitionists and Parliament. Although slave resistance had acted as a catalyst, slave demands for immediate freedom were ignored.

At the Cape, local gradualist schemes were thus overtaken by the externally-imposed apprenticeship system. In Britain, the term apprenticeship evoked images of training for a particular kind of skilled labour which 'combined education and labour with the promise of eventual self-employment.'[18] This suited the formulators of the Abolition Act who believed that slaves were to be trained in the 'discipline of labouring'. In practice, however, it was equivalent to indenture, merely ensuring a continued labour supply. No provision was made in the Abolition Act for any special education for the apprentices.[19] As was pointed out in the parliamentary debates of 1838 over the ending of slave apprenticeship, the Abolition Act had,

> but sunk the name of slavery in the hypocritical base, deceptive name of apprenticeship—a term intended to deceive the people of Great Britain—...they would learn that they had got apprenticeship for slavery—not apprenticeship as it was understood by the term in this country, but a vile system that exacted labour and fear of the lash.[20]

16   Holt, *The Problem of Freedom*, pp. 18–21.

17   *Ibid.*, pp. 42–53; D.B. Davis, *Slavery and Human Progress* (Oxford, 1984), pp. 204–7.

18   The quotation is from S. Salinger, *'To Serve Well and Faithfully': Labour and Indentured Servants in Pennsylvania, 1682–1800* (New York, 1987) cited in C. Malherbe, 'Indentured and Unfree Labour in South Africa: Towards an Understanding', *South African Historical Journal*, 24 (1991), p. 6.

19   Although in late 1835 Parliament did approve the granting of funds to match local financing of school buildings for the apprentices: Holt, *Problem of Freedom*, p. 72. In the Caribbean missionary societies carried out this function: G. Eisner, *Jamaica, 1830–1930* (Manchester, 1961), p. 327. At the Cape there was no equivalent of this activity. A school-room was built in Cape Town to commemorate emancipation in 1834, but education was overwhelmingly limited to the middle classes; *South African Commercial Advertiser*, 6 Dec. 1834; K. Elks, 'Crime and Social Control in Cape Town, 1830–50', *Studies in the History of Cape Town*, 6 (1988), p. 39. Contributions to schools were expected from parents, and it is thus hardly surprising that, as the Attorney-General stated in 1838, 'I believe no demand is made from the coloured population', CA, GH 26/96, Attorney-General's enclosure in dispatch of Napier to Glenelg, 22 June 1838, f. 131.

20   C.H. Wesley, 'The Abolition of Negro Apprenticeship in the British Empire', *Journal of Negro History*, 23 (1938), p. 164.

At the Cape, apprenticeship was occasionally used in the British sense. As in other colonies, it referred to pauper children placed in the care of colonists.[21] The Cape of Good Hope Philanthropic Society apprenticed those slave children whose freedom it had bought to colonists, including their previous owners, so that they should become 'useful members of society'.[22] However no skills training was provided and the distinction between this 'apprenticeship' and indenture remained unclear.

Indeed, to most Cape colonists, 'apprenticeship' meant indenture. In this they were influenced by the status of Khoi labourers. The Khoi had long worked alongside slaves on the Cape farms, although their legal status had varied from outright indenture as *inboekselings* in the eighteenth century, to relative freedom of movement after the passing of Ordinance 50 in 1828. Apprenticeship of Khoi children to farmers, ostensibly to learn skills for later employment, had been sanctioned in 1812, but was used as a means of tying both the children and their families to the farms in effective indenture.[23] After 1828 this continued on a voluntary basis and was even extended, in 1836, for male children to the age of 21 years.[24] Khoi labourers were thus frequently referred to as apprentices, although contemporaries clearly thought of them as indentured workers.[25]

Apprenticeship was used in similar ways to refer to slaves. Manumitted slaves were 'apprenticed' to their owners for a number of years, often until their employer's death.[26] The 'Prize Negroes', slaves captured from passing foreign slaving vessels and indentured to colonists for periods of up to 14 years, were known as apprentices.[27] None of these schemes intended that apprenticeship should include any kind of special training. Indeed Fairbairn, editor of Cape Town's *South African Commercial Advertiser*, made the identity of indenture and apprenticeship for slaves explicit when he advocated in 1831 that, 'the people [slaves] are to be apprenticed or bound by indenture to serve their former masters—so that the great wheel of labor shall not be stopped for a single hour.'[28] The coercive aspects of an indentured 'apprenticeship' at the

21   *The Australians, 1838* (Cambridge, 1988), p. 123.

22   CA, SO 3/20a, Confidential Report of the Protector of Slaves for the period ending 28 July 1830; Iannini, 'Slavery, Philanthropy and Hegemony', pp. 81–2, 95–7.

23   R. Elphick and V. Malherbe, 'The Khoisan to 1828', in R. Elphick and H. Giliomee (eds.), *The Shaping of South African Society, 1652–1840*, 2nd edn. (Cape Town and London, 1989), pp. 32, 41.

24   *Cape of Good Hope Government Gazette*, 4 Nov. 1836.

25   On the use of apprenticeship for such labour structures, see esp. W.M. Macmillan, *The Cape Colour Question* (London, 1927), pp. 167–8; Newton-King, ch. 9, and Crais, ch. 10 in this volume.

26   E. Hengherr, 'Emancipation—and After: A Study of Cape Slavery and the Issues Arising From It, 1830–43' (MA thesis, University of Cape Town, 1953), p. 45.

27   See Saunders, ch. 4 in this volume.

28   Editorial of the *South African Commercial Advertiser*, 2 Mar. 1831, cited in McKenzie, '*South African Commercial Advertiser*', p. 167.

Cape were also fully revealed in the ill-fated scheme of the Children's Friend Society to apprentice children from Britain to Cape employers. Whereas the Society anticipated that they would receive training for skilled work on the British apprenticeship model, they were alarmed to discover that many of the employers had been slaveowners and that 'their apprentices may have been looked upon in the same light as slaves'.[29]

Slave apprenticeship was thus readily perceived as indenture at the Cape. Wade, the Acting Governor, made a direct link between Khoi indenture and slave apprenticeship when he wrote, in late 1833, to the Colonial Secretary that the Khoi freed from indenture by Ordinance 28 set a bad example of indisciplined 'free labour' and warned that slaves should not be emancipated in a similar way.[30]

ADMINISTERING APPRENTICESHIP

The Abolition Act had broadly outlined the working of the system, but it was left to local legislative bodies to specify the details of apprenticeship in each colony in terms consistent with the Westminster legislation but appropriate to local circumstances.[31] The danger that these would be tantamount to the old slave codes was recognized, and the Colonial Office urged governors to ensure that the new laws did not give planters too much unbridled authority over their apprentices, stating that local laws could even be more lenient than those which existed to control labourers in England.[32] Codes which did not meet with the approval of the Colonial Office would be vetoed and no compensation money paid until acceptable legislation had been produced. Although the codes presented the relationship between employer and employee as more of a contract than had been the case under slavery, nonetheless their essential purpose was 'to make temporary provision for the continued cultivation of the soil and the good order of society, until all classes should gradually fall into the relations of a state of freedom.'[33]

Under these circumstances it is not surprising that the laws passed were concerned primarily with controlling the apprentices and were vague and inadequate about improvements in their status. The Cape's Ordinance 1 of

29 CA, GH 1/127, Glenelg to Napier, 29 Mar. 1839, f. 132. On this scheme, E. Bradlow, 'The Children's Friend Society at the Cape of Good Hope', *Victorian Studies,* 27 (1984), pp. 155–77.

30 CA, GH 23/10, Wade to Stanley, 6 Dec. 183, ff. 265–6.

31 And each colony was also permitted to move to direct emancipation. Only Antigua did so, because local circumstances meant that complete emancipation would not disrupt the existing system of labour: D. Watts, *The West Indies: Patterns of Development, Culture and Environmental Change Since 1492* (Cambridge, 1987), p. 470.

32 W. Green, 'Emancipation to Indenture: A Question of Imperial Morality', *Journal of British Studies,* 22 (1983), p. 100.

33 CA, GH 1/101, Circular to Governors of the Sugar Colonies, 19 Oct. 1833.

1835, which laid down the laws for apprenticeship (a full month after the start of the scheme), was particularly striking in this regard.[34] Most notably, the distinction established in the Abolition Act between praedial field workers and non-praedial urban and domestic slaves was not implemented at the Cape. Although such a division was made by the Protector of Slaves for the calculation of slave values in 1834, it was not deemed appropriate for the operation of apprenticeship, and all apprentices were defined by Ordinance 1 as non-praedial.[35] The Protector pointed out that the West Indian definition of gang slave was ill-suited to the work of Cape slaves who were 'scarcely ever allocated to one particular labor for any fixed time'.[36] A public meeting of slaveowners in Cape Town in early 1834 made the same point.[37] A detailed justification of the non-praedial classification, made by the Governor, pointed out that the hours worked by Cape slaves were, on average, less than those laid down for praedial apprentices, and they would furthermore gain from the shorter period of apprenticeship specified for non-praedials in the Abolition Act: four years rather than the six established for praedial apprentices. Any distinction between the two would lead to a splitting of praedial and non-praedial spouses and dissatisfaction at the freeing of only a portion of the apprentices after four years.[38] The former calculation was dubious, and the possible disadvantages of differential periods of termination were in the event nullified by the decision, in 1838, to end apprenticeship for all in that year.

Although Ordinance 1 laid down the maximum numbers of hours which apprentices could be compelled to work in garden or field labour, there was no clear distinction between the work that they performed on these tasks and on other employment broadly defined as 'domestic'. For this reason, most of the provisions which were set out under Section VI, 'On the Duties to be Performed by the Employers Towards their Apprentices', such as the rights to task work and payment for overtime, were unenforceable. As the *Zuid-Afrikaan*, no friend to the abolitionists in Cape Town or London, pointed out, non-praedial apprentices 'must perform domestic labor as before at any hour, and for any number of hours exactly as when in a state of slavery.'[39] The hours of work were thus less tightly controlled under apprenticeship than by earlier ameliorative legislation. Rather than paying wages to their apprentices, Cape employers were obliged to provide them with food, lodging and

---

34   Ordinance 1 of 1835, For giving due effect to the Provisions of…an Act for the Abolition of Slavery.

35   CA, SO 20/61, Returns of total number of slaves according to the several classes and values. Ordinance 1/1835, Sect. III.

36   CA, SO 3/20a, Report of Protector of Slaves for the period between June and Dec. 1832.

37   *De Zuid-Afrikaan*, 28 Mar. 1834.

38   Enclosure in CA, GH 23/11, D'Urban to Spring Rice, 7 Jan. 1835.

39   *De Zuid-Afrikaan*, 28 Nov. 1834.

maintenance at the levels required of them in the last days of slavery. And apprentices could still be bought and sold, although they were not to be publicly displayed at auctions, a concession to the perceived personal humiliation and brutalizing effect of such actions, and a response to the pressures of abolitionists against public sales.[40] In an attempt to inculcate 'self-improvement' at a price, apprentices also had the right to own property and to purchase their freedom.

The duties to be performed by the apprentices and the penalties for their non-performance laid down in Section V of Ordinance 1 were more directly enforceable. Apprentices were 'obliged to work and labor in every day of the year—Sundays and holidays hitherto usually allowed to the laboring population excepted—in the service and for the benefit of the employer.' Absence from work for longer than seven and a half hours per week was regarded as desertion and punishable as such. 'Wilful' absence was also to be made up by prolonged compulsory service after the termination of apprenticeship, and, in all, 954 apprentices were so sentenced, although their punishments were annulled in 1838.[41] In clauses reminiscent of the slave codes and later reinforced in the post-emancipation Master and Servants legislation, indolence, careless or negligent work, disobedience of orders, 'combined and open resistance', drunkenness, and the 'careless use of fire', were punishable offences.

Where the Abolition Act and Ordinance 1 did break with the past was in the removal of the right of employers to punish their servants themselves. This had been partially removed under the ameliorative legislation of the preceding years. However the apprenticeship laws brought the process to completion. They detailed the judicial and magisterial system which would be the sole authority for the administration of the regulations to both apprentices and employers. New stipendiary magistrates were to be specially appointed for the duration of apprenticeship, and it was intended that they should be outsiders to the colonies, untainted by acquaintance with slavery or the ex-slaveowners, and hence impartial implementors of the law.

The special magistrate system marked an important stage in the development of a concept of impartial 'rule of law' in the colonies. This paralleled attempts in Britain to limit the arbitrariness of justice administered by landowners, and men of power and influence in the local community.[42]

---

40   For instance, 'Sale of a Negro Family at the Cape of Good Hope', *New Monthly Magazine*, 1824. However this provision was difficult to enforce and was often ignored by employers, CA, CO 5177, Circular to Special Justices, 6 Jan. 1836.

41   CA, CO 476, nos. 61–75, Number of apprentices to serve employers after 1 Dec. 1838; Ordinance 3/1838, For Fixing the Termination of Certain Apprenticeships: Act to Amend the Act for the Abolition of Slavery in the British Colonies, 11 Apr. 1838.

42   D. Philips, '"A New Engine of Power and Authority": The Institutionalisation of Law-Enforcement in England, 1780–1830', in V. Gatrell (ed.), *Crime and the Law: The Social History of Crime in Western*

Although some abolitionists had compared the limits of custom and community consensus placed on Justices of the Peace in England favourably with the untrammeled power of slaveholders, both systems made the implementation of law more arbitrary than reformers of the 1830s thought desirable.[43] Rather all offenders should be punished for disobeying the law, although, of course, this was not accompanied by the belief that the laws themselves should be blind to class distinctions or that there should be universal rights enforceable by law. In the colonies, similar attempts were made in the 1820s and 1830s to override local partiality, and to establish more centralized and equitable control by state-appointed magistrates and police.[44] It was one of the achievements of the apprenticeship period, according to the Colonial Secretary in late 1837, that 'there has been a greater respect for the laws which have afforded more equal protection to the rights of all classes of the community.'[45]

Slaveowner authority at the Cape had never been completely arbitrary and uncontrolled. Some state intervention had always existed to control the extent to which slaves could be punished, although its effectiveness under the Dutch East India Company (VOC) had been limited. The most effective sanction against abuse of slaveowner authority was the loss of 'moral reputation' in the local community, but this did little to diminish the power of such domestic control.[46] During the late 1810s and 1820s, more effective intervention in the control of masters over their slaves emerged with the establishment of Slave Protectors, laws to limit permissible punishment, and giving slaves the right to lodge complaints against their abuse; and, in 1831, the requirement to record all punishments given, a move which led to a minor slaveholder revolt.[47] Ordinance 1 marked the final extension of this

Europe Since 1500 (London, 1980), pp. 155–89; C. Emsley, *Policing and its Context, 1750–1870* (London, 1983), ch. 4.

43   D.B. Davis, 'Reflections on Abolitionism and Ideological Hegemony', *American Historical Review*, 92 (1987), pp. 805–6.

44   The fullest account of this process is D. Neal, *The Rule of Law in a Penal Colony: Law and Power in Early New South Wales* (Cambridge, 1992). Neal makes overt parallels between the convict system and slavery, and the attack on employer arbitrary rule by a centrally-imposed state system of magisterial authority. On the police, see R. Hill, *Policing the Colonial Frontier: The Theory and Practice of Coercive Social and Racial Control in New Zealand*, vol. 1 (Wellington, 1986) and for the Cape, see K. Elks, 'Crime, Community and Police in Cape Town, 1825–50' (MA thesis, University of Cape Town, 1986).

45   CA, GH 1/117, Glenelg to Napier, 6 Nov. 1837, ff. 76–7. For the argument that the apprenticeship period saw an increasing impartiality of punishment and legal control between the races, see E. Bradlow, 'Emancipation and Race Perceptions at the Cape', *South African Historical Journal*, 15 (1983), p. 24.

46   R. Ross 'The Rule of Law at the Cape of Good Hope in the Eighteenth Century', *Journal of Imperial and Commonwealth History*, 9 (1980), pp. 5–16; W. Dooling, *Law and Community in a Slave Society: Stellenbosch District, South Africa, c.1760–1820* (Centre for African Studies, University of Cape Town, Communications, no. 23, 1992).

47   See Dooling, ch. 1 in this volume.

development by removing all rights of ex-owners to punish their ex-slaves. Not only did the Special Magistrates hold hearings in the main settlements of their districts, but they were also obliged to visit farms with more than 20 apprentices, to take testimonies and sometimes to deliver sentence on the spot.

However, as Edwards has pointed out, the transfer of this function to the Special Magistrates gave them a punitive, as much as a protective, role in the eyes of the apprentices.[48] Certainly some employers saw them in this light and attempted to control their apprentices by threats of the magistrate's arrival. This was not always successful. Christian, an apprentice on a farm in the Worcester district, told his employer that, 'I know the Justice comes here every six months, but you cannot frighten me with his coming.'[49] In some cases, employers attempted to retain some control over the dispensation of justice by bringing charges against their apprentices to the magistrates, but then appealing against the imposition of the sentence on their behalf.[50]

The main role of the Special Magistrates was to hear cases of infringe-ment of Ordinance 1 by both apprentices and employers, and to impose appropriate punishments. These were laid down in the Ordinance, thus limit-ing the arbitrary nature of punishment for particular offences. Male appren-tices were usually flogged, with a stipulated numbers of stripes according to the severity and frequency of the offence. Since the Special Magistrates were mainly retired naval and army officers, they were familiar with such punish-ments and imposed them with equal or even greater severity than the slave-owners had done.[51] Female apprentices were not to be whipped but to be placed in the stocks. This was in line with the ban on corporal punishment of females in Britain in 1817 and of women slaves at the Cape, established by ameliorative legislation, between 1826 and 1830.[52] In addition, offences committed by apprentices could be punished by set terms of imprisonment, usually with hard labour. The rise of the penitentiary in Britain during this period was paralleled by increasing attention to the prison as an institution of state control in the colonies.[53] The apprenticeship years intensified the

---

48   I. Edwards, *Towards Emancipation: A Study in South African Slavery* (Cardiff, 1942), p. 180.

49   CA, 1/WOC, 19/26, Worcester Court Record Book, 28 Apr. 1835, ff. 141–4. He was nonetheless accused successfully of disobedience and sentenced to 20 lashes by the magistrate.

50   For instance, CA, 1/WOC, 19/26, Worcester Court Record Book, ff. 163, 177, 195.

51   W.A. Green, *British Slave Emancipation: The Sugar Colonies and the Great Experiment, 1830–65* (Oxford, 1976), p. 135; Neal, *Rule of Law*, pp. 134, 139.

52   J. Hirst, *Convict Society*, p. 17; M. Ferguson, *Subject to Others: British Women Writers and Colonial Slavery, 1670–1834* (New York and London, 1992), p. 293; P. van der Spuy, 'A Collection of Essays on Gender and Slavery at the Cape of Good Hope in the 1820s' (MA thesis, University of Cape Town, 1993), pp. 34–5.

53   M. Ignatieff, *A Just Measure of Pain: The Penitentiary in the Industrial Revolution, 1750–1850* (London, 1978); C. Crais, *The Making of the Colonial Order: White Supremacy and Black Resistance in the Eastern Cape, 1770–1865* (Cambridge and Johannesburg, 1992), pp. 59–61.

process. The first task that the Cape Town Special Magistrate undertook on his arrival was an inspection of the local jail and he demanded that it be extended for his needs. His Swellendam counterpart also complained that the single cell in the local jail was inadequate.[54]

Not only did imprisonment give the state control over an arena previously in the hands of private individuals, but it fitted the abolitionist notion that discipline and self-control needed to be inculcated into the apprentices, if necessary by institutional means. In Jamaica, the treadmill was introduced in the apprenticeship period as a device to inculcate the notion of hard work amongst recalcitrant offenders. In the Cape Town jail, a treadmill had been used from at least 1825 for the punishment of slaves, although it is not specifically mentioned elsewhere in the colony.[55] Fairbairn had waxed eloquent about the inducement that the treadmill gave to discipline in 1831.[56] Despite its torturous effects, it seemed to provide both the surveillance of offenders in prison, and the notion of hard labour as a means of self-improvement.

Employers were also subject to the control of the Special Magistrates. Apprentices could bring complaints against abuse, usually when they had been physically punished, but also if they felt that they had not been given their due allowances of food and clothing. If found guilty, employers were usually fined, and occasionally forbidden to continue using the services of the aggrieved apprentice—although they could also be imprisoned in extreme circumstances.[57] Employers were also being schooled in the practice of future obligations within a contractual system of free labour.

The apprenticeship system was thus dependent on the Special Magistrates for its implementation. As in England and other colonies, the role of magistrates involved much more than hearing cases. They were also responsible for the administration of the jails, and for the active investigation of complaints—thus combining the functions of magistrate, lawyer and policeman. Their situation was not an easy one, however. They were paid and supported entirely out of a parliamentary grant made at the time of the Abolition Act, which was a burden on top of the £20 million to be paid out in compensation to owners.

The Treasury tried to cut these costs as much as possible. Only eight Special Magistrates were sent to the Cape, where they had to administer a

---

54 CA, CO 441, no. 2, Longmore to Colonial Secretary, 28 Jan. 1835; CO 441, no. 21, Report of Barnes on state of prison, 3 Mar. 1835.

55 Holt, *Problem of Freedom*, p. 106; M.D. Teenstra, *De Vruchten Mijner Werkzaamheden, Gedurende Mijne Reize, Over de Kaap de Goede Hoop Naar Java en Terug...* (Cape Town, 1943), pp. 195–6.

56 McKenzie, '*South African Commercial Advertiser*', p. 167.

57 For instance, CA, 1/WOC 19/27, unpaginated, case of Francois du Toit, 9 Jan. 1937, found guilty of tying an apprentice to a wagon-wheel and beating him, was sentenced to a fine of £5 and a month in prison.

widely-scattered population of apprentices and employers—the same number as was assigned to the small island of Barbados.[58] The Colonial Office refused to provide more since the total number of apprentices did not warrant it, and it turned down applications for the posts by local inhabitants. However by mid 1835 it was apparent that help was needed and a few of the regular magistrates were used, without extra pay.[59] Only four Special Magistrates had arrived by the Emancipation Day, the other four were to arrive several weeks later, and the Order-in-Council granting them authority to take up office was also delayed.[60] They were all retired army and naval officers, already receiving pensions or on half-pay, who were therefore only granted a small salary of £300 per annum and £75 for the passage.

It was soon apparent that the pay and allowances granted by the Colonial Office were woefully inadequate.[61] The Special Magistrates had to find their own accommodation, purchase horses, and employ a clerk and interpreter on very slender allowances. Many were unable to carry out their duties properly because of a lack of funds, and their correspondence with the colonial authorities is full of complaints and wrangles over money.[62] The Cape Town Magistrate complained, at the start, that he could not find a suitable clerk and interpreter for the wages he was allocated and, in 1835, the Magistrates of Cape Town, Tygerberg and Stellenbosch, petitioned the Governor for extra allowances to enable them to obtain adequate accommodation and wagon transport for journeys to farms in their districts.[63] This was a particular problem in the more geographically extensive regions. The Swellendam Magistrate temporarily stopped holding court sessions at Caledon, and complained that he could not visit farms with large numbers of apprentices because the Colonial Office refused to pay adequate travel allowances for himself, and nothing was provided for his clerk-interpreter and constable.[64] The extra police establishment required to assist the Magistrates was to be paid out of colonial funds, and was both patchy and inadequate.[65]

---

58   They were assigned to Cape Town, Tygerberg, Stellenbosch, Paarl, Worcester, Swellendam, Uitenhage and Graaff-Reinet. The Cape Governor complained at the inadequacy of this number for such a geographically extensive colony, CA, GH 23/10, Wade to Stanley, 6 Dec. 1833, ff. 264–5.

59   CA, GH 1/105, Glenelg to D'Urban, 15 June 1835, ff. 125–9; GH 1/120, Glenelg to Napier, 21 Apr. 1838.

60   CA, GH 1/100, letters of introduction of Stipendiary Magistrates appointed under the Abolition Act, ff. 100–22; GH 23/11, D'Urban to Spring Rice, 22 Nov. 1834, ff. 64–5.

61   For the financial difficulties of the Special Magistrates in the Caribbean, see Green, *British Slave Emancipation*, pp. 129–61.

62   B.J. Liebenberg, 'Vrystelling van die Slawe in die Kaap Kolonie en die Implikasies Daarvan' (MA thesis, Universiteit van die Oranje-Vrystaat, 1959), pp. 26–31.

63   CA, CO 441, no. 121, Longmore to Colonial Secretary, 23 Jan. 1835; CA GH 26/13, memorial of Longmore, Hill and Piers to D'Urban, 11 Mar. 1836.

64   CA, CO 465, nos. 8, 13, 23 and 27, Barnes to Colonial Office, 23 Jan. to 27 Mar. 1837.

65   CA, GH 1/105, Grant to D'Urban, 29 Apr. 1835, ff. 33–6.

In addition to financial problems, the Special Magistrates encountered difficulties arising out of their particular situation in the colony. Since all of them were outsiders, they could not speak Dutch-Afrikaans, the language of the employers and the apprentices, and they were dependent upon inter-preters. By contrast, several of the rejected local applicants had emphasized their 'familiarity with the habits and manners of the people as well as their language'.[66] One Special Magistrate admitted that he was unfamiliar with 'the colonial laws of the land'.[67] Moreover, many employers strongly resen-ted the imposition of outsiders and indicated their preference for local magis-trates and Justices of the Peace long before emancipation.[68] In Graaff-Reinet the position was exacerbated since the Special Magistrate did not arrive until three months after emancipation. The previous Slave Protector had carried out his functions in the meantime, and earned the support of the inhabitants who petitioned that he be kept in place of the outsider, since he had acquired 'complete knowledge of the Dutch language and customs which, Memorialists submit, pre-eminently qualifies him for the peculiar duties of the office of Special Justice'. Significantly, they also stressed that he 'dis-charged his duties in a manner well calculated to establish that good feeling which so happily exists in his district between the masters and their servants lately emancipated.'[69] They now preferred an official of the previously resented slave amelioration system to a new outsider whom they believed would have little sympathy towards employers or understanding of the local situation.

Such objections of employers to the agents of a new externally-imposed rule of law were widespread in the apprentice colonies. They were especially marked when a Special Magistrate was perceived to favour the interests of apprentices over employers.[70] At the Cape, most of the Special Magistrates were relatively well accepted. New men in a strange environment, especially in rural districts where almost all the colonists were ex-slaveholders, were unlikely to alienate those with whom they had to live by their judgements, and this was a major limitation to the impartiality of the apprentice system. Major Piers of Stellenbosch was even accused by one of the few English-speaking employers in the district, of 'seeking popularity with the Dutch at his expense'.[71]

66   For instance, Public Record Office, London (PRO), CO 48/154, Memorial of Lt. William Gilpillam, ff. 145–6.

67   CA, CO 441, no. 77, Sherwin to Colonial Office, 15 Aug. 1835.

68   For instance, at a public meeting of slaveholders in Cape Town, De Zuid-Afrikaan, 22 Mar. 1834.

69   CA, GH 26/78, Memorial of W. van Ryneveld and 96 other inhabitants of Graaff-Reinet, 15 Feb. 1845, ff. 152–4.

70   W.L. Burn, Emancipation and Apprenticeship in the British West Indies (London, 1937), pp. 220–30.

71   CA, CO 465, no. 95, Piers to Colonial Office, 30 Aug. 1837.

But some Magistrates found themselves in difficult circumstances. Barnes, the Swellendam Magistrate, complained of being 'grossly insulted' by employers in his district. Commander Sherwin (Royal Navy), in Uitenhage, was accused of being a 'slave magistrate'. Demands were made that he be 'kicked out', and one farmer stated in the market-place that he would willingly pay a fine 'for *sjambokking* the said Magistrate and that he was sure many persons would subscribe to pay it'. Sherwin received these anonymous warnings when going on circuit: 'do not sleep in a Boer's house but in your wagon and take with you persons you can trust; one may die; be careful how you cross a river...do not be seen out at nights alone'. It is scarcely surprising, in these circumstances, that he appealed to be transferred to Port Elizabeth, a move which placed him further away from the farmers, but also from the apprentices.[72]

Sherwin's predicament did not meet with much support from the authorities in Cape Town.[73] Indeed, there is a strong sense, in the records, that the local administration also resented the imposition of outsiders and the apparent contempt of the Colonial Secretary in London for local circumstances.[74] Although the Cape Governor approved of some of the new magistrates, four of whom were kept on the colonial establishment after 1838, he was less supportive of 'trouble-makers' such as Sherwin. And occasional disputes arose between the Special Magistrates and the local Justices of the Peace, who often co-existed in the same town or village. This was usually over who had authority to act in a particular case, but it reflected a deeper resentment by local officials against outsiders arriving in their area with authority from London.[75]

Some of the tension was caused by the affront to army and naval officers of their social position, and their need to 'maintain the respectability of their situations'.[76] Their appointments were intended to break down local paternalistic power, both of the kind practised by farmers over their slaves and servants, and that of the local Justices of the Peace and Resident Magistrates. They expected to be treated as social superiors. At least one, Major Barnes of Swellendam, had served as a local magistrate in Britain, and was sensitive to affronts to his rank from those he perceived to be of lesser social status.[77] As Holt has pointed out in the case of Jamaica, many of the Special Magistrates were imbued with the concepts of 'improving' the labour force and with

---

72   CA, CO 441, no. 60, Sherwin to Colonial Office, 8 June 1835; CO 441, no. 84, 12 Sept. 1835; GH 26/85, Sherwin to D'Urban, 1 June 1835.

73   CA, GH 26/85, D'Urban to Glenelg, 22 Nov. 1837.

74   See for instance, CA, GH 1/128, Glenelg to Napier, 16 May 1839, ff. 128–82.

75   For instance, CA, CO 476, no. 3, Mackay to Colonial Office, 9 Mar. 1838.

76   CA, GH 26/13, Memorial of Longmore, Hill and Piers to D'Urban, 11 Mar. 1836.

77   CA, CO 465, Barnes to Colonial Office, 3 Jan. 1837.

advising and instructing employers in the ways they considered to be appropriate. In this, the customary practices of their class ensured that they differed little from the English landlord addressing his tenant, or the army and navy officer giving orders to lesser rankings.[78]

The main role of the Special Magistrates was to be as judges and enforcers of penalties. During the first year of apprenticeship 1,140 apprentices were punished; over a 12-month period between October 1837 and September 1838, the figure returned was 811, although there were several omissions in the later records.[79] There were variations between districts. The Special Magistrates were more inclined to sentence apprentices to whippings and terms of imprisonment than those regular magistrates empowered to deal with such cases. The largest number of punishments were inflicted in the Cape Town district, where the highest proportion of apprentices lived, to which many rural apprentices who had deserted their owners fled, and where Major Longmore was an assiduous Special Magistrate.[80]

EXPERIENCING APPRENTICESHIP

Given these circumstances, how successful was apprenticeship in reconciling employers to the reduced legal powers they now held over their workers, and in inculcating a new sense of 'disciplined labour' amongst apprentices?

By 1833 many slaveowners realized that emancipation was inevitable. But they were only resigned to such a prospect if it were carried out on 'fair and equitable principles'.[81] Such principles included gradualist approaches and the assurance of adequate financial compensation. In the period from 1830, increased infringement of slaveowners' domestic authority—through ameliorative legislation and talk of immediate emancipation in London and the Cape newspapers—had led to greater hostility of slaveowners towards the government.[82] As the colonial authorities had hoped, promise of compensation and the transitional period of apprenticeship did pre-empt widespread slaveowner resistance to emancipation. But dissatisfaction remained over the amount and methods of compensation, the 'substitution of magisterial for domestic authority', and the perceived problems of securing sufficient labour after the end of apprenticeship. The Acting Governor concurred, in late

---

78   Holt, *Problem of Freedom*, pp. 76–7.

79   PRO, CO 48/166, ff. 95–113, Return of number and nature of punishments inflicted on apprenticed labourers, 1 Dec. 1834 to 30 Nov. 1835; CA, GH 26/97, ff. 22–37 and GH 26/99, ff. 54–65, Returns of punishments inflicted by the Special Magistrates, Sept. 1837 to June 1838, and July to Dec. 1838.

80   N. Worden, 'Slave Apprenticeship in Cape Town, 1834–8', *Studies in the History of Cape Town*, 7 (1994), pp. 32–44.

81   CA, GH 23/10, Wade to Stanley, 6 Dec. 1833, f. 260.

82   See for instance, CA, SO 1/6, Bergh to Rogers, Protector of Slaves, 14 Apr. 1831.

1833, that there was a need for 'a law, compelling [several thousand of the Free Blacks and Hottentots who are at present scattered over the colony without occupation] and all other vagrants to work for an honest liveli-hood'.[83]

But these slaveowner demands were not met. The level set for compensa-tion was considered to be low, and the means of obtaining the cash discrim-inated against local farmers. Instead, the main beneficiaries of compensation were the merchant houses of Cape Town.[84] Although a Vagrancy Bill was approved by the Legislative Council and gazetted in May of 1834, it was vetoed by the Colonial Secretary, following the advice of the new Governor, on the grounds that it would negate the rights of free movement granted to the Khoi by Ordinance 50 of 1828. Thus, in contrast to Jamaica or Mauritius, where vagrancy ordinances were allowed, Cape employers were unable to secure legislative control over unemployed inhabitants, which would have included the freed apprentices after 1838.[85] Other attempts by farmers to secure workers were also foiled by the government's opposition to any measure which smacked of forced labour, although some relief was provided by the indenture of Prize Negroes captured from foreign slaving vessels.[86]

The final removal of the domestic authority of employers over their apprentices, and the failure to secure an alternative coerced source of labour, had a marked impact on the nature of the bonds between ex-slaveowners and their workers. Apprenticeship legislation aimed at inculcating the notion of the work relationship as a voluntary contract between employer and em-ployee, even while rights of movement and wage compensation for workers were still denied. In the Caribbean many planters turned this attack by the state on their absolute control over labour to their advantage by removing some of the privileges previously granted as patriarchs to their slaves. Boons handed down from the owners, such as garden plots, allocation of time to work them and to sell the produce, exemption of pregnant women from labour, special additions to food rations and other allowances, were all curtailed under apprenticeship. Nothing in the Abolition Act could guarantee the maintenance of what owners perceived as bonuses, which they freely granted to their slaves but were reluctant to continue to give to workers who were being weaned away from their control. As some Caribbean historians

83   CA, GH 23/10, Wade to Stanley, 6 Dec. 1833, ff. 262–6; Report of meeting of Cape Town slaveowners, *Zuid-Afrikaan*, 28 Mar. 1834.

84   See Meltzer, ch. 7 in this volume.

85   R. Ross, *Beyond the Pale: Essays on the History of Colonial South Africa* (Hanover and London, 1993), p. 226, n. 181.

86   See Saunders, ch. 4 in this volume; N. Worden, 'Adjusting to Emancipation: Freed Slaves and Farmers in the Mid Nineteenth-Century South-Western Cape', in W. James and M. Simons (eds.), *The Angry Divide: Social and Economic History of the Western Cape* (Cape Town, 1989), p. 34.

have shown, the insistence on limited rights under quasi-contract removed from apprentices what little benefit they had been able to negotiate under slavery.[87]

At the Cape there were fewer overt markers of withdrawal of slave privileges; provision grounds and the marketing of produce by slave 'proto-peasants' was less developed than in the sugar colonies, and was confined mainly to the minority of slaves in the pastoral eastern districts of the colony.[88] Since no apprentices had been classified as praedial, disputes over wages or task work were pre-empted. But there are clear signs that at least some employers rejected state control over their domestic authority and took vengeance on their apprentices. In late 1833, the Acting Governor of the colony noted that many masters, 'looking upon the slaves as though they were the cause of the approaching crisis, upbraid them with having, as it were, carried this measure against their masters and transfer to them in ill-treatment no inconsiderable portion of their discontent.'[89] Such ill-treatment certainly included domestic physical punishment, which was now illegal, and demonstrated the refusal of owners to submit to the authority of the Special Magistrates in this sphere. As during the last years of slavery, some employers refused to permit their apprentices to take complaints to the authorities.[90] One defiantly declared that he would 'risk his money' in the form of a fine to give his apprentice a beating.[91] Another claimed that, because of the remote position of his farm, he did not know that it was now illegal to beat his workers.[92] Some employers denied apprentices medical treatment, refused to recognize advanced pregnancy as a reason not to work, and stinted on food rations.[93]

In these ways some employers rejected the provisions of the apprentice-ship system and clung to their prerogatives as slaveowners. But others turned the new situation to their advantage. Offences such as idleness, insolence, absence and inefficient work were now codified. Many employers took their recalcitrant labourers to the Special Magistrates on such charges and thus ensured their punishment at levels which, to the apprentices, must have

---

87   D.G. Hall, 'The Apprenticeship Period in Jamaica', *Caribbean Quarterly*, 3 (1953), pp. 147–53; W. Marshall, 'Apprenticeship and Labour Relations in Four Windward Islands', in D. Richardson (ed.), *Abolition and its Aftermath* (London, 1985), pp. 206–10; J. Ward, *British West Indian Slavery, 1750–1834: The Process of Amelioration* (Oxford, 1988), p. 223.

88   C. Crais 'Slavery and Freedom Along a Frontier: The Eastern Cape, 1770–1838', *Slavery and Abolition*, 11 (1990), pp. 190–215.

89   CA, GH 23/10, Wade to Stanley, 6 Dec. 1833, f. 261.

90   CA, CO 476, no. 26, Mackay to Colonial Office, 9 Mar. 1838.

91   CA, 1/WOC 19/26, Worcester Court Record Book, complaint of apprentice Flora, 5 June 1835.

92   CA, 1/WOC 19/26, Worcester Court Record Book, complaint of apprentice Pedro, 9 Mar. 1835.

93   CA, CO 465, no. 117, Sherwin to Colonial Office, 2 Dec. 1837; 1/WOC 19/26, Worcester Court Record Book, complaint of Charles van der Merwe, 6 Apr. 1835.

seemed little different from that under slavery, and may well have been even harsher. Other strategies were employed. Since their rights of ownership were now being removed, some employers considered that obligations to maintain apprentices who were not active should also end. Thus they were reluctant to support children born of apprentice women unless they were indentured formally until the age of 21 years, a provision made by the Abolition Act.[94] But no arrangement was made for elderly and infirm apprentices, and at least one employer demanded money to maintain them during the apprenticeship period.[95] The dissolution of the bonds of slavery made no provision for such situations. In the course of the apprenticeship period employers began calculating the benefits and drawbacks of holding on to their workers. Some were only too willing to be able to rid themselves of apprentices who were 'useless and depraved'.[96] Denied their domestic authority by the authorities, they accordingly refused to accept responsibility for their former slaves.

There were other employers who defied the apprenticeship system in more overt ways. Reports had been received in early 1834 that some colonists were planning to leave the colony 'with the view of preventing the liberation of their slaves' and in defiance of the Abolition Act.[97] During the apprenticeship period, and increasingly as its end approached, the Special Magistrates in Uitenhage, Graaff-Reinet, Worcester and Cape Town, reported cases of similar moves or signs that they were being planned.[98] The authorities were unable to patrol the borders of the colony and prevent a number of apprentices taking part in the process which later came to be identified as the 'Great Trek'. Although some apprentices were left behind, either by their employer's consent or by the insistence of the Special Magistrates,[99] others were not unwilling to go, and refused to return to the colony despite being 'assured of their freedom' by a special mission of Veldcornet Joubert in late 1838.[100] For them the colony they had only known as slaves was not an alluring place. Others did go back, either with Joubert or by escaping from their owners. Vivid accounts survive of the terrors they felt

94 A provision that was much abused; see below and Scully, ch. 8 in this volume.

95 CA, CO 476, no. 103, Lloyd to Colonial Office, 26 Nov. 1838; 1/WOC 19/26, Worcester Court Record Book, complaint of apprentice Sabria, 16 Mar. 1835.

96 CA, GH 23/11, D'Urban to Stanley, 19 Sept. 1837, f. 395.

97 CA, 1/CT 11/6, Colonial Office Cape Town to Civil Commissioner for the Cape District, 21 Feb. 1834.

98 For instance, CA, CO 452, no. 36, Sherwin to Colonial Office, 19 Apr. 1836; CO 465, nos. 67, 109 and 122, Sherwin to Colonial Office, 1 Feb., 8 July and 9 Dec. 1837; CO 465, no. 119, Molesworth to Colonial Office, 4 Dec. 1837; CO 476, nos. 41, 44, 46, 47, 49, 50, 78, Mackay to Colonial Office, 6 Apr. to 10 Sept. 1838; CO 476, no. 77, Longmore to Colonial Office, 7 Sept. 1838.

99 CA, GH 23/12, Napier to Glenelg, 21 Sept. 1838.

100 CA, GH 26/101, report of Veldcornet Joubert, Oct. 1838. For details of this episode, see C. Venter, 'Die Voortrekkers en die Ingeboekte Slawe Wat die Groot Trek Meegemaak Het, 1835–8', Historia, 39 (1991), pp. 14–29.

in alien surroundings as they made the journey back, the fear they felt for the Xhosa, as well as the hospitality that they received from them.[101]

Some apprentices also rejected the terms of apprenticeship while others worked within it to their advantage. Slave expectations of freedom had been evident before 1834, not least in the 1825 Bokkeveld revolt. This seemed to counteract the argument of the Acting Governor, in a dispatch to the Colonial Secretary in late 1833, that slaves in the remoter regions only desired their rights under amelioration and were 'unprepared' for anything more, although he did recognize that

> in the more populous parts of the colony the case is different, and in the districts nearest to Cape Town, an expectation has been awakened among the slaves that they are about to receive some more important, but to them as yet, undefined benefit than has hitherto been conferred upon them.[102]

In the period between the passing of the Abolition Act and the formal transition to apprenticeship, the Protector of Slaves had noted a marked increase in the rate of desertion.[103] Many slaves, and not just near Cape Town, recognized apprenticeship as a tactic on the part of their owners and the authorities to perpetuate slavery beyond its final end. Relieved press reports of 'tranquillity' on 1 December 1834 show that there was no organized revolt on the part of the new apprentices. But many showed their rejection of the system in other ways. The court record books of the Special Magistrates contain numerous cases of apprentices who deserted on 1 December and refused to return. For instance, Isaac, a Cape Town apprentice, left his owner's house in Strand Street on the morning of Emancipation Day, 'has been secreting himself about the city' for the following four months and when apprehended stated that he refused to stay with his owner.[104] Some apprentices justified their reactions by what others had told them. Jacob, a Cape Town joiner whose owner lived in Loop Street, was told by Mr Boring, to whom he had been hired in November 1834, that he should 'behave himself well as the time was near that he should receive his freedom'. Not surprisingly, Jacob interpreted this as meaning that he would be free after 1 December and left work on that day. When Boring met him in the street in mid January, he asked, 'Why have you not been to work with me?' to which Jacob relied, 'What have you to do with me?'[105] Nor were such cases confined to Cape Town. In Worcester magisterial district, three cases were brought to the Special Magistrate in early 1837 of apprentices who had deserted on

---

101 For instance, CA, CO 476, no. 24, testimony of Carolus, 28 Feb. 1838; CO 2778, testimony of Dina, 24 Sept. 1838, ff. 167–70.

102 CA, GH 23/10, Wade to Stanley, 6 Dec. 1833, f. 258.

103 CA, SO 3/20a, report of the Protector of Slaves for the period up to 24 June 1834.

104 CA, 1/WBG, Add. 1/1/1, complaint of Bertrand Daniel, 26 Mar. 1835, f. 95.

105 CA, 1/WBG, Add. 1/1/1, complaint of George Fisher, 29 Jan. 1835, f. 6.

1 December 1834 and had lived for over two years disguised as free people in Cape Town and other areas, far away from their owners.[106]

Other apprentices stayed with their owners after 1 December but showed new resentment at being forced to remain and refused to continue to accept the subordinate role they associated with slavery. Leentje, a Cape Town apprentice, was brought to the Special Magistrate by her employer at the end of February 1835 for her 'continued insubordination' since Emancipation Day and asserted defiantly that 'she did not care for anyone, nor for the *tronk*, nor for any punishment', and that 'if she should stay in the deponent's house a day longer she was certain she would hang herself.'[107] To other apprentices news of their frustrated freedom may only have occurred at the end of the year. In Worcester district, the apprentice Salida refused to clean the kitchen utensils as she had been accustomed to do as a slave, was 'sulky and obstinate' and 'insolent' 'nearly every day since 1st January'.[108] These responses may indicate a gendered character: desertion by men and 'insubordination' of women. Women may have had less opportunity for forging contacts and links outside the household which they could exploit as runaways, and there was less chance of casual employment for them where no questions were asked.[109]

In some cases more direct and united action was taken by apprentices, both male and female. Isaac van der Merwe reported, on 18 February 1835, that the four male and two female apprentices on his farm in the Vier en Twintig Rivieren region:

> forced me to send the wagon for wine for them, whenever I ordered them to do anything they refused, and with insolence—whenever I offer them clothes they refuse to take them. I sent the wagon for wine so as to induce them to cut the wheat—I was not sure of my life…they were all in disorder and they would not obey my orders. I consider them generally to have been in open resistance to my lawful commands. The cause of complaint has been since 1 December last.[110]

It is highly significant that not only did Van der Merwe's apprentices reject his authority as employer by refusing to obey his orders and intimidating him into providing wine for them, but they also refused his offer of clothing. Under slavery, new clothes were often distributed at New Year. They refused to accept the actions of the paternalist slaveowner, even when it was to their benefit.

---

106 CA, 1/WOC, 19/27, complaints of Jacobus de Wet contra Elias, 6 Feb. 1837; Christoffel Fischer contra Adrian, 8 Feb. 1837; Christian de Wet contra Adonis, 8 May 1837.

107 CA, 1/WBG, Add. 1/1/1, complaint of Otto Landsberg contra Leentje, 27 Feb. 1835, f. 54,

108 For instance CA, 1/WOC, 19/26, complaint of Schalk Burger contra Salida, 7 Mar. 1835.

109 P. van der Spuy, 'Slave Women and the Family in Nineteenth-Century Cape Town, *South African Historical Journal*, 27 (1992), pp. 66–71.

110 CA, 1/WOC, 19/26, complaint of Isaac van der Merwe contra his apprentices, Julie, America, Abel, New Year, Victoria and Lena, 18 Feb. 1835.

Such examples may have been exceptional, but amongst the wealth of individual cases some broad patterns emerge. Tables 5.1 and 5.2 show the offences for which apprentices were punished in the Cape Town and Worcester districts in the first year of apprenticeship.

TABLE 5.1

APPRENTICESHIP OFFENCES PUNISHED BY SPECIAL MAGISTRATE OF CAPE TOWN [111]

1 DECEMBER 1834 – 30 NOVEMBER 1835

Offence	Male	Female	Total	Percentage
Desertion/absence	178	51	229	64.3
Insolence	12	16	28	7.9
Drunkenness	21	7	28	7.9
Theft	21	2	23	6.4
Malicious complaints	11	3	14	3.9
Outrageous conduct	8	4	12	3.4
Disobedience	5	5	10	2.8
Wilful negligence	8	1	9	2.5
Cruelty to animals	2	0	2	0.6
Conspiracy	1	0	1	0.3
TOTAL	267	89	356	

Apart from the differences in the number of apprentices punished (which reflects, at least in part, the lesser total number in each district), there are important variations in the offences committed. Almost two-thirds of cases in Cape Town were for desertion or temporary absence. The urban environment gave an opportunity for apprentices, and especially males, to join other workers in the city or to find casual employment, and many runaways from the rural areas made for the town for these reasons.[112] In rural and remoter Worcester, desertion made up only just over a third of the offences. More prevalent were cases of 'insolence', 'negligence' and destruction of property

---

111 Figures calculated from Special Magistrate Record Books, CA, 1/WBG, Add. 1/1/1–2.

112 CA, CO, no. 441, Longmore to Colonial Office, 6 May 1835; Worden, 'Slave Apprenticeship in Cape Town'.

TABLE 5.2

APPRENTICESHIP OFFENCES PUNISHED BY SPECIAL MAGISTRATE OF WORCESTER [113]

1 DECEMBER 1834 – 30 NOVEMBER 1835

Offence	Male	Female	Total	Percentage
Desertion/absence	23	13	36	38.3
Unfounded complaints	5	4	9	9.6
Disobedience	1	1	2	2.1
Destroying property	5	4	9	9.6
Insolence	7	11	18	19.1
Negligence	7	1	8	8.5
Fighting	1	0	1	1.1
Feigning sickness	1	0	1	1.1
Drunkenness	8	1	9	9.6
Conspiracy	1	0	1	1.1
TOTAL	59	35	94	

(which included 'malicious damage'), offences which were typical of the slave period and reflected the kinds of hidden resistance more common on the farms.

In both districts, some apprentices were punished for making 'malicious' or 'unfounded' complaints. As under slavery during the amelioration period, apprentices used the Special Magistrates to bring complaints of ill-treatment against their owners. As the Magistrate in George put it, 'the apprentices are well aware of their rights, and assert them whenever they feel themselves in the slightest degree wronged', although as a regular rather than Special Magistrate he was more sympathetic to the employers and was concerned that enforcement of the laws 'tends to cause and augment a vindictiveness of feeling', which contrasted with his perception that 'reciprocity of interest and good feeling' had existed between masters and slaves and should continue.[114]

---

113 Figures calculated from Special Magistrate Record Books, CA, 1/WOC 19/26.

114 CA, CO 465, nos. 135 and 112, Bergh to Colonial Office, 8 Apr. and 13 Oct. 1837.

TABLE 5.3

COMPLAINTS BROUGHT BY APPRENTICES AND EMPLOYERS IN THE
CAPE TOWN & WORCESTER MAGISTERIAL DISTRICTS 1834–5 AND
1838[115]

	By Apprentices	By Employers
Cape Town		
(1/12/34–30/11/35)	18 [4.5%]	378 [95.5%]
(1/08/38–31/11/38)	0	32 [100%]
Worcester		
(1/12/34–30/11/35)	82 [44.1%]	104 [55.9%]
(1/08/38–31/11/38)	12 [66.6%]	6 [33.4%]

Although full records survive for only a few districts, a comparison of Cape Town and rural Worcester shows that there were striking differences in the incidence of apprentice complaints against their employers.

A far higher proportion of complaints was brought by apprentices in Worcester than in Cape Town. The circuit visits to farms of the Worcester Special Magistrate may well account for this. In Cape Town very few of the complaints were made by apprentices. Individual visitation and the sympathies of each Magistrate may have played an important role. But another cause was doubtless that urban apprentices had better means of dealing with their employers, by linking themselves to the underworld of the city, than by relying on a government official for aid. The higher levels of desertion or temporary absence shown in Tables 5.1 and 5.2 for the town in contrast to Worcester district confirms this impression. Clearly this was an option unavailable to those who were confined to the more isolated world of frontier farms. Most complaints against employers in Worcester were for beatings, although there were also cases of denial of food and clothing. Such cases demonstrate the general truth that farmers were less ready to loosen

---

115 Figures calculated from Special Magistrate Record Books, CA, 1/WBG, Add. 1/1/1–2, and 1/1/15–16; 1/WOC 19/26–27.

their hold as owners of labour than their urban counterparts.[116]

A provision of the Abolition Act which was used more in Cape Town was that by which apprentices could buy themselves out of their remaining period of indenture. The Special Magistrates were required to give valuations where this was sought by the apprentices, and to grant freedom where such amounts could be paid. In the year following 1 December 1834, a total of 85 apprentices did this, 73 of them from Cape Town. In a pattern which followed that of purchased manumission under slavery, most were freed by money put up for them by relatives in the city, and in a few cases by their employers.[117] The majority (47 out of the 73) were female; 14 (of equal number by gender) were freed by their owners without payment. But for the majority, access to financial resources was crucial. Although such a move was obviously more advantageous at the beginning of the four-year apprenticeship period, the desire for freedom was sufficiently strong that some apprentices continued to pay for the end of their indenture up to even a few months before its expiry. The desire to be united with kin, and especially with spouses and children, was a paramount factor in this, as Pamela Scully has shown.[118] Valuations could be causes of dispute and, on occasions, even the Governor was called in to act as umpire between the apprentice, employer and Special Magistrate.[119]

Together with variables of apprentice reactions according to place and gender, were changes over time. In Cape Town by the middle of 1838, the character of 'insubordination' was changing. Cases of desertion tended to be for longer periods than temporary absence, and some owners were content to be rid of troublesome servants so close to the end of apprenticeship. The number of employer complaints made to the Special Magistrate fell sharply in the final year of apprenticeship.

Other apprentices were making preparations for final emancipation by staying where they were and extracting all they could from their owners. In an ironic reversal of the claims which had been dominant for over a century under slavery, by 1838 some employers were now begging the Special Magistrate to free them of the burden of such troublesome apprentices. Thus Mrs Berstandig demanded that action be taken against her apprentice, Elsie, who 'despite every remonstration would not stir from her room...[when] sent word that she must pack up her things and go she would not do anything

---

116 For the lessening of domestic authority by Cape Town masters before the end of slavery, see Bank, ch. 3 in this volume.

117 PRO, CO 48/166, Returns of apprenticed labourers who have purchased the unexpired terms of their apprenticeship, compiled 16 Feb. 1836, f. 113. A. Bank *The Decline of Urban Slavery at the Cape, 1806 to 1834*, Centre for African Studies, University of Cape Town, Communications, no. 22 (1991), p. 177.

118 See Scully ch. 8 in this volume.

119 CA, GH 26/73, D'Urban to Glenelg, 15 Apr. 1836, enclosure 3A.

nor quit the house.' Clearly Elsie intended to continue to hold on to her room until the very end, and Longmore told her that she could avoid punishment only on condition that she quit her owner.[120] Sitie, a female apprentice of Mr Attwell, was more actively preparing for freedom. She stole handkerchiefs and cloth from her owner which she 'intended to dispose of at a house of reception for stolen things', and she stated under cross-examination that 'a Malay woman told her to bring her some handkerchiefs and any other things and that when she was free she could go and exchange these for clothing'.[121] Such actions, unlike those of escape and self-employment in the city, seem to have been made equally by men and women.

In contrast, Cape farmers anticipated that they would have difficulties persuading the freed apprentices to stay on the farms. In particular, they protested that the day of termination, 1 December 1838, fell just as intense work was required to bring in the grain harvest. Although the Governor expressed sympathy, the request for an extended period of apprenticeship was rejected decisively by a Colonial Office now anxious to end coerced labour once and for all.[122] And exceptions to this principle, such as the extended periods of indenture given as punishments by the Special Magistrates, and the indenture of children which forced parents to make a choice of either staying with their employers or abandoning their children, were removed by the repeal of both measures, despite the objections of some employers.[123]

In 1837, the grain farmers had threatened that without assured labour supplies for the harvest in the following year, they would sow less seed.[124] Although there is no direct evidence of the extent to which they carried out this measure of rural resistance, lower planting levels may have been the key explanation for the fall in grain output which took place in 1838–9. Wine production was not as directly affected and, indeed, grain production did recover in the following year.[125] In other words, drops in the harvest output came from farmer resistance rather than from a walkout by apprentices.

Historians have shown that in December 1838 some freed apprentices did leave their former owners, although in the absence of land, capital or alternative means of income, many subsequently went to work on other farms, or

---

120 CA, 1/WBG, Add. 1/1/16, complaint of Mrs Berstandig contra Elsie, 23 Oct. 1838, f. 19.

121 CA, 1/WBG, Add. 1/1/16, complaint of Attwell contra Sitie, 10 Sept. 1838, f. 5.

122 CA, GH 23/11, D'Urban to Glenelg, 19 Sept. 1837, ff. 394–6; GH 26/82, memorial of 113 farmers, 24 July 1837; GH 1/118, Glenelg to Napier, 4 Dec. 1837, ff. 134–7.

123 For instance, in Sept. 1838, 17 inhabitants of Wynberg, Constantia and Rondebosch petitioned against the fact that many of the apprentices sentenced to longer terms were runaways, and since the employers had lost the use of their services for a period of the apprenticeship years, they demanded recompense, CA, LCA 9, no. 17, memorial of Cape former slaveowners, Sept. 1838.

124 CA, GH 26/82, memorial of 113 farmers, 24 July 1837.

125 See Ross, ch. 6 in this volume.

joined the seasonal labour market and toured the farms during harvesting periods. Some were able to secure labour tenancy arrangements or share-cropping tenure in exchange for access to a plot of land or the right to keep their own livestock.[126] A few farmers offered their ex-apprentices cash inducements to stay, at least for as long as the harvest.[127] And in spite of the changes in the employer-apprentice relationship which the years between 1834 and 1838 had produced, many farmers were still able to invoke the bonds of loyalty and paternalism to keep their ex-slaves as their labourers.

Some farmers used the end of apprenticeship as an opportunity to rid themselves of those who were too old to be useful workers, while others refused to allow their apprentices to leave with their children, claiming the right to their indentured work after the maintenance they had provided for them.[128] Apprentices who had offended their owners in other ways were now forced to leave. The Worcester farm apprentice, Jan, recorded the events on the first Monday after the weekend of 1–2 December:

> It was very rainy that morning. My master had not asked me to remain in his service and therefore I did not know what he intended with us and I did not like to question him about it. In the early morning of that Monday I looked after the cattle as usually and after I had sent the cattle out of the kraal my master called me and told me to bring my tools—a spade, pick axe, and sickle to him which I did; he then told me that I was winding up the people to leave his place and ordered me to mention to all the others that those who intended to leave the place must do so immediately; we thereupon left the place tho' it rained very much; I did not ask my master to remain on the place until the weather cleared as I perceived he was angry.[129]

Jan was over 50 years old. He had lived on the farm all his life, and described his owner as a 'good master'. More than this, 'the fact is my master was my foster brother'. However, together with the 23 other apprentices who decided to go, Jan, his wife and children left in the drenching rain of the early morning.

For some the ending of apprenticeship thus broke the patterns of the slave years with a vengeance. The tensions and heightened expectations of the apprenticeship years were finally released. But the apprenticeship years had provided the freed slaves with little bargaining power or opportunities for a

---

126 J. Mason, '"Fit for Freedom": The Slaves, Slavery and Emancipation in the Cape Colony, South Africa, 1806 to 1842' (Ph.D. thesis, Yale University, 1992), ch. 8; Worden, 'Adjusting to Emancipation'; Ross, ch. 6 in this volume.

127 For instance, CA, CO 476, no. 112, Mackay to Colonial Office, 7 Dec. 1838.

128 The Graaff–Reinet Special Magistrate expressed concern at the end of Nov. 1838 that no provision had been made for the large number of aged and infirm apprentices who would be 'left destitute' by the neglect of their previous owners, CA, CO 476, no. 103, Lloyd to Colonial Office, 26 Nov. 1838. On the retention of children, see Scully, ch. 8 in this volume.

129 Testimony of Jan, CA, CO 476, no. 127, 2 Jan. 1839.

better life.

Most employers had learnt the impossibility of maintaining their absolute authority over coerced labour. However apprenticeship had heightened their dependence on the state to uphold their position as producers. This was to be upheld in the subsequent years. The termination of apprenticeship rendered Ordinance 1 invalid. However the Governor recognized the need for some legislation to regulate contracts between 'masters' and servants', particularly on farms, and also sympathized with the continued call of many colonists for vagrancy controls, although he stopped short at recommending laws of the kind which had been vetoed two years previously. The continued importance of Magistrates in regulating labour was shown by the creation of four new magisterial districts in areas where labourers were concentrated and where the apprenticeship years had shown that local Justices were required. They were administered by the Special Magistrates who had served in each area and were willing to remain in the colony.[130] In 1841, the Masters and Servants Ordinance was passed which regulated worker contracts with the backing of this magisterial system. Much of its content and administration derived from the apprenticeship scheme and it was to dominate the landscape of employer and employee relationships in the western Cape well into the twentieth century.[131]

130 The four Magistrates were Longmore (Cape Town), Hill (Tygerberg), Piers (Stellenbosch) and Barnes (Swellendam), who became Resident Magistrates in the newly-formed districts of Wynberg, Malmesbury, Paarl and Caledon respectively, CA, CO 5178, Circular of Colonial Office to Special Magistrates, 30 Nov. 1838.

131 Worden, 'Adjusting to Emancipation'; Ross, *Beyond the Pale*, pp. 104–5, and ch. 6 in this volume.

6

'RATHER MENTAL THAN PHYSICAL'
EMANCIPATIONS & THE CAPE ECONOMY

— ROBERT ROSS —

In 1838, James Backhouse, the Quaker traveller, was visiting the Cape, and thus witnessed the final emancipation of Cape slaves, when the period of 'apprenticeship' came to its end. His observation was that there were few, if any, clear changes in the relations between masters and their slaves. As he wrote, 'the benefit of emancipation was rather mental than physical.'[1] In this chapter I intend to test the correctness of his observation, at least as regards the organization of labour on the Cape's farms. This is, of course, a matter of deliberate choice. Slavery oppressed its victims economically, but also socially, politically and psychologically. To the extent that these matters can be disentangled, its legacy can be analysed along any of these lines. Backhouse believed that emancipation would lead to the psychological liberation of the slaves from bondage, even if their conditions of employment remained little changed. However, it should not be forgotten that in the great majority of those slave societies which derived from European colonial expansion, slavery was essentially an institution for the organization of production. Therefore, I will address the question of the effects of emancipation upon the levels of production, agricultural and other, within the Cape Colony.

In so doing, of course, it is important to realize that there were two emancipations at the Cape, not one. As in the rest of the British Empire (outside India)[2], slaves were freed in 1834, although for four years after this they were held as 'apprentices' under restrictions which differed little from those which had been imposed on them under slavery. However, before the promulgation of Ordinance 50 in 1828, the *de facto* position of the colony's Khoisan differed from that of the slaves only in that they could not be sold,

---

1 J. Backhouse, *A Narrative of a Visit to the Mauritius and South Africa* (London, 1844), p. 507.

2 S. Miers and R. Roberts, 'Introduction' to *idem* (ed.) *The End of Slavery in Africa* (Madison and London, 1989), p. 12.

or in any other ways transferred from one master (or mistress) to another. Thus emancipation, even as a legal concept, was not a single event but a process which covered at least a decade.

THE CONDITIONS OF BONDAGE

From its foundation in the mid seventeenth century, the Cape Colony had been largely dependent on slave labour. The households of Cape Town, both of the Company officials and of the burghers, soon acquired significant numbers of slave domestic servants. The Company needed slaves to work its gardens and to load and unload its ships. Slave artisans were employed in the various workshops that sprung up in the town. From around 1690, the shale hills of the Zwartland, north of Cape Town, were parcelled out into wheat farms, and the valley lands of Stellenbosch, Drakenstein and the Wagenmakers Valley (Wellington) were opened up as vineyards.[3] These were heavily dependent on slave labour. Indeed, through the eighteenth century, over 90 per cent of arable farmers owned at least one slave—a remarkably high proportion.[4] But the slaves were not the only labourers on the farms. As the eighteenth century progressed, the indigenous Khoisan of the Cape increasingly were robbed of any independent access to grazing lands and hunting territories. As a result they were forced to become labourers on the farms. By 1806, even in the largely arable districts of Stellenbosch and Drakenstein, over 30 per cent of the labour force was Khoikhoi.[5] In the pastoral districts to the east of the mountain chains, some 80 kilometres from Cape Town, this proportion would have been much higher. The expansion of trekboers into the South African interior, a process which marked the whole of the eighteenth century—and much longer—would have been inconceivable without the subjugation and use of Khoisan labourers.

In the early part of the nineteenth century the slave-based agrarian economy of the western Cape was fully intact. Indeed, the production of wine nearly doubled between 1808 and 1824 as wine farmers profited from the opening of the British market to Cape wines. Thereafter a period of decline set in, as the tariff advantages which Cape wine had enjoyed in Great Britain, as against French vintages, were very sharply reduced.[6] There was also a

---

3   The early settlement can best be followed in L. Guelke, *The Southwestern Cape Colony 1657–1750: Freehold Land Grants*, Occasional Paper, no 5, Geography Publication Series, (University of Waterloo, Ontario, 1987). See also *idem*, 'The Early European Settlement of South Africa' (Ph.D. thesis, University of Toronto, 1974).

4   N. Worden, *Slavery in Dutch South Africa* (Cambridge, 1985), p. 27.

5   Worden, *Slavery in Dutch South Africa*, p. 35.

6   M. I. Rayner, 'Wine and Slaves: The Failure of an Export Economy and the Ending of Slavery in the Cape Colony, 1806–34' (Ph.D. thesis, Duke University, 1986), chs. 2 and 5.

Plate 7 Groenekloof Mission Station, 1844, by James Backhouse. *South African Library.*

steady rise in grain production. In particular, the cultivation of barley, oats and rye increased very sharply—three to four fold between 1806 and 1834—in response to the improved market provided by the British army and its cavalry. The increase in wheat production, on the other hand, was much slower, so much so that a couple of bad years, as in the early 1820s, could make a trend, based on five-year averages, appear negative. Nevertheless, in general there was a steady rise in agricultural production throughout the first quarter of the nineteenth century.

This rise in production, sharper than at any stage during the eighteenth century, occurred despite the abolition of the slave trade in 1807. By the early nineteenth century, the Cape's slave population was just about reproducing itself, but the transition from a largely immigrant population, with a high over-representation of adult men, clearly entailed some decrease in the quantity of available labour. In 1806, 35 per cent of the slaves were children (defined as males under the age of 16 years and females under the age of 14); by 1824, under the same definition, this proportion had risen to 42 per cent.[7]

There were two other new sources of bonded labour for the agricultural districts. A certain number of slaves seem to have been sold from Cape Town to the country districts as owners profited from the increased prices in the latter sector.[8] Some recaptured Africans (or 'Prize Negroes') also found their way to the countryside, although the majority of these remained in Cape Town.[9] Nevertheless, these two groups were almost certainly too small to allow the labour force on the wine and grain farms to grow at a rate commensurate with the increase in production. The result would thus seem to have been an increase in the pressure on labourers to work harder.

In the other main sectors of the Cape's economy, Cape Town and the frontier, the early nineteenth century brought notably different developments. In the former, as Andrew Bank's recent research has shown, the institution of slavery was eroding away.[10] On the frontier, in contrast, bonded labour increased sharply, in step with the developing complexity of colonial economic life there. The number of legal slaves in the eastern districts grew slowly, though faster than that of the colony as a whole. Slavery never dominated labour relations in the east, though, particularly as the British settlers who arrived in 1820 were forbidden to own slaves. A number of Africans from north of the Orange River, conservatively estimated at 500, were held in contravention of the law and some may have been fraudulently registered as slaves. More importantly, many of the Khoisan of the southern and

---

7   G.M. Theal, *Records of the Cape Colony* (*RCC*), vol. 4, p. 75 and vol. 19, p. 375.

8   Rayner, 'Wine and Saves', p. 58.

9   See Saunders, ch. 4 in this volume.

10 See Bank, ch. 3 in this volume, and A. Bank, *The Decline of Urban Slavery at the Cape, 1806 to 1834*, Centre for African Studies, University of Cape Town, Communications, no. 22 (1991).

eastern Cape were reduced to *de facto* serfs.[11]

The enserfment of the Khoisan was a process which began with the extremely violent conquest of the Cape interior during the eighteenth century. Colonial settlement entailed the wresting of the land from the Khoisan, although, in general, those who had cattle and sheep were still able to run them on farms claimed by Europeans. Nevertheless, labour discipline was maintained by the use of force. The stories of brutality in early colonial Graaff-Reinet are widely confirmed in the archival record. The result was not just the Khoisan rebellion of 1799 but also considerable psycho-social dislocation among the Khoisan which manifested itself in a series of disturbing dreams and visions.[12]

With British conquest of the Cape, firmly established in 1806, the colonial government attempted to play Leviathan, to impose constraints on what they saw to be the farmers' unrestrained power. The codes of labour legislation issued by the Earl of Caledon in 1809 and by his successor, Sir John Cradock, as Governor in 1812, were ostensibly designed to protect the Khoikhoi from genocide. The application of the codes by the new civil and military administration in the eastern Cape certainly had its effects. After 1809 the reports of brutality on the farms of the eastern Cape die away sharply.[13] The price that was paid for this, however, was a code of labour legislation which tied the Khoisan to their white employers by one-sided contracts and a system of apprenticeship, which forced children (and by extension their parents) to remain on a farm until the the age of 25 years, and by prohibitions on mobility and land-ownership.[14] In addition, payment was often in stock, so that the refusal to allow men and women to leave a farm with their stock and the harassment of those who were on the road seeking work meant that a large proportion of the Khoisan were tied to particular farms. On these they were treated as slaves, but did not have the protection which slaves enjoyed as the living repositories of the masters' capital.

These practices were the target of John Philip's *Researches in South Africa*, the first great work of campaigning journalism to come from South

---

11   C. Crais, 'Slavery and Freedom Along a Frontier: The Eastern Cape, South Africa: 1770–1838', *Slavery and Abolition*, 10 (1990), pp. 190–215.

12   See Newton-King, ch. 9 in this volume, and 'The Enemy Within: The Struggle for Ascendancy on the Cape Eastern Frontier, 1760–99' (Ph.D. thesis, London University, 1992); S. Newton-King and V.C. Malherbe, *The Khoikhoi Rebellion in the Eastern Cape, 1799–1803* (Cape Town, 1984); E. Elbourne, 'To Colonise the Mind: Evangelicals and Missionaries in Britain and South Africa' (D.Phil., University of Oxford, 1991), pp. 255–6; A.A. van der Lingen, 'Bijzondere Droomen en Gezichten Gedroomd en Gezien door Hottentotten en Hottentottinnen', Archive of the Nederduitse Gereformeerde Kerk (now in Cape Archives), P/38.

13   On this, see D. van Arkel, G.C. Quispel and R.J. Ross, *De Wijngaard des Heeren? Een Onderzoek naar de Wortels van 'die Blanke Baasskap' in Zuid-Afrika* (Leiden, 1983), pp. 58–9.

14   R. Elphick and V.C. Malherbe, 'The Khoisan to 1828', in R. Elphick and H. Giliomee (eds.), *The Shaping of South African Society, 1652–1840*, 2nd edn. (Cape Town, 1989), pp. 40–2.

Africa.[15] Only those who managed to gain access to one of the mission stations had any chance of escape.

EXPECTATIONS AT EMANCIPATION

In 1828, Ordinance 50 was issued by the Cape Government, which removed all discrimination on the basis of race from the legal system. Six years later, slavery itself was abolished, though a four-year period of so-called 'apprenticeship' followed during which the ex-slaves laboured under more or less the same restrictions as before. There were those at the Cape (notably, the 'philanthropic' group led by Philip and his son-in-law John Fairbairn), whose views on the outcome of emancipation mirrored those of the British abolitionists.[16] Following Adam Smith in their economic doctrines, they believed slavery to be a highly-inefficient economic institution, for two reasons. Firstly, because of the absence both of economic rewards for harder and more efficient work and of economic penalties for laziness and incapacity, it provided no incentives to the labour force to maximize their productivity. Direct compulsion, rather than the iron laws of the market, was a thoroughly wasteful way of getting people to work. Secondly, slavery severely restricted the rational reallocation of labour in response to changing economic opportunities. Rather, it tended to keep labour tied up in enterprises which, though not unprofitable in an absolute sense—or they would have gone out of business—were certainly not operating at maximum profitability. In other words, slavery shielded some entrepreneurs from the effects of a competitive labour market and prevented others, namely those who did not initially possess slaves, from expanding as they would have wished, for want of sufficient labour. If these hindrances were removed, so it was thought, the only result would be economic progress, with concomitant benefits for both the ex-slaves and their former owners.

The slaveowners and their apologists, in contrast, argued that the mass emancipation of slaves would be disastrous for the colonial economy. The arguments which they used were essentially racist. They believed blacks to be too childlike, or too lazy, to work on a regular basis, except under the threat of punishment. Compulsion was, therefore, essential to the continuance of an economic system which had brought such benefits to the metropolis—and, not

---

15   J. Philip, *Researches in South Africa*, 2 vols. (London, 1828).

16   On Fairbairn, see J.L. Meltzer, 'The Growth of Cape Town Commerce and the Role of John Fairbairn's *Advertiser*, 1835–1859' (MA thesis, University of Cape Town, 1989), esp ch. 2, and ch. 7 in this volume; Philip did not directly discuss slavery to any extent, but his *Researches in South Africa* are shot through with Smithian economics; on the British abolitionists, see D. Eltis, 'Abolitionist Perceptions of Society after Slavery', in J. Walvin (ed.), *Slavery and British Society, 1776–1846* (London and Basingstoke, 1982), pp. 195–213.

coincidentally, to themselves.[17] Such racist arguments cannot, of course, be accepted today, though the concomitant argument that the state had no right to interfere in the enjoyment of property is still very much with us. Nevertheless, it is quite possible to translate the slaveholders' arguments into terms which are both reasonable and plausible. The ending of slavery, it might be supposed, would be accompanied by such a revulsion on the part of the ex-slaves for the system of labour organization under which they had been exploited, that they would withdraw their labour on a massive scale for estate-organized agricultural labour. Obviously enough, they could only do this if alternative ways of acquiring a living were available to them, presumably primarily as subsistence-orientated peasant farmers. If the choice had been simply one of starvation versus continued work for their own, or some other, former masters, there would have been few ex-slaves who would have chosen the former. But if other alternatives had been available, then, on these premises, it could be predicted that the result would have been a massive fall in the production of agricultural commodities for the commercial and, above all, the export market. This was certainly the case in certain of the Caribbean sugar colonies, notably Jamaica and Surinam.

Therefore there were two diametrically opposed predictions: the one suggests that emancipation would increase the efficiency of slave economies, and the other that it would decrease it. In both cases, the validity of the prediction can be ascertained by examining production statistics. However, matters are not quite that simple. Three further possibilities exist. In all of these the result would be that levels of production would remain more or less constant, or at least that the trend which had preceded emancipation would continue. The first possibility is that the agricultural enterprises continued very much as before, because the ex-slaves were unable to find any alternative employment so they continued to work under conditions similar to those experienced while they were still slaves. The second is that the ex-slaveowners were able to find (and afford) an alternative source of labour or labour-saving capital goods to replace their slaves.[18] The third possibility is that natural and agronomic conditions allowed the old systems of slavery to be replaced by another system, but that the ex-slaves were constrained, by whatever means, to continue producing the same commodities in more or less the

---

17 R.L. Watson, *The Slave Question: Liberty and Property in South Africa* (Hanover and London, 1990), esp. pp. 106–9, 117–35; J.E. Mason, 'Hendrik Albertus and his Ex-Slave Mey: A Drama in Three Acts', *Journal of African History*, 31 (1990), pp. 423–45. Probably as a result of my ignorance, I do not know of any modern study of the ideology of the British anti-abolitionists and planters, except for L.J. Bellot, 'Evangelicals and the Defence of Slavery in Britain's Old Colonial Empire', *Journal of Southern History*, 27 (1971), pp. 19–40. Studies of those in the United States, on the contrary, are relatively numerous.

18 The importation of Asian labourers into Trinidad, Guyana and Cuba, and of Italians into the coffee counties of Brazil, are examples of this possibility.

same quantities—as was the case in the southern United States, where share-cropping replaced plantation agriculture in the production of cotton.

Clearly there is no reason to suppose that any one of these possibilities obtained in all the European colonies which had been organized on the basis of slave, or quasi-slave, labour. The outcome depended on the specific economic and political circumstances in each case.[19] It has been argued that the level of population density in the slave colonies at emancipation is a very good predictor of the course of the post-emancipation economy. In densely populated small islands, notably Antigua and Barbados, estate production continued to expand after 1838. Given a slave population of 500 and 269 to the square mile, respectively, the ex-slaves were unable to escape from this labour since there was no land available for peasant agriculture, and also no tradition of slaves working and controlling their own provision grounds.[20] However, in Jamaica, with only 74 slaves to the square mile, ex-slaves were able to find the land on which to build up 'reconstituted peasant' communities, and thus to resist the pressure which their former owners placed on them to continue to work on the sugar estates.[21]

But, as Nigel Bolland has argued, such a simple correlation of population density and post-emancipation sugar production is an insufficient explanation. Rather it is necessary to look at the whole complex of methods of labour control after emancipation. Repressive measures may have been easier to apply in colonies where land shortages reduced the options of the ex-slaves, but there were cases such as Belize, Bolland's focus of study, where circumstances allowed the imposition of severe restrictions on the ex-slaves, despite an apparent abundance of land.[22]

POST-EMANCIPATION PRODUCTION AND POPULATION

How, then, does the Cape Colony fit into this pattern? Essentially, if one discounts the inevitable but relatively minor annual fluctuations, the two

---

19 For a valuable discussion of these matters, see S.L. Engerman, 'Economic Adjustments to Emancipation in the United States and British West Indies', *Journal of Interdisciplinary History*, 13 (1982), pp.191–220 and *idem*, 'Slavery and Emancipation in Comparative Perspective: A Look at Some Recent Debates', *Journal of Economic History*, 46 (1986), pp. 35–9.

20 A further complication in this case relates to the fact that sugar production on the long-established and worn-out estates was raised by the application of considerable amounts of Peruvian guano from the 1840s onwards; W.A. Green, *British Slave Emancipation: The Sugar Colonies and the Great Experiment, 1830–65* (Oxford, 1976), p. 202.

21 Population figures are taken from Green, *British Slave Emancipation*, p. 193.

22 O.N. Bolland, 'Systems of Domination after Slavery: The Control of Land and Labour in the British West Indies After 1838', *Comparative Studies in Society and History*, 23 (1981), p. 591–619; W.A. Green, 'The Perils of Comparative History: Belize and the British Sugar Colonies after Slavery', *Comparative Studies in Society and History*, 26 (1984), pp.112–19 and Bolland's 'Reply' in the same journal, pp. 120–5.

decades after the emancipation of slaves saw a boom in the agricultural economy of the colony. This can be shown most clearly from the production figures presented in Tables 6.1 and 6.2. Table 6.1 gives production figures, derived from the Cape Blue Books,[23] for the main crops, grain (wheat, barley, oats and rye) and wine, with its derivative brandy, grown on the farms with slave labour. It shows that the production of grain was scarcely affected, even in the medium term, by the emancipation of slaves, and, if anything, emancipation led to an increase in production. In the immediate aftermath of effective emancipation, in 1838, production of both wheat, and oats and rye (which for reasons of recording have to be taken together) were lower than in any year in either the previous or the subsequent decade, while the production of barley was only marginally higher than that of the previous year, which was the minimum for the period 1828–46.[24] The heavy drought no doubt exacerbated labour problems.[25] In the subsequent one or, perhaps, two years, production was also low. However, if the period 1829–34 (excluding 1832) is compared with that between 1842–6, then the speed of the recovery from the effects of emancipation becomes clear. The production of both wheat, and oats and rye is 35 per cent higher in the latter period than in the former, while that of barley is lower, but only by 7 per cent.

For grape products the situation is complicated, but in an interesting way. The figures demonstrate that the period around and immediately subsequent to emancipation saw the high point of both wine and, in particular, brandy production. More wine was pressed between 1838 and 1841 than in any other four-year period, for which there is information, between 1806 and 1855, while more than twice as much brandy was distilled in each of those four years than in any other year before the 1850s. In part this may represent a recovery from the depression which had followed the ending of the wine boom in the 1820s.[26] More importantly, this phenomenon was, paradoxically enough, a response to a temporary labour shortage. In general, there is a trade-off between the quantity of the wine produced in any vineyard and its quality. If there is a reduced input of labour at certain crucial stages of the agricultural year, notably when the vines have to be pruned, then the amount of juice which can be pressed from the grapes will be considerably higher,

---

23   These figures probably suffer from a certain degree of under-reporting, but nevertheless provide an accurate assessment of the relative performance of the agricultural economy in particular years.

24   There is an exception to these statements for wheat in 1832. However, the district totals show that production in the major wheat-producing district of the colony, the Cape district, was less than 10% of that in neighbouring years (11,000 as opposed to 120,000 in 1831 and 142,800 in 1833), while no other crop or district shows such a pattern. The most likely reason for this is thus a clerical error, with one digit being omitted from the tabulation before calculation of the total was made.

25   J. Marincowitz, 'Rural Production and Labour in the Western Cape, 1838 to 1888, with Special Reference to the Wheat Growing Districts' (Ph.D. thesis, University of London, 1985), p. 30.

26   On which, see Rayner, 'Wine and Slaves'.

but, since its sugar content will be lower, the wine that can be made from it will be of an inferior quality. What seems to have happened, then, is that a decrease in the husbandry of the vineyards increased the total supply of wine, but that much of it was so bad that farmers had no option but to convert it into brandy, aptly known as 'Cape Smoke'.[27]

The other main sector of the colony's agriculture was stock farming. As a general rule, the sheep and cattle which were held on the enormous ranches of the Cape's interior were herded mostly by Khoisan, whose positition in the first quarter of the nineteenth century was, if anything, worse than that of the slave. It follows that the lifting of all civil disabilities on the Khoisan, and other free 'coloureds', by the measure known as Ordinance 50 of 1828, was probably more important in many of the eastern districts of the colony than the emancipation of slaves.[28] As is shown in Table 6.2, there was no fall-off in production as a result of Ordinance 50 or, indeed, of the emancipation of slaves a decade later. The figures are less self-evident than in the case of agriculture because frontier wars, notably those of 1835, 1846 and 1850–3, could have reduced the colony's flocks and herds fairly drastically, and it could have taken several years for them to recover. All the same, it is clear that the colony's herds and flocks increased steadily, if unevenly, and that the export of wool rose dramatically in the years after emancipation, from around 500,000 pounds in 1838 to about 12,000,000 pounds in 1855.[29]

After 1855, any pretence at an annual reporting of agricultural production disappeared. The decennial censuses of 1865 and 1875 do give production figures for the previous year, but clearly random fluctuations, caused by the weather and so forth, make it more difficult to derive any trend from such information. Moreover, there is less reason to suppose that the incidence of

---

27   The increase in brandy production eliminates the possibility that Blue Book production figures in fact represent sale figures, and that post-1838 increases were caused by decreasing on-farm consumption as the ex-slaves departed. There is no reason to believe that slaves received large quantities of brandy—as opposed to wine—before emancipation.

28   S. Newton-King, 'The Labour Market of the Cape Colony, 1807–28', in S. Marks and A. Atmore (eds.), *Economy and Society in Pre-Industrial South Africa* (London, 1980) pp. 171–207; Van Arkel, Quispel and Ross, *De Wijngaard des Heren?*; Crais, 'Slavery and Freedom'; W. Dooling 'Slaves, Slaveowners and Amelioration in Graaff-Reinet, 1823–30' (BA Hons. thesis, University of Cape Town, 1989); V.C. Malherbe, 'Diversification and Mobility of Khoikhoi Labour in the Eastern Districts of the Cape Colony Prior to the Labour Law of 1 November 1809' (MA thesis, University of Cape Town, 1978).

29   The figures for the colony's wool exports are to be found in R. Ross, *Adam Kok's Griquas: A Study in the Development of Stratification in South Africa* (Cambridge, 1976), p. 141.

30   The census of 1875 commented as follows: 'The numbers in this part [Agriculture and Livestock] are defective because of ignorance and fear of taxation influencing the returns. Moreover, occasional drought, disease, insect plagues, rains and floods had wrought such damage to crops and to large and small cattle [i.e. sheep] that the numbers here returned may be estimates as one-forth, perhaps one-third, less than the numbers which would have been arrived at under more favourable circumstances.' Results of a census of the Colony of the Cape of Good Hope taken on the night of Sunday, the 7th March, 1875, Cape Parliamentary Paper, G42–1876, p. 21. The first part of this comment applies *a fortiori* to the Blue Book returns, but does not, I believe vitiate their use for the discernment of trends.

TABLE 6.1 PRODUCTION OF AGRICULTURAL COMMODITIES IN THE CAPE COLONY

Year	Wheat bushels	Barley bushels	Oats/Rye bushels	Wine leggers	Brandy leggers
1806	376,721	189,568	26,385	9,643	974
1807	323,565	143,126	24,668	9,443	841
1808	350,628	130,368	68,160	9,525	823
1809	546,674	145,307	77,035	8,411	774
1810	339,456	151,780	88,165	10,400	977
1811	358,774	158,253	77,871	11,010	1,014
1812	472,298	180,311	119,705	11,279	933
1813	370,431	158,580	99,618	6,724	579
1814	327,278	142,880	125,394	8,697	729
1815	508,776	193,647	129,640	14,365	1,167
1816	513,188	212,801	129,364	15,398	1,303
1817	407,332	185,561	142,217	10,713	860
1818	446,210	176,869	141,174	12,382	914
1819	486,210	186,445	168,223	13,543	1,059
1820	528,078	238,455	206,530	15,210	1,152
1821	271,021	191,829	193,030	16,254	1,205
1822	229,615	229,858	222,552	15,348	1,169
1823	381,998	360,720	267,707	21,147	1,656
1824	445,064	281,856	235,449	16,183	1,326
1825	NA				
1826	NA				
1827	NA				
1828	322,635	351,188	329,928	20,405	1,413
1829	520,768	300,625	321,570	15,539	1,060
1830	410,472	224,676	283,785	14,977	1,845
1831	443,693	271,147	282,182	18,467	1,382
1832	306,063	282,380	275,106	16,973	1,394
1833	528,147	286,197	237,012	14,501	1,207
1834	540,528	257,602	276,553	12,005	1,075
1835	NA				
1836	NA	218,490	241,185	16,693	1,282
1837	494,280	220,534	211,535	18,103	1,373
1838	463,691	180,847	187,860	21,915	5,846
1839	395,329	203,323	185,759	22,899	5,861
1840	433,454	244,600	197,663	20,229	6,190
1841	471,804	295,718	215,006	25,312	6,161
1842	592,054	271,983	286,075	18,299	1,653
1843	705,647	242,662	392,672	13,426	1,386
1844	771,760	293,569	419,587	16,412	2,075
1845	650,849	262,912	436,526	17,156	1,996
1846	579,421	180,856	350,159	18,640	2,069
1847	NA				
1848	516,219	233,667	248,615	10,308	1,671
1849	585,325	265,663	249,307	19,943	2,151
1850	NA				
1851	NA				
1852	721,775	244,432	451,981	16,261	2,418
1853	864,272	302,753	846,520	23,705	3,393
1854	1,012,488	424,134	925,235	23,088	3,891
1855	994,273	400,237	NA	23,640	3,797
1865	1,389,766	308,318	607,359	21,299	2,835
1875	1,687,935	447,991	1,132,754	29,511	7,025

Source: Opgaaf returns in G. Theal (ed.), *Records of the Cape Colony*, 36 vols. (London, 1895–1906); Cape Colony Government Blue Books; Census of the Cape Colony, 1875, CPP G42–1876.

TABLE 6.2   STOCK NUMBERS IN THE CAPE COLONY

Year	Oxen	Other cattle	Wooled sheep	African sheep
1806	69,487	138,958	14,233	1,240,151
1807	69,060	130,601	18,282	1,476,174
1808	63,596	130,808	11,622	1,596,642
1809	85,378	148,186	23,921	NA
1810	87,762	144,831	22,325	1,961,607
1811	92,943	171,500	43,479	2,107,615
1812	84,264	158,541	41,021	1,821,631
1813	88,992	166,728	40,824	1,817,387
1814	74,417	135,674	11,508	1,227,835
1815	90,375	167,627	15,465	1,577,543
1816	93,888	166,850	10,620	1,557,017
1817	99,016	172,269	9,546	1,604,736
1818	103,968	181,692	14,325	1,624,113
1819	99,489	233,433	11,361	NA
1820	111,228	232,048	13,708	1,942,749
1821	116,002	253,435	12,177	1,843,391
1822	109,395	237,276	14,151	2,082,996
1823	112,553	240,475	17,883	1,103,665
1824	115,415	236,925	10,241	2,192,470
1825	NA			
1826	NA			
1827	NA			
1828		357,531		2,181,952
1829		322,021		1,839,402
1830		311,938		1,905,728
1831		315,355		1,087,614
1832		334,907		1,923,132
1833		343,644		1,960,886
1834		312,569		1,919,778
1835	NA			
1836	NA			
1837		279,818		1,923,082
1838		266,255		2,030,145
1839		306,809		2,339,191
1840		334,201		2,456,176
1841		377,803		3,008,613
1842		451,852		3,706,791
1843		452,886		3,949,354
1844		471,635		4,513,534
1845		466,558		4,557,227
1846	122,720	210,082	1,502,611	1,740,835
1847	NA			
1848	169,877	249,189	2,093,074	2,042,767
1849	198,899	390,485	2,283,232	2,114,919
1850	NA			
1851	NA			
1852	203,058	291,600	2,651,136	1,679,941
1853	198,542	273,112	3,476,209	1,528,386
1854	NA			
1855	157,886	292,142	4,827,926	1,625,857
1865	249,307	443,207	8,370,179	1,465,886
1875*	421,732	689,951	9,986,240	990,423

Source: Opgaaf returns in G. Theal (ed.), *Records of the Cape Colony*, 36 vols. (London, 1895–1906); Cape Colony Government Blue Books; Census of the Cape Colony, 1875, CPP G42–1876.

*   The 1875 stock figures are distorted by the inclusion for the first time of the Ciskeian districts of Wodehouse, King Williamstown and East London in the census.

under-reporting was relatively constant.[30] Nevertheless, despite these caveats, it is clear that the steady expansion evident before 1855 continued. Even though it was taken after several years of drought and in the middle of a sharp depression,[31] the 1865 census recorded wheat production substantially higher than in any year before 1855, though significantly this was not the case for forage grains or for wine. Equally, stock numbers had increased substantially. By 1875, when the effects of the diamond boom were making themselves felt, the production of forage grains had recovered and wine and, particularly, brandy production had increased sharply—though the increase in the wheat crop was probably due more to better weather than to an expansion of cultivation.

On the basis of production figures, especially as there was no significant change in the size of the units of production,[32] the experience of emancipation at the Cape appears to be similar to that of Barbados and Antigua.[33] If all other things were equal—which of course they were not—it would be tempting to conclude that the Cape Colony had a high population density, since in many ways its history resembles that of these New World societies. But that would be absurd.

The absurdity lies in this: in comparative and, indeed, absolute terms, the Cape was very underpopulated. In 1829, there were 1.07 people, slave and free, to every square mile in the colony, and by 1842 there were only 1.45.[34] Even in the agricultural heartland of the Cape and Stellenbosch districts, there were only 3.3 people to the square mile in 1829 and 4.6 in 1842.[35] Compare this to a density of 74 slaves to the square mile in Jamaica in 1834, and of 12 per squale mile in Trinidad.[36] Indeed, when in 1833 the officials of the Colonial Office in London were predicting the likely outcomes of emancipation, they included the Cape among those colonies where there was a great expanse of free land and where 'the facility of procuring land has invariably created a proportionate difficulty in obtaining hired labour.'[37] In

31   Marincowitz, 'Rural Production and Labour', p. 159.

32   There are some indications that forms of share-cropping and labour tenancy were emerging in the aftermath of emancipation, but never to any great extent. See the petition on the Masters and Servants Bill from the inhabitants of Wagenmakers Valley, 7 Sept. 1839, Cape Archives, LCA 10/17.

33   The Cape did not receive any major imports of indentured labour at this stage, and only after the cattle killing of 1856–7 did Xhosa labourers begin to reach the agricultural heartland of the south-west Cape. For this reason comparisons with, say, Trinidad or Cuba are not in order.

34   These figures are based on the populations given in the Blue Books for the two years, and the area given for 1842. The area given in 1829 was considerably larger, presumably as a result of the lack of good surveyors.

35   The district comparisons given here are illegitimate, because there had been considerable boundary shifts between the two dates, but the basic point of the low density of even the agricultural heartland of the Cape still holds.

36   Green, *British Slave Emancipation*, p. 193.

37   'Heads of a Plan for the Abolition of Negro Slavery, and for the Securing of the Continued Cultivation of

this, of course, they were describing the experience which successive governments had had with white, non-slave settlers. After the emancipations, though, the Khoisan and the ex-slaves should have had the same opportunities as the white trekboers, if all other things had been equal, which of course they were not.

Clearly, then, it is not possible to explain the Cape's agricultural production by its population density. Other explanations have to be found. Clearly, it would seem that an investigation of post-emancipatory forms of labour organization could provide an answer, but it would be mistaken to assume *a priori* that it is sufficient in itself. Therefore it is necessary to investigate first those other economic factors which may have had a considerable, or even a decisive, influence on production.

THE MARKET

The first of these, of course, is the market. In analysing the trends in the market for Cape produce, it is necessary to make a sharp distinction between the various sectors of agricultural and pastoral production. Wine farmers were by far the most dependent on exports before the 1840s. Between 1825 and 1829 as much as 50 per cent of wine produced in the colony was exported, most of it to Great Britain, although there were growing, if temporary, markets in the southern hemisphere, notably in Australia. These exports seem to have been the most heavily hit by emancipation. At the high point of wine exports, in the 1820s, on average more than 5,500 leggers of wine were sent to Britain annually. This had declined to just over 3,500 by the early 1830s, and by 1840–4 had dropped to no more than 2,365 leggers a year.[38] This may in part have been a result of a perceived decline in the quality of Cape wine as labour became short, but it is more likely that rumours of British tariff changes were responsible. In 1831, the British government passed a law which greatly reduced the differentials on duties between Cape wine and that from continental Europe, and in 1840 rumours reached Cape Town that a tariff agreement between Britain and France would further weaken the competitive position of Cape wine in its major export market. The result was that Cape wine merchants were unwilling to risk shipping wine to Britain where it might prove to be unsaleable.[39] Even though these rumours proved to be untrue, Cape wine was unable to recapture the market share that it had once held.

---

the Estates by the Manumitted Slaves', Public Record Office (PRO), CO 320/8, cited by Engerman, 'Slavery and Emancipation', p. 328.

38 D.J. van Zyl, *Kaapse Wyn en Brandewyn 1795–1860* (Cape Town, 1974), pp. 169–70.

39 *Ibid.*, pp. 143–4, 149–50.

The result for Cape wine farmers was a period of decline. In 1843 and 1844 wine production was lower than it had been for two decades. It should be noted that this fall did not occur until well after emancipation. Moreover, perhaps as early as 1846, and certainly by the 1850s, there were clear signs of recovery, even though wine exports continued to fall sharply. The internal market of the Cape evidently was able to absorb significantly more wine, and the vineyards of Stellenbosch and surrounding areas could produce it.

Grain farming, on the other hand, which in financial terms was by far the largest sector of the colony's agricultural economy, suffered no such problems. The dependence on the internal market which had always characterized this sector, except for a short period in the 1770s,[40] stood it in good stead. It is difficult to provide precise figures on the proportion of grain production which was exported, since the largest proportion of those exports were in the form of flour, and in the milling process the volume of the grain was reduced and its value increased. However, it is unlikely that during the second quarter of the nineteenth century more than about a tenth of the colony's grain production was ever exported, even by way of sales to provision the ships in Cape Town harbour.

In the final major section of the rural economy, that of pastoral production, two distinct trends can be observed. The investment in merino sheep was very strong during the 1840s and 1850s, buoyed up by the demand of the British market. During this period wool overtook wine as the colony's largest export, and Port Elizabeth, with its pastoralist hinterland in the east of the colony, exceeded Cape Town as a port for the outward, though not the inward, trade of the colony.[41] However, even by the mid 1850s, wool accounted for no more than between 30 and 45 per cent of the value of pastoral production—and well under a quarter of the total rural production—in the colony.[42] The greater proportion of the rest consisted of meat and draft oxen, and in the nature of things these had to be consumed, or utilized, within the colony itself.[43]

At mid century, a decade or more after the emancipation of slaves, and two decades after that of the Khoikhoi, the colony's agrarian economy depended primarily on the local market. Growth in one part of the economy stimulated demand for other products. It is possible that the demand itself

---

40 P. van Duin and R. Ross, *The Economy of the Cape Colony in the Eighteenth Century* (Leiden, 1987).

41 A. Mabin, 'The Rise and Decline of Port Elizabeth, 1850–1900', *International Journal of African Historical Studies*, 19 (1986), pp. 275–303.

42 On this, see R. Ross, 'The Relative Importance of Exports and the Internal Market for the Agriculture of the Cape Colony, 1770–1855', in G. Liesegang, H. Pasch and A. Jones (eds.), *Figuring African Trade* (Berlin, 1985), p. 259.

43 There was a certain trade in salt meat, to the passing ships and for export to the Mascareignes, but this was comparatively negligible.

could have been sufficient to alleviate the problems that emancipation might have caused, by providing income sufficient to satisfy landowner and labourer alike. But, for this to have happened, prices would have had to have risen dramatically in the 1840s, whereas, in fact, they seem to have stayed fairly stable. Post-emancipation economic expansion was thus not demand driven, although demand was sufficient to sustain the expansion achieved.

CAPITAL

The other possibility is that farmers were able to compensate for the loss of labour by sharply increasing their productivity. This would have entailed a considerable injection of capital. The capital was, indeed, available in the form of the compensation money paid at the emancipation of slaves. There were complaints, which have been exaggerated in later historiography, that Cape slaveowners did not receive the full value for their slaves, largely because the money had to be collected in London and the agents obviously took a commission. Nevertheless, since there was considerable competition between those vying for agency,[44] and since the number of absentee slaveowners at the Cape was minimal, the majority of the £1,193,085 8s. 6d. granted by the British government to the Cape slaveowners as compensation money certainly reached the Cape.[45] Some of this obviously had to be used to redeem mortgages secured on slave property, but the farmers would nevertheless have had a clean slate and thus have been able to raise capital again on the credit market against the security of their landed property. This would have been available, since their pre-emancipation creditors were largely residents of the colony.[46]

The injection of capital into the Cape Colony which resulted from emancipation allowed, and in many ways gave rise to, the development of the Cape's banking system. The first private bank in the colony was established in 1837, and within a few years several others had followed. The government-run Lombard and Discount Banks were driven out of business as a result.[47] The farmers found that credit had become easier to obtain, and thus cheaper. In this context, though, what needs to be asked is how did a ready availability of capital improve the productivity of Cape farms? The most likely possibility is that guano, from Malagas Island to the north of Cape

44 In 1834, the Cape newspapers, notably the *South African Commercial Advertiser* and *De Zuid-Afrikaan*, contain numerous advertisements from those merchants who were buying up compensation claims.

45 British Parliamentary Paper (BPP) 215 of 1837–8, Accounts of Slave Compensation Claims, pp. 351–3.

46 This was pointed out by John Fairbairn in the *South African Commercial Advertiser*, 11 Sept. 1833, cited by Meltzer, p. 175 in this volume.

47 E.H.D. Arndt, *Banking and Currency Development in South Africa, 1652–1927* (Cape Town, 1928); J.L. Meltzer, 'The Growth of Cape Town Commerce and the Role of John Fairbairn's *Advertiser*, 1835–59' (MA thesis, University of Cape Town, 1989).

Town, gave at least some farms the added fertility they needed. The government, which shrewdly took a monopoly on the sales, made a profit of nearly £150,000 over an unspecified period in the 1840s, but it is impossible to estimate how much manure this would have been, or how effective it was. Since guano revenues were concentrated heavily in a single year, 1845, it cannot have been of major importance.[48] It may have been that farmers could now buy machinery which they previously either could not afford or saw no reason to purchase, given sufficient labour. They also might have introduced new systems of husbandry in an attempt to compensate for the labour shortage. Only a close study of the equipment actually on the farms at the time, which as yet has not been undertaken, could test the accuracy of this supposition.[49] However, even in Europe, both grain and wine farming remained extremely labour-intensive throughout the nineteenth century, so the possibility of technological improvements at that date seems slight. Equally, even though they lauded 'progress' in virtually every other sphere of life, such journals as the *Cape Almanac* or the *South African Commercial Advertiser* do not seem to have focused on agronomic improvement. Dangerous as it is to argue from such negative evidence, it would seem that they did not have a great deal to applaud.[50]

THE BIFURCATION OF THE RURAL LABOUR FORCE

All in all, then, it seems unlikely that either the development of new markets by itself or the import of capital could have maintained the level of agricultural production in the wake of the emancipations. It has to be assumed, therefore, that the labour supply remained sufficient to allow the farms of the Cape Colony, both in the (largely) agricultural west and in the (largely) pastoral east, to continue at much the same level. This 'happy' result—for the farm owners at least—was in part the result of the concerted action of the landowning class, in conjunction with the colonial state, but was also, to a large degree, the result of contingent historical circumstances which were at once unplanned, unexpected and propitious.

The landowners' offensive was successful because it was based on experience, acquired over two or three decades, of holding the officially free Khoisan effectively in bondage. The supposedly emancipatory Ordinance 50

---

48   W.A. Newman, *Biographical Memoir of John Montagu* (London and Cape Town, 1855), p. 57. The figure which Newman gives does not tally with the much lower figures in the Cape Blue Books. I am grateful to Andrew Bank for his investigations of the latter for me.

49   Given the number of wills and inventories, such a study is not doomed for lack of evidence.

50   On the limits of technical progress in grain agriculture see Marincowitz, 'Rural Production and Labour', pp.108–11; on the progressive movement in general, see J. du Plessis, 'Colonial Progress and Countryside Conservatism: An essay on the Legacy of Van der Lingen of Paarl, 1831–75' (MA thesis, University of Stellenbosch, 1988), pp. 30–83.

was subverted fairly systematically at the local level. Even had they been willing to enforce it fully, which is most doubtful, the courts simply did not have the staff to do so.[51]

With the emancipation of slaves the number of those who were free, but whom the landowners still considered to be subservient, increased dramatically. The result was a two-pronged offensive by landowners. The first prong was legislative. This took three forms. The first, contemporary with the abolition of slavery, was the attempt to have a legislation controlling vagrancy introduced into the colony. The Ordinance in question, which was published on 14 May 1834, empowered and required 'every field-commandant, field-cornet and provisional field-cornet [the local officers of law and administration, elected from among the wealthiest farmers of a district]...to apprehend all persons found within his jurisdiction, whom he may reasonably suspect of having no reasonable means of subsistence, or who cannot give a satisfactory account of themselves.'[52] This Ordinance was passed by the Cape's Legislative Council, largely by the votes of the 'unofficial members, that is to say those who did not owe their membership to their tenure of a high position in the administration. It was then submitted to the Colonial Office in London for approval before enactment.

Even before it had been tabled, Colonel T.F. Wade, who had been Acting Governor of the Cape and was the Ordinance's main sponsor, had, rather disingenuously, informed the Colonial Office that laws would be introduced with, as their objects

> the prevention or punishment of vagrancy...and for securing [sic] a sufficiency of labourers to the colony by compelling not only the liberated apprentices to earn an honest livelihood, but all others who, being capable of doing so, may be inclined to lead an idle and vagabondizing life.[53]

In other words, the Vagrancy Ordinance was explicitly designed to re-establish the control of slaveowners over their erstwhile slaves, and also of landowners in general over the Khoisan. Indeed, Ordinance 50 had already been followed by an offensive along these lines.[54] For this reason, the Vagrancy Ordinance was greeted both with a large-scale movement of those Khoisan who were able to the mission stations, where they expected a degree of protection,[55] and with a storm of protest—from the missionaries and other

---

51   L.C. Duly, 'A Revisit with the Cape's Hottentot Ordinance of 1828', in M. Kooy (ed.), *Studies in Economics and Economic History: Essays in Honour of Professor H.M. Robertson*, (London, 1972), pp. 34–46.

52   Report of the Select Committee on Aborigines (British Settlements), Together With the Minutes of Evidence, British Parliamentary Paper (BPP) 538 of 1836, pp. 723–4.

53   Cited in W.M. Macmillan, *The Cape Colour Question: A Historical Survey* (London, 1927), p. 234.

54   'Evidence of Major W.B. Dundas', BPP 538 of 1836, p. 128.

55   Macmillan, *Cape Colour Question*, p. 238.

defenders of Khoisan and slave rights, as well as from a substantial group of the Khoisan themselves.[56] Essentially, as they were all too well aware from past experience, the passing of such an ordinance would allow a farmer to arrest any employee who left the farm on which he or she worked. This would prevent any form of bargaining as to wages or conditions, by weighting the scales far too heavily in the farmer's favour. As a result, the Colonial Office disallowed the Vagrancy Ordinance as being incompatible with Ordinance 50.

If the vagrancy measures failed to achieve the desired control over the labouring population, the subsequent Master and Servant Ordinance did so, to a large degree. It, too, had a difficult passage. The first draft which was submitted to London was rejected because its operation was limited to 'people of colour'.[57] However, shorn of such racial excrescences, a revised version became law in 1841, and indeed remained so, in somewhat amended form, until the 1960s.[58] The basic import of the measure, as John Marincowitz has noted, was that it transferred numerous aspects of an essentially civil law contract between an employer and an employee into the sphere of criminal law. This was because the Ordinance made 'misconduct' on the part of the employee a punishable offence. Misconduct was an elastic concept, defined to include 'refusals or neglect to perform work, negligent work, damage of a master's property through negligence, violence, insolence, scandalous immorality, drunkenness, gross misconduct'[59] and so forth. The punishments were not so vague; offenders could be docked one month's wages, or imprisoned, with or without hard labour, for 14 days. The result was thus a more stringent labour code than that imposed on the emancipated slaves of the Caribbean or Mauritius.

Nevertheless, this was thought to be not enough. The third measure of labour control was the Bill to prevent the practice of squatting on government lands, which was introduced into the Legislative Assembly on 10 October 1851. Rightly or wrongly, many farmers thought that government land and the farms of their less scrupulous colleagues[60] were being used by

---

56 For the former, see the evidence before the Select Committee on Aborigines, notably that provided by Capt. C. Bradford, the Rev. H.P. Hallbeck and Dr. J. Philip; for the latter, see E. Bradlow, 'The Khoi and the Proposed Vagrancy Legislation of 1834', *Quarterly Bulletin of the South African Public Library*, 39 (1985), pp. 99–105, and S. Trapido, 'The Emergence of Liberalism and the Making of "Hottentot Nationalism", 1815–34', in Collected Seminar Papers of the Institute of Commonwealth Studies, London: *The Societies of Southern Africa in the Nineteenth and Twentieth Centuries,* 17 (1991).

57 Otherwise, so it was argued, no European workmen would ever be prepared to emigrate to South Africa.

58 Marincowitz, 'Rural Production and Labour', pp. 57–65; C. Bundy, 'The Abolition of the Master and Servants Act', *South African Labour Bulletin,* 2 (1975), pp. 37–46.

59 Master and Servant: Documents on the Working of the Order-in-Council of 21 July 1846 (Cape Town, for the Legislative Council, 1849), p. 3.

60 W.F. Bergh, Resident Magistrate of Malmesbury to Secretay to Government, 20 Feb. 1849, in Master and Servant: Addenda to the Documents on the Working of the Order-in-Council of the 21st July 1846

potential labourers to escape the necessity of regular labour. Once again, there was considerable protest against the Bill, and it was dropped at the final moment of its passage through the legislature. The western Cape landowners believed, rightly or wrongly, that its enactment would be the signal for an armed uprising among their labourers, and they panicked.[61] One cynical official wrote of the panic that 'It has been good for the dealers in gunpowder here.'[62]

The remarkable thing about the Squatting Bill was that it was largely unnecessary. The second prong of the landowners' offensive had seen to that. As the Caribbean experience showed clearly, ex-slaves—and for that matter the emancipated Khoisan— needed independent access to land if they were to reconstitute themselves as a peasantry and thus escape their former masters' control. There were a few areas of the eastern Cape where this was possible for a time, both as squatters on Crown lands[63] and, above all, in the Kat River Settlement.[64] Even before emancipation a number of Free Blacks and their descendants had set up as market gardeners in the neighbourhood of Cape Town.[65] In general, however, the land of the Cape had been taken over by the landowning class to such an extent that this was impossible. This could be done, despite the low density of population, because of the highly uneven distribution of water throughout the Cape countryside. Without access to a reasonably permanent stream, an independent existence as a peasantry was not feasible, and the small communities which attempted this were few and poverty stricken.[66] Slave gardens, worked mostly on Sundays, as

(Cape Town, for the Legislative Council, 1849), p. 191; *De Zuid-Afrikaan*, 28 Sept. 1848, cited in Marincowitz, 'Rural Production and Labour', pp. 84–5.

61   For divergent views on the reality of the planned uprising, see J. Marincowitz, 'From "Colour Question" to "Agrarian Problem" at the Cape: Reflections on the Interim', in H. Macmillan and S. Marks (eds.), *Africa and Empire: W.M. Macmillan, Historian and Social Critic* (London, 1989), pp. 155–60; E. Bradlow, 'The "Great Fear" at the Cape of Good Hope, 1851–2', *International Journal of African Historical Studies*, 23 (1989) pp. 401–22. In general, I believe that the evidence favours Bradlow's argument that the panic was without foundation.

62   John Rainier to John Montagu, 3 Jan. 1852, in Further Papers Detailing an Alarm in the District of Riversdale in Reference to the Proposed Ordinance 'To Prevent the Practice of Settling or Squatting on Government Lands' (Cape Town, for the Legislative Council, 1852), p. 28, CA, LCA 26/8, 10.

63   S. Dubow, *Land, Labour and Merchant Capital: The Experience of the Graaff-Reinet District in the Pre-Industrial Economy of the Cape (1852–72)*, Centre for African Studies, University of Cape Town, Communications, no. 6 (1982), pp. 63–70.

64   T. Kirk, 'Progress and Decline in the Kat River Settlement', *Journal of African History*, 14 (1973), pp. 411–28; J.B. Peires, 'The British and the Cape, 1814–34', in R. Elphick and H.B. Giliomee (eds.), *The Shaping of South African Society, 1652–1840*, 2nd edn. (London, 1989), p. 484; J.C. Visagie 'Die Katriviernedersetting, 1829–39' (Ph.D. thesis, University of South Africa, 1978); C. Crais, *White Supremacy and Black Resistance in Pre-Industrial South Africa: The Making of a Colonial Order in the Eastern Cape, 1770–1865* (Cambridge, 1991), pp. 79–86.

65   Bank, *Decline of Urban Slavery at the Cape*.

66   Proceedings of Evidence Given Before the Committee of the Legislative Council Respecting the Proposed Ordinance 'To Prevent the Practice of Settling or Squatting Upon Government Lands (Cape Town, for the Legislative Council, 1852), esp. pp. 8–10, 19, 40–1.

they had been before emancipation,[67] could thus only continue, as they had started, by the grace of the landowner. These then formed extra bonds, tying the ex-slaves to the farms on which they worked.

The main alternative for those seeking a modicum of independence were the mission stations. During the 1840s, the number of those who were prepared to accept the discipline imposed by the missionaries increased sharply. Between around 1838 and the early 1850s, the population of the missions of the western Cape doubled, from about 6,000 to around 12,000.[68] In particular, the southern plains of Caledon and Swellendam districts had a number of very large such stations, especially at Genadendal and Elim, but there were also a number of smaller stations in the Stellenbosch and Cape districts, in addition to the old established village of Mamre in the Groenkloof, in the heart of the wheat-growing Zwartland.

The mission stations could not in any way directly support the hundreds of ex-slaves who thronged to them. They could provide a house and a vegetable garden but not sufficient land to provide subsistence for a family. There might have been a certain amount of employment on the stations itself, as teachers, or in workshops such as the famous Genadendal knife works. But the great majority, at least of the men, had to find work outside on the farms. Those who were able returned to the stations every weekend, but many had to work at greater distance, and were away from home for weeks at a time. The missions could provide security from the exactions of over-exploitative farmers. Children and women—at least outside peak harvesting—spent most of their time there, but the men were absent for long periods.[69] The population figures for the stations cannot be treated as a true census, except during such holidays as Christmas and Easter, but rather represent those who were registered as belonging to the station.

There were some alternatives. A few farmers did hire out living space to labourers who were working elsewhere.[70] Presumably these landowners were prepared to flout any pressure from their fellows in exchange for the rent they received and, no doubt, for an assured supply of labour for themselves. Refugees were also to be found in the villages and small towns of the Cape, and even in Cape Town which grew considerably in the years immediately after emancipation. However, places such as Stellenbosch, Paarl, Swellendam or George could not provide regular employment for the hundreds of ex-slaves who came to live there. Seasonal employment on the

---

67 Isaac Bissieux to Directors, 22 nov. 1830, *Journal des Missions Evangeliques*, 6 (1831), p. 67. It may be significant that this report came from Wellington, the location of the short episode in post-emancipation share-cropping mentioned above.

68 Marincowitz, 'Rural Production and Labour', p. 41.

69 Master and Servant: Addenda contains an occupational census of the mission stations in 1848.

70 Master and Servant: Addenda, p. 191.

surrounding farms was, therefore, the only way to make a living. There was even a regular exodus from Cape Town for the wine and wheat harvests. The towns provided more freedom than the mission stations, though the living conditions were probably inferior.[71]

It was here that the serendipity of the Cape's labour situation after emancipation was to be found. The mission stations and, to a lesser extent, the towns of the colony were much hated by the farmers. They were seen as repositories of idleness. One farmer noted that they 'have been called "reservoirs of labour" but they are more like stagnant pools, engendering pestilential vapours and requiring immediate purification.'[72] However, at least in economic terms, this does not seem to have been an accurate assessment. Grain, wine and wool production all have sharp peaks in their labour requirements, for pruning, harvesting, shearing and so forth. In the Cape, these did not coincide. For example, the timing of the wheat harvest varied in the different regions of the Cape, as can be expected given the country's great distances and high relief. As a result, it is at least arguable that the most efficient use of labour under such circumstances would have been the combination of a small number of tied labourers on each farm, coupled to a large pool of men and women who travelled round the countryside and worked where they were needed at any given moment. Under slavery, this was difficult to organize, even though the Khoisan might be employed as casual labourers and farmers frequently hired each other's slaves for peak periods.[73] With emancipation, this was achievable. The mission inhabitants played the role of travelling labourers, while those held in place by the contracts of the Masters and Servants Ordinance formed the fixed core of labourers on each farm. As a result it was possible for the farmers to compensate for any shortfall in labour caused by the withdrawal of many women and children from the labour force. What labour there was, was used more efficiently.

CONCLUSION

It might seem, then, as though the Cape Colony was about the only case where the economic predictions of the abolitionists actually came true, and where freedom raised all-round productivity. Clearly, this would be overstating the matter considerably. The restrictive legislation, such as the Masters and Servants Ordinance, and a welter of restrictive practices kept a high

---

71 On Cape Town, see in particular S. Judges, 'Poverty, Living Conditions and Social Relations: Aspects of Life in Cape Town in the 1830s' (MA thesis, University of Cape Town, 1977).

72 Master and Servant, pp. 74–5, cited in Marincowitz, 'Rural Production and Labour', p. 85. This sort of reaction was a clear psychological residue of slavery. The former slaveowners could not countenance their labourers not being directly under their own control.

73 Worden, *Slavery in Dutch South Africa*, pp. 87–8.

proportion of the erstwhile slaves and Khoisan in bondage. It was not for nothing that Dr John Philip spent the rest of his life campaigning against the dilution of both Ordinance 50 and the emancipation of slaves. After the establishment of the Cape Parliament in 1854, which entrenched the power of Cape gentry, the Masters and Servants Ordinance was strengthened, to tie those labourers who were held on the farms ever closer to the landowners.[74]

This was not a maintenance of the pre-emancipation patterns of labour organization. Rather, the Cape's post-emancipation trajectory created a new division of labour, a process analogous to, though very different from, what happened in the cotton belt of the United States. What the post-emancipation settlement clearly did do was divide the Cape's rural working class into those who were tied to the farms and those who had at least one foot in the relative freedom of the mission stations or country towns, which gave them the possibility of social mobility denied to their fellows. There may not have been much difference between the two groups in terms of the standard of living they enjoyed in the years immediately after emancipation. Those who remained on the farms, even if they changed employer, at least knew what to expect, and were guaranteed a minimum of subsistence. Those who went to the towns risked abject poverty, while those on the mission stations had to submit to a form of discipline which, although it differed from that experienced under slavery, was perhaps no less restricting for some, notably in its enforced sobriety. However, in the long term, the two groups came to grow apart, both in economic terms and matters of culture. The inhabitants of the mission stations, the country towns[75] and Cape Town had the chance to acquire education and to work their way up out of their status as agricultural labourers—or at least their descendants did. Symbolically the first school for the training of ex-slaves, Khoi and, indeed, African teachers was opened in Genadendal in 1838.[76] The products of this and other such institutions became among the most typical examples of the 'Cape coloured' élite. In contrast, those who remained as farm labourers had few, if any, opportunities to escape from the cycle of bondage, debt peonage and alcohol addiction, so characteristic of Cape rural life.[77] The results of this bifurcation are still evident today.

---

74 Marincowitz, 'Rural Labour and Production', pp. 125–9.

75 The diaries of the Rhenish missionaries in Stellenbosch, Worcester and Tulbagh, published in the *Jahresbericht der Rhenische Missionsgesellschaft* show them to have worked mostly as schoolteachers.

76 *Dictionary of South African Biography*, vol. 4 (Durban, 1981), p. 207.

77 See, for example, P. Scully, 'Criminality and Conflict in Rural Stellenbosch, 1870–1900', *Journal of African History*, 30 (1989), pp. 289–301; *idem*, 'Liquor and Labour in Stellenbosch District, 1870–1900' in C. Ambler and J. Crush (eds.), *Liquor and Labour in Southern Africa* (Athens, Ohio, 1992), pp. 56–77; and numerous studies on twentieth-century rural Cape labour.

Plate 8   Heerengracht, c.1850, by Johan Schonegevel. *William Fehr Collection.*

7

EMANCIPATION, COMMERCE & THE ROLE OF JOHN FAIRBAIRN'S *ADVERTISER*

— LALOU MELTZER —

The emancipation of the slaves at the Cape in 1834 resulted in a quickening tempo of commercial life in Cape Town. The arrival of the slave compensation money created a minor economic boom in the late 1830s, in spheres such as property sales and company formation. The combined long-term effects were to expand the base of the commercial classes and contribute significantly to the opening up of the agricultural and commercial economy of Cape Town and the south-western Cape to market forces. The newspaper editor, John Fairbairn, played a pivotal role in guiding the colonists through this transitional period.

The first section very briefly sketches the state of commerce in the period before 1834 to establish a context for a discussion of the changes brought about by emancipation. It also introduces the key role player in the discussion, John Fairbairn.

COMMERCE AT THE CAPE BEFORE 1834

The importance of merchant capital and the commercial bourgeoisie in the shaping of modern South Africa has frequently been acknowledged, but investigation of their origins and growth in the period before the discovery of diamonds and later gold is still in its infancy.[1]

The closing decade of the eighteenth century at the Cape saw the final withdrawal of a bankrupt Verenigde Oostindische Compagnie (VOC) from a

---

1 This chapter is based mainly on ch. 2 of my MA thesis: J.L. Meltzer, 'The Growth of Cape Town Commerce and the Role of John Fairbairn's *Advertiser*, 1835–59' (University of Cape Town, 1989). See Meltzer, *ibid.*, pp. 1–2, 9–12 for an appraisal of the available source material for the early period of Cape commercial growth; B. Bozzoli, *The Political Nature of a Ruling Class: Capital and Ideology in South Africa 1890–1933* (London, 1981), p. 107; S. Marks and S. Trapido, 'The Politics of Race, Class and Nationalism in Twentieth Century South Africa', in S. Marks and S. Trapido (eds.), *The Politics of Race, Class and Nationalism in Twentieth Century South Africa* (Harlow, 1987), pp. 3–4.

poorly-developed economy characterized by company-regulated, highly-restricted commerce. In response to the VOC's mercantilist restrictions, trade largely took refuge in various semi-legal and illegal forms, with some legal participation. The latter was in the form of trade in locally-grown agricultural commodities, via the Company's pacht or concession system.[2] Generally, much of the private trade under the VOC was conducted from home by individual settlers from different walks of life. Private specialist or full-time trading activities remained in basic contradiction to the Company's own needs and policies.[3]

The policies of the British colonial government and the English East India Company during the First British Occupation (1795–1803) were not qualitatively different from those of the VOC, though in some aspects the outlook for the development of commerce did improve. The period of the Batavian Republic rule at the Cape (1803–6) was too brief to achieve any of the well-intentioned reforms.[4]

Trade opportunities for Cape Town merchants increased considerably in the early years of the Second British Occupation after 1806. New markets became available on the Mascarene Islands and St. Helena. The settlement in Albany also provided fresh opportunities. After 1813, when preferential tariffs for Cape wines were implemented in Britain, farmers and merchants threw their energies into increased production and sale. A series of measures passed in 1813 and during the 1820s continued to improve opportunities for local merchant participation in the re-export trade of Eastern goods and made way for the development of Cape Town as a free port. In 1834 an Act was

---

2   Meltzer, 'The Growth of Cape Town Commerce', pp. 17–18; G.J. Erasmus, 'Die Geskiedenis van die Bedryfslewe aan die Kaap 1652–1795' (Ph.D. thesis, Universiteit van die Oranje-Vrystaat, 1986), pp. 204–5, 211–12, 220–1; W. Blommaert and J.A. Wiid (eds.), *Die Joernaal van Dirk Gysbert Van Reenen 1803* (Kaapstad, 1937), pp. 1–8 for a biographical sketch of such a pacht concessionaire; R. Ross, 'The Origins of Capitalist Agriculture in the Cape Colony: A Survey', in W. Beinart, P. Delius and S. Trapido (eds.), *Putting a Plough to the Ground: Accumulation and Dispossession in Rural South Africa 1850–1930* (Johannesburg, 1986), p. 68; G. Schutte, 'Company and Colonists at the Cape', in R. Elphick and H. Giliomee (eds.), *The Shaping of South African Society, 1652–1840* (Cape Town, 1989), pp. 298–303; H. Giliomee, *Die Kaap Tydens die Eerste Britse Bewind, 1795–1803* (Kaapstad, 1975), p. 142.

3   Meltzer, 'The Growth of Cape Town Commerce', pp. 18–19; Erasmus, 'Die Geskiedenis van die Bedryfslewe', pp. 235, 239–42; C. de Jong, *Reizen naar de Kaap de Goede Hoop, Ierland en Norwegen, in de Jaren 1791 tot 1797... met het, onder zijn Bevel Staande, 's Lands Fregat van Oorlog, Scipio* (Haarlem, 1802–3), p. 156; J.L.M. Franken, ''n Kaapse Huishoue in die 18de Eeu uit Von Dessin se Briefboek en Memoriaal', *Argief-jaarboek vir Suid- Afrikaanse Geskiedenis*, 1940 (1), pp. 13, 17, 19–20.

4   Meltzer, 'The Growth of Cape Town Commerce', pp. 19–21; Giliomee, *Die Kaap Tydens die Eerste Britse Bewind*, pp. 137, 173–4; M. Arkin, 'John Company at the Cape: A History of the Agency Under Pringle 1794–1815 Based on a Study of the "Cape of Good Hope Factory Records"', *Archives Year Book for South African History*, 1960 (II), pp. 197, 206–7, 210, 212, 217–18; T.R.H. Davenport, 'The Consolidation of a New Society: The Cape Colony', in M.H. Wilson and L. Thompson (eds.), *Oxford History of South Africa*, vol. 1 (Oxford, 1969), pp. 288–9; P.H. Philip, 'The Vicissitudes of the Early British Settlers at the Cape', *Quarterly Bulletin of the South African Library*, 40, no. 4 (1986), p. 165.

5   Meltzer, 'The Growth of Cape Town Commerce', pp. 22–9, 35–7, 116; M. George, 'John Bardwell

passed which rescinded all the remaining privileges of the English East India Company.[5]

During the early years of the British occupations the Company's records continued, however, to reflect the predominance of trade with English merchants, though in the retailing sphere trade was not the sole prerogative of the English.[6] Despite the improvements initiated during this period, the growth of the economy should not be exaggerated.[7] It is in the context of the general increase in economic horizons and the optimistic beliefs in future great prosperity, on the one hand, and, on the other, the basically poor nature of the Cape agricultural-based economy, dwarfed by the might of the British industrializing economy, that the emergence of the early Cape merchants must be understood.

The first steps taken by the small, newly-emerging group of Cape Town merchants were to create institutions to increase their social and economic influence. They began by establishing the Commercial Exchange and formalizing their links with London merchants, organized in the Cape of Good Hope Trade Society, which could lobby the British government. It was a significant achievement in a period marked by the absence of local Cape government representation.[8] After its establishment in 1825, the Commercial Exchange undertook a great number of commercial and economic tasks, projects and battles on behalf of commerce. From the start its members were ably assisted in their campaigns by a sympathetic Cape Town newspaper editor, John Fairbairn.

Between 1824 and 1829 Fairbairn had, together with Thomas Pringle and George Greig, championed a successful battle against the autocratic British colonial government to establish a free press in the Cape Colony. The struggle was, *inter alia*, over Fairbairn's liberal *South African Commercial Advertiser*, the first private newspaper in South Africa and destined to become Cape Town's leading paper of the period.[9] Fairbairn was editor

Ebden: His Business and Political Career at the Cape 1806–49' (MA thesis, University of Cape Town, 1980), pp. 8–10, 24–30, 74–6; Arkin, 'John Company at the Cape', pp. 237, 250–2, 257–60, 299–301, 303 n. 71, 304, 318–19; M. Arkin, *Storm in a Teacup: The Later Years of John Company at the Cape 1815–36* (Cape Town, 1973), p. 3; B.A. le Cordeur, *The Politics of Eastern Cape Separatism 1820–54* (Cape Town, 1981), pp. 37–40; A.J. Christopher, *Southern Africa* (Folkestone, 1976), p. 59; D.J. van Zyl, *Kaapse Wyn en Brandewyn 1795–1860* (Kaapstad, 1975), *passim*, esp. pp. 9–11, 126.

6   Giliomee, *Die Kaap Tydens die Eerste Britse Bewind*, p. 201.

7   Arkin, 'John Company at the Cape', p. 315; C.G.W. Schumann, *Structural Changes and Business Cycles in South Africa 1806–1936* (London, 1938), pp. 67–70; W. Bird, *State of the Cape of Good Hope in 1822*, facsimile of original edn. of 1823 (Cape Town, 1966), p. 129; R.P. Beck, 'Edward Hanbury—Cape Town Ship Chandler and Merchant 1819–25', part 2, *Quarterly Bulletin of the South African Library*, 39, no. 2 (1984), pp. 77–9; A.P. Buirski, 'The Barrys and the Overberg' (MA thesis, University of Stellenbosch, 1952), p. 48.

8   Meltzer, 'The Growth of Cape Town Commerce', pp. 29–38.

9   A.M.L. Robinson, *None Daring to Make Us Afraid: A Study of English Periodical Literature in the Cape*

between 1824 and 1859 and sole editor and owner after 1835. The columns of the *Advertiser* reveal Fairbairn's role as energetic campaigner in promoting the growth of the economy and commerce at the Cape during the first half of the nineteenth century. His editorial comments and articles reveal his intense interest in and identification with commercial developments, whether in debates concerning the advantages of free trade, slave emancipation, the usury law, joint-stock companies, or his reporting of relevant extracts from overseas papers, government economic statistics and company reports. Despite the political and editorial importance and liberal achievements accorded Fairbairn, it is surprising how little his role in the economic sphere has been acknowledged.[10]

THE *ADVERTISER* AND THE ABOLITION OF SLAVERY

On 16 September 1835, Fairbairn pronounced with delight and relief: 'This is the brightest page in the history of the colony—in the history of England—perhaps in the history of human governments... After God, then let our affections be drawn out towards our Mother Country. May she long set an example of humanity, justice and honor to all nations!'[11] Prompting Fairbairn's praise on this occasion was not the abolition of slavery throughout the British Empire, as one might expect from his moral tone, but instead the British government's award of slave compensation money.

Editorial discussion in the *Advertiser* of the question of abolition intensified in the wake of Ordinance 19 of June 1826, which provided for improved conditions for slaves, including the appointment of a Guardian of the Slaves. Modelled on the 1824 Trinidad Order-in-Council, the Ordinance resulted in uproar amongst slaveowners at the Cape.[12] In July 1826 Fairbairn admitted his reluctance to discuss the topic of slavery before Ordinance 19 was passed:

> We have hitherto avoided, as much as possible, all discussion on the subject of SLAVERY, although it was one of much interest to most of our readers, who have frequently blamed our silence, and called for some observations upon it. There were two reasons for this line of conduct... The first was, that we did not

---

Colony from its Beginnings in 1824 to 1835 (Cape Town, 1962), pp. 22–3; H.C. Botha, *John Fairbairn in South Africa* (Cape Town, 1984), pp. 17–18, 23, 31, 46–52, 133.

10   Meltzer, 'The Growth of Cape Town Commerce', pp. 10–11, *passim*. Fairbairn's recent biographer has devoted a very small section to his promotion of various enterprises, see Botha, *John Fairbairn*, pp. 147–57.

11   *South African Commercial Advertiser* (henceforth *SACA*), 16 Sept. 1835.

12   M.I. Rayner, 'Wine and Slaves: The Failure of an Export Economy and the Ending of Slavery in the Cape Colony, South Africa 1806–34' (Ph.D. thesis, Duke University, 1986), pp. 260–67; Davenport, 'The Consolidation of a New Society: The Cape Colony', pp. 306–7; A.F. Hattersley, 'Slavery at the Cape 1652–1838', in E. Walker (ed.), *Cambridge History of the British Empire*, vol. VIII (Cambridge, 1963), pp. 272–3.

understand the case, nor could see any method of obviating the difficulties apparently inseparable from every scheme that had been devised for effecting the final abolition of slavery, nor had we met with any modest person who pretended to be much wiser than ourselves on these heads; and the second was, that, in our opinion, the question could not be agitated without deteriorating the value of slave property.[13]

The most striking characteristic of Fairbairn's discussion of slavery is the virtual absence of any moral or social condemnation of the institution. Yet, in this respect, his position was in complete alignment with English abolitionists. Biblical interpretation had seldom been an important issue in controversies over the slave trade. 'Despite the predominantly religious motivation of British Quakers and evangelicals, the abolitionists, with a few exceptions like Granville Sharp, made little use of scriptural argument.' Wilberforce even cautioned against introducing this aspect into discussions in the House of Commons. The main defence of the anti-slavery argument was secular, lying instead along lines of national interest and foreign competition.[14] However, here and there a pious statement, to be expected perhaps of Fairbairn as friend of the missionary movement, is to be found. For example:

> The Abolition of the Slave Trade was an open recognition of the principle that man ought to have no property in man... The religious public, those who think nobly of the soul, and who anticipate the reign of Faith, Hope and Charity upon earth, have therefore cause to rejoice above all others, at the removal of this impassable barrier [slavery] which has so long stopt [sic] the progress of all spiritual improvement. And we trust to see them on the morning of the First of December, in their churches and chapels, offering up praises to the GREAT DELIVERER for this manifestation of his GOODNESS.[15]

This line of editorial discussion was, however, exceptional. That he deliberately avoided a moral viewpoint (in line with attitudes abroad), he acknowledged in March 1831:

> In treating this question [slavery] we have from the beginning (1824) carefully abstained as much as possible from touching on the moral and religious grounds from which so many able writers have drawn their arguments in favor of liberty. Not that we overlooked or were insensible of their paramount importance, or slighted the authority which the sanction of our holy religion sheds over every great design. But in discussing the propriety of political arrangements we prefer, for ordinary use, the more generally intelligible principles of political science. The

13   *SACA*, 8 July 1826.

14   D.B. Davis, *The Problem of Slavery in the Age of Revolution 1770–1823* (Ithaca, 1975), p. 525.

15   *SACA*, 26 Nov. 1834. See Botha, *John Fairbairn*, pp. 64–75, for an account of Philip and Fairbairn's tour of the eastern frontier and Fairbairn's marriage to Philip's daughter, Eliza. There was close co-operation between the two men. A correspondent to the *Zuid-Afrikaan* (henceforth ZA), called 'ZXL', mentions the Philipine party or faction—the party of Dr Philip. With this faction Fairbairn was, according to the correspondent, far too involved, see 21 Nov. 1834.

Ten Commandments, with the New Testament addition of universal benevolence, may be employed by others; we are content with the multiplication table.[16]

With what yardstick was Fairbairn measuring the propriety of 'political arrangements' that he could reduce political science to the laws of multiplication? His approach is revealed as pragmatic and materialistic. While he agitated hard for the cause of emancipation after 1826, often in opposition to the representatives of the slaveowners,[17] his great concern remained the matter of adequate compensation for freed slave property, a concern, I would argue, inextricably bound up with his perception of the need for the appeasement of the slaveowners in the interests of stable, united colonial rule.

Fairbairn's wish for reconciliation can be understood against the background sketched by Rayner in her study of slavery and Cape wine farming, more particularly in her concept of the 'weakening of the British-Dutch alliance'.[18] She characterizes those features of the early period of British occupation, which generally brought new possibilities of personal aggrandizement for the local gentry, as follows: offices in local government; pleasant social relationships between this gentry and British officials; official stimulus of wine farming; improved regulation of Khoi labour in Caledon's 1809 law, and the regulations of 1812 and 1817; the establishment of the circuit court system in 1811; and a paternalistic but unsystematic intervention in the master-slave relationship.[19] She then contrasts this with developments in the late 1820s and early 1830s which witnessed a reversal.

The effect of the reduction of privileged tariffs on the import of Cape wine into Britain in 1826 and the resultant failure of the wine industry, was compounded by a series of orders regarding slavery, particularly Ordinance 19.[20] Rayner thus concludes:

> For Cape slaveowners, the realization of the powerlessness of the local government in the face of a Colonial Office committed to a comprehensive amelioration programme and ultimately to the abolition of slavery, led to a re-evaluation of the alliance which had served the interests of the slaveowning élite and the local government for several decades. The crisis over slavery was one more element on top of economic failure engendering disillusionment with British rule.[21]

It was thus as mediator and property owner that Fairbairn formulated the problem of abolition—which was to engross his attention—namely the question of the conflicting rights of slave and master, further complicated in the colonial context.

---

16   *SACA*, 2 Mar. 1831.

17   Botha, *John Fairbairn*, pp. 85–6.

18   Rayner, 'Wine and Slaves', p. 295.

19   *Ibid.*, pp. 91–129.

20   *Ibid.*, ch. 4, *passim*, esp. pp. 190–221, also 260–94.

21   *Ibid.*, pp. 295–6.

The abolition of slavery, or regulations for ameliorating the condition of slaves, form but one side of the question. If the just rights of the masters are left out of view, these things can be easily accomplished by so a powerful nation as England. But the question before us is not a question of power, but of justice. It is—how these most desirable objects be gained for the one class, without inflicting an unmerited punishment on the other? How can the slave obtain his freedom, while the property of the master, which is of at least as much importance to him as Freedom is to the other...*how to make Abolition or Amelioration coincide with the rights of Property is the problem*, and it is one which readers will admit to be a very hard one. [My emphasis.][22]

Satisfied that emancipation in itself would be adequate protection for the slaves, Fairbairn turned his attention exclusively to the slaveowners. He set about proposing 'a scheme which shall enrich the slave-holder—furnish the colonies with an abundance of the cheapest, most manageable, and most profitable species of labor, and bind all classes of men throughout the Empire by the bonds of an equal, personal, and immediate interest in the support or order, and due administration of *all* the Laws.'[23]

Once convinced of the viability of emancipation, he began a campaign to persuade his readers of the advantages. He instituted in the newspaper in a variety of ways a process of opinion-forming. Finally, Fairbairn began to prepare the Cape for the great change heralded by emancipation and compensation. His detailed formulation of a plan for slave compensation was evolved from an early date and, as he pointed out in 1835, it was almost identical to the scheme eventually sent out by the British government.[24] In 1833 he was already outlining the rosy prospects for the Cape economy once the compensation money arrived:

One million sterling...is to be *added* to the capital of the colony at once, every thing else remaining as it is. In the West India colonies the glut of money will be much less sensibly felt as a very large proportion of the grant destined for them will remain with the mortgagees in England. Here the mortgagees are resident, and the whole sum in hard cash will enter Table Bay.

Passing over immediate and temporary effects, such as the advance of prices and the decline in the rate of the interest, the ultimate effect will be a great improvement in the style of living throughout the country districts. We do not refer merely to the farmers. The numerous class of laborers will lay out their gains on food, clothes, and furniture to an extent far beyond their present accommodation. There will be a great increase of buildings, both in town and country.

---

22   *SACA*, 8 July 1826.

23   *SACA*, 12 Feb. 1831.

24   *SACA*, 16 Sept. 1835, referring to an earlier editorial, 9 Feb. 1831.

25   *SACA*, 11 Sept. 1833

Capitalists will be glad to invest their money in *Joint Stock Concerns*, where there is a fair prospect of a moderate return—for not only will the borrowers be reduced in number, but what is more effective, securities will be diminished, laborers being no longer subjects of mortgage. The result of all this will be a vast increase of demand for labor, an advance in wages, an increase in the number of laborers by emigration, and the conversion of idlers... In conclusion it is perhaps not too much to say that this sudden influx of capital will raise the colony as much in five years, in point of wealth, as we could have hoped to see it rise in fifty under the present system of stinted labor, and deficient capital.[25]

Simultaneously, cognizant of the large amounts of money due to the Cape, Fairbairn began to voice cautionary concern for the colony's economy. The sudden influx, an amount he estimated at six times the value of money circulation at the Cape, he warned, could result in the unsettling of 'the whole financial arrangements of the colony'.[26]

Thus in the years preceding emancipation Fairbairn campaigned for abolition in such a way as to placate slaveowners and when news of the compensation money arrived at the Cape, he immediately began preparing his readers for the effects of this huge amount of money.

SLAVERY AND COMMERCE AT THE CAPE BEFORE 1834

The question that comes to mind is how far Fairbairn's concern with the issue of slavery and emancipation was reflected by Cape commerce generally. The Genoveses developed the argument of what they term the 'Janus face of merchant capital', to refer to merchant capital's ability because of its base in relations of exchange, not production, to feed off and coexist within different types of relations of production, that is capitalist and pre-capitalist forms of property such as slavery. Was the commercial bourgeoisie at the Cape able to adjust to and promote relations of advancing capitalism, yet at the same time remain tied to pre-capitalist forms of social relationships, simultaneously looking forward and backward, as Janus of ancient Roman mythology was believed to have done?[27]

The views of the smaller general trader at the Cape (mainly Dutch/Afrikaans) are generally difficult to reconstruct as they lacked the organizational, economic and social power enjoyed by merchants.[28] Judging

---

26   *SACA*, 3 May 1834; see also editorials in *SACA*, 19 Mar. and 30 Apr. 1834.

27   E. Fox-Genovese and E.D. Genovese, *Fruits of Merchant Capital: Slavery and Bourgeois Property in the Rise and Expansion of Capitalism* (Oxford, 1983), ch. 1, esp. pp. 5–6.

28   For an indication of the ZA's role and its posturing in the interests of the small shopkeeper, see ZA, 19 Dec. 1834; *SACA*, 27 Dec. 1834; Meltzer, 'The Growth of Cape Town Commerce', p. 156, n. 99. According to B.J.L. Liebenberg, 'Die Vrystelling van die Slawe in die Kaapkolonie en die Implikasies Daarvan' (MA thesis, Universiteit van die Oranje-Vrystaat, 1959), p. 128, by 1835 even news of the amount of compensation money was received calmly by the ZA.

from Fairbairn's account of the dinner of 1 December 1834 held to celebrate the abolition of slavery that day, the organized merchant sector, represented by the Commercial Exchange, certainly had no misgivings. Fairbairn talks of the 'Noble Britons'—chiefly merchants—who assembled that night at the George's Hotel in the Heerengracht 'and in true English fashion expressed their gratitude for this crowning mercy'. During that day the meteor flag of England had been unfurled on the Commercial Exchange.[29]

Merchant dominance of the celebratory dinner was underscored by the speech of Mr Venning, merchant and member of the London-based Cape of Good Hope Trade Society, in which he mentioned 'being surrounded almost exclusively by the merchants of Cape Town'.[30] In his toast that night, Merrington indicated that the accusation of 'party meeting' had been levelled at the dinner and he talked of the estrangement between the British and their fellow colonists. He tried, rather unsuccessfully, to counter the accusation that the Commercial Exchange represented the partisan interests of the English merchants.[31]

Yet, despite the festivities held by English merchants to mark slave emancipation, both English and Dutch/Afrikaans merchants had individually joined with slaveowners in public meetings and petitions during the events leading to emancipation. Prominent English merchants, Hamilton Ross and Stephen Twycross, for instance, feature amongst the memorialists 'concerned and affected by Ordinance No. 19'. Hamilton Ross and James Carfrae & Co. are mentioned in the original request for permission to hold a meeting, in order to draw up a petition against Ordinance 19.[32] Amongst such petitioners, however, Dutch/Afrikaans retailers, businessmen and, most especially, wine merchants, predominate. The names of P. Woutersen, J.J. van den Berg, G.J. Vos, J.F. Beck, J.J. Vos, R.A. Zeederberg, J.A. Smuts and J.W. Hurter, all wine merchants, appear; L.W.C. Beck and P.G. van der Byl, retail shop owners, and G.E. Overbeek, member of the Orphan Chamber, are also listed.[33] Evidence of merchant participation in the 'Town House Committee' formed to have Ordinance 19 suspended has been highlighted by Rayner.[34] Yet attention has not been drawn to the fact that the main impetus came from a specific sector of commerce, that is the group of smaller Dutch/Afrikaans wine merchants, closely involved as they were with wine farming in the south-western Cape which formed the slave-based sector of the economy *par excellence*.[35]

29   *SACA*, 3 Dec. 1834; *Almanac*, 1835.

30   *SACA*, 6 Dec. 1834; *Almanac*, 1835.

31   *SACA*, 6 Dec. 1834.

32   G.M. Theal, *Records of the Cape Colony (RCC)*, vol. 29 (1905), pp. 356–9.

33   *Almanac*, 1827.

34   Rayner, 'Wine and Slaves', pp. 260–4.

English merchants were very much in agreement with Fairbairn's agitation for satisfactory conditions of compensation payment. The memorial to the Slave Compensation Office sent by the London affiliate of the Commercial Exchange, the Cape of Good Hope Trade Society, wished 'to represent that great excitement and distrust exist in the Colony of the Cape of Good Hope, with regard to the slave compensation money, and that the mortgagees of slave property are in a state of alarm as to the probable value of their securities.'[36] Were merchants here admitting their commercial affairs to be extensively linked to slave property via mortgage and general credit, were they acknowledging their own slaveownership, or were they merely worried about the effects of emancipation on colonial property and capital generally?

The first question is, to what extent were merchants involved in transactions in which slave property was employed for raising loans? Obviously this would be an aspect stressed by slaveowners during the process leading to abolition. Shell's study of slavery at the Cape in the seventeenth and early eighteenth centuries has indicated the important role of slave mortgage. 'Since there were no public lending institutions at the Cape, some individuals used the slaves as a peripatetic bank. Such owners sold slaves when they needed to make a "withdrawal".' Over the course of the eighteenth century this scheme became an increasingly important feature of Cape slave society, especially for elderly slaveowners. By 1806, Samuel Hudson, an English slaveowner, talking of slavery at the Cape, flatly claimed: 'for the aged, 'tis their bank'. Thanks to the domestic market, slaves were a negotiable commodity at the Cape, giving a fiscal meaning to the word 'bondsman'.[37]

Van Zyl has also stressed that, during the early nineteenth century, slaves were frequently accepted as security by money lenders and that it was on the basis of slave property that the expansion of wine farming between 1813 and 1823 took place.[38] In 1823, according to the Commissioners of Enquiry, the mortgages on 4,089 slaves stood at 12,375,000 guilders (4,125,000 rixdollars).[39] Slaveowners stated in a petition, drawn up in 1827 (information which Van Zyl accepts unquestioningly), that by that year about 15,000 (that

---

35   The economic significance of this Dutch/Afrikaans wine sector should not be overestimated. Many of them exported in smaller retail quantities—see C.L. Leipoldt, *300 Years of Cape Wine*, 2nd edn. (Cape Town, 1974), p. 84. Documents in the Wine Taster's group reflect many names of Dutch/Afrikaans wine exporters; a register of Cape wine exports, in which both wine merchant and exporter are listed for each shipment, indicates that the exporter was more frequently a member of a big English merchant house, such as J. Collison, Nisbet and Dickson, J.R. Thomson of Thomson, Watson & Co. and Stephen Twycross—Cape Archives (CA), WT 7, 'Register of Shipments of Cape Wine Exported', 5 Aug. 1822 to 24 June 1826.

36   *SACA*, 22 Nov. 1834.

37   R.C.H. Shell, 'Slavery at the Cape of Good Hope 1680–1731' (Ph.D. thesis, Yale University, 1986), vol. 1, pp. 87–8.

38   D.J. van Zyl, 'Die Slaaf in die Ekonomiese Lewe van die Westelike Distrikte van die Kaapkolonie, 1795–1834', *South African Historical Journal*, 10 (1978), p. 24.

39   *Ibid.*, quoting Theal, *RCC*, vol. 35 (1905), pp. 375–6.

is roughly half) of the slaves were mortgaged.[40] Contemporary Dutch/Afrikaans opinion at the time of emancipation held that by the year of emancipation (1834), an amount of £400,000 or 5,333,333 rixdollars was mortgaged on the basis of slave property.[41]

While Van Zyl stresses the heavy mortgaging of slaves and does not indicate the source of this mortgage credit, Rayner gives a different emphasis regarding the security used by wine farmers of the south-western Cape to raise mortgages. She also specifically analyses the source of this credit. From her examination of estate records for the year 1823, she deduces that 'Two-thirds of the 374 wine-farming estates were heavily mortgaged primarily on the basis of their fixed assets rather than of slave property.'[42] 'The value of their [wine farmers] mortgages on slaves amounted to only 5 per cent of the four and one quarter million rixdollars which the colonists as a whole had borrowed up to 1823, and only 18 per cent of the total value of loans taken out by wine growers.'[43] Regarding the source of mortgage credit, Rayner furthermore states:

> Most of the mortgages had been contracted with the government-controlled Lombard and Discount Banks and to a lesser extent with the Orphan Chamber, which administered and settled intestate estates, and with private individuals. *Large-scale farmers, district officials and annuitants, rather than merchants, were involved as individual lenders of capital.* [My emphasis.] The records of the insolvent estate of Dirk Gysbert van Reenen, for instance, indicate that he owed Rxds 35,221 in unpaid principal interest on mortgages contracted with the Lombard Bank, the Orphan Chamber, J.J.L. Smuts, an Orphan Chamber official [a member, as will be seen, of the Dutch/Afrikaans commercial bourgeoisie]; Michiel van Breda, a leading agriculturalist; and P.H. van Reede van Oudtshoorn, a relative of the only Dutch nobleman resident in the colony.

She concludes:

> Merchants were apparently discouraged from investing in mortgages of fixed farm property by the great delays attendant on the recovery of the principal. During a period of rapid depreciation in the colonial currency, such delays could prove very costly to the lender of capital on a fixed interest rate of 6 per cent per annum.[44]

The Slave Office Day Books of Mortgages covering the period 1818–36, list those mortgages secured on the basis of slaves.[45] These were examined with

40   *Ibid.*, quoting Theal, *RCC*, vol. 34, p. 85.

41   *Ibid.*, quoting an 1834 edn. of *Het Nederduitsch Zuid- Afrikaansch Tijdschrift.*

42   Rayner, 'Wine and Slaves', pp. 211 and 35a, Table 1.9.

43   *Ibid.*, pp. 35–6

44   *Ibid.*, pp. 211–12.

45   CA, Slave Office, SO 9/1 'Day Book of Mortgages' 1818–21, SO 9/2 'Day Book of Mortgages' 1829–35, and SO 9/3 'Day Book of Mortgages', 1835–6. A study of the counter-claims register, in which contested claims advanced by mortgagees and others are listed, also reveals few clear interventions by

a view to further establishing how important a factor merchant capital was in such transactions. The result generally confirmed Rayner's proposition that merchants were infrequent creditors in relation to slave mortgages. The Government Discount and Lombard Banks, indeed, appear very frequently as mortgagees; and most mortgagees are Dutch/Afrikaans private individuals, many having no apparent business connection. Nevertheless, a group of Dutch/Afrikaans merchants and businessmen often with wine-trade connections does appear fairly frequently, while there is scattered mention of big English merchants, mainly exporters of wine.

English merchant mortgagees include the well-known firms: Stephen Twycross; J. Collison; Thomson, Watson & Co.; Borradailes, Thompson & Pillans; S.B. Venning & Co.; Simpson Brothers, William Gadney; William Heideman for James Carfrae & Co. and Ewan Christian.[46] But more frequent in the records is mention of Dutch/Afrikaans wine merchants, traders and agents. These include, *inter alia*: Andries Brink; Wicht family members; H.G. Muntingh; R.A. Zeederberg; J.J.L. Smuts and G.E. Overbeek of the Orphan Chamber; Wolff & Bartman and F.G. Watermeyer.[47]

The appearance, therefore, of names such as Twycross, Zeederberg, Overbeek and several other mortgagees as petitioners against Ordinance 19, is not surprising.

Commerce, therefore, did not participate extensively in transactions based on the mortgage of bonded human property, though the wine merchant sector as a whole, and the Dutch/Afrikaans group of wine merchants, agents and moneylenders, in particular, was more heavily involved.

A second aspect of the commerce-slave relationship, the extent of which is difficult to gauge, was commerce's advance of credit for the purchase of slaves. The business sector, particularly in the absence of a formal banking structure, performed a banking function by discounting bills of exchange, so

commerce. The majority of names appear to be Dutch, the two sides often seeming family—see CA, SO 20/57, 'Receipts for Counter Compensation Claims Paid', July 1836 to Nov. 1837, and SO 20/58, 'Book of Counter Claims'.

46 CA, SO 9/1, 2 Dec. 1818, 26 Apr., 20 Oct., 30 Aug., 30 Nov. 1819; SO 9/2, 19 Dec. 1833; SO 9/2, 16 Feb. 1835; CA, WT 7; George, 'John Bardwell Ebden', p. 29; Leipoldt, *300 Years of Cape Wine*, p. 84; Van Zyl, *Kaapse Wyn en Brandewyn, passim*, esp. pp. 62, 140; Meltzer, 'The Growth of Cape Town Commerce', p. 25.

47 CA, SO 9/1 and SO 9/2, *passim*; CA, SO 9/1, 4 May 1820; SO 9/2, J.H. Wicht—22 Feb. 1831, 31 Mar. 1831; J.A.H. Wicht—14 Mar. 1831, 5 Mar. 1831; Watermeyer—15 Nov. 1830, 1 Mar. 1833; SO 9/1, Muntingh—18 Sept. 1820; SO 9/2, Wolff and Bartman—9 Feb. 1830, 7 Mar. 1832, 17 Mar. 1832, 28 Nov. 1832, 16 Aug. 1834; *Almanac*, 1824, 1827–8, 1831, 1834; C.C. de Villiers en C. Pama, *Geslagsregisters van die Ou Kaapse Families*, deel 2 (Kaapstad, 1981), pp. 1128–9.

48 *SACA*, 29 May 1839. See also *SACA*, 6 Nov. 1839, where Advocate Musgrave, during the usury debate in the Legislative Council, describes the common use of bills of exchange by merchants in relation to shopkeepers; and *SACA*, 2 Nov. 1839, where the Hon. H. Cloete, in the same regard, marks out the distinguishing characteristic of that great 'capitalist' of Cape Town, Jonas van der Poel, who refuses to negotiate bills of exchange but accepts money only on first mortgage.

perhaps loans for the purchase of slaves were more general than the isolated case mentioned here. The instance that stands as example was related in correspondence to the *Advertiser*'s editor. Major Parlby, an English farmer, detailing his financial distress as a result of the reduced compensation awards, explained that he had borrowed the original capital for purchasing his slaves from Hamilton Ross & Co., to whom he had paid 6 per cent interest over a period of seven years.[48]

Finally, what of the basic relationship between the propertied classes, including commerce, and the slaves, namely that of master and slave? One would expect merchants and businessmen, a wealthy section of the ruling class, to employ slaves as domestic workers as well as labourers in their shops and firms. These urban workers at home and in the service sector formed an important section of the slave class. Therefore, the appearance of commercial men as claimants in the lists of compensation awards is not surprising, especially if ownership in the lists also represented mortgage-related transactions undertaken by them before emancipation. However, compensation awards to commerce will be dealt with later. At this stage it is sufficient to state that commerce certainly encompassed slaveownership.

Fairbairn had rightly stated in April 1834 that it was not only slaveholders who would be affected by emancipation; other 'classes in the community too, to the extent of their property and transactions, were involved not only as mortgagees, creditors, or partners with the holders of slaves, or simply partaking of the good or ill fortunes of so important a class of customers, or employers, or neighbours engaged in the same occupations with themselves, but directly and immediately in their own property and business.'[49] Commerce's involvement in slave property during the pre-emancipation period has been sketched. The general characteristic of commercial capital's Janus face is confirmed by its involvement in slave property relations and transactions, albeit not on an extensive scale. Yet, if in the years before slave compensation money, the fortunes of Cape commerce were not that closely tied up with slave property, in the years during the actual payment its fortunes were to become intimately linked.

EFFECTS OF ABOLITION AND COMPENSATION ON THE ECONOMY

On 16 September 1835, Fairbairn informed his readers that Cape slaveowners had been awarded £1,247,401. 0s. 7d. in compensation for their 38,427 slaves, valued at an average price of £73. 9s. 11d. each, calculated on the basis of prices obtained during the period 1823–30.[50] These calculations were made in London on the basis of information supplied by the local

---

49 *SACA*, 30 Apr. 1834.

Board of Assistant Commissioners, which was set up in Cape Town in early 1834.[51] The Board consisted of the Governor, Attorney-General and, of the six unofficial members, four were well-known merchants—Ewan Christian, W. Gadney, H.A. Sandenbergh and P.M. Brink—as well as the money-dealer, J.J.L. Smuts.[52] Encouragement for this selection of men came from London. In instructions to Governor D'Urban, Stanley recommended that the Board include men with 'a practical knowledge of slaves, which you will not find except amongst persons who are themselves interested in that species of property.'[53] That this recommendation was followed is proved by the naming of Christian, Sandenbergh, Brink and Smuts in the lists of the slave compensation awards and in the mention already made of Gadney, Christian and Smuts as slave mortgagees.[54]

The reduced compensation awards, the delays in the arrival of the money, the inability of the rural slaveowners to travel to Britain, their lack of business connections and acumen, their dependence on mainly British-connected merchants to collect the money and general financial failure, are all writ large in the annals of traditional historiographical interpretations of this period.[55]

In fact, once a serious look is taken at the period after emancipation, the picture that emerges is not one of depression and bankruptcy but rather a stimulated economy approaching, if not attaining, boom conditions. While some scholars who have studied the period, such as Liebenberg and Hengherr, have identified it as a period of expansion and growth, its main features have never been discussed in detail.[56]

MONEY SUPPLY

In November 1839 Fairbairn spoke of the abundance of money at the Cape 'in return for the abolition of a law—for a change in the relation of master and servant'. Despite his earlier quoted statement that an amount equal to six

---

50   *SACA*, 16 Sept. 1835; Liebenberg, 'Die Vrystelling van die Slawe', pp. 127–8. The Cape was awarded the fifth largest amount and the average value of a Cape slave was fourth highest.

51   E. Hengherr, 'Emancipation and After: A Study of Cape Slavery and the Issues Arising from it 1830–43' (MA thesis, University of Cape Town, 1953), p. 53; Liebenberg, 'Die Vrystelling van die Slawe', pp. 114–27.

52   *SACA*, 11 June 1836; *Almanac*, 1837.

53   Liebenberg, 'Die Vrystelling van die Slawe', p. 116.

54   CA, SO 20/47, 'Lists of the Awards of the Commissioners of Compensation', 1836–7, claim no. 5544 Ewan Christian, 6404 P.M. Brink, 6473 H.A. Sandenbergh, and 6555 J.J.L. Smuts.

55   Liebenberg, 'Die Vrystelling van die Slawe', pp. 183–4.

56   While it is not the intention to examine the situation of the slaveowners as such, even here the traditional idea that emancipation resulted in severe poverty and bankruptcies among former slaveowners, has been refuted. According to Liebenberg's graph showing levels of bankruptcies at the Cape between 1830 and

times the circulating medium of the Cape was to arrive in compensation, the whole amount of over £1,000,000 certainly never reached the Cape. But his prediction of 1833, regarding the effects of the compensation on the economy, proved remarkably accurate.[57]

Government figures relating to the currency, though inconsistent, reveal both an increase in specie import over the period, especially in the years 1837–8, and a great increase in the component of privately-imported specie. No private imports of specie occurred in the period between 1825, the year British sterling was introduced, and 1835. The £25,000 introduced privately in 1835 cannot be explained in terms of the slave compensation money inflow. Certainly, some of the 1836 imports (£18,000) and all the 1837 imports (£192,680) can be attributed to the compensation, as claims began to be processed in late 1836.[58]

Regarding the total amount of coin in circulation, government figures indicate that the circulation of specie doubled during 1837 (£300,000), the first proper year of arrival of the compensation money, remaining at that level in the immediate aftermath, beginning to decrease in 1840 and falling to roughly 1836 levels by 1843.[59] In 1840, therefore, the government was still referring to 'The great and sudden increase in the circulating medium by payment of the slave compensation claims.'[60] However, the increase in specie in the period to 1840 cannot be explained entirely in terms of the compensation money. Increased monetary importations, the first large-scale rewards of eastern Cape merino farming and the establishment of the first private bank in 1837, the Cape of Good Hope Bank, must also have played a role.[61]

IMPORTS

It is obvious that much of the compensation money due to the Cape never left London. No doubt the money was used by commerce to pay off existing debts, which had been a problem because of the difficulties of remitting

1840, a peak was reached in 1833–4. The years of emancipation until 1838, in fact, witnessed a continuous downturn in the number of bankruptcies, with the year 1838 showing the lowest number over the whole period. He demonstrates, furthermore, that of the 146 bankruptcies in 1834, only 18 were farmers, see 'Die Vrystelling van die Slawe', pp. 187–8, 193–9; see also Hengherr, 'Emancipation and After', pp. 65–71.

57 *SACA*, 9 Nov. 1839, 3 May 1834, 11 Sept. 1833.

58 Hengherr, 'Emancipation and After', pp. 57–8; Colony of the Cape of Good Hope Blue Book (CCGHBB), 1835–8; Meltzer, 'The Growth of Cape Town Commerce', p. 57, Table 2.1 and 2.2.

59 CCGHBB, 1835–8; Meltzer, 'The Growth of Cape Town Commerce', p. 57, Table 2.3.

60 CCGHBB, 1840.

61 Christopher, *Southern Africa*, p. 59; E.H.D. Arndt, *Banking and Currency Development in South Africa 1652–1927* (Cape Town, 1928), p. 236; CCGHBB, 1835–40.

money. Some money must also have found its way into the London branches of the merchant houses as agency fees. Another probable explanation is that many merchants brought in goods instead of bringing back actual money, or immediately returned the money to England in payment for new goods.

Imports show an enormous increase during the period in which the slave compensation money was paid. Though again the reason for this increase cannot be assigned solely to the compensation, but was also a reflection of generally expanding market demands, compensation must be seen as a major factor and was widely hailed as such at the time. The Commercial Exchange's annual report published in the *Advertiser* in mid 1837, remarks on the unusual increase in imports which may be partly ascribed to the payment of the slave compensation money.[62] The Cape Colony Government Blue Book for 1836 stated: 'The importation of goods from the United Kingdom has been very greatly increased of late, owing mainly to the payment of the slave compensation money.'[63]

Trade (imports and exports combined) through Cape Town in the first half of the nineteenth century has recently been tabulated. This shows that between 1831 and 1835 the annual average stood at £630,000; between 1836 and 1840 at £1,596,000 (more than doubling) and between 1841 and 1845 it had fallen back slightly to £1,017,000.[64] Imports and exports through the port of Cape Town, separately tabulated, show that they both increased during the period of the slave compensation money, peaking in the 1839–40 period. Compare, for instance, the value of imports and exports in 1835, before the arrival of the money (£498,564 and £328,579 respectively) with 1839 (period of slave compensation) figures (£1,231,362 and £706,769 respectively).[65] In the Legislative Council the Hon. H. Cloete mentioned the slave compensation money as the probable reason for the increase of shipping in Cape Town's harbour.[66]

INTEREST RATE

The influx of money resulted in a reduction in the interest rate. In August 1838 Fairbairn attributed the fall to the inflow of compensation money and the lack of investment of that money in productive undertakings, such as harbours and agricultural improvements.[67] The 1837 Blue Book noted that the rate of discount had been lowered from 6 per cent to 4.5 per cent and even to

62 *SACA*, 6 May 1837.

63 CCGHBB, 1836–8.

64 Christopher, *Southern Africa*, p. 95, Table 4.

65 Meltzer, 'The Growth of Cape Town Commerce', p. 60, Table 2.4; CCGHBB, 1834–43.

66 The proceedings of the Legislative Council reported in SACA, 9 Sept. 1837.

67 *SACA*, 11 Aug. 1838.

4 per cent because of the substantial increase in the money supply, adding that the establishment of the new private bank had not been without its influence. The Blue Book for 1840 also explained that the great and sudden increase in the 'circulating medium' was due to the slave compensation money, noting that the interest rate was now reverting to 6 per cent because of a shortage of money.[68]

On 12 September 1838, the Savings Bank, following the Government Bank, reduced the interest on deposits from 4 to 3 per cent, and on bonds in favour of the bank in the western division, from 5 to 4 per cent. In its annual report published in the *Advertiser* in January of the next year, the bank stated that the reduction of interest had not been an adequate remedy for its large amounts of idle reserves, and because of the difficulty of finding investment opportunities on good security, it had been decided to limit deposits to £75 per annum or £5 per month.[69]

PROPERTY

The property market was also affected by the compensation money. The colonial government reported as early as 1836 that land policy was to be affected by the sudden increase of money. 'For two reasons, and in order to take advantage of the recent influx of money into the colony, opportunities have been given for the redemption of quit-rent lands at 20 years purchase, and the granting of lands on that tenure has been checked in order that all persons desiring to acquire lands, may do so by purchase.'[70]

Emancipation itself also stimulated the property market. Fairbairn alluded to new areas of poor housing inhabited by artisans/labourers, many obviously former slaves. He reported in 1838: 'To the low-browed, damp, unventilated cellars, and narrow lanes inhabited by the poor of Cape Town, a number of small "cottages", as they are called, in the form of a bisected triangle, are making their appearance in the vicinity, constructed apparently for the purpose of proving, by direct experiment, that pure air, light and cleanliness are not necessary to health in this climate.'[71] When the smallpox epidemic struck Cape Town in 1840, the worst affected areas were obviously these poor areas. Fairbairn wrote indignantly: 'The upper ranks would discover that they are reposing over a magazine of death in which the torch is always smouldering... What do you think of ten, twenty, or even thirty human beings sleeping night after night in an apartment twelve to fourteen

---

68 CCGHBB, 1837 and 1840.
69 *SACA*, 4 Aug. and 12 Sept. 1838; 30 Jan. 1839.
70 CCGHBB, 1836.
71 *SACA*, 1 May 1838.

foot square—the floor damp clay—and many in the last stages of confluent small pox?'[72] He described the overcrowded housing conditions, a result of 'the capitalists...[having] not yet built proper houses... They [the tenants] are, therefore, apparently from necessity, crowded in dozens into cellars, back courts and cavern-like holes.'[73] This new breed of landowning commercial bourgeoisie, with landlord wealth based firmly on these working-class areas and holding the future reins of municipal power, will be touched on later in the discussion of the expansion of the local commercial bourgeoisie during the emancipation period.

In addition, the phenomenon of accelerated subdivision of existing plots in Cape Town and the suburbs, particularly the southern suburbs, is indicated in the flurry of property advertisements placed in the *Advertiser* during 1838 and early 1839. The advertisements reveal both the transactions of future members of the Cape Town municipality indicating their steadily increasing ownership of property in the poor areas of Cape Town and provide evidence of urban subdivision and rapid suburban expansion of Cape Town during 1838 and early 1839.

Thus, in March 1838, the *Advertiser* carried advertisements for two property lots belonging to F.S. Watermeyer, Municipal Commissioner in 1842. One of the lots was an alley issuing at Rose Street in the present Bo-Kaap, containing '5 newly-built neat hire houses, and two more dwelling apartments.'[74] Later that year, P.J. Pentz, Municipal Commissioner in 1844, advertised on his estate 'Schotsche Kloof' in the same Lion's Rump area, six lots of land. Forming part of these were: 'Two pieces arable land, producing annually a very rich crop, and having the advantage of a passage to Lion's Rump, and fronting Leeuw-street. This is an excellent opportunity for building houses cheaply, as there is plenty of stone and clay on the spot.'[75]

Expansion in the southern suburbs was a noteworthy feature of the property market at this time. While the extent to which this expansion was linked to the compensation money is difficult to establish, it is highly likely that the two were connected. One cannot neglect the significance of the timing of these advertisements which so neatly correspond with all the other expansionary effects around the years 1837 and 1838. A study of the advertisements reveal a great concentration around 1838 and early 1839, with few preceding, and decreasing numbers after the period. Interesting too, is the emphasis in these advertisements on the suitability of the plots for small

---

72   *Ibid.*, 15 Apr. 1840.

73   *Ibid.*, 23 May 1840.

74   *SACA*, 31 Mar. 1838; D. Warren, 'Merchants, Municipal Commissioners and Wardmasters: Municipal Politics in Cape Town 1840–54' (MA thesis, University of Cape Town, 1986), p. 255, appendix H.

75   *SACA*, 10 and 17 Oct. 1838; Warren, 'Merchants, Municipal Commissioners', p. 256, appendix H.

cottages, perhaps indicating the growth in numbers of a white petty bour-geoisie and lower middle class as a result of the general growth in the economy.[76] The loss of slaves, it may be speculated, resulted in the ownership of large suburban and urban erven becoming a non-viable financial proposition.

In October 1839, a correspondent to the *Advertiser* mentioned that substantial quantities of land had been exchanged in the past two years and great improvements made to existing buildings.[77] Government statistics for the period attest to this too. Transfer dues to the government rose from £17,791 in 1837 to £23,636 in 1838 and, in the Blue Books' lists of the colony's industries, the number of brickfields in Cape Town shot up from four in the 1834–7 period to ten in 1838,[78] offering proof of the increased building activity in that year, and obviously also indicating the increased number of freed workers in the town. Interestingly enough, according to news carried by the *Advertiser* on two separate occasions at this time, property prices in Barbados witnessed a similar rise after the abolition of slavery, showing an increase at one point of some 30–50 per cent and, at another, of 10–15 per cent.[79]

The second half of the 1830s, therefore, witnessed an economic boom in Cape Town, providing the context for the expansion of the commercial bour-geoisie, including both old and new layers, and a great spurt in company formation.

COMPENSATION MONEY AND THE MERCHANT SECTOR

In January 1837 Fairbairn informed readers of the latest decision of the British government, namely that the money was to be paid in 3.5 per cent government stock.[80] As a result of the new decision former slaveowners became dependent on merchants with largely English connections to collect the compensation funds. As Hengherr has stated: 'The firms and the individuals transmitting the compensation have been represented as callous profiteers exploiting the plight of the helpless claimants by charging exorbitant agency fees or buying claims far below their value.'[81] In August 1835, the *Zuid Afrikaan*, voice of the Dutch/Afrikaans community and of the slaveowners, already mentioned the losses that would be incurred by the appointment of agents in London. A meeting was therefore called in the Commercial

---

76 *SACA*, 1838–40; for a fuller treatment of the subject, see Meltzer, 'The Growth of Cape Town Commerce', p. 63.

77 *SACA*, 23 Oct. 1839.

78 CCGHBB, 1834–8.

79 *SACA*, 29 June and 4 Dec. 1839.

80 SACA, 4, 7 and 11 Jan. 1837; Liebenberg, 'Die Vrystelling van die Slawe', pp. 172–4.

81 Hengherr, 'Emancipation and After', p. 61.

Exchange and a petition drawn up and forwarded to the King.[82] Interesting is the fact that several of the merchants who were to become compensation agents, have been encountered earlier as slave mortgagees.

As early as February 1835, two English merchant firms began advertising as intermediaries for the compensation money. J.B. Ebden announced that he would accept compensation claims as payment at an auction of Saxon and merino sheep, newly imported from Sydney, New South Wales. Heideman, Carfrae and Co. announced they would accept transfer of compensation claims in payment for their assortment of merchandise. And in January 1836 the same firm offered its services and those of its London office in receiving sums due from compensation, as agents by power of attorney. They stated they would also purchase claims on reasonable terms and offered in exchange manufactured goods.[83] Thus, side by side with Heideman, Carfrae and Co. of Cape Town ran the connected London firm of Carfrae, Heideman and Co.[84]

A London connection characterized many of the Cape Town merchant houses handling the claims. The first bank at the Cape began operations only in August 1837[85] and this belated appearance must have contributed to commerce gaining the agency of claimants. A further advantage to collecting the money in London was the opportunity it afforded merchants to make payments in London for goods purchased there, the problem of remittance being a perennial one.[86] London merchants with Cape Town links were typically members of the Cape of Good Hope Trade Society. A look at the surviving Power of Attorney Registry Book (1836–7) amongst the records of the Cape Town Slave Compensation Office,[87] reveals the frequent presence of such dual-connected (that is Cape Town/London) merchant houses.

Simpson Brothers, Maynard and Blackburn, Venning, Busk and Co., Hudson, Donaldson and Dixon, Ewan Christian, Borradailes, Thompson and Pillans, Thomson and Watson, and several others are mentioned frequently in the Power of Attorney Registry Book.[88] Their overseas connection is clearly evidenced in the campaigns of their London partners on matters such as the formation of a new bank in Cape Town, slave compensation money and frontier compensation to Albany residents.[89]

82 ZA, 23 Aug. 1835.

83 SACA, 21 Feb. 1835 and 20 Jan. 1836.

84 CCGHGG, 11 Mar. 1836.

85 Arndt, Banking and Currency Development, p. 236.

86 Arkin, Storm in a Teacup, p. 129; R.B. Fisher, The Importance of the Cape of Good Hope as a Colony to Great Britain (London, 1816), pp. 46–7.

87 CA, SO 20/59, 'Power of Attorney Registry Book', 1836–7.

88 Meltzer, 'The Growth of Cape Town Commerce', pp. 65–7.

89 Ibid.; SACA, 22 Nov. 1834; 11 Mar. 1835 and 11 June 1836.

However, the most frequently mentioned triad appointed by power of attorney is that of Silvanus Phillips, John King and Charles Phillips, partners of the London firm Phillips, King & Co. which was to play a major role in the early development of Namaqualand's copper mining.[90]

Thus the advantage fell to the London-connected Cape merchants who (as the able French Consul to the Cape, Monsieur E. Blancheton, noted in an exhibition pamphlet in 1855), often enjoyed the facility of world-wide correspondents.[91] The scope of London-based merchant involvement in the exercise was thus much wider than indicated by Hengherr. In this period the role of the corresponding firm and the world-wide multi-branch commercial house, the latter a unique feature of British colonialism, was crucial.[92]

The activities of compensation agents took three forms: agency, purchase, and exchange. The already-mentioned advertisement of Heideman, Carfrae & Co. offered all three types of service. Hengherr has stated that though the sums handled by the firms as agents were very large, most of the colonists obtained their compensation money by selling their claims for cash. This was a less favourable method for claimants because of the heavy discounts demanded, but was often unavoidable because of more immediate financial pressures.[93] A study of the Power of Attorney Registry Book reveals some 2,870 entries. Bearing in mind that the Book covers 1836–7 only, but that this period is probably the one during which most of the agency arrangements were made, it can be calculated that between 45 per cent and 59 per cent of the approximately 4,880 to 6,400 awards made were handled by power of attorney—45 per cent if 6,400 and 59 per cent if 4,880.[94]

---

90   J.N. Smalberger, *Aspects of the History of Copper Mining in Namaqualand* (Cape Town, 1975), esp. p. 49, n. 10, for mention of partners; Warren, 'Merchants, Municipal Commissioners', p. 246, lists an August John Phillip, and the *Almanac*, 1838, mentions a John King, merchant; South African Library, Manuscripts collection, MSB 375, 'Phillips Power of Attorney to John King', in which Silvanus and Charles Phillip give power of attorney to John King, 1838; see Meltzer, 'The Growth of Cape Town Commerce', pp. 103, 105–6.

91   E. Blancheton, *Exposition Universelle Colonie de Bonne Esperance: Vade-Mecum* (Cape Town, 1855), pp. 45–56.

92   Hengherr, 'Emancipation and After', p. 60; P.L. Cottrell, 'Commercial Enterprise', in R.A. Church (ed.), *Dynamics of Victorian Business* (London, 1980), pp. 239–40; for the importance of wool correspondents in London, see Meltzer, 'The Growth of Cape Town Commerce', p. 111. The role of the corresponding firm at the Cape awaits future investigation. The more global context, as sketched by Cottrell, has thus far been neglected by historians of the Cape.

93   Hengherr, 'Emancipation and After', pp. 61–2; *SACA*, 20 Jan. 1836.

94   CA, SO 20/59, 'Power of Attorney Registry Book', 1836–7. According to additions made by the author on the basis of the lists of awards, some 4,880 awards were made, SO 20/47–49, 'Lists of the Awards of the Commissioners of Compensation' 1836–7, 1837–8 and 1838–40. According to Hengherr, 'Emancipation and After', p. 56, some 6,093 claims were at stake, and according to Liebenberg, 'Die Vrystelling van die Slawe', p. 168, some 6,400. The percentage figures, 45 per cent and 59 per cent, representing compensation agency, were calculated on the basis of a possible 6,400 awards and a possible 4,880, respectively.

It is difficult to establish accurately the rate of profit earned by merchant houses in agency and purchase of the compensation awards. In a letter to the editor of the *Advertiser* in October 1835, 'an old emigrant' mentioned the costs involved in obtaining the money as the following: 5 per cent commission for power of attorney in London, another 5 per cent for freight, insurance and so on, while a country person would, in addition, have to employ a town agent at further cost. In 1836 Thomas Sutherland advertised a 2.5 per cent commission fee, as did Hudson, Donaldson & Dixon, while in 1837 Fairbairn mentioned a total fee of 5 per cent for agency.[95] The 5 per cent commission figure is confirmed by the disgruntled slaveowner, Major Parlby, in a letter to the *Advertiser*, in which he presented the detailed account of his agent, Hamilton Ross.[96] In June 1837, Hamilton Ross & Co. advertised that it wished to purchase £300 worth of slave compensation claims. Earlier that year in the *Advertiser*, R.A. Zeederberg, Home, Eager & Co., and J.A. le Sueur jointly advertised that they had received £10,000 on account of the slave compensation fund. In other words, in that period the triad probably received the tidy sum of some £500, giving us an example of the fair-sized cash amounts which must have accrued to agents at this time.[97]

Regarding the outright selling of claims to merchants, Fairbairn wrote in 1837 that he had heard of claims being sold at between a 10 and 20 per cent discount, and later that year he reported claims being sold at 7 per cent discount.[98] Major Parlby protested that slaveowners in outlying rural areas were particularly hard hit by unscrupulous agents travelling the country and interior districts.[99] No doubt the rate of discount varied according to how urgently the slaveowner required ready cash. The offer of credit facilities under power of attorney arrangements, as was done by Ebden and Hudson, Donaldson & Dixon, may have further increased the merchants' profit rate.[100]

Finally, besides activities as agents and purchasers of the slave compensation money, several English merchants are mentioned as owners of slaves in the Lists of Awards of the Commissioners of Compensation. Names such as Hamilton Ross, C.S. Pillans, Ewan Christian, A. Chiappini, J.B. Ebden and G.W. Prince, crop up.[101] Such awards represented compensation to merchants as slaveowners and also perhaps ownership as a result of mortgage

---

95 *SACA*, 28 Oct. 1835; 25 June 1836; CCGHGG, 23 Dec. 1836; *SACA*, 11 Oct. 1837.

96 *SACA*, 29 May 1839; see *ZA*, 24 Mar. 1837 for same percentage.

97 CCGHGG, 9 June 1837; *SACA*, 25 Feb. 1837.

98 *Ibid.*, 11 Mar. and 19 July 1837.

99 *Ibid.*, 29 May 1839; for another contemporary criticism of agency activities, see 'A Traveller', *The Cape of Good Hope: A Review of its Present Position as a Colony: Information Which May be of Advantage to the Intending Settler* (Glasgow, 1844), p. vii.

100 *SACA*, 10 Feb. 1836; CCGHGG, 23 Dec. 1836; Hengherr, 'Emancipation and After', p. 61.

101 CA, SO 20/47, claim 5676, 5219, 5544, 5552, 5561, 6192 and SO 20/49, claim 6105A.

transactions. It is clear that through both agency and actual awards, English merchants emerged from the compensation period with substantial increases in liquid wealth.

ABOLITION, COMPENSATION & NEW LAYERS OF THE COMMERCIAL BOURGEOISIE

What were the effects of emancipation and slave compensation money on the non-London connected layers of the commercial bourgeoisie? Abolition and the consequent influx of money resulted in a general boost to commerce, a stimulus to the development of new layers of the commercial bourgeoisie and the spread and diversification of commercial power, which challenged the monopoly of trade enjoyed by the established British-connected Cape Town merchants. Such consequences will account partly for the arrival on the scene of a more locally-based, increasingly vocal, commercial bourgeoisie, whom Kirk and Warren have characterized as being typical membership material of the Cape Town municipality (established in 1840).[102]

In September 1831, Fairbairn took up discussion of the need for the production of exportable goods, agitating for increased local production and appearing to persuade merchants to integrate more fully into the local bourgeoisie, on the basis of local production. He stated:

> The offspring of merchants and traders, the enterprising and ingenious capitalists of this colony, seem to have directed their attention too exclusively to trade. Wealth, after which all aspire, appeared more within their reach when engaged in the rapid movements of buying and selling, than when chained to a plough or waiting the slow increase of herds and flocks. This was natural for men who still looked to a retreat in their native country as the final object of their colonial labors and speculations. *But the present generation is in very different circumstances. This colony is their birth-place, their home, and here they must lay their bones.* [My emphasis.] They must and will of course devote themselves entirely to its improvement—to rendering it a fruitful sphere for every species of industry, and a fit abode for *free men.* [Fairbairn's emphasis.][103]

Fairbairn is here clearly emerging as spokesman for a more locally-based bourgeoisie.

The conflict between the merchant sector and representatives of more locally-based commerce existed from an early date. Arkin has indicated that on the closure of the East India Company Agency in 1834 and the consequent need to dispose of the Agency's stocks, a group of shopkeepers with

---

102 T.E. Kirk, 'Self-Government and Self-Defence in South Africa: The Inter-Relations Between British and Cape Politics 1846–54' (D.Phil. thesis, Oxford University, 1972), p. 142; Warren, 'Merchants, Municipal Commissioners', esp. 45 ff.

103 *SACA,* 28 Sept. 1831.

mainly Dutch names, appealed to the Company's Agent, Hawkins, not to allow tea to fall into the hands of a group of larger, established merchants.[104] Evident in correspondence to the editors of the *Zuid-Afrikaan* and the *Advertiser*, was the anti-merchant position of the *Zuid-Afrikaan*. It played host to the idea that the interests of British-connected merchants conflicted with those of local shopkeepers, reasoning which coincided with its politicking in the interests of the Dutch/Afrikaans propertied element in general.[105]

Though the abolition of slavery and the arrival of the slave compensation money were not the sole causes of the growth and diversification of the commercial bourgeoisie, the two contributed in various significant ways to its expansion.

Abolition prompted an extension of commodity relations in the town and countryside. Slaves in the towns and on the farms were the artisans, craftspeople and the working class. Emancipation and the final freeing of the apprentices in 1838, therefore, must have stimulated consumer demand from a newly-created class of wage earners and an enlarged artisan class. The boom in property in the poor areas of Cape Town in this period, which will be dealt with later, is evidence of the new presence of wage earners and artisans. Similarly, the rise in the number of brickfields is also indirect proof of the increased numbers of urban wage earners. While no direct evidence of the effect of freed slaves on consumption has been gathered, Worden's study of slavery in the Dutch period has given an earlier indication of the role of slave consumer demand. He quotes the example of a Stellenbosch miller who complained about the loss of trade experienced during the 'slave mortality crisis' of the 1740s and subsequently reported a stimulus to corn production as a result of an increase in the slave population during the 1770s.[106]

Slaveowners occupied a variety of professions and hence slave labour was distributed throughout the economy. While farmers employed the majority of slaves, recent research has highlighted the considerable numbers employed in the urban area, particularly in the manufacturing and service sectors. Slaves worked in the docks, shops, warehouses, as coachmen, porters, domestic labourers, in ale houses, bakeries, butcher shops and as masons, bricklayers, blacksmiths, carpenters and tailors.[107] Evidence points to the considerable variety of functions slaves were forced to carry out. These may not have been their primary functions and would not normally

---

104 Arkin, *Storm in a Teacup*, p. 116.

105 *ZA*, 19 Dec. 1834, correspondent 'Shopkeepers', taken up in *SACA*, 27 Dec. 1834, by 'A Subscriber', reflecting this conflict; for reflection of tensions between merchant and shopkeeper, see Meltzer, 'The Growth of Cape Town Commerce', p. 59 and p. 192, n. 99.

106 N. Worden, *Slavery in Dutch South Africa* (Cambridge, 1985), p. 84.

107 Shell, 'Slavery at the Cape of Good Hope', pp. 198–208; Worden, *Slavery in Dutch South Africa*, pp. 36–9.

show up in records. A small example is found in the *Memoriaal*, kept by Joachim Nicolaas von Dessin, a member of Cape Town's most select urban gentry. Entries during the 1750s noted how he had put his slaves to work to knit stockings and make caps and shirts.[108] Shell made a similar point:

> The major manufacturing categories of slaves do not encompass all slaves used in a manufacturing capacity throughout the colony. The transfers of slaves to the large plantations do not disclose which slaves did what. The estate inventories which list all farm equipment, down to the butter churns in the pantry, reveal that many of the wealthy plantation owners specialized in manufacturing sidelines, investing their capital laterally in building, transport and handicrafts.[109]

Maclear attested to these same circumstances in 1834:

> The expense of erecting any building here is enormous, excepting among Dutch farmers—who employ their slaves and purchase timber and lime. Each farmer has among his slaves a butcher, baker, shoemaker, stonemason, carpenter etc., and is thus independent of regular tradesmen. Society thence has no link in the grades of farmer and tradesman, nothing of that self-interest from material dependence that cements these classes in England. An Englishman at the Cape by not possessing slaves has recourse to regular artizans [sic] who make a market of him because he cannot do without them. When time shall have further increased the population and the emancipation of the slaves shall have severed them from their former masters, an assimilation to the English system, must be the consequence.[110]

Farmers and townsmen were therefore equipped with a variety of multi-purpose labour to provide them with a miscellany of commodities and a means to satisfy diverse service needs. On abolition, they lost a permanent supply of labour and consequently were forced to rely on the market for the satisfaction of wants such as shoes, furniture, clothing and house-building. Presumably then, abolition in this respect also provided a stimulus to markets and the extension of commodity relations, particularly in the countryside, where there had previously been a much greater degree of self-sufficiency.

Abolition improved the opportunities for the expansion of the locally-based commercial bourgeoisie in a third way. Warren has pointed out that many of the municipal commissioners became extensive owners of urban property, particularly in the poorer areas of Cape Town. He recounts that by the second quarter of the nineteenth century a number of these commissioners had become landlords of rows of cheap houses in the densely-populated 'steegs' (narrow lanes) and streets of Cape Town. The Waterfront, Constitution Hill and Lion's Rump, were three particular areas dominated by

---

108 Franken, ''n Kaapse Huishoue in die 18de Eeu', p. 66.

109 Shell, 'Slavery at the Cape of Good Hope', p. 206.

110 B. and N. Warner, *Maclear and Herschel: Letters and Diaries at the Cape of Good Hope 1834–8* (Cape Town, 1984), pp. 35–6.

such men. Their names featured prominently on the urban landscape: Jarvis's Building, Mechau's Buildings, Watermeyer Lane and Pentz Street. By 1865, for instance, one man, J.A.H. Wicht, owned no fewer than 374 houses, housing some 4,000 tenants.[111]

By the late 1830s and 1840s these three areas contained significant sections of poor housing for workers and tradesmen. 'The Waterfront area (Districts One and Two), embracing the portion of the town on the shore side of Strand Street, contained a substantial fishing and labouring population, and a smaller group of artisans and tradesmen... Many of the habitations, especially in the "rear" of Strand Street (where there was a row of "steegs") were dirty, overcrowded "hire houses", while the drains were "filled with putrid masses of filth" and the neighbourhood stank of dying fish.'[112] According to Warren, the Lion's Rump area (Districts Four, Six, Seven and Eight), the portion of Cape Town on the Signal Hill side of the Buitengracht and on the Table Mountain side of Wale Street, contained a high concentration of artisans, craftsmen, domestics and labourers. A 'Malay Quarter' was already emerging there.[113] The Constitution Hill area (District Twelve) behind the Castle, likewise, contained a sizeable 'coloured' population of workers and artisans. 'The growth of the Constitution Hill area (the heart of future District Six) during the mid-century period was phenomenal.'[114]

In the late 1830s many of the tenants in these poor areas were newly-freed slaves or apprentices. Most privately-owned slaves in Cape Town had slept in the attic, kitchen or outhouses of the master's house. Even in the rural areas only large farms included separate slave quarters. Thus, according to Ross, 'emancipation led to a definite shift within the spatial arrangements of the town. Once they were fully free in 1838, the slaves were no longer prepared to live on their ex-master's premises. The memory of slavery was too fresh, so they moved out into the slums, alongside their friends and kin who had been free before 1838. They were joined by a large number of ex-slaves who had moved into Cape Town from the countryside, so that overcrowding became worse.'[115] In other words, the growing wealth of these local property-owning capitalists at this time can be seen as arising out of emancipation, based on a new form of exploitation of the former slaves, now in their capacities as tenants, workers and artisans, and intensified by conditions in the period which witnessed a property boom.

---

111 Warren, 'Merchants, Municipal Commissioners', pp. 65–6, 253, appendix F.

112 *Ibid.*, pp. 31–2.

113 *Ibid.*, p. 34.

114 *Ibid.*, p. 36.

115 Worden, *Slavery in Dutch South Africa*, pp. 92–3; R.J. Ross, 'Cape Town 1750–1850: Synthesis in the Dialectic of Continents', in R.J. Ross and G.J. Telkamp (eds.), *Colonial Cities* (Dordrecht, 1985), p. 116; see also S. Judges, 'Poverty, Living Conditions and Social Relations: Aspects of Life in Cape Town in the 1830s' (MA thesis, University of Cape Town, 1977), pp. 77, 80.

It was not only the effect of abolition on increased commercialization and property ownership which favoured the fortunes of locally-based commerce. Actual compensation payment proved as beneficial to the local commercial bourgeoisie, as it had to the British-connected merchant sector. Although the preponderance of merchants listed as slave-compensation agents in the Power of Attorney Registry Book is English,[116] several Dutch/Afrikaans names do occur. In fact, one of the most frequent, second perhaps to the English Phillips & King, is a triad formed by R. Zeederberg, J.A. le Sueur and Robert Eager.[117] Other Dutch/Afrikaans agents included Johannes Smuts, Servaas de Kock and J.H. Hofmeyr.[118]

There were also a significant number of wine merchants and various traders who, like their English counterparts, were awarded substantial compensation for slaves once owned by them or mortgaged to them. Such men, including J.A.H. Wicht, Andries Brink, P.M. Brink, J.A. Bam and G.E. Overbeek. J.J.L. Smuts, received particularly large amounts.[119] Finally, Rayner has stressed the patterns of intermarriage amongst Cape-Dutch families evident in the early nineteenth century, particularly among farmers and officials. She has attributed this to 'the partible Roman-Dutch inheritance law requiring the distribution of property amongst all the children, whether male or female, at the death of one or other of the parents'. Marriage alliances, she postulates, 'helped consolidate valuable property within the hands of a small number of families'.[120] Because of this family network, some former slaveowners may have been ready to provide cash from their newly-acquired stocks for family members to start off businesses in the town and country.

Together, all these factors contributed to the burgeoning of a local commercial bourgeoisie, evident most vividly in the great increase of Dutch/Afrikaans businessmen and their increasing presence in companies in the years around 1838. The names of men discussed above in connection with the compensation money, thus recur in the section dealing with com-pany expansion. In other words, as Hengherr has remarked: 'Because compensation had brought relatively small amounts of money into the hands of many people, rather than very large sums among only a few capitalists, a type of establishment was needed which would provide small holders with an outlet for their money on a more

---

116 CA, SO 20/59.

117 R.F.H. Immelman, *Men of Good Hope: The Romantic Story of the Cape Town Chamber of Commerce 1804–1954* (Cape Town, 1955), p. 59, for a reference to a P. Home at the 1825 Cape of Good Hope Trade Society meeting.

118 *SACA*, 25 June 1836; J.H. Hofmeyr was an advocate and notary, see *Almanac*, 1839; see advert *ZA*, 9 Dec. 1836.

119 CA, SO 20/47, claim 5953; 5759; 6343, 6404; 5765, 5754; 6190; 6555, 5390, 4786, 4086; *Almanac*, 1838; for the doubtful possibility of this being another Petrus Michiel Brink, see De Villiers and Pama, *Geslagsregisters*, deel 1, pp. 102–4.

120 Rayner, 'Wine and Slaves', p. 101; also pp. 95–102.

profitable basis than merely banking it.' This was the essential explanation for the growth of Dutch/Afrikaans-speaking capitalists in joint-stock companies in Cape Town after 1838, something on which Warren had remarked without offering an explanation.[121] Emancipation and the money that came into the Cape in the form of compensation gave an injection to the economy which, as has been shown, stimu-lated a great spending spree, enriching old and new layers of the commercial bourgeoisie and giving a boost to property selling and speculation. It is against this background that the commercial bourgeoisie both expanded and diversified in the years before 1840.

ABOLITION, COMPENSATION & COMPANY FORMATION

In July 1837, Fairbairn reported that most of the compensation had reached Cape Town.[122] Until that point, Cape Town (that is the Cape) had very few companies. The 1837 *Almanac* listed six companies: South African Fire and Life Assurance Company (established 1831); Cape of Good Hope Savings Bank (established by law 1831); South African Association for the Administration and Settlement of Estates (1834, ratified by law 1836); Cape of Good Hope Fire Assurance Company (established December 1835); Cape of Good Hope Steam Navigation Company (established 1836); and the Cape of Good Hope Bank (1836/7). The 1838 *Almanac* added the Committee of the Cape Town Joint Stock Company, while the 1839 *Almanac* indicated the formation during the course of 1838 of five new companies, namely: South African Bank (1838); Cape of Good Hope Marine Assurance Society (1838); De Protecteur Fire and Life Assurance Company (1838); Board of Executors (1838), and the Rondebosch Joint Stock Company (1838). Omitted was the Commercial Wharf Company (previously the Shipping and Landing Company), whose formation was reported in the *Advertiser* towards the end of 1838.[123] In the course of 1838, therefore, six companies were formed, doubling the number in existence.

The relationship between the accelerated growth of companies in 1838 and the arrival of the compensation money during 1837 and 1838 was not coincidental. Certainly, both the editor of the *Advertiser* and the commercial community were aware of the correlation. Considerable excitement was aroused by the increase in the commercial tempo, evident in the formation of these several companies.

In July 1838, G.W. Silberbauer announced the start of his publication, *Price-Current,* which included amongst its commercial information dividends of the

---

121 Hengherr, 'Emancipation and After', p. 68; Warren, 'Merchants, Municipal Commissioners', p. 47.

122 *SACA*, 19 July 1837.

123 *Almanac*, 1837–9; *SACA*, 25 Aug., 29 Aug., 19 Sept., 17 Nov. 1838.

joint-stock companies. Shares were advertised for sale by private brokers such as the same Silberbauer, or by public auction. A letter to the editor of the *Advertiser* in September 1838 remarked that Cape Town had become a vast stock exchange.[124] Cape Town was, undoubtedly, running a high commercial fever, despite the fact that considerably less than £1,000,000 in compensation had arrived.

Interestingly, of the six companies formed during 1838, three (South African Bank, De Protecteur and the Board of Executors) were dominated by Dutch/Afrikaans-speaking shareholders.[125] Previously the only one to have had primarily Dutch/Afrikaans names was the South African Association for the Administration and Settlement of Estates, which was formed in 1834 to fill the gap of the long-standing, but recently disbanded, Orphan Chamber.[126] Other companies, in which a limited number of such businessmen gained experience, were the South African Fire & Life Assurance Company in which F.S. Watermeyer, F.G. Watermeyer and S. Oliver featured and the Cape of Good Hope Savings Bank, in which J.J.L. Smuts and F.S. Watermeyer were mentioned.[127]

The link between emancipation, compensation money and the increasing presence of Dutch/Afrikaans-speaking capitalists was reflected in the appearance, during 1838, of a new layer of shareholders in companies such as the South African Bank, De Protecteur and the Board of Executors. There was, in turn, a connection between these new shareholders and the Cape Town municipality.

Wine merchants, corn chandlers, linen drapers and ironmongers who had received compensation money became shareholders in one or more of the three new companies. They included Andries Brink, P.M. Brink, J.A. Bam, J.A.H. Wicht and J.H. Wicht. Servaas de Kock and the advocate/notary J.H. Hofmeyr were important compensation agents who similarly became active in the new companies.[128]

Brink, Bam and the Wichts in turn became leading members of the newly-established Cape Town municipality, as did F.S. Watermeyer, a compensation claimant and Chairman of the South African Bank.[129] Even those municipal

---

124 *SACA*, 6 Aug. 1838, 11 July 1838, 30 May 1838 and 17 June 1837, 12 Sept. 1838.

125 *Almanac*, 1839.

126 This was the forerunner of Syfrets. It had been formed in 1834 to fill the gap of the long-standing but recently disbanded Orphan Chamber. A couple of ex-Orphan Chamber members, such as the already-mentioned G.E. Overbeek and J.J.L. Smuts became shareholders in the SAAA & SE—see unsorted archival papers, South African Association for the Admininistration and Settlement of Estates, housed in the University of Cape Town Archives, for full lists of members. Like wine merchanting, the Orphan Chamber may have been an early, important avenue of business experience for the local bourgeoisie. A study of this key institution of Dutch rule at the Cape still needs to be made.

127 *Almanac*, 1833 and 1834.

128 CA, SO 20/47, claim 5720; *Almanac*, 1838.

men who did not become company shareholders received compensation awards which increased their liquid assets and improved their business status.[130]

The events of emancipation, therefore, can be seen as an important facet in the expansion of the local commercial bourgeoisie who formed a significant power base of the municipality. The municipality was, in turn, exploited by them as a stepping stone for further expansion.

In 1838 Fairbairn remarked on the difference between Cape Town company shareholders before and after 1838. He contrasted the capital of the men of the South African Bank (1838), which consisted of money and property, with that of the Cape of Good Hope Bank (1836), which was composed of merchant capital and what he termed 'merchant skills'.[131] Despite the fact that some of these later company shareholders were wine merchants, Fairbairn did not characterize their wealth as merchant-derived but rather as capital accrued via property and money. He was thereby pointing to a *nouveau riche* layer of the commercial bourgeoisie which had not risen to a position of strength via established merchant channels. Fairbairn's distinction can best be understood in terms of the argument that property acquisition as a result of abolition and the compensation money, contributed significantly to the growth of these new shareholders and companies.

Initially, the group consisting of the South African Bank, De Protecteur and the Board of Executors aimed much of their advertising at agricultural landowners. On 1 September 1838, the South African Bank notified the public that it would be opening early in the morning in order to please the 'agricultural interest', who arrived for the morning market. Apparently, the South African Bank and the Board had shared offices for some time, pointing perhaps to some kind of collaboration.[132] Country agents were a regular feature of a company such as De Protecteur, for example, which almost immediately on establishment began advertising its agents in Malmesbury, Koeberg, Tygerberg, Stellenbosch and George.[133] The rural connection of certain companies in Cape Town was a distinguishing characteristic. In fact, the links of these new shareholders to rural landowners may be regarded as an important facet in the make-up of at least some members of the new commercial bourgeoisie and, in turn, of members of the municipality. This relatively closer link with the farmers is a feature which could distinguish the interests of the more locally-based commercial bourgeoisie from the merchant sector.[134]

---

129 CA, SO 20/47, Watermeyer—claim 6450, £289 16s. 3d. and 6484, £350 5s. 2d., and Hofmeyr, 4808, £40 19s. 5d.; Warren, 'Merchants, Municipal Commissioners', pp. 255–8, appendix H.

130 Names such as H.C. Jarvis, E. Landsberg, C.F. Juritz and J.J.L. Smuts occur, see CA, SO 20/47; Warren, 'Merchants, Municipal Commissioners', pp. 255–8, appendix H; *Almanac*, 1839.

131 *SACA*, 8 Aug. 1838.

132 *Ibid.*, 1 Sept. 1838 and 31 Aug. 1839.

133 *Ibid.*, 17 Oct. 1838.

134 See *ibid.*, 26 Oct. 1839, a letter from 'An Enquirer', describing a link between the Dutch and South

CONCLUSION

By the first quarter of 1839 the boom effects of the compensation money were already vanishing[135] and a great deal of the money eventually found its way back into the coffers of London export merchants and English manufacturers. Abolition and the compensation money set a changed tempo in commercial life, engendered a new confidence in the commercial class, presenting new experiences and creating fresh opportunities for business at the Cape. The boom in the wake of emancipation seems largely to have been the result of a chain reaction within the economy, set in motion as a result of the freeing of labour. As the Genoveses have stated in relation to the American South:

> The South had a plantation economy embedded in a world market, but it also had a huge subsistence sector that severely circumscribed the penetration of market relations into the regional economy as a whole. The South, in other words, may be said to have had a market economy only in a very restricted sense. And it did not have a market society. At the roots of the restrictions on a regional market economy and of the absence of a market society lay the absence of a market in labor power.[136]

It is interesting in this regard that it was in the eastern Cape, where slave relations of production were outlawed and pre-capitalist forms of production not entrenched, that capitalist agriculture first took off on a large scale.

The radical changes set in motion after the 1870s' mineral discoveries should not, therefore, obscure the fact that substantial capitalist advance, albeit only in colonial terms, had been made in the preceding period. This was chiefly the result of eastern Cape merino wool farming, but with important commercial gains having been made in the wake of slave emancipation. The developing maturity of local agriculture and a locally-based commerce found its reflection in the determined moves for self-government by these groups after 1848.[137]

A 'waveless calm, that slumber of the dead' was how Fairbairn had described life in Cape Town during the 1820s.[138] By the time he retired as editor of the *Advertiser* in 1859 though, the sleepy hollow had undergone a substantial transformation for which, in part, credit is due to him. His continual editorial intervention had played a key part in propelling, guiding and advising Cape Town's inhabitants through the unprecedented commercial growth that started with the period of slave emancipation.

African Bank vs English merchants and their banks.
135 *SACA*, 30 Mar. 1839, 2 and 9 Nov. 1839.
136 Fox-Genovese and Genovese, *Fruits of Merchant Capital*, p. 17.
137 Meltzer, 'The Growth of Cape Town Commerce', esp. ch. 3–4.
138 *SACA*, 4 Nov. 1835.

Plate 9 Genadendal Mission Station, 1847, by George Angas. *South African Library*.

PRIVATE & PUBLIC WORLDS OF EMANCIPATION IN THE RURAL WESTERN CAPE, c.1830-1842[1]

– PAMELA SCULLY –

The focus of this chapter is the family, both as 'a place and an idea'.[2] Focusing primarily on the rural districts of Worcester and Swellendam, the chapter looks at the processes of apprenticeship (1834–8) and emancipation from 1838 through the 1840s, and at the choices and values that both apprentices, masters, missionaries, and the colonial state brought to those experiences. I contend that the coincidence of a metropolitan belief in the family as an anchor of class stability, slaves and dependent labourers' concerns with protecting and reinforcing personal relationships, and slaveholders' patriarchal and familial conception of power, helped privilege 'family' as the dominant discourse of emancipation. The struggles and debates about child labour, the family, and marital relationships thus both engendered and resulted from the language within which people articulated their beliefs about the meaning of freedom.

The role of the family as a mode of control during the slaveholding period in the western Cape remains an area of debate, but no one has yet systematically examined the extent to which ideas and practices of gender and family helped shape post-emancipation social and economic relations in the Cape Colony.[3] In general the domestic arrangements and emotional lives of colonial subjects have remained uninterrogated. The family emerges as an important locus around which definitions of freedom were forged in the apprenticeship period. Jeffrey Weeks has suggested that most family studies have made the mistake of seeing the family as a 'discrete historical object, usually a biological reality which society acts upon'.[4] The family is rather a

---

1   This chapter is an early version of ideas developed in my dissertation, 'Liberating the Family? Gender, Labor, and Sexuality in the Rural Western Cape, South Africa, 1823–53' (Ph.D., University of Michigan, 1993). I am grateful to Fred Cooper, Clifton Crais, Sita Ranchod-Nilsson, and members of the Post-Emancipation Seminar at the University of Michigan for help with this chapter.

2   The term is S. Coontz's, see *The Social Origins of Private Life* (London, 1988), p. 14.

3   See R. Shell, 'Slavery at the Cape of Good Hope, 1680–1731', vol. 1 (Ph.D. thesis, Yale University, 1986).

set of choices and relationships which exists in relation to other dictates such as economic context, ideas of personal liberty, and the particular gender systems with which notions of family articulate.[5] I conceptualize the family as a site of struggle, rather than idealizing the family as a haven from, or alternative to, harsh social and economic relations.[6]

The historiographical silence on the subject of family, gender and emancipation is curious, since the emancipation experience was so affected by a metropolitan world-view which perceived the nuclear patriarchal family as a crucial foundation of social stability.[7] Little regard has yet been paid to the significant conjuncture of emancipation and a new and self-conscious metropolitan concern regarding the underclass family. Apprenticeship and emancipation occurred precisely when the evangelical anxiety regarding the effects of industrialization on women and children, and on the family, was at its peak.[8] This was to have significant implications for the dynamic of emancipation in the British Empire. Competing notions of the family thus have much wider implications than a study of people's inner emotional worlds. In the post-emancipation period they were a central element in the reconstruction of colonial society.[9]

An analysis of the rural worlds of Worcester and Swellendam districts reveals some of the ways in which emancipation in the British Empire was premised not only upon particular views of class hierarchy, but also was fundamentally imbricated with ideas about family, gender relations, and a belief in the existence of discrete private and public realms. The post-emancipation period witnessed a significant reformulation of familial and gender relations,

---

4   J. Weeks, *Sex, Politics and Society: The Regulation of Sexuality Since 1800* (London, 1981), p. 26.

5   For a discussion of gender in a colonial context see A. Stoler, 'Carnal Knowledge and Imperial Power: Gender, Race and Morality in Colonial Asia', in M. Di Leonardo (ed.), *Gender and Political Economy: Feminist Anthropology in the Postmodern Era* (Berkeley, 1992), and A. Stoler, 'Rethinking Colonial Categories: European Communities and the Boundaries of Rule', *Comparative Studies in Society and History*, 13, 1 (1989), pp. 134–61.

6   Cf. Shell, 'Slavery at the Cape'.

7   The underpinnings of free labour ideology in the abolitionist movement have begun to be given due attention and we now have a sense of how emancipation in the British Empire emerged out of an ideological tradition dating back to the late eighteenth century, which centered on the abolition of slavery and the construction of the wage labouring individual. See D.B. Davis, *The Problem of Slavery in the Age of Revolution: 1770–1823* (Ithaca, 1975) for a discussion of the implicit assumptions in abolitionist ideology regarding the 'duty' of the lower classes to engage in regular wage labour. See also R. Blackburn, *The Ending of Colonial Slavery* (London, 1988), ch. 1, for a discussion of the genealogy of anti-slavery thought. And D.B. Davis, *The Problem of Slavery in Western Culture* (Ithaca, 1966). Also F. Cooper, *From Slaves to Squatters* (New Haven, 1980) for discussion relating to Africa. Also see the debate regarding the relationship between capitalism and the humanitarian sentiment: T. Haskell, 'Capitalism and the Origins of the Humanitarian Sensibility, Part 1, *American Historical Review*, 90 (1985), pp. 339–61; Part 2, *American Historical Review*, 90 (1985), pp. 547–66; and the critiques by D.B Davis and J. Ashworth, and Haskell's response in *American Historical Review*, 92 (1987), pp. 797–878.

8   Weeks, *Sex*, p. 57.

9   See Scully, 'Liberating the Family?', intro. and ch. 2; also P. Scully, 'Gender, Emancipation, and Free Wage Labor Ideology', (paper presented to the Eighth Annual Graduate Women's Studies Conference, Ann Arbor, Michigan, 7–8 Mar. 1991).

most clearly seen at the discursive level, but also unfolding in daily social practice. Former masters, missionaries, law makers, and freed people all sought to make the family their terrain of domination. In ambiguous ways all succeeded. To some extent freed people saw the independence of their families from farm labour as one of the meanings of freedom, while former slaveholders saw control over the family as a crucial means of exercising power in the post-emancipation world. Moravian missionaries—the dominant missionaries in the districts with which this study is concerned—had their own agenda, and sought to make marriage accessible to greater numbers of people while also setting up a strict model of the nuclear patriarchal family on the mission stations. The rest of this chapter will explore how these visions of family played out with the start of apprenticeship period in 1834 and how they were imbricated in the elaboration of other colonial discourses concerning gender and labour.

LANDSCAPES OF EMANCIPATION

In 1806 the British formally took over the Cape from the Dutch who had controlled the Cape of Good Hope almost continuously from 1652. A British occupation at the turn of the nineteenth century had prefaced some of the attitudes to gender and family which the British later began instituting in their new colony.[10] By the mid eighteenth century the indigenous people of the western Cape, the Khoisan pastoralists and hunter-gatherers, had been reduced to dependent status. Slaves were introduced to the colony in the 1650s and by 1834 there were 36,169 slaves in the Cape. They came from diverse origins including Madagascar, Mozambique and the East Indies. By 1833, 53.2 per cent of slaves had been born in the Cape since the ending of the slave trade, and the ratio of men to women was 1.18:1 in 1834. The Worcester and Stellenbosch districts had 14,365, or 39.7 per cent of the slave population, while Swellendam and George had only 5,661 or 15.7 per cent of the total.[11]

The Worcester and Swellendam districts lay within two days horseback ride to Cape Town, the capital of the Cape Colony. At the start of the apprenticeship period in 1834, Worcester still exhibited some of the features of a colonial frontier zone. As in the neighbouring districts to the east, a small and sparse white population involved predominantly in pastoral production ruled over slaves and dependent Khoisan, 'bastards' (the children of

---

10   John Barrow travelled the colony during the First British Occupation and left eloquent testimony both to British attitudes at the time, as well as chronicles of Dutch and Khoi social life. See particularly, J. Barrow, *Travels into the Interior of Southern Africa in the Years 1797 and 1798*, vol. 1, 1st reprint edn. (New York, 1968).

11   J.C. Armstrong and N.A. Worden, 'The Slaves, 1652–1834' in R. Elphick and H. Giliomee (eds.), *The Shaping of South African Society, 1652–1840*, 2nd edn. (Cape Town, 1989), pp. 109–62, 109, 121, 133.

slave/slaveholder, or Khoi/slaveholder unions), and 'bastard hottentots' (the offspring of Khoikhoi and slaves) with relatively little intervention from the state. The free population of Worcester in 1832 was 5,198 (including whites, Khoikhoi and Bastard Hottentots), while slaves numbered 2,770.[12] Population density was highest near the village of Worcester. In 1832, 136 owners lived within 20 miles of Worcester village and owned 1,005 slaves. The field cornetcies (administrative units) in the interior of the district had smaller populations and lower ratios of slaves to slaveowners. In one field cornetcy in the Middle Roggeveld, for example, there were 21 managers or owners and 81 slaves.[13]

Swellendam, a large district bordering on Stellenbosch with a coastal boundary on the Atlantic Ocean, embodied both the characteristics of the frontier and of the more settled areas of the western Cape. In the northern areas pastoral farming predominated, while in the south-west region around Caledon village, wheat farming was primary, particularly after the decline of wine exports in the 1820s. Swellendam had very few slaves, with the majority owned by the wheat farmers near Caledon village in the west. Both slave and dependent labour was used and these labourers seem to have shared a common experience of exploitation vis-à-vis the settlers.[14] Moravian mission stations had long dominated the southern half of Swellendam, particularly around Caledon. The Moravian Church, or United Brethren, was a Calvinist church of German origins. The Moravians were the first missionaries at the Cape, their first station being established, for a short period, in 1738.[15] After the visit of Latrobe in 1816, the Society underwent a renaissance which lasted till 1840 with the death of Superintendent Hallbeck.[16] These missions were originally intended to minister to the Khoisan population but the stations of Genadendal and Elim played a significant role in Caledon's post-emancipation world as many apprentices and freed people moved onto the missions looking for land.

FARM AND FAMILY

Social boundaries in the rural western Cape were produced and reproduced in part through a discourse on the family: these boundaries were inherently

---

12   *South African Almanack and Directory for 1832* (Cape Town, 1832), p. 154.

13   Cape Archives (CA), CO 2737, no. 81, 4 Sept. 1832, Letter from P. Poggenpoel, Assistant Protector of Slaves, Worcester.

14   Some instances of intermarriage between freed slaves and settlers occurred, but this does not necessarily undermine an awareness of exploitation. See P. Scully, 'Liberating the Family? Gender, Labor and Sexuality in the Rural Western Cape, South Africa, 1823–53' (Ph.D. thesis, University of Michigan, 1993), for discussion of this point.

15   B. Kruger, *The Pear Tree Blossoms: A History of the Moravian Mission Stations in South Africa, 1837–69* (Genadendal, 1966), p. 19.

16   J.W. Raum, 'The Development of the Coloured Community at Genadendal Under the Influence of the

ambiguous and frequently contradictory. Dutch slaveholders represented the farm as a single household which joined slaves and slaveholders in one field of authority. The household and family were seen as synonymous: Boers did not automatically conceptualize family in nuclear terms.[17] In practice, various nuclear and extended families coexisted enjoying different degrees of slaveholder recognition. Families defined by genetic relationship frequently straddled the perimeters of a number of more clearly socially-constituted families: for example, a child of a slave mother and slaveholder father fell within the social boundary of the slave/Khoi family even while being a half-sibling to the master's acknowledged children. The slaveholder might see the household of the farm as his family, but this did not mean that all members of the household were defined as kin.

For most of the slaveholding period the law, and slaveholders, did not accord recognition to the slave nuclear family: parents and children were sold separately and, up to the 1820s, slave marriages were not legally acknowledged. Partly because of the lack of state concern with slaves' emotional ties, the records on slaves' intimate lives are very scarce prior to the 1820s. 'Among an unknown, but certainly not negligible proportion of slaves, long-lasting, monogamous relationships formed both the ideal and the general practice.'[18] Nigel Worden has argued that, during the VOC period, where two-parent slave households did exist the role of the father was very weak.[19] Indeed the matrilocal family was the most common slave family formation.[20] Certainly, by the time slavery was coming to an end, stable relationships between slaves, and between slaves and nominally free labourers were evident, and in the early 1840s many freed people went to the churches asking to be legally married.[21]

In contrast, the Boer family was highly visible both in Boers' self-representation and in the diaries of British travellers.[22] Boer nuclear families were large. John Barrow, who travelled in the Cape in 1797 and 1798, said that 'six to seven children per family is considered very few; from a dozen to twenty are not uncommon'.[23] Boer kinship patterns were commonly

Missionaries of the Unitas Fratrum, 1792–1892' (MA thesis, University of Cape Town, 1953), p. 22.

17   See R. Shell, 'The Family and Slavery at the Cape 1680–1808', in W. James and M. Simons (eds.), *The Angry Divide: Social and Economic History of the Western Cape* (Cape Town, 1989), pp. 20–30.

18   R. Ross, 'Oppression, Sexuality, and Slavery at the Cape of Good Hope', *Historical Reflections*, 6 (1979), pp. 421–33; p. 426.

19   N. Worden, *Slavery in Dutch South Africa* (Cambridge, 1985), p. 258.

20   See P. van der Spuy, 'Slave Women and the Family in Nineteenth-Century Cape Town', in *South African Historical Journal*, 27 (1992), pp. 50–74, for a very helpful discussion of the dominance of the matrilocal family among slave women in Cape Town.

21   See H. Gutman's *The Black Family in Slavery and Freedom, 1750–1925* (New York, 1977), ch. 1 for a discussion of the slave family in the US South. Gutman argues that slaves had a far richer, and more stable family life than historians had previously believed.

22   Barrow, *Travels*, vol 1.

23   Barrow, *Travels*, p. 81; also see G. Botha, *Collected Works. General History and Social Life at the Cape*

virilocal—brothers, uncles, fathers, and sons and their wives lived together on the same farm. Boers thus recognized the slaveholder family as a complex whole incorporating many degrees of kin relations—a strong contrast to the lack of recognition accorded to the nuclear slave family. Under Roman-Dutch law children of both sexes inherited equally—Barrow argued that this meant that children were less 'subject to the caprice of parents than elsewhere' and that, unlike in England, the first-born son was not necessarily favoured over other children in the family.[24] Roman-Dutch law gave women of wealthy families considerable economic power owing to the equitable inheritance system and marriage was thus an important component of economic planning: it occupied a dominant place in the legal, social and economic life of Dutch farmers.

The farm was organized along interconnecting and referential hierarchies of class, gender, and different forms of social status. Unmarried women were more likely to help with farm work than their married peers, and poorer Boer families were also more likely to depend on women's labour.[25] Our knowledge of Boer women's lives in the outlying districts is gleaned mostly from British travellers' accounts of events at the turn of the nineteenth century, and must be read with care: gender relations were scrutinized almost as if they were a formula whereby Dutch and indigenous societies could be rated in comparison to British norms. Barrow, for example, sought to represent the Boers as slothful and backward *vis-à-vis* the Khoi, whom he portrayed as 'noble savages', and the British whom he saw as paragons of civilization. Gender functioned as a significant symbolic system through which Barrow harnessed his discussions of civilization. He portrayed married Dutch women as living lives of 'listless inactivity'[26] and argued that Boer women were seen as too delicate even for leisure activities such as horseriding.

Regional variations also played a part in shaping Boer women's lives. Henry Lichtenstein, writing about six years later than Barrow, commented on the distinctions between the genteel lifestyle of women in the families of the western Cape gentry and the more work-oriented life of Boer women living in the more expansive and less-settled regions such as the Roggeveld areas of Worcester. Of the women in Eerste Rivier, in the Stellenbosch district, he stated that compared to Cape Town[27]

of Good Hope, vol. 1 (Cape Town, 1962), p. 131.

24 Barrow, *Travels,* p.77. R. Ross, 'The Development Spiral of the White Family and the Expansion of the Frontier', in Ross, *Beyond the Pale: Essays on the History of Colonial South Africa* (Hanover, London and Johannesburg, 1993), pp. 138–51.

25 R. Ross, 'The Rise of the Cape Gentry', *Journal of Southern African Studies,* 11 (1983), pp. 193–217. My comments on regional differences in white women's work are tentative based on insights gleaned from criminal records for the Circuit Court of Stellenbosch.

26 Barrow, *Travels,* p. 80.

27 H. Lichtenstein, *Travels in Southern Africa, in the Years, 1803, 1804, 1805, and 1806,* 2 vols. (Cape Town, 1928), vol. 1, p. 140.

From living in the country, there reigns…a much greater simplicity and modesty in their whole demeanour. At the same time, they are instructed in every branch of domestic economy necessary for forming good wives; and have, for the most part, an adequate knowledge of African husbandry, without being like the girls of the distant parts, mere peasants; or, as has been especially remarked of those who inhabit the countries where the prevailing occupation is the breeding of cattle, where, consequently they are unaccustomed to any hard work, sinking into habits of sloth and indolence. Here we find them constantly busied, either with household affairs or needle-work; and it is no uncommon sight to see all the women of the house, mother, daughters, and female slaves, collected together in the cool apartment at the back of the house, sewing, knitting, or executing several kinds of fine ornamental works.

On the poorer and more isolated farms, both married and single women worked in the household and, when needed, in agricultural work as well. Dutch farmers did not see this state of affairs as desirable, however. During times of perceived labour shortage in the post-emancipation period, farmers bemoaned the fact that their wives and daughters were having to work on the farm as the final outrage. A memorial from farmers of the Clanwilliam, Worcester and Swellendam districts stated, in the 1850s, that 'from year to year we see our farms retrograde and are inevitably necessitated to employ our sons as labourers and herds and our wives and daughters to perform the meanest field and domestic services.'[28] During slavery, manual labour was perceived by Boers as being ideally the preserve of slaves and dependent labourers. Boers constructed gender rather differently with regard to slave women and men. The farmhouse retained its feminine spatial associations and slave women worked in the house, while men worked in the fields: slave and dependent female labourers, however, were called to the fields in the peak seasons of the agricultural calendar. People on the farm thus occupied discrete subject positions, differentially yet simultaneously aligned along intersecting hierarchical axes such as gender, slave or non-slave status, racial categorization, and religion.[29]

These hierarchies also constituted part of a larger ideological and spatial invention: the patriarchal household of the farm. A patriarchal mythology permeated the Boer representation and practice of master/slave and master/servant relationships, and joined in ambiguous and often contradictory ways all members of the farm.[30] In many respects the boundaries of the farm were synonymous with the boundaries of this definition of the family.

---

28 Cited in Marincowitz, 'Rural Labour', p. 115.

29 This was particularly important on the wine and wheat farms of Stellenbosch and Swellendam. Worden, *Slavery*, p. 238. For comments on settler women, see Barrow, *Travels*, pp. 49, 80, and Botha, *Collected Works*, p. 178: 'the young man, as he grew into manhood, considered himself superior to everyone'.

30 I use the term patriarchy in a feminist sense: the domination of men over women through the legitimation of male superiority over women in a gender hierarchy. I also mean it in the sense of the rule of the father over members of his family. See G. Lerner, *Women and History: The Creation of Patriarchy*, vol. 1

Boer masters represented all members of the farm as children ruled over by the senior male.[31] Boers perceived their farms as territories, or spaces falling within their personal power.[32] For slaveholders, the private sphere was thus coterminous with the boundaries of the farm rather than with the social boundaries of domestic versus civic life which the British were assembling in the course of the nineteenth century. A certain paradox existed in the conceptualization of public/private distinctions. The Boer interfered at will in his slaves' personal lives, but he equally resented the penetration of the British legal order into his domain.

The British introduced a new conceptualization of power to the Cape and sought to put limits on the personal authority of the slaveholding class. Particularly from the 1820s both masters and slaves were brought under the ambit of the rule of law.[33] Power was to flow henceforth from state institutions that were sanctioned by law and that had the authority to regulate punishment. The British sought to put an end to what they saw as an arbitrary exercise of power: that emanating from the individual will of the slave-holder.[34] The slave amelioration measures, apprenticeship, and finally emancipation, were part of this project to reformulate social relations in the furthest reaches of the British Empire as well as in Britain itself.[35] The 1820s witnessed transformations in peoples' emotional and material connections to one another as the Colonial Office increasingly scrutinized previously hegemonic practices regarding labour, space, and authority. The slave amelioration laws, which accorded the slave and slaveholder nuclear families similar recognition, helped to structure the discourse on family which was such a feature of the subsequent period of apprenticeship. The state recognized slave marriages and abolished the separate sale of husband and wife in 1823 while Section 66 of the Order-in-Council of November 1831,

---

(New York, 1986) for a feminist perspective.

31   I have not yet found an indication as to how Boer women as opposed to men might have perceived this family. The rural archival record is overwhelmingly masculine. I hope to investigate this aspect further in my forthcoming research. Shell, 'Slavery', initiated the discussion of the patriarchal family and its relationship to slaveholding at the Cape. He errs, I think, in seeing as fact (the way that Dutch slaveholders spoke about their slaves as children and as being members of the family) what I would argue is rather slaveholders' representation. See C.C. Crais, *White Supremacy and Black Resistance in Pre-Industrial South Africa: The Making of the Colonial Order in the Eastern Cape, 1770–1865* (Cambridge, 1991) for a critique of Shell. For a discussion of paternalism at the Cape see J.E. Mason, 'The Slaves and Their Protectors: Reforming Resistance in a Slave Society, 1826–1834', *Journal of Southern African Studies*, 17 (1991), pp. 104–28; 'Hendrik Albertus and His Ex-Slave Mey: A Drama in Three Acts', *Journal of African History*, 31 (1990), pp. 423–45.

32   Crais, *White Supremacy and Black Resistance*, ch. 3.

33   M. Rayner, 'Wine and Slaves: The Failure of an Export Economy and the Ending of Slavery in the Cape Colony, South Africa, 1806–1834' (Ph.D. thesis, Duke University, 1986).

34   See M. Foucault, *Discipline and Punish: The Birth of the Prison* (New York, 1977) for a discussion of new conceptualizations of power which arose in the eighteenth and nineteenth centuries. For a discussion of Foucault and some of the discursive implications of British rule at the Cape see Crais, *White Supremacy and Black Resistance*.

35   See Davis, *Problem of Slavery*.

'distinctively stated that husbands and wives and parents and children shall not be separ-ated from each other.'[36] Privacy was now accorded to the slave family and slaveholding conceptions of the patriarchal farm household were challenged.

What information we have on how slaves perceived their emotional lives is mostly drawn from this period of amelioration and the cases which came before the Guardian (from 1830, the Protector) of Slaves. This office was established in 1826 with the aim of looking after the interests of slaves and adjudicating in conflict between them and their owners.[37] Many slave complaints to the Assistant Protector coalesced around the issues of personal relationships and the limits of slaveholder power: possibly slaves saw a demarcation between 'private' and 'public' not shared by their masters, but maybe compatible with the rule of law as instituted by the British. The emphasis on issues of family and sexuality might also have reflected the pre-occupation given to these matters in the amelioration legislation.[38]

The extent to which the Protector did defend the interests of slaves remains a matter of debate, but slaves used the space provided by this office to prosecute their masters and many complaints were registered within the discourses of family and sexuality.[39] Saartje, a slave from Worcester district, complained to the Assistant Protector of Slaves that she did not want to return to her owner, stating that 'my mistress wishes me to cohabit with one of her slave boys, and in consequence of my not complying, I have been continually illtreated by her'.[40] In 1828 a free woman, also called Saartje, asked permission to buy a slave Salomon with whom she was 'connected'. She hoped to finance the purchase through money owed to her by Salomon's master for her care of a free child.[41] Two years later, Fortuin ('Fortune') testified how, under a former owner, he had received food that was 'neither enough to let him live, nor to let him die'. The Protector stated 'Fortuin is sickly, and when confined to bed gets no food but what his wife saves from him out of her portion and brings home to him from the field.'[42] These cases suggest that relationships with lovers and family were very important to slaves; they also tell us of the intersection of various boundaries— slave/free—and the creation of shared histories.[43]

---

36 Armstrong and Worden, 'The Slaves', p. 147; CA, 1/WOC, 19/60, 23 July 1835, Special Justice Peake to Nicholas van Wyk of Middle Roggeveld.

37 See Mason, 'The Slaves and their Protectors' for discussion of the office and slave complaints.

38 See Van der Spuy, 'Slave women', p. 56–60, for a discussion of the impact of amelioration legislation on slave marriages in the 1820s.

39 See Rayner, 'Wine and Slaves' for a cynical view, and Mason, 'Hendrik Albertus' for a more positive evaluation.

40 CA, 1/WOC, 19/24, Day Book of the Assistant Protector of Slaves, 8 Oct. 1827.

41 CA, 1/WOC, 19/24, 5 Apr. 1828. See also 1/WOC, 19/24, 29 Nov. 1827; 1 Sept. 1829 etc.

42 CA, 1/WOC, 19/24, 2 Sept. 1830.

43 For discussion of the interconnected worlds of slaves and dependent labourers, see Crais, White Supremacy and Black Resistance, and Scully, 'Liberating the Family?'.

APPRENTICESHIP AND CHILD LABOUR, 1834-8

On 7 January 1834, the Acting Lieutenant-Governor of the Cape Colony sent out a circular in which he outlined the desired responses of masters and slaves to the declaration of apprenticeship: 'Proprietors should distinctly understand that a cheerful acquiescence in the provisions of the law is not only required of them as a positive act of duty, but that their own individual interests…are deeply involved.' From slaves, Wade argued, 'His Majesty is entitled to expect and demand the most tranquil and orderly submission to such laws as shall be framed for their future government, …and they will display their gratitude for the favour they are about to receive by carefully abstaining from any insolence or insubordination towards their masters.'[44]

The apprentices greatly appreciated the significance of apprenticeship, but not in the way that the Acting Lieutenant-Governor would have liked. Apprentices pursued the avenue of prosecution that had been first opened up with the creation of the office of the Guardian of Slaves, but which received greater credibility with the appointment of Special Justices by the Colonial Office.[45] Complaints by apprentices centered on those issues which had been central to their experience as slaves and forced separation from children and spouses was particularly protested.[46] Freed people's desires to unite families, or to maintain existing relationships conflicted with former slaveholders' ambitions to retain some authority over their former slaves. Some farmers responded to the introduction of apprenticeship and the lessening of their bonds of authority over their slaves by deliberately making apprentices' lives more miserable. For example, Jacobus Stoffberg, a farmer at Goudini near Worcester village, attempted to send off his farm a baby still nursing at her mother's breast, while another farmer, Charles de Wet, would not allow his apprentice's husband to come and visit her.[47] The numerous incidents of abuse by farmers of apprentices who had complained to the Special Justices is awful testimony to the hardships which apprentices were prepared to face in order to win respect for their persons and their personal relationships.[48] Most apprentices in Worcester had to travel many hours, if not days in order

---

44   CA, 1/WOC, 11/12, circular from Government House, dated 7 Jan. 1834.

45   These officers were ideally meant to come out from England, although in reality most did not, so as to have a modicum of impartiality when dealing with relations between apprentices and former masters. In the case of the western Cape, these officials seem to have acted with integrity; both Mackay of Worcester and Harry Rivers, Special Justice of Caledon, were embroiled at one time or another in arguments with local village officials and former masters. For detailed examination of the Special Justices and apprenticeship see Worden, ch. 5 in this volume.

46   CA, 1/WOC, 19/60, 16 June 1835, Peake to Jacobus Theron; 24 Oct. 1835, Peake to Charles de Wet, Waterfall; 5 Apr. 1835, Peake to Adriaan Van Wyk, Cold Bokkeveld etc.

47   CA, 1/WOC, 19/60, 16 Feb. 1836, Peake to Stoffberg, Goudini; 24 Oct. 1835, Peake to Charles de Wet, Waterfall.

48   See 1/WOC 19/24 and 19/27 for cases brought before the Assistant Protector of Slaves and the Special Justice, Worcester.

to lodge complaints with the Protector or Special Justice. In the years 1834 to 1838, as the spectre of free labour loomed, the control of apprentice children became a crucial battle site between apprentices and former slaveholders. The various ploys to retain access to labour suggest that farmers had not come to terms with the transformations in power: they perceived a right to the labour of children who had belonged to them a few years previously.

The principal actors in the contest over children were apprentice women, farmers, and the Special Justices. Silent and ignored in much of the nineteenth-century historical archive, women emerge as the spokespeople of the apprentice class in the period 1834 to 1838. The centrality of slave women in the battle over children partly arose out of family dynamics in slavery, but was reinforced by abolition legislation. The legal determination of childrens' status according to that of the mother under slavery had bolstered the maternal relationship and weakened that of the slave father. Abolition legislation strengthened this bias in favour of the mother's legal claim to the children. The Abolition Act of 1833 explicitly charged mothers with responsibility for the welfare of children under six years of age.[49] The Act provided for the indenture of children below the age of six with the consent of the mother, or without her consent if it appeared to the Special Justice that the children were otherwise likely to be destitute.[50] In the three-and-a-half-year period ending in April 1838, for example, 1,464 children were indentured in the western Cape. The majority of children indentured in Worcester in 1836 were infants. Between 1 December 1834 and 30 September 183,697 children under the age of six years were indentured in the Worcester district alone.[51]

The implicit affirmation of mothers' rights over young children provided apprentice women with a powerful ideological weapon against the claims of farmers, and of other freed people, regarding the control of children's labour. Freed people fought for their children in part for economic reasons— children's labour was needed to supplement wages or, in the case of a family owning land, as farm labour. A Khoikhoi woman living in the Swartberg contested the indenture of her son saying that she needed her son's service 'very much', while Eva, a free woman of Swellendam district, petitioned the Governor to order her grandchild to come and live with her, 'chiefly to support me when I am sick'.[52] The child's aunt told the Governor that her

---

49 Mothers were, perhaps, most prominent in these cases because the paternity of the children could be uncertain—this would accord with the sexual abuse of slave women by masters.

50 Indentureship consisted of engaging a child's services to a farmer until the age of 18 years. Indentureship had a long history in the Cape, being used as early as the late eighteenth century to bond Khoi children to farmers. For discussion of this history, see V.C. Malherbe and R. Elphick, 'The Khoisan to 1828', in Elphick and Giliomee, *Shaping*, p. 32. For a comparative angle, see R. Scott, 'The Battle over the Child: Child Apprenticeship and the Freedmen's Bureau in North Carolina', *Prologue* (1978), pp. 101–13. CA, 1/WOC, 19/60, 11 Mar. 1835, Special Justice Peake to Isaac de Vries, Hex River.

51 CA, 1/WOC, 19/60, 11 Oct. 1836, List of Indentures in Worcester District.

52 CA, CO 2799, no. 118, 11 Sept. 1838, Clerk of the Peace, Worcester to Secretary to Government; CA, CO 2801, 9 Mar. 1841, from Clerk of the Peace, Swellendam, to Secretary to Government.

mother merely wanted the child in order to exploit her and that the child was well brought up by the farmer who was raising her. This child was described as being 'white' so possibly the aunt saw an opportunity for the child to be assimilated into white society—indeed it might even have been possible that this child was the daughter of the farmer with whom she was said to get on with so well.

The endorsement of motherhood was a double-edged sword: it constructed apprentice women in public discourse as mothers only, and suppressed other identities. For example, women entered the post-emancipation world as workers only by default. In addition, the responsibility placed on mothers to organize or protest the indenture of their children also meant that women had to confront some of the most painful decisions cast by the ending of slavery. The complexities of the emancipation period meant that apprentices were often faced with tragic choices. Sometimes an apprentice's need to be free conflicted with his or her role as a parent: sometimes the freedom of one family member could only be gained at the expense of another. In May 1836, an apprentice named Leea, mother of three children, came to an agreement with her master, Daniel Rossouw of Paarl, to buy her freedom and that of her children for 250 rixdollars. Upon receiving this freedom, Leea was to indenture her two boys, Tommie and Caarl for five years each to Rossouw. The Special Magistrate worried about legalizing the discharge as it placed 'the minor children of the discharged apprentice in such situation as will protract the term of their service much beyond that fixed by the Abolition of Slavery'.[53] The Attorney-General said the discharge could go ahead. What considerations led Leea to indenture her two boys as the price of her and her daughter's freedom? Was the boys' indenture also the price of keeping her daughter away from the sexual abuse of women so often inherent in relationships of economic domination where men hold power?[54]

Ironically, the freedom that had been bestowed on children born after 1834, carried a potential for bondage which was all too frequently enacted. Free status was transformed into a condition for extended servitude. By law, children born after August 1834 were free, and slaveholders used this as leverage against apprentices.[55] In 1836, a Mr Mostert of Paarl threatened to throw the children of two of his women apprentices off his farm unless they indentured their children to him.[56] W. C. Rossouw, also of Paarl, demanded that his apprentice Sarah indenture her child to him, but she refused his

---

53   CA, CO 452, no. 51, 28 May 1836, Special Justice, Paarl, to Secretary to Government.

54   A similar scenario was played out in the case of Caroline, an apprentice in Tygerberg, who despite the urging of the Special Justice made a verbal agreement with her master to buy her own freedom 'leaving the two eldest and taking her youngest child with her'. CA, CO 465, no. 69, 10 July 1837, Special Justice to Secretary to Government.

55   I am grateful to Mary Beth Jones for alerting me to this provision.

56   CA, CO 2799, no. 65, Acting Special Justice, Paarl, to Secretary to Government.

request. When the child became ill Sarah agreed to the indenture. In the end, however, this did not occur. Rossouw declined to indenture the child because it was ill, and sent it off the farm.[57] Sarah deserted the farm to be with her child who subsequently died.[58] These threats represented practical application of the economic power held by the former master class after emancipation, even in the years before the state came to their aid with the Masters and Servants Ordinance.

In cases of illegal indenture, power to decide between the claim of the employer or the mother lay with the Special Magistrate. The first Special Justice of Worcester, Peake, stated in 1836 that[59]

> the general condition of the apprenticed children [sic] as regard treatment is highly creditable to their employers... The article of clothing in some cases has not been quite so good as it ought to have been, the consequence of some mothers being averse to have their children apprenticed. To which, I consented to, until I was satisfied of the incompetency of the mothers to support their offspring... I am of the opinion that a vigilant control cannot be maintained and enforced in this district over the employers without a great increase and expense to the government... I am satisfied there is every inclination on the part of the employer to do all in his power to make good subjects of the rising generation.

Owing to a loophole in the original Abolition Act of 1833, farmers were able to indenture children for periods extending considerably beyond 1838. Complaints about illegal indenture of children came from apprentices all over the western Cape. Lea, of Tulbagh in the district of Worcester, protested that her child was illegally detained by her former master Jacobus Theron, while an apprentice in Worcester bought the remaining years of her and two of her children's period of service and wanted a third freed from indenture.[60] In the last year of apprenticeship, Special Justice Mackay stated that 'it appears from the records of this office that very many children...have been indentured against the wishes of the mothers.'[61] In the Stellenbosch and Worcester districts, out of 122 indentures in 1838 for which records remain, 30 children were indentured despite the explicit objections of their mothers.[62] The Abolition of Slavery Act of 1838 outlawed such indentures of apprentice children beyond 1840, and Governor D'Urban abolished child

---

57 CA, CO 452, no. 74, 27 Aug. 1836, from Acting Special Magistrate, Paarl, to Secretary to Government.

58 CA, CO 5177 (no number), 18 Aug. 1836, from Secretary to Government to Acting Special Justice at Paarl. Also see Sarah's memorial in CO 3990, no. 31.

59 CA, 1/WOC, 19/60, 11 Oct. 1836, no name, but I presume it is Peake as it is in letters despatched by the Special Magistrate.

60 CA, 1/WOC, 19/60, 16 June 1835, Peake to Jacobus Theron; 1 Dec. 1837, Molesworth, Acting Special Justice, to Colonel Bell, Secretary to Government.

61 CA, 1/WOC, 19/61, 30 Mar. 1838, Mackay to Wouter de West.

62 See CA, 1/WOC, 16/40, Contracts of Apprenticeship, 1836. The volume gives detailed information on ages and names of all parties involved.

indentureship as a whole on the day of emancipation owing to the outcry over child labour, although the practice continued in a different guise under the Masters and Servants Act.[63]

EMANCIPATION

On 1 December 1838, Cape slaves woke up as free people, no longer unequivocally the possessions of others. The immediate post-emancipation period presented both ex-slaves and their former owners with dilemmas and concerns with regard to the future. As in the United States, ex-slaves experienced a much flawed emancipation deprived of an economic base which would have helped equate freedom with economic independence. Apprentices were freed into poverty. The Civil Commissioner of Worcester wrote in 1837 that 'the free colored population constitute an indigent class'.[64] Economic context thus profoundly shaped decisions about work and freedom.

Masters sought to maintain their social, economic, and political dominance in a new era where slaveholding was no longer the basis of status and accumulation. The ill-fated Vagrancy Ordinance of 1834 and the more successful Masters and Servants Ordinance of 1841 were some of the legislative means whereby former masters sought to guarantee a cheap and accessible labour force. Freed people had different concerns. Above all they sought self-sufficiency, often moving to mission stations in search of land which would give them security from reliance on farm labour. In the late nineteenth century, children and grandchildren of slaves moved to the villages and to Cape Town to try to avoid the legacy of servitude which lingered on in the rural areas.[65] Freed people's actions in the time of apprenticeship demonstrate clearly that freedom meant being free of their former masters' control. It is striking that even in the last months of 1838 many apprentices came to the Special Justices seeking to buy out their remaining months of service.[66]

In 1838, approximately 25,000 slaves were emancipated in the western Cape. In the next ten years, 7,000 left the farms and moved to villages and mission stations, while about 1,000 lived on public land.[67] In the six weeks

---

63   Isobel Edwards provides helpful detail on this subject in *Towards Emancipation: A Study in South African Slavery* (Cardiff, 1942).

64   CA, CO 2773, no. 77, 4 July 1837, from P.J. Truter, Civil Commissioner, Worcester, to Secretary to Government.

65   See J.C. Marincowitz, 'Rural Production and Labor in the Western Cape, 1835–88 with Special Reference to the Wheat Growing Districts' (Ph.D. thesis, University of London, 1985); P. Scully, *The Bouquet of Freedom: Social and Economic Relations in the Stellenbosch District, 1870–1900*, Centre for African Studies, University of Cape Town, Communication, no. 17 (1990).

66   CA, 1/WOC, 19/60, 11 Nov. 1837, Molesworth to Wouter de Wet, Justice of the Peace, Worcester; CA, 1/WOC, 19/61, 13 Mar. 1838, B. de Labat, Clerk to the Special Magistrate, to Charl du Toit, fieldcornet, Bokkeveld; 13 Sept. 1838, Mackay to Ernest P. Kruger, fieldcornet of Roggeveld, etc.

67   Marincowitz, 'Rural Production', p. 38.

following emancipation on 1 December 1838, 456 people moved to Genadendal alone.[68] Despite evidence of flight from the farms, in the New Year farmers in the Worcester district still fostered 'the hope that by some means or other the coloured class may come under their former control'.[69] However, one former owner in Worcester was so bitter at the loss of his slaves that at dawn on Emancipation Day, in the midst of a terrible storm, he threw all his former apprentices, including a family with a newborn child, off his farm.[70] Freed people appear to have been much happier with the prospect of emancipation than were their masters. The Special Justices of Stellenbosch and Worcester reported that 1 December passed without incident on the part of the apprentices, and in Stellenbosch 'not withstanding the inclemency of the weather, the missionary chapel…was crowded to excess at three different services during that day and many who could not gain admittance, remained outside, near the door, and windows endeavouring to catch some portion of the service'.[71]

In the months leading up to emancipation in December of 1838, apprentices began to make explicit demands regarding their coming freedom. Ideals of freedom revolved around obtaining land, giving their children an education, and being free of former masters' control.[72] In 1838. freed men who made an application for allotments near to the village of Worcester stated that they wanted 'an opportunity of sending their children to the Missionary Chapel'. They also wanted to avoid labour on the farms as[73]

> some of them have wives and children, and [unintelligible word] they engage themselves with their family, the person hiring them will scarcely give them any wages, telling them that as they have also to feed their children, they cannot give them more than four or five Rxd per month, and that if any of their children are able to perform the most trifling service for the family, such children are prevented from attending school.

Freed people in other areas of the colony shared their peers' concerns. The population of Genadendal mission station in the Caledon district grew from 1,446 in 1837 to 2,846 12 years later. Ex-slaves were at the bottom of

---

68 T. van Ryneveld, 'Merchants and Missions: Developments in the Caledon District, 1838–50' (BA Hons. thesis, University of Cape Town, 1985), p. 46.

69 CA, CO 2788, no. 31, 12 Feb. 1839, from Resident Magistrate, Worcester, to Secretary to Government.

70 CA, CO 476, no 127, 16 Dec. 1838, Special Justice, Worcester, to Secretary to Government.

71 CA, CO 476, no. 123, 10 Dec. 1838, Special Justice, Stellenbosch, to Secretary to Government.

72 See School of Oriental Studies Library (SOAS), University of London, Records of the Methodist Missionary Society (MMS), FBN 7, no. 260, 1 Mar. 1838, Letter from Hodgson, missionary at Stellenbosch to MMS in London; CA, CO 475, no. 50, 8 Nov. 1838, Reverend J. Ballot of George to Secretary to Government; CA, CO 476, no. 123, 10 Dec. 1838, H. Piers, Special Justice, Stellenbosch, to Secretary to Government.

73 CA, CO 2788, no. 31, 12 Feb. 1839, Civil Commissioner, Worcester, to Secretary to Government. The document is marked confidential and private. See also CA, 1/WOC 19/61, 25 June 1838, for evidence of apprentices wanting land.

the social and economic rung at the mission as much of the land had been taken by the time they entered. There was a dramatic increase in population in 1838, and the baptism class grew from 52 candidates in 1835 to 'three times that number' in 1839.[74] In February 1839, Genadendal and Elim missions were 'full, almost to an overflow'.[75] The Special Justice at Stellenbosch stated that 'it would seem that their concern, was to obtain religious instruction'.[76]

Freed people found one distinction between slavery and freedom which former masters had been far less willing to recognize: control of personal relationships. Formal marriage represented one way of making claim to a private relationship. The Marriage Order-in-Council, in force in the colony from 1 February 1839, was partly promulgated because of 'the increased desire for lawful matrimony felt by a large number of persons recently released from slavery' in the British Empire.[77] The Cape Order increased the number of people qualified to perform marriages (formerly only ministers of religion could do so) by appointing marriage officers. The Order also sought to recognize the (de facto) marriages of former slaves '...which have never been sanctioned by any public ceremony or formally registered'. By making such a declaration, freed people could gain legal recognition of their marriage and have their children recognized as legitimate, and possibly therefore more acceptable to missionaries. Reverend Hallbeck of Genadendal perceived such a strong desire for formal marriage among freed people that he was paradoxically induced to postpone solemnizing declarations 'by the consideration that many of these, who are employed on the farms, might have been led to leave their masters at an inconvenient season, if they had been invited to appear here for such a purpose'.[78] Subsequently over 100 such marriages were performed at Genadendal.[79] Marriage licence fees remained an obstacle to marriage among the underclass. A missionary from George stated that 'payment...acts as a heavy tax on marriage on the very poorest part of the community and prevents many getting married who would otherwise wish it'.[80] Church legislation eliminated the payment of marriage fees to the poor.[81]

At the time of emancipation, missionary and freed people's concerns

---

74   See Van Ryneveld, 'Merchants and Missions', p. 45; also Raum, 'Development'.

75   CA, CO 2784, no. 33, 19 Feb. 1839, Acting Resident Magistrate, Caledon, to Secretary to Government.

76   CA, CO 476, no. 123, 10 Dec. 1838, H. Piers, Special Justice, Stellenbosch, to Secretary to Government.

77   CA, Cape Colony Publications (CCP), 6/6/1/1, 7 Sept. 1838, Marriage Order-in-Council; D. Ward, *A Handbook to the Marriage Laws of the Cape Colony, the Bechuanaland Protectorate, and Rhodesia* (Cape Town, 1897).

78   CA, CO 485, no. 44, 5 Aug. 1839, Hallbeck to Secretary to Government.

79   Raum, 'Development', p. 126.

80   CA, CO 2741, no. 72, 18 July 1833, Missionary Meyser to Civil Commissioner of George and Uitenhage.

81   I have as yet been unable to find the specific order. Archival evidence refers to such an order but no

seem to have coalesced to some extent around the issue of marriage. Yet the context of emancipation in the western Cape problematizes the issue of marriage. Was marriage a way of giving primacy to relationships hitherto not respected by colonial society; a symbolic act in the constitution and reconstitution of identity by freed people; possibly a way of finding favour with missionaries who had land to offer?[82] How did missionary ideas about a 'normal Christian family' bear on the manner in which freed people created their intimate worlds? And why did the colonial authorities do so much to encourage marriage among the rural underclass?

GENDER AND FAMILY

From the early 1840s the public voice of freed women disappears from the historical record of emancipation, indeed from much of the nineteenth-century archive. A discursive shift occurred in the public representation of family decisions and concerns from a context in which women spoke as mothers, to a post-emancipation setting which privileged men. Mothers remained primary guardians for younger children, but the battle over the child faded in labour discourse from the 1840s. The challenges by ex-slave and Khoi mothers to farmers' control of child labour possibly faded along with their optimistic visions of freedom and alternatives to a life of rural labour.

It is difficult to tease out the discrete sources of this new mode of representation. The need to stabilize a class of workers newly freed from slavery clearly occupied the Colonial Office, the missionary establishment and employers in the Cape from at least the 1820s to the end of the nineteenth century.[83] Both missionaries and the state advocated the nuclear family and Christian marriage as a means of steadying what they perceived as a potentially threatening sector of the underclass. The desirability of the free wage labourers was connected to their foundation in a nuclear family. Family represented stability, and particular kinds of family arrangements represented more stability than others.[84] As a Dutch Reformed minister stated with regard to marriage in a nuclear monogamous family, it afforded 'a powerful stimulus to their acquiring property—binding parents to provide for their children, and being one grand step towards the admission of

---

details are given.

82 A comparison of marriage rates between mission stations and villages would be helpful in determining the significance of the mission context. The missionary at George stated that 'it is an undoubted fact that more marriages take place at our different stations than at this village'. CA, CO 2741, no. 72, 18 July 1833, Missionary Meyser to Civil Commissioner of George and Uitenhage.

83 For a longer treatment of this topic see Scully, 'Gender, Emancipation and Free Wage Labor'. For the 1820s see Van der Spuy, 'Slave Women'.

84 C. Hall, 'The Early Formation of Victorian Domestic Ideology' in S. Burman (ed.), Fit Work for Women (New York, 1979).

85 CA, CO 454, no. 81, 15 Nov. 1836, W. Robertson, minister at Swellendam, to Secretary to Government.

baptism'.[85] This concern with reliability was especially pertinent to colonial labour officials and farmers who saw in labourers an unwillingness to work.[86] The domestic reformers in Britain, and the colonial authorities in the Cape, thus looked to the inculcation of habits and social practices conducive to the reproduction of a self-reproducing working class.[87]

The drive to reformulate private relationships in the colony started with the amelioration measures in the 1820s and gained more momentum when slavery was finally abolished in 1838. The family model around which legislators, evangelicals, and middle-class reformers chose to focus their efforts was one 'which carried heavy ideological concepts of what the distribution of power should be in the family'.[88] This formulation invested ultimate power in the father and accorded the mother prime responsibility for child-rearing and maintaining emotional harmony in the home. The conception derived some of its legitimacy from the separation of spheres: masculinized public space and feminized private space which had begun under industrialization and received ideological sanction in the nineteenth century.[89] The reformulation of gender relations in the Cape was pursued particularly in the legal sphere through marriage, inheritance, and labour legislation.

Yet if free wage labour ideology was premised upon these assumptions, it was introduced into a context (both in Britain and the colonies) in which these assumptions were not necessarily held by all the actors. The British had walked into the slaveholding world of the Cape Colony bringing with them very different ideas about the exercise of power, free wage labour, the management of the underclasses—partly through a 'cult of respectability'—and gender relations. It is difficult to accurately comprehend how free wage labour, and the separation of gendered spheres was conceived by the various actors in the Cape. Many freed women retreated from permanent farm labour, possibly because of the long history of sexual abuse from masters which had been a persistent feature of slavery. Female domesticity was encouraged on the Moravian mission stations, but the low wages paid to men, and the lack of land on the stations meant that many married women did work on the farms.[90] Women also worked in the villages doing piece-

---

86 See E. Foner, *Nothing But Freedom: Emancipation and Its Legacy* (Baton Rouge, 1983); also Marincowitz, 'Rural Production'.

87 See P. Bourdieu, *Outline of a Theory of Practice* (New York, 1977) and E.P. Thompson, 'Time, Work-Discipline and Industrial Capitalism', *Past and Present*, 38 (1967), pp. 56–97 for a discussion of the importance of habit and time management in the creation of a working class. For discussion of these issues in a colonial context, see Crais, *White Supremacy and Black Resistance*.

88 Weeks, *Sex*, p. 27.

89 See L. Tilly and J. Scott, *Women, Work, and Family* (New York, 1978); I. Pinchbeck, *Women Workers and the Industrial Revolution, 1750–1850* (London, 1969); Poovey, *Uneven Developments: The Ideological Work of Gender in Mid-Victorian England* (Chicago, 1988).

90 E. Boddington, 'Domestic Service: Changing Relations of Class Domination, 1841–1948: A Focus on Cape Town' (M.Soc.Sci. thesis, University of Cape Town, 1983).

work as washerwomen and seamstresses. Freed women's perception of work outside of the home was related as much to the context of that work as it was to the notion of work itself.[91]

Many freed men appear to have had different perceptions. From the few direct records which I have encountered in which freed men speak of their vision of family and freedom, they articulate a desire to divide home and work and to have their wives staying at home: they are constructing a gendered notion of waged work. Historians of gender relations under industrialization have stressed that people entered the labour market with ideas shaped by previous experiences.[92] Certainly both freed men and women engaged in wage labour in the shadow and particular meanings of harsh farm-based slavery. Freed men might have wanted to keep their wives free from abuse by employers, and might also have seen, in the distinction between slavery and freedom, a right to exert power over their wives. In 1836, Widow Moses Meers stated that her slave, Cobus, had said that 'he is now no more slave...is as good as she is, and will have her daughter a girl of about 14 years also for his wife—nay he even insisted on it, that he would have a white wife'.[93] Cobus saw freedom as being able to marry a member of the race which had heretofore harnessed power to the colour of their skin. This is the only example I have, so far, found in the records of an explicit comment linking 'white' skin colour to domination.[94] It suggests, however, that apprentices clearly saw the significant connection between whiteness, masculinity, and power in the colony. For Cobus, race and gender came together in a weapon for reassertion of his selfhood: he sought possibly to affirm freedom through marriage to whiteness, and to give meaning to freedom through subordination of a wife.

In the second half of the nineteenth century, a respectable class of people who distinguished themselves as separate from the squalor and degradation of the farms emerged, particularly in Cape Town, but also on the Moravian mission stations in the rural western Cape, such as Mamre, Genadendal and Elim. They, like their African peers to the east, drew on Christian principles

---

91   See J. Scott's observation regarding French tailors in 1848. They argued for such a separation based on an equivalency between skill, workplace, and masculinity. However they did not deny women the right to work in their homes—i.e. they did not subscribe to a middle-class equation of the home and the domestic sphere. 'Work Identities for Men and Women' in Scott, *Gender and the Politics of History* (New York, 1988).

92   J. Quaetaert, 'The Shaping of Women's Work in Manufacturing: Guilds, Households, and the State in Europe, 1647–1870', *American Historical Review*, 90 (1985), pp. 1122–48; also J. Scott and L. Tilly, 'Women's Work and the Family in Nineteenth Century Europe', *Comparative Studies in Society and History*, 17 (1975), pp. 36–64.

93   CA, 1/CAL, no. 21, 16 Feb. 1836.

94   For discussions of race and class stratification at the Cape, see G. Fredrickson, *White Supremacy: A Comparative Study in American and South African History* (New York, 1981); also R. Elphick and R. Shell, 'Intergroup Relations: Khoikhoi, Settlers, Slaves and Free Blacks, 1652–1795' in Elphick and Giliomee, *Shaping*, pp. 184–239.

of marriage, family, and gender relations to forge a new and distinctive identity.[95] The notion of family—with male authority over women intrinsic to
that notion—was a central defining trope of the Moravian mission stations.
The Moravians organized their stations around the nuclear family with each
family having access to land. Strong penalties were incurred for having children out of wedlock.[96] The fact that most land made available to ex-slaves
was within the boundaries of mission stations had significant implications
for the nature of the worlds that freed people fashioned after 1838. In comparison to other colonial missionary societies, the Moravians had particularly
strong injunctions regarding morality and family life. The Moravians represented the community of missionaries on a station as a family, and wives
were literally distributed by lot among the male missionaries.[97] The missionaries perceived a connection between the patriarchal nuclear family and the
efficiency of the male worker, and between religion and hard work. The
Society enjoyed fairly good relations with farmers and the government into
the 1850s because of its encouragement to freed men to work on the white
farms.

EMANCIPATION AND LABOUR, 1838-56

Many farmers regarded the transition to wage labour with hostility and
apprehension, and practices common under slavery guided their actions in
the first three decades subsequent to emancipation. Male workers were
employed throughout the year but on the understanding that their families
had to be available when needed during the peak seasons. In the Cape, male
workers were paid more than women, partly in recognition of their status as
'head of household'. However, the idea that married women should not
work, was bent in accordance with class location: women of the working
class, married or not, overwhelmingly worked. Women of the rural underclass were to remain in the domestic sphere only as long as their labour was
not needed on the farms. At the Cape, the ideology of domesticity for
women, and work outside the home for men, was also shaped by racial

95   For a discussion of the importance of mission stations in Cape history see C. Bundy, *Rise and Fall of the
     South African Peasantry* (Berkeley, 1979); also Crais, *White Supremacy and Black Resistance*, and
     Marincowitz, 'Rural Production'. See Scully, 'Liberating the Family?' for an extended discussion of the
     rise of a rural respectability among ex-slaves and their descendants.

96   See P. Scully, 'Infanticide and the Humanitarian Sentiment at the Cape' (paper presented at the Africa
     Seminar, Centre for African Studies, University of Cape Town, 29 April 1992). CA, GH 23/14, no. 152,
     no. 209; CA, GH 28/20, no. 1; CA, GH 28/19, no. 1, no. 2, for cases of infanticide at Zuurbraak and
     Groenekloof (later Mamre) mission stations. I am grateful to John Mason for telling me of these cases.
     Also see Raum, 'Development', p. 126.

97   Raum, 'Development', p. 8. Robert Ross, personal communication. For an impatient statement on the
     Moravians' inflexible gender morality see CA, GH 23/14, vol. 1, no. 152, 10 Aug. 1842, Statement of
     the Governor to the Secretary of State regarding the case of infanticide perpetrated by Franscina Louw, a
     member of Zuurbraak mission station.

dynamics particular to the colonial experience. The association of labour with slavery, or other bonded forms of labour had served to degrade that work in the eyes of many of the former slaveholding class.[98] In the colony, settlers associated rural labour with demeaned status, and increasingly with people categorized as 'coloured' or 'black'.

The extent to which certain notions of gender relations and family pervaded the construction of social and economic relations in the post-emancipation period is clearly revealed in the labour legislation passed in the two decades immediately following emancipation. Concern with the intractability of agricultural labour in the 1830s led to calls both for a Vagrancy Act and a Masters and Servants Act. The former Act never saw the light of day after the Colonial Office in London became squeamish at the coercive measures it entailed, but farmers' calls for labour legislation were more successful and the Masters and Servants Ordinance was passed in 1841. This was revised in 1856 as the infamous Masters and Servants Act which was abolished only in 1974.[99] Clauses allowed for the apprenticeship of destitute children and also gave fathers authority to contract their children for service. Farmers' need for cheap and relatively acquiescent labour was thus structured into the law. The battle over children thus continued into the post-emancipation period.

The fierceness of farmers' methods to keep women and children in farm employment during apprenticeship and after indeed only makes sense if one tries to understand the premises upon which rural labour relations were built, and the significance of emancipation for the development of state power in the Cape Colony: the end of slavery occurred at the same time as, indeed was in part a precondition for, the creation of the modern bureaucratic state in South Africa. The family was a social and economic construct in which were embedded assumptions about the way labour power was accessed and harnessed. Former slaveholders were faced with a loss of power in a society increasingly divided along the axis of public and private spheres. State functionaries such as Magistrates and Justices of the Peace became paramount in arbitrating relations between master and servant. Simultaneously the law guaranteed the authority of the master and elevated paternal authority in the family. Slaveholders exchanged power over the bodies of slaves for greater power of men over children and women within the family, and for greater power in the public sphere.[100]

The separation of spheres was, however, somewhat ambiguous. While

---

98 Thus, when farmers bemoaned rural labour shortages, what they were really bemoaning was the lack of labourers willing to work for poverty wages, and they were making a statement about their own reluctance to engage in labour themselves. See Marincowitz, 'Rural Production', and Scully, *Bouquet*, ch. 4, for discussion of perceptions of labour shortages.

99 See C. Bundy, 'The Abolition of the Masters and Servants Act', *South African Labour Bulletin*, 2 (1975), pp. 37–46. Marincowitz, 'Rural Production' provides a detailed discussion of the proposed Vagrancy Ordinance.

100 See C. Pateman, *The Sexual Contract* (Stanford, 1988) for a discussion of the fraternal basis of contract

the state sought to bring the discipline of servants from the private into the public realm, it simultaneously gave employers the right to intervene into labourers' private lives. The colonial state claimed labour relations as its preserve; once this was acknowledged, much power was, in fact, handed back to former slaveholders and other employers.

The Masters and Servants Ordinance of 1841, and the later Masters and Servants Act of 1856, were legislated as a result of intense pressure both from former slaveholders in the western and eastern Cape, as well as from British settlers (who were prohibited from owning slaves) who resented the ability of Xhosa to resist labour on the farms.[101] The Ordinance placed the servant in a subservient relation to the master and made insolence a criminal offence. The Ordinance also sought to intervene in the private world of the servant placing 'scandalous immorality' in the realm of misconduct.[102] Its chapters II and IV demonstrate the underpinnings of a gender system which invested the working father with ultimate authority over a nuclear family.[103] The terms of this legislation replaced maternal power to indenture or contract of children with paternal power. This represents a larger shift in the Cape legal system which increasingly subordinated married women to their husbands.[104]

The hidden assumption of agricultural employment remained that when a male labourer was contracted so too was the potential labour of his wife and children.[105] Working-class women were routinely called to work, particularly in the wine-growing district of Stellenbosch. They thus acted as a reserve labour force upon which the farmer could depend at any time. This clearly had implications for the kinds of employment in which rural women could engage.[106] Only other temporary or unsteady work would allow a woman to go to work on the farm at a moment's notice; most freed women therefore worked as laundry women or in domestic service. Farmers did not conceive an autonomous existence of women and children. It is possible that freed men participated in this restructuring of rural relations which gave them some authority through the control of women, even if they, as rural 'coloured' men, were placed near the bottom rungs of the class and racial hierarchies of the Cape

theory, and of the modern state.

101 Crais, *White Supremacy and Black Resistance*.

102 Boddington, 'Domestic Service'. I have relied quite heavily on Boddington's interpretation.

103 In other terms of the Ordinance the father was now able to contract his children and at his death his wife and children's contracts expired after a month. Another clause allowed an employer to dismiss a woman should she become pregnant or get married, while a newly-wed man could have his wife's contract ended should he so desire. CA, CCP 6/2/1/1, Masters and Servants Ordinance, 1 Mar. 1841, cap. II, clauses xiii, and cap. IV, clauses xii and xiii.

104 See the Cape Inheritance Commission of 1865 which vividly demonstrates the eroding of married women's power under the influence of British law, and the relatively egalitarian views held by Dutch farmers in comparison to their English-speaking peers. Cape of Good Hope, Governor, Legislative Council, *Law of Inheritance Commission for the Western Districts*, G15–65 (Cape Town, 1866).

The magisterial records give evidence of disintegrating relationships, desertion of children by parents, alcoholism, and domestic violence in the ex-slave communities.[107] The archival record is, however, prejudiced in recording the abuses in working-class lives as opposed to those of the dominant classes.[108]

The records are much clearer in demonstrating that ex-slaveholders operated within a world-view which assumed the legitimacy of hierarchies of domination and that they perceived and exploited a gender system which operated both in the larger society and within underclass families. The elaboration of a British-influenced legal system provided employers with the legal means to enforce such class and gender hierarchies. After Responsible Government was given to the Cape Colony in 1872, additional amendments were made to the Masters and Servants Act which tightened even further the controls on rural labourers.[109]

CONCLUSION

We have been accustomed to interpreting the Cape experience through the lenses of class and race. One of the aims of the project, of which this is a part, is to explore the malleability of notions of the family, and of relations between men and women over time. Ideas of the family, and of gender, were crucial components of post-emancipation society. They influenced state policy, struggles within newly-formed households of emancipated slaves, between labourers and employers, life on the mission stations, and the way that people interpreted their lives. The emotional lives of people in the nineteenth-century Cape deserves attention, if only because emotion was so important to them. On the day of emancipation, Booy Floris, a member of Pacaltsdorp Mission Station, collected his wife, two daughters, and their eight children from their former master and brought them home.[110]

---

105 This hidden agreement is very similar to the bondage system of nineteenth-century England which also arose in a context of people's flight from rural labour. Pinchbeck, *Women Workers*, ch. 3.

106 K. Young, 'The Sexual Division of Labor: A Case Study From Oaxaca, Mexico', in A. Kuhn and A.M. Wolpe (eds.), *Feminism and Materialism* (London, 1978).

107 CA, 1/CAL, 21, 24 Mar. 1836; 4 Apr. 1836; 24 Dec. 1836; 1/CAL, 1/1/1. 16 Mar. 1842, preliminary examination, etc.

108 For analysis of the creation of 'facts' about violence in the archival record, see Scully, 'Liberating the Family?', chs. 6, 7 and 8. The evidence is skewed in so far as the underclass only emerge in archival records mostly once they have been criminalized through the ambit of colonial law. See P. Scully, 'Criminality and Conflict in Rural Stellenbosch, South Africa, 1870–1900', *Journal of African History*, 30 (1989), pp. 289–300, for consideration of this issue.

109 Bundy, 'Abolition of the Masters and Servants Acts'; Scully, *Bouquet*, p. 60.

110 CA, CO 485, no. 29, 21 Mar. 1839, Revd Anderson, Pacaltsdorp, to Revd John Philip, Cape Town.

Plate 10   Boers returning from the hunt, 1804, by Samuel Daniel. *South African Library.*

9

THE ENEMY WITHIN

— SUSAN NEWTON-KING —

It is now nearly two decades since I first encountered a slim green volume by the late J. S. Marais, entitled *Maynier and the First Boer Republic*,[1] but the issues raised in that book preoccupy me still. Like all Marais' work, it is thoroughly grounded in archival research—indeed, it brings the motley cast of frontier characters alive in a way few subsequent works have done—but it also had a moral purpose. In seeking to vindicate the actions of the unfortunate Landdrost Maynier, reviled and rejected by his Afrikaner subjects and expelled from his drostdy in the frontier district of Graaff-Reinet, Marais was hoping to strike a blow for reason against blind passion, and for the rule of law against anarchy.[2] Marais shows a frontier community at war with its own best interests, short-sightedly pursuing a policy of naked aggression towards Xhosa and Khoisan alike, thereby provoking both parties to vengeful retaliation and unleashing a chain of events with which it was not equipped to cope. When, in 1799 and again in 1801, the burghers of Graaff-Reinet were forced to abandon their homes and flee westwards to escape the wrath of a 'combined confederacy' of 'vagabond Hottentots' and their Xhosa allies, Maynier knew that he had been right: the Boers' persistent maltreatment of their Khoisan servants had been not merely unjust, but also impolitic. Had it not been for the timely intervention of the British, the greater part of the district would have been lost to the rebels.[3]

Marais' study thus presents the reader with an unsolved problem: why, if Maynier's counsel was wise, did his Afrikaner subjects reject it with such vehemence? Why, in the language of the modern historian, should a thinly

---

1   Published by Maskew Miller (Cape Town) in 1944.

2   Cf. C. Saunders, *The Making of the South African Past: Major Historians on Race and Class* (Cape Town, 1988), p. 117.

3   S. Newton-King and V.C. Malherbe, 'The Khoikhoi Rebellion in the Eastern Cape, 1799–1803', Centre for African Studies, University of Cape Town, Communications, no. 5 (1981), pp. 28–9.

scattered and poorly armed settler population so antagonize the indigenous inhabitants as to put its very survival at risk? How was it possible, as Robert Ross has asked,

> that men and women who at one moment were treated with a certain measure of respect and trust and on whom the Boers were dependent to a considerable degree for the daily functioning of their farms, could the next moment be flogged to death at the slightest provocation?[4]

As the reader may recognize, similar questions have been asked repeatedly of the frontiersmen's descendants, with reference to the apartheid policies of the mid twentieth century, and historians still argue about the answers. The late eighteenth-century Cape was a very much simpler society than mid twentieth-century South Africa, but still such questions can be a useful tool with which to probe the inner workings of the colonial world. One could, of course, sidestep the problem by responding that violence was not a regular or characteristic feature of relations between master and servant on the frontier. Thus Martin Legassick, whose paper on 'The Frontier Tradition in South African Historiography' initiated a major re-assessment of frontier history, suggested that it might be possible to distinguish between 'violence *within* the master-servant relationship' and the several forms of coercion which were used to procure servants and prevent them from leaving.[5] 'Cape colonists in general', he conceded, 'expected to employ labour in a slave capacity', but there was no evidence that servants on the frontier were more frequently assaulted by their masters than were those in the western Cape. Indeed, he suggested, in a footnote pregnant with possibilities, an over-reliance on the evidence of missionaries and travellers may well have led scholars to erroneous conclusions in this regard.[6] 'If there was a trend in class relationships,' he concluded, 'it was a trend away from master-slave towards chief-subject or patron-client on the frontier.'

Legassick's challenge to the traditional view of the frontier as a place of irreconcilable racial conflict and stark social divisions was taken further by Hermann Giliomee in an influential article published in *The Shaping of South African Society* in 1979.[7] Giliomee formulated a two-phase model of frontier history. During the initial 'open' phase, when no one group held

---

4   D. van Arkel, G.C. Quispel and R.J. Ross, '"De Wijngaard des Heeren?": Een Onderzoek naar de Wortels van "die Blanke Baasskap" in Zuid-Afrika', *Cahiers Sociale Geschiedenis*, no. 4 (Leiden, 1983) p. 40.

5   M. Legassick, 'The Frontier Tradition in South African Historiography', in S. Marks and A. Atmore (eds.), *Economy and Society in Pre-Industrial South Africa* (London, 1980), p. 67. This article first appeared in the form of a seminar paper, delivered to the seminar on the Societies of Southern Africa (Institute of Commonwealth Studies, London) in 1971.

6   *Ibid.*, n. 123.

7   'The Eastern Frontier, 1770–1812', in R. Elphick and H. Giliomee (eds.), *The Shaping of South African Society, 1652–1820* (London, 1979), pp. 291–337; (2nd edn., Cape Town, 1989).

undisputed power over the frontier zone, many Khoisan were able to enter service with the Boers on terms acceptable to both parties. There *were* some cases in which 'trekboers used violent methods against Khoikhoi', but on the whole, Giliomee suggests, relations between Europeans and Khoisan more closely resembled clientship than slavery. As the frontier closed, however, the Khoisan found their options reduced and they increasingly fell prey to 'labour-repressive methods'. 'At the furthest extreme some colonists abducted Khoisan or Xhosa children and sold them or kept them in bondage almost like slaves.'[8]

This two-phase view of inter-ethnic relationships on the frontier has now become a new orthodoxy. It has, indeed, much to recommend it. In particular, its stress upon the complexities of the colonists' relations with the Xhosa chiefdoms of the Zuurveld has done much to correct the distortions of an earlier school of historians preoccupied with inter-racial conflict. However, where the Khoisan are concerned, it is doubtful whether the notion of transition from a fluid 'open' phase of inter-group contact to a 'closed' phase marked by 'labour repression' and increasingly rigid class divisions has much validity. It is not that such a model is implausible; on the contrary, it is reasonable to assume, as Giliomee does, that the low density of the settler population during the 1770s and 1780s would have made it easy for servants to desert and hence inclined the colonists to a labour policy based on the voluntary principle rather than the use of naked force.[9]

One might add, moreover, that many colonists lived in daily fear of 'Bushman' attacks and were in need of loyal servants. To alienate them through maltreatment would, as Ross suggests, seem counter-productive. But this was precisely Maynier's point. And yet the evidence of maltreatment is overwhelming; and it comes not from missionary sources (for the first missionaries arrived in Graaff-Reinet only at the turn of the century), but from the routine correspondence of the Drostdy and the archives of the Court of Justice at *de Kaap*. One could, perhaps, argue for the existence of a brief honeymoon period from 1768 to 1775 or thereabouts, as the first colonists marked out places for themselves in the coastal forelands and on the plains of Camdeboo to the north, but even then, as I have shown elsewhere, the ugly phenomenon of enslavement (or attempted enslavement) was already undermining the voluntary principle.[10]

We are returned, then, to the question with which we began: why did the burghers of Graaff-Reinet (as that part of the colony which lay east of the

8   *Ibid.*, 2nd edn., p. 451.

9   *Ibid.*, p. 430.

10   S. Newton-King, 'The Enemy Within: The Struggle for Ascendancy on the Cape Eastern Frontier, 1760–99' (Ph.D. thesis, University of London, 1992), ch. 2. In press, Cambridge, as *Masters and Slaves on the Cape Eastern Frontier*.

Gamtoos and Gamka rivers became known in 1786) defy both the counsel of their Landdrost and the logic of their historians, eschewing the role of patron (and perhaps even that of patriarch) and establishing instead a reign of terror over the Khoisan who lived among them? In the limited space available I can offer only a partial answer to this question, focusing more upon what Roland Barthes has called 'consecution' (an explanation of *how* something happened) than 'consequence' (an explanation of *why* it happened). As Barthes observed, it is in the nature of narrative (and thus of history, which is but one form of narrative) to confuse the two, though that is not my intention here.[11] It is simply that, like most historical phenomena, the nature of master-servant relations on the Cape frontier requires explanation on several levels, and only the first, the 'consecutional', can be properly treated here. An exploration of the *circumstances* under which the behaviour of the boers towards their Khoisan servants came to be characterized by extreme brutality will not lay the question 'why?' to rest, but it will advance the argument.

RAIDERS OF THE CENTRAL ESCARPMENT

An investigation of coercive labour practices in the district of Graaff-Reinet should begin, in my opinion, with the so-called 'Bushman War' on the northern frontier. The colony had suffered from intermittent attacks by raiding bands of 'Bushman-Hottentots' since the beginning of the eighteenth century. The first attacks began immediately after Willem Adriaan van der Stel opened the cattle trade to freemen and permitted the establishment of settlers across the Roodezand Pass, in *'t Land van Waveren* (present-day Tulbagh). On this and subsequent occasions, it was clear the raiders comprised dispossessed Khoekhoe (Khoikhoi) as well as San.[12] There was a further outbreak of hostilities in 1715 and again in 1728 and 1731. The growing determination of the raiders and the increasing savagery of the conflict was evident in these encounters: the 'Bushman-Hottentots' began to kill unwary herdsmen and destroy those animals they could not take with them in their retreat, while the commandos formed to oppose them adopted the methods of 'search and destroy' which would become characteristic of the conflict in future decades. In 1731, moreover, the first captives were taken from among the survivors.[13]

11   'Everything suggests, indeed, that the mainspring of narrative is precisely the confusion of consecution and consequence, what comes *after* being read in narrative as what is *caused by*; in which case narrative would be a systematic application of the logical fallacy denounced by Scholasticism in the formula *post hoc, ergo propter hoc*—a good motto for destiny, of which narrative all things considered is no more than the "language".' Quotation taken from R. Barthes, 'Introduction to the Structural Analysis of Narratives', in S. Sontag (ed.), *A Barthes Reader* (New York, 1982), p. 266.

12   R. Elphick, *Kraal and Castle: Khoikhoi and the Founding of White South Africa* (New Haven and London, 1977), ch. 11.

13   Newton-King, 'The Enemy Within', ch. 3.

In 1738 a band of 'Bushmen' one hundred strong, who had stolen the cattle of Augustus Louwerensz behind the Piketberg, explicitly declared that their intention was to

> chase [the Dutch] out of their country, since they were living in their country: and that this was only a beginning, but that they would do the same to all the people living thereabouts and if that didn't help, and they did not leave, they would burn all the corn presently standing in the fields, once it was ripe; that then the Dutch would be compelled to leave their country.[14]

The attack on Louwerensz's place heralded a wave of interconnected attacks on the persons and property of colonists in the Sandveld and Bokkeveld during the following year. Collectively, these raids and the commando reprisals which followed them have come to be know as 'the Bushman War' of 1739. Its origins, according to Nigel Penn, lay in an illegal cattle bartering expedition to Namaqualand.[15] At the conclusion of a successful stay in the country of the Great Namaqua, the European barterers had turned upon their hosts and stolen their cattle. This act, and the Europeans' subsequent failure to reward their Khoisan servants for their part in the expedition, provoked a furious response. By the autumn of 1739 there was 'a general panic...throughout the north west' and the authorities were obliged to pardon those who had derived illegal gain from the original expedition so as to obtain their support for the commandos.[16] Finally, after several commandos had scoured the Bokkeveld, attacking every encampment they discovered and killing 101 Khoisan, 'peace' returned to the north-west frontier. The Khoisan of the Sandveld and Bokkeveld had suffered a crushing defeat and thereafter, according to Penn, their status deteriorated markedly.[17]

Following the burgher victory in the war of 1739, there was a prolonged lull in hostilities between the Khoisan and the colonists. Apart from a brief outburst of resistance in November 1754, there were no further reports of armed conflict until 1770, and the colonists were able to stake out places for themselves in the Onder Bokkeveld, the Hantam and the Roggeveld with little opposition.[18]

By the 1760s, the sons and daughters of Roggevelders and Bokkevelders had begun to settle in the Nuweveld and the Camdeboo, on the north-eastern marches of the colony. Then all of a sudden, in April 1770, the alarm was

---

14 Cape Archives (CA), C 453, Louwrens to Governor, 22 Oct. 1738.

15 N. Penn, 'Land, Labour and Livestock in the Western Cape During the Eighteenth Century', in W. James and M. Simons (eds.), *The Angry Divide: Social and Economic History of the Western Cape* (Cape Town, 1989).

16 N. Penn, 'The Frontier in the Western Cape, 1700–40' (paper presented to a workshop organized by the Spatial Archaeology Research Unit, University of Cape Town, 1984), p. 19.

17 Penn, 'Land, Labour and Livestock', p. 9.

18 Newton-King, 'The Enemy Within', ch. 3.

sounded by the Veldcorporaal Adriaan van Jaarsveld, then living in the Sneeuberge, 'beyond the Salt River, behind the Coup'. 'The Hottentots residing thereabouts', he wrote, 'had robbed the farmer Casper Schols of thirty-four cattle.' The commando sent after them had recovered the carcasses and shot six of the robbers. The remainder had been taken prisoner, 'excepting two, who, as they would not surrender, were then shot'.[19] The following year, Van Jaarsveld sent word that 'the Hottentots living thereabouts had become so wicked that on several farms they had surrounded the houses at night and tried to break into them'. They had stolen 900 sheep from Jacob Joubert, murdered three of his servants and 'shot his house full of arrows from the outside'.[20] Similar reports emanated from the Nuweveld and Roggeveld. By December 1773, appeals for assistance were reaching the Drostdy in Stellenbosch from all quarters of the Roggeveld and the Hantam. Commandos were hastily organized and nearby 'Bushman' encampments were attacked and their occupants destroyed, but to no avail. In June 1774, Van Jaarsveld reported that 'the stealing daily becomes worse…and the people on the Sneeuwberg are of one mind to abandon their farms…' Even the 'General Commando' of 1774, during which 499 Khoisan were shot dead and 231 captured, was unable to subdue the robbers. Within months of its end, the raids began again with renewed intensity.[21]

And this, to borrow a phrase from the Piketberg raiders of earlier times, 'was only a beginning'. The conflict on the northern borders of the colony was to continue, almost without respite, for a further 30 years. The Hantam and the Roggeveld were never entirely free of depredations, but the worst hit areas were further east, in the Nuweveld, the Sneeuberge and the Camdeboo. By 1795 the inhabitants of the northern wards of Graaff-Reinet district were on the verge of despair, having lost an estimated 19,161 cattle and 84,094 sheep since the foundation of the district in 1786, not to mention guns captured, horses destroyed and slaves murdered.[22] They in their turn had exacted a savage revenge: over the same period, according to the records of militia officers, 2,504 'Bushmen' were shot dead and 669 captured.[23] And not every Veldwagtmeester bothered to record the number killed, wounded or captured. Given the low density of hunter-gatherer populations in the Karoo (and, as I shall explain below, I believe the great majority of the raiders to

19 Landdrost of Stellenbosch to Governor Tulbagh, 4 July, 1770, in D. Moodie (ed.), *The Record; or, a Series of Official Papers Relative to the Condition and Treatment of the Native Tribes of South Africa* (Cape Town, 1838), part III, pp. 7–8.

20 CA, C 565, Landdrost Faber to Governor, 3 May 1771.

21 Newton-King, 'The Enemy Within', ch. 3.

22 Newton-King, 'The Enemy Within', ch. 5.

23 K. Wyndham Smith, 'From Frontier to Midlands: A History of the Graaff-Reinet District, 1786–1910', *Occasional Papers*, no. 20, Institute of Social and Economic Research, Rhodes University, Grahamstown, p. 17.

have been of hunter rather than herder origin), a death toll of this magnitude can only be described as genocidal. And yet, as we have seen, the raids continued until the end of the century, preventing the colonists from establishing themselves on the Karoo plains behind the Escarpment.

Who were these indomitable resisters and what was the secret of their resilience? In my opinion, their ethnic composition was different from that of the raiders of the Sandveld and Bokkeveld. Many of the latter were clearly of Khoekhoe origin, whereas the people of the Central Escarpment (the chain of mountains which stretches east-west across the Great Karoo) seem to have been mainly San or *soaqua*.[24] The archaeology of the Great Karoo behind the Nuweveld- and Roggeveldberge is still under-researched, but that of the Zeekoe River valley, behind the Sneeuberge, is much better known, thanks to an extensive survey conducted by Garth Sampson and his associates in the Zeekoe Valley Archaeological Project (ZVAP).[25] The ZVAP has shown that the valley of the Zeekoe River has been inhabited periodically by man and his hominid ancestors for more than a quarter of a million years. The final occupation episode commenced some 4,000 years ago, following a mid-Holocene abandonment which, it seems, lasted for some millenia.[26] Throughout this period the valley (which has many springs and fountains) supported a much larger population than during any preceding episode, but the greatest increase seems to have taken place about 1,000 years ago, at the time when the archaeological residue designated 'Interior Wilton' was replaced by the Smithfield industry.[27] The latter is generally assumed to be the archaeological trace left by the San of the central South African plateau, the immediate forebears of the San or *soaqua* of historic times. During the ninth century AD, the Zeekoe valley San were joined by herders who entered the valley from the south and remained in the upper valley (the area called Agter Sneeuwberg by the Boers) until approximately AD 1500 . Following their departure, the valley was reclaimed by hunter-foragers, who remained in sole occupation until colonial times.

One should not assume, however, that the San who inhabited the valley in the wake of the herder withdrawal and who, in my opinion, were primarily responsible for the opposition to European settlement in the Sneeuberge and the Camdeboo, were necessarily the direct descendants of the first Smithfield

---

24   I use the latter term here in the sense coined by John Parkington, that is to say 'residual hunter-gatherers', clinging to their traditional lifestyle 'in the interstices of pastoralist society', J. Parkington, 'Soaqua and Bushmen: Hunters and Robbers', in C. Schrire (ed.), *Past and Present in Hunter-Gatherer Studies* (New York, 1984).

25   The project is co-ordinated by Garth Sampson, Professor in the Department of Anthropology, Southern Methodist University, Dallas.

26   C.G. Sampson, 'Atlas of Stone Age Settlement in the Central and Upper Seacow Valley', *Memoirs* of the National Museum, Bloemfontein, no. 20, (1985), pp. 12–13, and personal communication, 14 Jan. 1989.

27   Sampson, 'Atlas', pp. 93, 108–9.

settlers, in either a cultural or a biological sense. The long period of interaction with herders had brought about changes in their settlement patterns and subsistence strategies, and, during the eighteenth century, the age-old lifeways had been further disrupted by the intrusion of refugees from the spreading colony, among whom, no doubt, were many individuals of Khoekhoe origin.

The people of the Zeekoe valley were thus no strangers to change and adaptation. And yet the coming of the *veeboeren* was an event to which they could not adapt, except at the expense of their very being.[28] The immigrant Europeans brought with them a set of attitudes to man and nature which were entirely different from those of the San. For the *veeboeren*, the natural world was primarily an economic resource, to be privately appropriated and exploited for material gain. It had few spiritual or even (during the early phase of settlement) cultural connotations.[29] For the San, by contrast, the natural world and the world of spirit were one: land and culture, matter and spirit, nature and community, were aspects of a whole and could not be separated. The potency or 'supernatural energy' activated in the shamanistic rituals common to San groups throughout southern Africa was channelled through ordinary and familiar objects: animals and (from our point of view) inanimate substances which, while 'sacred' in their capacity as 'strong things' endowed with a peculiar potency, were also very much a part of everyday life.[30] Thus the eland antelope, favourite of the trickster god /Kaggen,[31] and principal among the 'maieutic creatures' of /Xam trance performance, was also a valued source of food. Moreover, humans and animals were closely linked in a single moral community, 'for the people of today were the animals of the past and the animals of today were the dawn-time people'.[32] The first order of creation had been reversed because it was flawed, but the people of today still carried within themselves aspects of their 'dawn-time' animal identity and the animals retained certain human characteristics. Such beliefs, as the anthropologist Mathias Guenther has observed of the Nharo of present-day Botswana, amounted to 'a cogent doctrine of communion between man and beast'.[33] Features of the landscape,

28   I prefer the term *veeboer* to the more commonly used *trekboer*, since the latter suggests a mobility which I think would not have been characteristic of European stock-farmers in the eighteenth century.

29   This instrumentalist attitude to nature seems to have changed during the course of the next century. By the 1930s, it seems, inherited land had come to acquire an almost mystical significance for the Afrikaner intelligentsia. Cf. J.M. Coetzee, *White Writing: On the Culture of Letters in South Africa* (Sandton, 1988), ch. 4.

30   For further explanation of the expression 'strong things', see J.D. Lewis-Williams, *Believing and Seeing: Symbolic Meanings in Southern San Rock Paintings* (New York, 1981), p. 77.

31   *Ibid.*, pp. 84, 123.

32   *Ibid.*, p. 88.

33   M. Guenther, 'The Nharo Bushmen of Botswana: Tradition and Change', *Quellen zur Khoisan-Forschung*, no. 3 (Hamburg, 1986), pp. 227, 238.

such as fountains, pans and ridges, seem also to have had a symbolic meaning for the southern San, although they do not seem to have regarded certain
places as sacred in the same sense as the Australian Aborigines.[34]

Under these circumstances, the loss of territory, or the invasion of hunting grounds, would involve more than an economic loss; it would provoke a
spiritual crisis as well. If we say, then, that the *soaqua* of the Escarpment
were fighting to preserve their land from annexation and their hunting
grounds from violation, we must understand that, in doing so, they were
fighting for their very identity. Hence, I believe, the extraordinary tenacity of
their resistance in the face of what, in the end, were overwhelming odds.

PRISONERS OF WAR

The most direct and visible link between the Bushman frontier and the structure of social relations in the Boer domain was embodied in the persons of
the captives taken by the commandos and distributed among the men at the
close of an expedition.[35] Contrary to the impression created in Giliomee's
text, these war captives (sometimes explicitly called *krijgsgevangenen* in the
records) made up a significant proportion of the total labour force in frontier
districts. It is nearly impossible to make an exact assessment of their number,
since the primary source of information—the reports of Veldwagtmeesters—
sometimes omitted to mention the taking of captives, listing only the number
of 'Bushmen' killed. And the other major source of information—the registers of *inboekselingen*[36] compiled by the local authorities—did not always
distinguish clearly between 'Bushman' captives, *huisboorlingen* (Khoisan
children indentured to the European on whose farm they were born), and
Bastard Hottentotten (the offspring of slaves and 'Hottentots'), all of whom
were indentured to their masters until the ages of 18 or 25 years.[37] Moreover,
several entries in the registers refer simply to children 'without father or
mother', who could be either captives or orphaned *huisboorlingen*.[38]

---

34   J. Deacon, 'The Power of Place in Understanding Southern San Rock Engravings', *World Archaeology*,
     20 (1988); J.D. Lewis-Williams, 'Reply', *Current Anthropology*, 23 (1982), p. 447.

35   According to the instructions issued to Godlieb Rudolph Opperman in 1774, and again to Adriaan van
     Jaarsveld, Commandant of the Eastern Country, in 1780, the prisoners were to be divided among the
     members of the commando 'to serve for their subsistence for a fair term of years, according to the prison-
     er's age'; or, failing this, they were to be divided among the other inhabitants, 'always preferring those
     who are the poorest'. (Moodie, *The Record*, part III, pp. 29, 101.) In practice, however, prisoners were
     nearly always allocated among the members of a commando before it disbanded.

36   Best translated as 'indentured servants'.

37   See CA, 1/GR 15/43, Lijst van de Ingeboekte Hottentotten beginnende met de maand December 1786;
     Aantekening der Ingeboekten Hottentotten, beginnende van Primo September 1795 tot 1799; Register
     van zodanige Hottentotten die als huisboorlingen gehouden zijn, hunne hieronder gespecifeerde meesters
     den tijd van 25 jaaren te dienen.

38   *Ibid.*

Nevertheless, despite the less than satisfactory nature of the sources, one can establish that at least 548 'Bushmen' were taken captive by commandos sent out from the district of Stellenbosch between 1774 and 1786,[39] while 669 were captured by the militia of Graaff-Reinet during the following decade (1786–95).[40] Of these latter, 332 were formally registered as *inboekselingen*. Since a good number of the men involved in the Stellenbosch commandos were actually resident in divisions (such as the Sneeuberg and the Camdeboo) which in 1786 became part of the new district of Graaff-Reinet, one can reasonably assume that by 1795 there were upwards of 1,000 war captives among the labour force of this district. To these should be added the small number of captives taken by commandos operating from the district of Swellendam before 1786, and the unknown number of 'Bushmen' and Khoekhoe kidnapped by unauthorized raiding parties.[41] Unfortunately, it was not until 1798 that the authorities began to record the total number of 'Hottentots' in service with the Boers, but even if we make the unlikely assumption that their number in the 1780s had not been much lower than the 1798 figure of 8,635 men, women and children, it is apparent that war captives made up a very substantial segment of the total servant population.[42] By the last decade of the eighteenth century they probably outnumbered the officially acknowledged slave population of Graaff-Reinet by nearly two to one.[43]

The majority of these captives were women and children, for men of fighting age did not often survive an engagement with a Boer commando. However it is wrong to suggest that mature men were never taken captive. According to the lists of inboekselingen, the children's ages could range from just a few months to 16 or even 20 years.[44] The rules governing the apprenticeship of 'Bushman' children were not formally codified during the period of Dutch East India Company rule[45] and they appear to have varied

---

39   This figure is a sum of the numbers given in the reports of Veldwagtmeesters from the Stellenbosch district between 1774 and 1786. Reports dated Mar. 1774 to July 1781 can be found in Moodie, *The Record*, part III while those dated July 1781–July 1786 are in the series CA, 1/STB 10/163, 13/13 and 13/43. Whereas reports compiled in the 1770s regularly list the number of 'Bushmen' killed and captured, those compiled in the early 1780s do so less often.

40   Wyndham Smith, 'From Frontier to Midlands', p. 17.

41   See, for example, CA, CJ 362, Documents in Criminal Cases (1753), pp. 148–9; 1/GR 3/16, Criminal Interrogatories, 1786–92: Statement of the female Hottentot Hester, 25 Nov. 1791; Statement of the Hottentot Captain Ruijter Platje, ? Nov. 1791; Statement of Theunis Botha Jacobzoon, 7 Nov. 1792; Statement of Christiaan Kok, 29 Dec. 1792. See also A. Sparrman, *A Voyage to the Cape of Good Hope Towards the Antarctic Polar Circle Round the World and to the Country of the Hottentots and the Caffres from the Year 1772–6*, vol. I, V.S. Forbes (ed.) (Cape Town, 1977), pp. 198–9.

42   The figures for 1798 can be found in CA, J 115 and those for 1800 in J 118.

43   In 1787 there were 470 slaves in the district of Graaff-Reinet; by 1791 there were 672 and in 1796 there were 579. See the Graaff-Reinet Opgaafrollen, CA, J 107 (1787), J 108 (1788) and J 113 (1796).

44   CA, 1/GR 15/43, Lijst van de Ingeboekte Hottentotten, etc.

45   At any rate, I could find no record of such rules in the *Kaapse Plakaatboeke* (Cape Town, 1944, 1948,

according to the whim of the local authorities (thus between 1786 and 1790 'Bushman' children were usually apprenticed *until* the age of 18 or 25 years, whereas after 1790 they might be apprenticed *for* 25 years), but it was always in a master's interest to give the lowest possible estimate of an apprentice's age. In the eighteenth century such subterfuges went undetected, but we may assume that the gross irregularities exposed by members of the London Missionary Society early in the nineteenth century had a long history. 'I have frequently had my attention called', observed Dr John Philip in 1828,

> to cases in which young people, who had arrived at the ages of fourteen and sixteen years, have been rated, at that period of life, as being eight years of age only, and then apprenticed for ten years. In one case of this nature, after being assured by the local authorities of the district that an apprenticed boy was not more than eight years of age, I proved, by the evidence of the farmer at whose place he was born, that he was fifteen years of age at the very time he was apprenticed by them as a child not exceeding eight years of age. This fact, however, would not have been so easily established, if it had not been that the magistrate had used his dispensing power in this case, in taking the boy from the farmer with whom the father lived.[46]

Moreover every now and again, in documents appended to the reports of Veldwagtmeesters, one finds incontrovertible evidence that adult men and women were included among the captives parcelled out to commando members. In the aftermath of the General Commando of 1774, for example, Nicolaas van der Merwe distributed seven male captives whose ages (according to his estimates) ranged from 20 to 50 years. With three of them were paired three women, aged respectively 30, 40 and 50 years, who may have been their wives.[47]

In general, however, the commandos preferred to avoid taking grown men captive. A harassed militiaman who had coaxed and bullied an undermanned expedition through four or five weeks in the open veld could do without the burden of adult captives. There was often no means of restraining them—even the General Commando had not received its full complement of handcuffs and leg-irons—and they had to be kept under constant guard.[48] Not every Veldwagtmeester had had the unfortunate experience of Andries van der Walt, whose 82 captives attempted to escape under cover of night, 'while some of the males attacked the wagon in which their bows and arrows had been placed'; but many, one suspects, shared Van der Walt's

---

1949, 1950 and 1951).

46   J. Philip, *Researches in South Africa: Illustrating the Civil, Moral, and Religious Condition of the Native Tribes* (London, 1828; reprinted New York, 1969), vol. I, p. 180.

47   CA, 1/STB 10/162, Notitie, Jan. 1775.

48   See for example CA, 1/GR 12/1, Statement of D. du Toit.

opinion that the taking of prisoners was altogether too much trouble and that it would be far better 'to destroy the robbers without giving quarter'.[49]

Sentiments like these do not accord with a view of the burgher commando sometimes espoused by historians, namely that slave-raiding was one of its primary functions.[50] There is little doubt that some men banded together explicitly for the purpose of taking captives, while others made occasional kidnapping forays as a diversion from the hunt.[51] Indeed, Anders Sparrman has left us a vivid account of the *modus operandi* on such occasions. Although not an eye-witness account, it is worth quoting in full because of the unusual detail with which it describes the process of enslavement. 'The capture of slaves from among this race of men ['Boshies-men'] is by no means difficult,' he explained,

> and is effected in the following manner. Several farmers, that are in want of servants, join together, and take a journey to that part of the country where the Boshies-men live. They themselves, as well as their Lego-Hottentots,[52] or else such Boshies-men as have been caught some time before, and have been trained up to fidelity in their service, endeavour to spy out where the wild Boshies-men have their haunts. This is best discovered by the smoke of their fires. They are found in societies from ten to fifty and a hundred, reckoning great and small together. Notwithstanding this, the farmers will venture on a dark night to set upon them with six or eight people, which they contrive to do, by previously stationing themselves at some distance round about the craal. Then they give the alarm by firing a gun or two. By this means there is such a consternation spread over the whole body of these savages, that it is only the most bold and intelligent among them, that have the courage to break through the circle and steal off. These the captors are glad enough to get rid of at so easy a rate, being better pleased with those that are stupid, timorous, and struck with amazement, and who consequently allow themselves to be taken and carried into bondage. They are, however, at first, treated by gentle methods; that is, the victors intermix the fairest promises with their threats, and endeavour, if possible, to shoot some of the larger kinds of game for their prisoners, such as buffaloes, sea-cows and the like. Such agreeable baits, together with a little tobacco, soon induce them, continually cockered and feasted as they are, to go with a tolerable degree of cheerfulness to the colonists's [sic] place of abode. There this luxurious junketing upon meat and fat is exchanged for more moderate portions, consisting for the most part of butter-milk, gruel and porridges .[53]

49   Report of Commandant Opperman, 1 May 1775, in Moodie, *The Record*, part III, p. 67, Supplementary Papers.

50   Cf. S. Trapido, 'Reflections on Land, Office and Wealth', in Marks and Atmore (eds.), *Economy and Society*, pp. 351–2. Legassick does not specifically refer to slave-raiding, but stresses the general economic functions of the commando. (Martin Legassick, 'The Northern Frontier to *c.*1840: The Rise and Decline of the Griqua People', in Elphick and Giliomee (eds.), *Shaping*, p. 361.) See also J. Barrow, *Travels into the Interior of Southern Africa in the years 1797 and 1798* (London, 1801), vol. I, p. 292, and Philip, *Researches*, vol. II, p. 274.

51   See, for example, CA, CJ 362, Documents in Criminal Cases (1753), Duplicq of Jacobus Botha

However, despite the great value of Sparrman's account, it would be a mistake to view the slaving activities of most commandos in these terms. In the majority of cases, slaving was a by-product of a commando's activities, not its primary goal. Were it otherwise, militia officers would have made some attempt to curb the random slaughter so as to maximize the supply of young and tractable prisoners. How, for example, if slaving were the prime concern of the commandos, would one account for behaviour such as that of the Veldcorporaal Dirk Marx, who, after overcoming a 'Bushman' band in the Little Karoo, had all but six of the survivors shot in cold blood?[54] And how would one explain the massacre orchestrated by Adriaan van Jaarsveld at the Blaauwbank in August 1775?[55] The only reasonable conclusion is that the primary objective of the commandos was to incapacitate their enemies, not to take captives, though captives were a most useful by-product of their exertions.

The authorities in Cape Town were ambivalent about the taking of Bushman captives. The Council of Policy had long abandoned hopes of a negotiated settlement with the mountain raiders and therefore lent its support to the commandos, yet its members recoiled from the immoderate and 'vindictive' conduct of the militiamen and constantly exhorted them to avoid unnecessary bloodshed.[56] The taking of captives was seen as an alternative to wanton bloodshed and was therefore encouraged.[57] On the other hand, the Company had always been mindful of the consequences which might follow from the enslavement of the native population. The instructions issued to Jan van Riebeeck in 1651 had enjoined him to avoid injury to the persons and property of the natives, lest 'they be rendered averse to our people' and this had remained Company policy from that time onwards.[58] Van Riebeeck's

Jacobuszoon, 28 Oct. 1751, pp. 148–9.

52 That is, hired Hottentots.

53 Sparrman, *Voyage to the Cape of Good Hope*, vol. I, pp. 198–9.

54 CA, CJ 362, Documents in Criminal Cases (1753), Trial of Jacobus Botha Jacobuszoon, Statement of the Hottentot Ruijter, 30 Dec. 1750.

55 Van Jaarsveld and his men shot 12 hippopotami and left the carcasses at the Blaauwbank on the Zeekoe River. The commando returned the following night, having heard that 'a great number of Bosmans' had gathered at the site of the kill. At dawn the men attacked, killing 122 'robbers' and taking 21 prisoners. (Moodie, *The Record*, part III, pp. 44–5.)

56 See, for example, Instruction...to...the newly-appointed Field Commandant Godlieb Rudolph Opperman...19 Apr. 1774; Extract of Records of the Landdrost and Militia Officers Stellenbosch, 5 Mar. 1776; Extract from Resolution of Council, 5 June 1777; Instructions for the Commandant of the Eastern Country, 5 Dec. 1780, in Moodie, *The Record*, part III, pp. 29, 52–3, 7, 101.

57 Instructions...to...the newly-appointed Field Commandant Godlieb Rudolph Opperman, 19 Apr. 1774; Instructions for the Commandant of the Eastern Country, 5 Dec. 1780, in Moodie, *The Record*, part III, pp. 29, 101; A.J. Böeseken, 'Die Nederlandse Kommissarisse en die 18de Eeuse Samelewing aan die Kaap', *Archives Year Book for South African History* (1944), pp. 84–5.

58 R. Ross, 'The Changing Legal Position of the Khoisan in the Cape Colony, 1652–1795', *African Perspectives*, no. 2, 1979. One might note that similar considerations had induced the Carolina Proprietors to restrict the enslavement of native Americans in the 17th century. (P. Wood, *Black*

proposal to enslave the Peninsular Khoekhoe had not been rejected out of hand, but it had not been approved either.[59]

One hundred and forty years later, the Veldwagtmeester Petrus Pienaar was sharply rebuked for his over-zealous response to the Company's offer of a premium, payable in rixdollars, for every Bushman taken alive by the commandos. The intention of the Council of Policy, its members insisted, had been solely to 'prevent the unnecessary shedding of human blood', not to encourage a trade in human beings. Pienaar was informed that his proposal to raise commandos at his own expense, specifically for the purpose of taking captives, was entirely contrary to Company policy; such actions would merely 'incite the natives to further hostilities' and bring 'the greatest disorders and confusion' upon the colony.[60] Again, in 1795, O.G. de Wet, President of the Council of Justice and special commissioner to the troubled district of Graaff-Reinet, firmly vetoed a request from the Krijgsraad of that district to the effect that those who did commando duty should be allowed to sell their captives 'by legal transfer even as slaves', upon payment of a sum of money into the Company's chest. De Wet was no less concerned than were local officials about finding a means of rekindling the 'departed military ardour' of frontiersmen, but he could not countenance so radical a departure from Company policy.[61]

However, while the authorities may have shrunk from giving sanction to the deliberate enslavement of Bushmen, they knew only too well that war captives made up a steadily increasing component of the labour force on the farms of the interior. (De Wet, indeed, had gone out of his way to find a means of securing the farmers' hold over their captives, short of granting them the rights of slaveholders.)[62]

Company officials found refuge, perhaps, from the disturbing implications of their paradoxical stance, in the comforting fact that Bushman captives remained free persons in the eyes of the law. Unlike slaves, their status as voluntary servants was neither permanent nor heritable; they would be freed at the expiry of 'a fixed and equitable [but unspecified] term of years'; and whilst in service they would (according to the instructions issued to Veldcommandant Opperman in 1774) be well treated and properly maintained.[63] Moreover, as we have seen, they were not to be bought or sold.

Majority: Negroes in Colonial South Carolina from 1670 through the Stono Rebellion (New York, 1975), pp. 38–9.

59   Ross, *ibid.*, and Elphick, *Kraal and Castle*, p. 102.

60   CA, C 221, Resolusies, 11 Jan. 1794.

61   CA, VC 68, Extract from Minutes of Krijgsraad, 2 June 1795, pp. 132–7. See also 1/GR 1/1, Minutes of a Meeting of Heemraden and Militia Officers, 16 Mar. 1795, pp. 300–5.

62   CA, VC 68, Extract from Minutes of Krijgsraad, 2 June 1795, pp. 132–7.

63   Instructions…to…the newly-appointed Field Commandant Godlieb Rudolph Opperman, 19 Apr. 1774,

Good treatment was particularly emphasized by the authorities: they noted that war captives had been maltreated 'more than once' in the past and 'thus excited to wicked revenge'.

Alas, these provisions were, for the most part, a dead letter, and the authorities must have known it. Certainly the visiting Commissioners, Nederburgh and Frijkenius, knew it.[64] It is true that the local registers of captives and other *inboekselingen* specified a fixed term of indenture, but only a small proportion of captives was actually entered in these registers, and of those whose names *were* recorded, many were apprenticed *for* 25 years rather than until the age of 25.[65] In the case of adult captives, 25 years would have entailed a lifetime of servitude. Moreover, there is little positive evidence that Bushman captives were ever released at the expiry of their term of indenture. Indeed, it is peculiarly difficult to follow the lives of captive Bushmen for any distance in the historical record; all too often they disappear without trace after the moment of capture. The reason, I believe, is not that there was a conspiracy of silence, or that the majority of them escaped, but rather that as they were absorbed into the servant body on the farms they lost their distinctive identity, at least in the eyes of their masters, and were subsumed within the general category of 'Hottentots', along with the other servants of indigenous origin. 'The Hottentots at Graaff Reinet...[were] mostly generated from the Bosjesmen,' explained the elder Andries Stockenstrom in 1807, 'and only trained to be herdsmen'.[66] And Stockenstrom's son, who knew the frontier even better than his father, echoed the latter's opinion: the Bushmen 'that had lived for a length of time among the farmers,' he explained, '[and become] accustomed to a more civilized mode of life...were in general accounted as Hottentots' and should not be confused with 'the wild Bushmen without the limits of the colony'.[67] As a rule, then, adult captives cannot be distinguished in the historical record, for they have become one with other 'Hottentots'. Their fate, one supposes, was similar to that of many *huisboorlingen*, who, though nominally free at the age of 18 or 25 years, were *de facto* tied to their masters for life.

Occasionally one catches a brief glimpse of their condition. In the summer of 1798, for example, Jacobus Jooste had laid a complaint against his stepfather, Johannes Schalk Hugo, regarding a slave girl whom Hugo was

in Moodie, *The Record*, part III, p. 29.

64 A.J. Böeseken, 'Die Nederlandse Kommissarisse, pp. 84–5.

65 CA, 1/GR 15/43, Register van zodanige Hottentotten die als huisboorlingen gehouden zijn, hunne hieronder gespecifeerde meesters den tijd van 25 jaaren te dienen.

66 CA, GH 28/1, Magistrate of Graaff-Reinet to Governor, 17 July 1807, enclosed in Despatch no. 11, Caledon to Colonial Secretary, 1807.

67 Stockenstrom to Mr Smit, 20 Oct. 1815, cited in W.M. Macmillan, *The Cape Colour Question: A Historical Survey* (Cape Town, 1968), p. 129.

allegedly withholding from him. Hugo admitted the charge, but explained that 'his Hottentot' was 'coupled' with the girl and that if he were to give her up he would surely lose his Hottentot too, something he could not afford. 'It is a Bushman Hottentot', he explained,

> whom my wife's late husband brought as a child from the Zeekoe River... I am not unwilling to give up the girl, if I could but be sure that my Hottentot would not abscond...but that will be the upshot of it and I cannot do without him as I have few volk.[68]

As to the heritability of slave status, the children of Bushman captives were *de jure* exempt from this fate, but in practice such children would have been indentured as *huisboorlingen* to their masters, or their masters' descendants, along with the children of other 'tame Hottentots'. As Orlando Patterson has so convincingly argued, the heritability of slavery was a function of the 'natal alienation' or radical deracination of the victims of enslavement. The slave was 'a socially dead person. Alienated from all rights or claims of birth, he ceased to belong in his own right to any legitimate social order.'[69] It followed that,

> having no natal claims of his own, he had none to pass on to his children. And because no one else had any [recognized] claim or interest in such children, the master could claim them as his own essentially on the grounds that whatever the parents of such children expended in their upbringing incurred a debt to him.[70]

As we shall see, the extent to which Bushman captives were really 'natally alienated' was precisely the issue around which the ferocious struggle between master and servant revolved. But the very existence of the *inboekseling* system presupposed an assumption on the part of the masters that their 'Hottentot' servants had lost their independent social existence and with it their capacity to assert their claims upon their kin.

Of the several measures instituted to protect the Bushmen against enslavement, only the prohibition on the sale of captives appears to have been adhered to. Company officials, as we have seen, had consistently stood firm on this point, perhaps because they considered chattel status to be the determining characteristic of slavery.[71] Thus, while O.G. de Wet had been willing to support whatever measures were necessary to secure a captor's hold over his *inboekseling* for the full 25-year term, he had stopped short at purchase and sale.[72]

---

68   CA, 1/STB 10/152, Inkomende Brieven, 1798–9, Johannes Schalk Hugo to Landdrost van der Riet, 13 Nov. 1798. For the relationship between Hugo and Jooste, see C.C. de Villiers and C. Pama, *Geslagsregisters van die Ou Kaapse Families* (Cape Town, 1966), vol. I, pp. 339, 368.

69   O. Patterson, *Slavery and Social Death: A Comparative Study* (Cambridge, Mass., 1982), p. 5.

70   *Ibid.*, p. 9.

71   Many eminent students of slavery would agree with them. Moses Finley, for example, is uncompromising on this point. (*Ancient Slavery and Modern Ideology*, London, 1980, pp. 73–5.) Patterson, however, regards chattel status as a by-product of the more fundamental characteristic of the slave-natal alienation.

There is no doubt, however, that the Company's stance was deeply resented by the *veeboeren*. On De Wet's arrival in Graaff-Reinet in April 1795, the rebellious citizenry had presented him with a *Klachtschrift*, or written statement of their grievances. A rambling and irreverent document, written in a tone of high indignation, it gave vent to the freeburghers' great anger against the officials who had been placed over them, in particular Landdrost Maynier, whom they had recently evicted from the Drostdy.[73] Maynier, they alleged, was an upstart and a rogue, an oppressor of widows and orphans, a thief and a 'destroyer of the land and people' who had put the interests of the heathen above those of his Christian subjects.[74] His Hottentot policy was a particular source of grievance. Not only had he opened his court to the complaints of 'deserters' from service; he had also, so his critics alleged, allowed the district gaoler, a certain Bodenstrom, to sell arrested runaways 'by way of prison expenses'. 'Is this right?' they demanded to know,

> As these men [their former masters] had brought them up from childhood? It may be answered they are a free people—then why may one sell them, and not another? If a burgher may not do that, still less may a gaoler—Granted, there is a show of right about the expenses—but what have we for our trouble? Almost all of them were deserving of death—we have risked our lives; and must see them taken away, after all our trouble and risk.[75]

No sooner had De Wet in his turn been expelled from the district, than the rebel leaders declared their intention to remedy this defect in the law. Henceforth, they declared,

> Bushman Hottentots, male or female, taken on commando, or by individuals, [were] to remain the property from generation to generation, of those with whom they reside.[76]

This innovation presumably survived no longer than the short-lived 'republic' which had spawned it; however, lest we place too much trust in the power of the newly-installed British authorities to suppress an illegal trade, we should recall that, in 1817, Landdrost Stockenstrom had felt obliged to inform government of the existence of a widespread traffic in Bushman children. Referring to the 'ancient custom', by which the farmers procured Bushman children from their parents in exchange for 'trifles', he confessed

---

72 CA, VC 882, Moodie's Afschriften, vol. 19, Extracts from the Records of the Military Court, Graaff-Reinet, 2 June 1795.

73 Honoratus Christiaan David Maynier, christened at the Cape on 20 July 1760, son of Horatius Conrad Maynier of Leipzig; appointed to the secretaryship of Graaff-Reinet in 1789 and to the magistracy in 1792. For a full account of the Graaff-Reinet burgher rebellion, see Marais, *Maynier and the First Boer Republic*, ch. 7

74 CA, VC 871, Moodie's Afschriften, vol. 8. Complaints of 276 Boers of Graaff-Reinet against Maynier, 16 Apr. 1795.

75 *Ibid.*

76 CA, VC 887, Moodie's Afschriften, vol. 24, p. 676.

to a strong suspicion that this custom

> was beginning to be seriously abused; that these children…are transferred from one hand to another, and that payment is secretly taken; that many, by these means, are gradually taken from the frontier, brought into the inner districts, and passed off as orphans; that itinerant merchants are beginning to be supplied with them, through some channel or other.[77]

As to the question of proper maintenance and 'good treatment', it was a non-starter in the context of violent domination established by the forcible seizure and subsequent detention of Bushman captives. The problem, at root, was precisely that which the authorities had foreseen but failed to confront: it was imprudent to enslave the local population; it was unwise to take their children; it was dangerous to hold them captive in their native land. No amount of legal cant could disguise the fact that the Dutch had ignored a cardinal maxim in the annals of slavery: that 'neighbours made difficult slaves'.[78] Throughout the history of enslavement, Orlando Patterson reminds us, there has been 'a strong tendency on the part of a conquering group not to enslave a conquered population *en masse* and *in situ*'. There have been exceptions to this tendency, he observes, but

> the exceptions bring us to a second generalization, which can be stated in much stronger terms: attempts by a conquering group to enslave a conquered population *en masse* and *in situ* are almost always disastrous failures.[79]

For Patterson, the primary reason for the failure of such attempts lies in the inversion of the critical outsider or alien status of slaves in the slaveholding society. He explains:

> When a people was conquered, it was by definition the conquerors who were the outsiders to the local community and the conquered who were the natives. In this situation one of the most fundamental elements of slavery—natal alienation—was almost impossible to achieve.'[80]

In such a situation it was the master, not the slave, who was the intruder, the one without ancestral claims to belonging. Or at least this is how it would appear to the slave, and, though they might not care to admit it, to many members of the master class as well. The 'moral community', from which in the normal course of events the slave would be excluded, was in this case defined by the conquered as much as by the conqueror. Who, in such circumstances, was 'the enemy within'? The very phrase—which describes the position of the slave in those societies where slaves were externally

---

77 Cited in Philip, *Researches*, vol. II, pp. 265–6.

78 R. Blackburn, 'Slavery—its Special Features and Social Role', in L. Archer (ed.), *Slavery and Other Forms of Unfree Labour* (London, 1988), p. 268.

79 Patterson, *Slavery and Social Death*, pp. 110, 112.

80 *Ibid.*, p. 111.

recruited, often as prisoners of war—took on a new meaning in cases where the slave was himself a native. It was not simply in a negative sense—by virtue of his alienation from the community of the conqueror—that he was the enemy within, it was also in a positive sense—by virtue of his kinship with the still existent (albeit damaged) community of the conquered.

MIGHT WITHOUT RIGHT

In such circumstances, the very basis of slavery was under threat. The power of the slaveholder, as Patterson has emphasized, rests not only on brute force, but also, crucially, on authority, by which force is transformed into right and obedience into duty; and authority, in turn, derives from the master's control of symbolic and ritual processes. It was this control which allowed him to define the slave as a non-person, alien, dishonoured and degraded. And the slave, cut off from his own cultural heritage and lacking the social support which could reinforce an alternative definition of himself, came to obey the master, 'not only out of fear, but out of the basic need to exist as a quasi-person, however marginal and vicarious that existence might be'.[81] However, where the slave was held captive on his native terrain, he had access from the outset to an alternative symbolic universe and to a living cultural heritage on which he could draw in his struggle to combat and contradict the master's conception of himself. He was not obliged to create a new community on foreign soil as was the case with slaves uprooted and transported far from home.[82]

How true this was of San captives! Every krans, every fountain, every pool of water carried reminders of a cosmic order whose foundations had been laid long before the coming of the Europeans. The *veeboeren* had blundered into this world, ignorant of its principles, unaware of its secrets, recklessly careless of its prohibitions. They had desecrated its landscape and destroyed its most precious treasures, killing eland like cattle, piling the carcasses high on their wagons, without regard to the meaning of their actions. In time perhaps, like the Nharo of Botswana, the San would come to accept and rationalize the superiority of the intruders, integrating their explanations into the old cosmology;[83] or worse, like the Inca of Peru and the Aztecs of Mexico, they might conclude that their gods had failed them and their world was lost:

> Let us die then,
> Let us perish then,
> For our gods are already dead![84]

---

81 *Ibid.*, pp. 39–41.

82 Please note: I am not arguing here that slaves who were true outsiders had no sense of dignity, merely

But, to the best of our knowledge, no such sense of moral collapse had taken root among the /Xam of the Central Escarpment before the end of the eighteenth century. On the contrary, as we have seen, the hegemony of Europeans was resisted tooth and nail; nowhere, until the nineteenth century, did the mountain people concede defeat. (And even then, as the very existence of the Bleek collection demonstrates, indigenous culture and cosmology displayed an extraordinary durability.)[85] 'Of all those people whom the avarice of the Europeans has treated with cruelty,' declared Le Vaillant,

> there are none who preserve a stronger remembrance of the injuries they have sustained, or who hold the name of the whites in greater detestation... Their resentment is so violent that they have always the dreaded word 'vengeance' in their mouth.[86]

Indeed, so resilient was the 'moral community' of the conquered in this case, that, in 1799, more than 30 years after the first occupation of their territories by Europeans, the rebel leader Klaas Stuurman could rally hundreds of 'Hottentot' servants to his cause with his powerful restorationist vision, saying:

> Restore the country of which our forefathers were despoiled by the Dutch and we have nothing more to ask... We have lived very contentedly...before these Dutch plunderers molested us, and why should we not do so again if left to ourselves? Has not the Groot Baas given plenty of grass-roots, and berries and grasshoppers for our use; and, till the Dutch destroyed them, abundance of wild animals to hunt? And will they not return and multiply when these destroyers are gone?[87]

Clearly, in such a context, 'good treatment' and 'proper maintenance' would not suffice to reconcile the captured to their condition, nor restrain them from 'wicked revenge'.

On a more practical level too, the enslavement of natives was a peculiarly 'arduous option'.[88] Members of a conquered population held captive on their own terrain could resist captivity in numerous ways which were not available to 'natally alienated' slaves. Here again, one should stress that the decisive factor is the existence of an alternative 'moral community'. In every slave society many slaves were native born; in some societies even newly-

---

that they had to fight against greater odds to achieve it. I think this is Patterson's meaning too. Indeed, he argues that the greater the sense of alienation, the greater the striving to overcome it.

83 Guenther, *The Nharo Bushmen of Botswana*, pp. 232–3.

84 Libros de los Coloquios de los Doce, in W. Lehmann, *Sterbende Gotter und Christliche Heilsbotschaft* (Stuttgart, 1949), p. 102, cited in N. Wachtel, *The Vision of the Vanquished*, p. 27.

85 The Bleek collection comprises more than 12,000 pages of oral testimony, songs and folklore, as told to the German linguist W.H. Bleek and his sister-in-law, Lucy Lloyd, by /Xam informants imprisoned on the breakwater in Cape Town in the late 1860s. The collection is housed at the University of Cape Town.

86 Le Vaillant, *New Travels*, vol. II, p. 347.

87 Barrow, *Travels*, vol. II, p. 111.

88 Blackburn, 'Slavery', p. 268.

recruited slaves were natives—'fallen' persons who had been excluded from the community because they had breached its norms; but in such cases the ideological hegemony of the master class usually ensured that there were few free persons to whom a runaway could turn. Only communities of former slaves, such as Free Blacks in the Americas, or outlawed maroon bands, might be expected to shelter the recalcitrant slave. Where slaves were drawn from a conquered group, however, runaways would be welcomed as heroes by those who had as yet escaped enslavement. They would, moreover, bring skills and information which could be put to good use in the service of continuing resistance. And their intimate knowledge of the environment would enable them to survive the dangerous passage to freedom far better than those whose roots lay in another land and whose only experience of the local terrain had been gleaned in captivity.

The role of the natal community of the war captive in relation to the slaveowner was not unlike that of maroon communities in the Americas. Like the maroon community, but perhaps more starkly, it represented 'the antithesis of all that slavery stood for'; its presence on the fringes of the colonized domain rendered the master's hold over his slave critically insecure, and ensured that, as in Brazil or the Caribbean, 'the most brutal punishments were reserved for recaptured runaways.'[89]

These factors go a long way, I would argue, towards explaining the peculiar violence which punctuated relations between a master and his *volk* on the Cape frontier. Captive Bushmen could and did desert with relative ease. Some escaped repeatedly, despite the ordeal they faced on recapture.[90] And while most escapees may have chosen to steal silently into the night, there were some who made a more dramatic departure, or who, having gone, returned with reinforcements to wreak a noisy revenge.

There was, for instance, the 'Hottentot' Claas, who absconded from the service of Christiaan Bock in the Hantam, and returned with 'a gang of Hottentots' to shoot poisoned arrows at Bock and set fire to his house. Claas was apprehended some weeks later and sent up to Cape Town, where he was subjected to an exemplary punishment, being

> condemned to be bound to a post and severely flogged by the public executioner, with rods upon the bare back, and thereupon branded and riveted in chains, in order therein to labour for life at the Company's public works on Robben Island, without wages.[91]

This public chastisement may have helped to allay the anxieties of those

---

89   R. Price (ed.), *Maroon Societies: Rebel Slave Communities in the Americas*, 2nd edn. (Baltimore, 1979), pp. 2–3.

90   See, for example, E.C. Godee-Molsbergen, *Reizen in Zuid-Afrika in de Hollandse Tijd*, vol. IV (The Hague, 1932), p. 76.

91   Extract of the Journal, Colonial Office, 25 Mar. 1773, in Moodie, *The Record*, part III, p. 17.

in authority, but it had little effect on the behaviour of others who were moved to act as Claas had done. In 1777, for example, on the very night that Stephanus Naude was robbed of 15 oxen and his herdsman murdered,

> a Hottentot of Naude's ran off, hid himself about the farm for some days, and coming to the farm by night, killed Naude's principal Hottentot with a poisoned arrow.[92]

Again, in 1778, a 'Hottentot' named Carel deserted with a gun and joined a band of 'Bushman' robbers in the Roode Berg (Agter Renosterberg).[93] In October the following year, Carel was rumoured to have been among the sheep of Johannes Jurgen de Beer in the Camdeboo, together with another runaway who spoke 'good Dutch and had lived with Barend Burger'. No effort was spared in the attempt to recapture the elusive Carel, but, with the aid of an unknown companion, who paid with his life for misleading the avenging commando, Carel escaped to rob again: on 25 October De Beer's entire flock was stolen and barely one third was recovered.[94]

Perhaps the most flamboyant of the runaways was a man known to the colonists as Dikkop, who in July 1781 'deserted from Lodewyk Pretorius with a gun'. Dikkop's wife stole the gun from him and returned it to Pretorius, but Dikkop, undaunted by this betrayal,

> contrived to procure another gun from one of his master's Hottentots, named Vlaminck, and went on the hill behind Pretorius' house, at which he fired seven shots; the balls fell among the servants, and when Pretorius the same day went away to his other place, stationing another Hottentot to fire upon Dikkop, so as to keep him from the path,—he [Dikkop] fired a bullet under the horse on which Pretorius' wife was mounted, and then went back and set fire to the house; but was at last caught while asleep.

These events were reported by Adriaan van Jaarsveld, in whose jurisdiction the incident occurred. 'I beg', concluded Van Jaarsveld, 'that this Hottentot may, at least, be placed on the island;[95] for if such things go on, it will not be possible to oppose the public enemy.'[96]

But alas, the enemy was already within, and Van Jaarsveld, among others, had had a major hand in bringing this about. Moreover Robben Island, although a veritable chamber of horrors for those acquainted with it, was too far away to inspire fear among the servants of the interior. Without authority, then, and lacking even the primitive instruments of state repression available

---

92   Report of Commandant R.G. Opperman, in Moodie, *The Record*, part III, p. 68.

93   Report of Field Sergeants H.M. van den Berg and Adriaan van Jaarsvelt to the Landdrost and Militia Court, 11 Sept. 1779, in Moodie, *The Record*, part III, p. 85.

94   Report of Corporal Albertus van Jaarsvelt to Sergeant D.S. van der Merwe, 24 Nov. 1779, in Moodie, *The Record*, part III, p. 87, n. 1.

95   Robben Island.

96   Commandant A. van Jaarsveld's Report of the Expulsion of the Kafirs, 20 July 1781, in Moodie, *The Record*, part III, p. 112.

to slaveholders in the arable districts, the man who would be master of his Bushman servants was compelled to rely in large part on naked force—on what Machiavelli has called the 'beastly' aspect of power.

There *were* other strategies available to him, notably the option which Patterson has termed 'divide and partially enslave',[97] which in this case would involve an attempt to differentiate between captive Bushmen and voluntarily contracted Khoekhoe servants; however such strategies were largely ignored by the *veeboeren*. Voluntary arrangements (such as labour tenancy and various forms of wage labour) did exist; indeed such arrangements had probably predominated during the initial period of white settlement east of the Gamtoos, but they were soon swallowed up in the atmosphere of fear and tension which rapidly enveloped the whole sphere of relations between Europeans and native Khoisan. Very soon, as we shall see, the same forces which had created an inherent instability in the relations between Boer master and Bushman captive would engender a 'static electricity of violence' in nearly every household on the frontier.[98]

Runaway Bushmen were relentlessly pursued: '...as soon as they have eloped,' noted Sparrman,

> men are set to lie in ambush for them at such places by the rivers sides, as it is supposed they must take in their way, and by this means they are often retaken.[99]

Those recaptured were summarily and often cruelly punished. Nevertheless, despite the risks attendant on recapture, many runaways, driven perhaps by their failure to find refuge at a safe distance from their former masters, would return to the farmstead to seek food or companionship from the other servants. Thus the 'Bushman Hottentot' Dwa, who in 1788 had absconded from Johannes van der Walt, returned frequently to the *werf* at night 'to visit his mates'. One evening, while he was begging tobacco at the *strooijhuijs* of the Hottentots Legtvoet and Mannel, he was betrayed by the Hottentot Ruijter, whom Van der Walt had set to watch for him. Van der Walt then ordered his *knecht*, Jacob Nieman, to have the Bushman caught and beaten 'so that he could not leave the farm again'. So faithfully did Nieman execute this order that Dwa quickly lost consciousness and died the very same night—the next morning his body was found in the veld 'by a pool of water' and 'the following night was devoured by the wolves and jackals'.[100]

According to the Hottentot Jan Bries, Van der Walt had been overheard to say 'that, by order of the Veldwagtmeester, whenever a strange Hottentot

97   Patterson, *Slavery and Social Death*, p. 111.

98   The phrase is borrowed from Robin Lane Fox, *Pagans and Christians* (Harmondsworth, 1988).

99   Sparrman, *Voyage to the Cape of Good Hope*, vol. I, p. 201.

100 CA, 1/GR 3/16, Criminal Interrogatories, Statement of the Hottentot Piet, living with Johannes van der Walt; Statement of the Hottentot Jan Bries, 30 Dec. 1788; Statement of the Hottentot Willem, 30 Dec. 1788; Statement of the Hottentot Ruijter, 6 Jan. 1789.

came upon the *werf*, he should be driven away with a beating'.[101] Such an order had indeed been issued some years before by the Veldwagtmeester Hendrik Schalk Burger.[102] The intention of the order was to deter 'Hottentots' from 'wandering about'; but in this case it apparently failed, for, soon after the incident involving Dwa, another servant of Van der Walt's, a Hottentot named Bakker, who had testified during the preparatory examination into the death of the Bushman Dwa, ran off and joined the 'Bushman robbers', in whose company he stole and destroyed 'a considerable number' of sheep and cattle belonging to members of the Van der Merwe family, who lived, like Van der Walt, in the Agter Sneeuberg.[103]

If naked force was the primary means by which Bushman captives were prevented from escaping, it was scarcely less important in the everyday management of the relationship between master and bondsman. In the case of a captive child, the exercise of force might not amount to more than 'a few curses and blows', accompanied by the constant 'maundering and grumbling of his master and mistress', who might abuse him verbally, calling him *t'guzeri* or *t'gaunatsi* (which meant, according to Sparrman, 'young goblin' and 'evil spirit').[104] But in the case of adults, the imposition of a master's will frequently involved a tense physical confrontation, culminating all too often in explosive violence.

Thus the dramatic confrontation recalled so vividly in the circuit court at Graaff-Reinet in 1817 had been played out many times before, though with minor variations. The occasion was an inquiry into the death of the Bushman Hottentot Klaas, who had been one of five 'Bushman' servants on the farm of Petrus Coenraad van der Westhuizen in the Agter Sneeuberg.[105] In December 1816, Petrus Coenraad had gone up to the Cape with his *bijwoonder*, Leendert Louw, leaving his farm in the care of his sons, Pieter Willem and Nicolaas Johannes van der Westhuizen. One hot summer evening, 'shortly before New Year', as the Bastard Hottentot Klaas later recalled, bad blood had erupted between the Bushman Klaas and his young master, Nicolaas Johannes. Needless to say, the witnesses could not agree on the cause of the confrontation, except that it involved a ewe which had recently lambed. According to the Veldcornet Michiel Adriaan Oberholster, who was called to inspect the body, Klaas had 'thrown away' the lamb, causing distress to its mother and arousing the wrath of Nicolaas Johannes van der

---

101 CA, 1/GR 3/16, Statement of the Hottentot Jan Bries, 30 Dec. 1788.

102 CA, 1/GR 3/16, Order to Whip Wandering Hottentots, *c.*1784.

103 CA, 1/GR 3/16, Statement of the Hottentot Jager, in service with the Heemraad Hendrik van der Walt Schalkzoon.

104 Sparrman, *Voyage to the Cape of Good Hope*, vol. I, p. 199.

105 The farm was called Jakkalsfontein and was situated 'agter de Groot Tafelberg'. (CA, M 3i [Miscellaneous], Proceedings of the Circuit Court of Graaff-Reinet, 1817.)

Westhuizen, who threatened to 'klap' him. The next morning at daybreak, as Oberholster understood it, Nicolaas had 'given him [Klaas] a push' when the ewe came up to the kraal, and Klaas had at once sprung over the fence and fetched his bow and arrow from the *strooijhuis*.[106] According to Nicolaas Johannes, Klaas had twice refused to come when he was called to fetch the ewe and had instead approached him with a kierie in his hand. Nicolaas Johannes thereupon seized the kierie, while Klaas picked up a stone. Both then went to fetch their arms, Nicolaas to the house whence he returned with a *sjambok* and a gun, Klaas to the *strooijhuis* whence he fetched an assegai and his bow and poison arrows. Nicolaas seized the bow and arrow and called to the other Hottentots to grab hold of Klaas. 'While he stood thus captive', testified the *Kleinbaas*, 'I gave him six or seven blows'.

The Bushman Hottentot Snel who, with three others had been forced to hold Klaas down while he was beaten, omitted to mention the act of defiance, saying instead that '*Kleinbaas* Nicolaas' had come up to them, shaken Klaas's kierie from his hand and hit him with it. Klaas 'had done nothing', testified the Bushman Booij; but Snel agreed that Klaas had attempted to defend himself with poison arrows. He had spread his arrows out in front of himself, said Snel, and his bow was taut. All the witnesses agreed, however, that Klaas had received in excess of 40 lashes with a handsjambok, one finger thick and four and a half feet long. Snel had counted 230 lashes, he said, while Oberholster had found the marks of 44 *sjambok* blows upon his body, all of which had cut through his skin and some of which had injured his genitals. By midday Klaas was dead. He was buried immediately after the Veldcornet's inspection, wrapped in his kaross. He was 'hit too high up', said Oberholster, and rode away in anger.[107]

Incidents like this were not unusual on the frontier. On the contrary, they were a common part of daily life. Each phase of the colony's expansion had brought its harvest of domestic violence.[108] Whippings might occur in response to what a master or mistress perceived as idleness or negligence, as well as outright defiance. Shepherds and shepherdesses unlucky enough to lose a sheep in the veld, albeit to a beast of prey, were particularly at risk, but so were kitchen maids who rose too late in the morning, or tarried too long in the garden.[109] However, it should not be assumed that the familiarity of such punishments rendered them any the less shocking to the victims. On the

---

106 CA, M 3i, Proceedings...1817, Report of the Field-Cornet Michiel Adriaan Oberholster, 3 Feb. 1817.

107 *Ibid.*, Statement of the Bastaard Hottentot Klaas, 19 Apr. 1817.

108 See, for example, in connection with the whipping of Bushman servants: CA, CJ 362, Documents in Criminal Cases (1753), statement of the soldier Jan Hendrik Klem van 't Graafschap Lippe, 10 Dec. 1750, and 1/STB 10/150, Incoming letters, a letter unsigned and undated, but *c.*1800.

109 See, for example, CA, CJ 3387, Circuit Court, Uitenhage, 1812, Testimony of the Bastaard Hottentot Jan Mager, 10 Nov. 1812; Testimony of the slave September, 10 Nov. 1812.

contrary, it seems that the memory of these brutal incidents was sometimes burned so deeply into the psyche of the victims and their relatives that they could be recalled decades later, by people who had never known the prot-agonists.[110]

'DIVIDE AND PARTIALLY ENSLAVE?'

It is clear then that direct physical coercion, which in practice often meant the infliction of life-threatening injuries, was integral to the everyday rela-tionship between European masters and their 'Bushman' servants. But how did it come to play so large a role in the interaction between the *veeboeren* and the servant population as a whole, even those who were not originally war captives? The colonists themselves drew a distinction, albeit imprecise, between 'thieving Bushmen' on the one hand and 'good natives or Hottentots' on the other. And they frequently reminded themselves that these 'good natives' despised and disliked the Bushmen as much as they did them-selves.[111] Indeed, in 1777, the Council of Policy, issuing one of its many warnings against the abuse of Bushman captives, had seen fit to lay the blame for much of the cruelty already perpetrated at the door of the com-mandos' Hottentot attendants, 'as these last', opined the councillors, 'being in general very much ill-used by the Bushman nations, may be naturally inclined to take revenge'.[112]

There is indeed a fair amount of evidence that servants of Khoekhoe ori-gin were willing participants in the capture and enslavement of San women and children. Thus Sparrman reported in the 1770s that the Khoekhoe Captain Ruiter used to help his European neighbours 'to make slaves of such straggling Boshies-men as did not live under his jurisdiction'.[113] And Ruiter was not alone in this. In 1751, for example, when Elias Campher was accused by his neighbour, Jacobus Botha, of involvement in slave-raiding in Outeniqualand, he replied: 'It wasn't I who did it, but my Hottentots'.[114] Again, in an appendix to a list of captives distributed in the aftermath of Gerrit van Wyk's commando of 1774, it was noted that the commando had 'liberated twelve women, with six sucklings, and five girls besides, whom

---

110 See for example the story of Doortje and her mistress Trina de Klerk in UCT Manuscripts Collection, BC 151 (Bleek Collection), LV III–19, pp. 7657–70. I am indebted to Dr Janette Deacon for drawing my attention to this reference.

111 See, for example, CA, C 1266, Memorien en Rapporten, Landdrost and Krijgsraad of Stellenbosch to Governor, 7 May, 1776 and CJ 362, Documents in Criminal Cases (1753), Eijsch ende Conclusie of Landdrost J.A. Horak.

112 Extract from Resolution of Council, 5 June 1777, in Moodie, *The Record*, part III, p. 71.

113 Sparrman, *Voyage to the Cape of Good Hope*, vol. II, p. 124.

114 CA, CJ 362, Documents in Criminal Cases (1753), Trial of Jacobus Botha Jacobuszoon, Duplicq of Jacobus Botha Jacobuszoon, 28 Oct. 1751.

some of our Hottentots took to wife'.[115] Finally, we should recall Sparrman's encounter with an unnamed 'Hottentot' on the Coerney River in December 1777: 'this Hottentot', he noted, 'had caught, and then had in his custody, three old Boshies-women with their children, with an intention to take them home to his master for slaves'. The man 'had been brought up in a village near the Christians, in the service of whom he had always been' and professed to feel nothing but contempt for the 'savage manners' of his Bushman captives. He was unperturbed by their attempts to bewitch him, he said, for he 'had no faith in witchcraft'.[116]

Such sentiments could, one assumes, have been successfully exploited by a master class seeking to implement the strategy of 'divide and partially enslave' to which Patterson referred. And indeed, a careful scrutiny of the documentary record does suggest that Khoekhoe servants—or at least (since the record seldom allows so definite an attribution of identity) servants of non-captive origin—did feel their status to be different from that of Bushman captives. '*Baas, dat is niet bosjesmans of drosters kinderen dat baas die met de ketting om de hals moet vast maaken*' ['Baas, these are not Bushmen children or runaways whom baas should chain by the neck'], protested the Hottentot Jacob to his master, Johannes Roos, the latter having chained Jacob's children to a tree with a brake chain.[117]

One must also remember that 'Hottentot' servants were the chief victims of 'Bushman' attacks on colonial herds and flocks,[118] and that they often bore the brunt of the fighting when commandos were in the field. One might expect, then, that they would come increasingly to identify with their masters' view of themselves as loyalists, willing defenders of the colonial order against 'land-destroying' savages. Most herdsmen carried guns, though they were not allowed to own them,[119] and many a *veeboer* was saved from ruin by the timely action of his armed servants: 'On the 31st March', reported G.R. Opperman in 1776, 'the robbers attacked the place of Willem Jansen and tried to take the livestock by force from the kraals, but they failed because the *volk* on the farm shot at them from evening until morning'.[120]

However, before we accept too readily the notion of an emerging dichotomy between loyal and freely-contracted Hottentots on the one hand

---

115 Unsigned paper appended to the journal of the commando under the orders of Gerrit van Wyk, 2 Sep. 1774, in Moodie, *The Record*, part III, p. 38, n. 1.

116 Sparrman, *Voyage to the Cape of Good Hope*, vol. II, p. 34.

117 CA, 1/GR 3/16, Criminal Interrogatories, Statement of the Hottentot Jacob, 10 Jan. 1791.

118 Newton-King, 'The Enemy Within', ch. 5.

119 For evidence of the authorities' efforts to restrict Khoisan access to guns, see, for example, CA, C 492, Landdrost Horak to Governor, 20 May, 1755; Sparrman, *Voyage to the Cape of Good Hope*, vol. 1, p. 228, n. 20; CA, 1/STB 10/162, Gerrit Maritz and 30 Landholders to Landdrost, 3 Mar. 1787.

120 CA, C 1266, Memorien en Rapporten, G.R. Opperman to Governor, 13 Apr. 1776.

and persecuted Bushmen on the other,[121] we should consider that among the defending 'Hottentots' there were many who were themselves of Bushman origin.[122] And of those who were not, the great majority, I would argue, were bound to their masters in almost as rigid a fashion.

In the first place, many Hottentots, although not of captive origin, had been *ingeboekt* as *huisboorlingenen* or *Bastard Hottentotten*, legally obliged to serve the same master for anything up to 25 years.[123] And even those who had voluntarily contracted themselves were liable to find their children indentured under one or other of these two headings. Male slaves outnumbered females in the outlying districts of the colony (though the gender imbalance was less marked in the purely pastoral districts than in the mixed arable and pastoral districts),[124] so that liaisons between slave men and Khoisan women were fairly common. Consequently those children who escaped indenture as *huisboorlingenen* were quite likely to be *ingeboekt* as *Bastaarden* instead. The registers of Graaff-Reinet district show that at least 581 children were indentured under one or other category between 1787 and 1800.[125]

This system of 'apprenticeship', as several contemporary observers, from Anders Sparrman to John Philip, had clearly perceived, served to bind whole families to the person who had apprenticed the children.[126] Should the parents abscond or obtain permission to leave, they were faced with enforced separation from their offspring. Philip's florid prose and his tone of righteous indignation have led many a modern researcher to doubt the authenticity of his evidence, but in truth his account of the desperate struggle of an unnamed Hottentot woman to recover her children from the farmer who had purchased their slave father is matched in the records by numerous documented cases.[127]

Few perhaps leave as lasting an impression on the reader as that of the Bastard Hottentot, Sara, who cut the throats of her two youngest children rather than return with them to the family of her mistress, Christina van der Merwe, the widow of Hans Jurgen de Beer. Sara had been in the service of Hans Jurgen de Beer for 12 years , during which time, she said, she had been

---

121 Cf. D. van Arkel, G.C. Quispel and R. Ross, '"De Wijngaard des Heeren?" Een Onderzoek naar de Wortels van "die Blanke Baasskap" in Zuid-Afrika', *Cahiers Sociale Geschiedenis*, 4 (1983), p. 40.

122 See above, p. 239.

123 See above, *idem.*

124 N. Worden, *Slavery in Dutch South Africa* (Cambridge, 1985), pp. 54–5 and Table 5.3. Worden notes that in 1787, 37% of the slave population of Graaff-Reinet was female.

125 CA, 1/GR 15/43, Hottentot Contracts.

126 Sparrman, *Voyage to the Cape of Good Hope*, vol. I, pp. 200–1; Barrow, *Travels*, vol. II, pp. 406–7; Philip, *Researches*, vol. I, ch. 9.

127 Philip, *Researches*, vol. I, ch. 9, pp. 185–8.

reasonably well-treated.[128] She had stayed on after his death in 1784 because she had children by the Hottentot Flink, who was contracted to one of her master's sons, Andries Jacobus de Beer. However, soon after the old man's death, Andries Jacobus, unbeknown to his mother, had, Sara said, impregnated a Hottentot servant named Feitje, and the Widow de Beer, in her determination to discover the identity of the child's father, had beaten and maltreated Feitje until Sara could bear it no more and encouraged Feitje to name Andries Jacobus. For this, Sara declared, she had been persecuted by the widow and her sons, 'and forced to undergo the severest chastisements for trivial reasons'.[129] Following the break-up of her relationship with Flink (which he himself ascribed to the intervention of Andries Jacobus), she determined to leave 'and seek her fortune elsewhere'. The widow eventually gave her permission, but only on condition that Sara leave her eldest daughter, Leentje, behind. This Sara refused: 'my children are my cattle, aren't they?' she said, 'and everything that I possess'.[130] And shortly thereafter she left secretly, with all three of her children.

However Dawid de Beer (Andries Jacobus's elder brother) caught up with them on the big wagon road and, ordering Sara to follow with the two smaller children, he drove Leentje back to the house before his horse.[131] Some hours later Christina van der Merwe's nephew Willem arrived at the farmhouse with the news that he had found two Hottentot children beside the road with their throats cut. Sara was with them, badly wounded. When confronted by Dawid de Beer and a party of burghers, she admitted the murders and, as though 'to prove that she herself had done it', she cut herself in the throat and stomach.[132] Two years later the Court of Justice sentenced her to death, despite Commissioner-General Sluyksen's conviction that 'grief and desperation' had driven her to this 'unnatural deed'.[133]

Fortunately very few parents were driven to such extremes of desperation. Others caught in a similar dilemma to that of Sara opted either to stay, or to leave without their children. Either way, the consequences could be severe: staying might entail the endurance of further persecution, or the

128 CA, CJ 446, Statement of the Hottentot Sara, 12 June 1792, pp. 311–15.

129 CA, CJ 446, *idem.* The other witnesses all denied that there had been a carnal connection between Feitje and Andries Jacobus de Beer.

130 CA, CJ 446, Statement of the Hottentot Leentje, 5 Nov. 1792; 1/GR 3/16, Statement of the Hottentot Flink, 3 Feb. 1789.

131 CA, CJ 446, Statement of A.J. de Beer, 5 Nov. 1792; Statement of the Hottentot Leentje, 5 Nov. 1792. David de Beer, incidentally, was the son-in-law of Adriaan van Jaarsveld. (De Villiers and Pama, *Geslagsregisters*, vol. I, pp. 32, 352.)

132 CA, 1/GR 3/16, Statement of the burgher Matthys Booyens, 26 Jan. 1789. Orlando Patterson's comments on self-inflicted violence among slaves may be useful here, see *Slavery and Social Death*, p. 12. See also the magnificent novel *Beloved*, by Toni Morrison, which deals with a similar theme.

133 Marais, *Maynier and the First Boer Republic*, pp. 76–7.

forfeit of improved conditions elsewhere; going might initiate a prolonged or even permanent separation of family members. In 1834, during a meeting at Philipston in the Kat River valley, the Hottentot Magerman recalled his experience of such a separation: 'In Mr Fischer's time,'[134] he said,

> I was *ingeboeked* for ten years, when I was so young [here showing his height then], to my baas Dawid van der Merwe in the Camdeboo—my baas promised then to bring me up and instruct me as his own children—but I had to lie among the dogs in the ashes—I was many a time lifted out of the ashes by the arm and flogged well so that when I ran from the hearth the ashes were strewed and the coals after me, and the dogs, alarmed, would pursue me—I got no instruction and no clothes—I know nothing—my mother was obliged from the bad treatment to run away and leave me—and my father soon after—and when he would attempt to get a sight of me, the dogs were sent after him—O! my poor father!

Magerman eventually escaped, and was reunited with his mother in the neighbourhood of Cape Town.[135] In this he was lucky, for the Boers pursued their runaway *huisboorlingenen* with as much fervour as they did their 'Bushman' apprentices. Thus Christiaan Rudolph Opperman waited two years for an opportunity to recapture his 'little Hottentot' Hendrik who had absconded in the Hex River valley during a journey to the Cape in 1789.[136] In 1791 Opperman travelled to the Cape again and, while traversing *de straat*, a rock-walled defile at the top of the Hex River pass, came to hear that Hendrik was with the widow Daniel van der Merwe in the Bokkeveld. He at once sent his son, Godlieb Rudolph, to catch him, truss him and bring him home, without so much as a 'by your leave' to the Widow van der Merwe.[137]

In the second place, even those Khoisan who had not been entrapped by the *inboek* system could find their freedom of movement restricted by masters whose attitudes had been shaped within the dominant slave mode of production and whose urgent need for labour in any case predisposed them to ignore the finer distinctions between Khoisan and slaves. Company officials reminded such men repeatedly that the Hottentots were a free people—'fellow human beings', as the Landdrost of Stellenbosch boldly declared in 1800, 'having equal right with us to the protection of the law;'[138] but their

---

134 Fischer was Landdrost of Graaf-Reinet from 1812 to 1815.

135 CA, ACC 50(4), Letters from James Read, Report of a meeting held at Philipston on 4 Aug. 1834.

136 CA, 1/GR 3/16, Statement of Christiaan Rudolph Opperman, 18 July, 1792. Christiaan Rudolph was the son of Godlieb Rudolph, who had led the General Commando of 1774.

137 CA, 1/GR 3/16, Statement of Godlieb Rudolph Opperman, 18 July 1792. For similar cases, see 1/GR 3/17, Criminal Interrogatories, 1787–1800, Statement of Johannes de Wit and Johan Hendrik Vos, 1 Aug. 1788; 1/GR 1/2, Minutes of Board of Landdrost and Heemraden, 1 June 1795, and VC 887, Moodie's Afschriften, vol. 18.

138 CA, 1/STB 20/30, Outgoing Letters, Landdrost to Veld-Cornet Jan Hugo, 29 Mar. 1800. See also CJ 362, Documents in Criminal Cases (1753), trial of Jacobus Botha, Eisch ende Conclusie of Landdrost

pronouncements too often fell on deaf ears: *'Het is ons volk,'* ['They're our people,'] explained the brothers Johannes and Stephanus Schoeman as they captured and bound a Hottentot family who had deserted them six years before, *'wij kunnen daarmee leeven zo als wij willen.'* ['we can do with them what we want.'][139]

The Landdrosts' attempts to intervene in disputes between a master and his 'volk', or even between rival masters, were deeply resented, except where the *veeboeren* felt they could turn the ambiguous status of the Khoisan to their advantage. 'You can't frighten me with your Landdrost of Graaff-Reinet', the Schoeman brothers had said to Johannes Nel, who had earlier caught their runaway servants in the veld and now wished to keep them:

this Landdrost means nothing to me; I don't want to be bothered with this Landdrost.

And they added,

who makes such orders that if a Hottentot has been six years away, the baas must give him up? No! Even if this Hottentot had been seven years away, I must have him back, because he's done me too much damage .[140]

The Landdrosts' position was made the more difficult by the absence of any codified regulations governing the relationship between the freeburghers and their 'Hottentot' servants. Written contracts appear to have been unknown before Maynier's reforms of 1799 (except in the case of apprentices)[141] and even verbal contracts were not made in the presence of witnesses. The Khoisan themselves clearly believed their relations with the *veeboeren* to be governed by contract: 'I asked the *oude nonje* for permission to leave,' Sara had said to Dawid de Beer, 'why should I have asked you too? Am I placed under you then?' [*'staan ik dan onder jou?'*][142] But when the terms were in dispute, it was one person's word against another and, despite the stated intentions of government, the words of white men and Hottentots seldom carried equal weight in court.

The resultant vulnerability of Khoisan servants can be clearly discerned in the court records of the period. One could cite, for example, the case of the Landdrost of Swellendam versus Francina Vosloo who, in 1753, was 'graciously pardoned' for her part in the death of the Hottentot Pieter, who had been accidentally shot during a scuffle on the *werf* of her homestead, De

Horak; R. Ross, 'The Changing Legal Position of the Khoisan in the Cape Colony, 1652–1795', *African Perspectives* (1979), pp. 80–1.

139 CA, 1/GR 3/16, Criminal Interrogatories, Statement of Johannes Nel Willemzoon, 15 Dec. 1790.

140 *Idem.*

141 Cf. Ross, 'Changing Legal Position of the Khoisan', p. 86, and Newton-King and Malherbe, 'Khoikhoi Rebellion', pp. 30, 32.

142 CA, CJ 446, Statement of the Hottentot Leentje, 5 Nov. 1792.

Riet Vallij, early one October morning in 1752. Pieter and a fellow-servant, named Kieviet, had intended to leave the employ of Vosloo and her husband, Hans Jurgen Gilbert, and were in the process of leading their cattle from the kraal when Gilbert discovered them and disputed their right to leave. According to Kieviet, Gilbert hit Pieter with his stick and dagger and Pieter attempted to parry the blows with his kierie and his kaross.[143]

Vosloo testified, however, that Pieter had overpowered her husband, who was old and weak, and that she had believed his life was in danger. She had therefore taken a musket from the house 'so as to assist her husband with it'. The Hottentot Kieviet had, she said, immediately sprung forward to disarm her and during the ensuing struggle, the gun had gone off, fatally wounding Pieter.[144] The court concluded that there was no case against Vosloo—she had merely been doing her duty in going to the aid of her husband—and that even if her husband had initiated the brawl by raising his hand against Pieter, he was justified in doing so, for the two Hottentots were guilty of insolence and annoyance, having

> molested aforesaid Gilbert on his own farm, not only in that they had tried to leave secretly and without reason, *before the expiration of their contracted time,*

but also in that, through the 'stealthy opening' of the kraal, they had exposed Gilbert's cattle to risk.[145] No contract was submitted to the court in support of this judgement, nor was one requested by the bench. A master's word had been enough.

It should not be supposed, however, that the absence of written contracts left the Khoisan entirely unprotected. Like slaves, they had the right to lay complaints against their masters and (as is evident from the cases cited above) the right to testify against them in court. A Hottentot was generally not considered to be an 'irreproachable witness'—his evidence was frequently subject to 'objections to credit' raised by the accused[146]—but, as Robert Ross has argued, the evidence of 'heathens and slaves' was essential to the maintenance of the VOC's control over its extensive and thinly-settled colony and the courts consequently continued to make use of such evidence.[147] 'Yes', insisted Landdrost Horak, prosecutor at the trial of the alleged disturber of the peace, Jacobus Botha, Jacobuszoon,

---

143 CA, CJ 361, Documents in Criminal Cases, Case no. 5, Statement of the Hottentot Kiewiet, 30 Nov. 1752.

144 *Ibid.*, Statement of the burgher Hans Jurgen Gilbert, 28 Oct. 1752; Statement of Francina Vosloo, 28 Oct. 1752.

145 *Ibid.*, Eisch ende Conclusie of Landdrost Horak; emphasis added.

146 Ross, 'Changing Legal Position of the Khoisan,' pp. 82–5; CA, CJ 362, Documents in Criminal Cases (1753), Eisch ende Conclusie of Landdrost Horak, 11 Feb. 1751.

147 R. Ross, 'Changing Legal Position of the Khoisan', pp. 84–5; 'The Rule of Law at the Cape of Good Hope in the Eighteenth Century', *The Journal of Imperial and Commonwealth History*, 9, (1980), pp. 6–9.

if such witnesses were never acceptable, the most gruesome crimes would, at least in this country, go unpunished.

And in support of his position he cited the esteemed legal scholar, Benedictus Carpzovicus, who had written that

when it is a question of crimes committed in deserts, forests, mountains and other isolated places, even inhabiele [incapable?] witnesses are admissible, if one cannot get at the truth by other means .[148]

Khoisan servants made enthusiastic use of this privilege, often braving hostile farmers and wild beasts in order to reach the Landdrost's seat. 'If you want to go there,' Johannes Roos had warned his servant Jacob when the latter had threatened to report the abuse of his children, 'you'd better take your gun, because it's too dangerous to go from here to there without a gun, because of the Bushmen.'[149] In some cases, it seems, aggrieved Khoisan entertained exaggerated expectations of the benefits to be derived from access to the courts. 'Listen,' the Bastard Hottentot Jantje had said to his fellow-servant Draabok, as they travelled to the Cape with Jantje's master Okkert Goosen,

now you must help me to nail Baas Okkert, now that he has beaten me—then we will be free people, then no Christian person can ever hire us again—we must just say that Baas Okkert shot Witbooij dead and cut him in pieces.[150]

Okkert Goosen had indeed shot the Hottentot Witbooij, but he had not cut him in pieces; he had merely left the corpse for the vultures.[151] And Draabok, finding himself haltered and led to the Drostdy, was soon to regret his testimony: he had, he confessed, 'to his utmost sorrow', been misled by the Bastard Hottentot Jantje.[152]

If access to the courts could not bring freedom, it could at least provide some protection against the worst excesses of arbitrary power. In the case of corporal punishment, for example, while there were no rules which referred specifically to the Khoisan, the Landdrosts of the country districts appear to have been guided by the regulations governing the punishment of slaves. These regulations, based partly on Roman Law and partly on the Statutes of India of 1642,[153] laid down that a master 'cannot at his pleasure dispose over

---

148 CA, CJ 362, Documents in Criminal Cases (1753), Eisch ende Conclusie of Landdrost Horak, 11 Feb. 1751.

149 CA, 1/GR 3/16, Criminal Interrogatories, Statement of the Hottentot Jacob, 10 Jan. 1791.

150 CA, 1/GR 3/18, Criminal Interrogatories, 1793–1802, no. 69, Statement of the Hottentot Draabok, 7 Oct. 1794.

151 CA, 1/GR 3/18, Criminal Interrogatories, Statement of Okkert Goosen, 7 Oct. 1794.

152 *Ibid.*, Statement of the Hottentot Draabok, 7 Oct. 1794. Draabok's efforts were not entirely in vain, however: in June 1795 Goosen was summoned to appear before the Court of Justice in Cape Town, but his case was postponed to a later date and, as far as I can establish, was never tried. (Cf. CA, CJ 77–80, Minutes of Proceedings in Criminal Cases, 1795–8.)

the life or limbs of his slave, but is obliged when they behave well recip-
rocally to behave well to them.'[154] Admittedly, the limits of good behaviour
were narrowly defined: a slave who got drunk, ran away, wilfully disobeyed
a command (provided such command was not illegal or immoral), stole
domestic property, occasioned loss to his master through neglect or careless-
ness, or was believed to be guilty of negligence or impudence, was deemed
to have overstepped the limits and could be subjected to 'domestic punishment'.[155] Domestic punishment, however, was not to exceed 39 lashes and,
though it was not specified 'in what manner and with what instrument' such
punishment was to be inflicted, it was 'recommended', according to Fiscal
Denyssen, that a slave not be beaten on the naked body, 'or otherwise than
on the back or buttocks,' and that no other instruments but *sjamboks*, leather
thongs, or rattans be used for the purpose.[156]

A master who transgressed these norms, or failed to provide his slaves
with adequate food and clothing, could, at least in theory, be brought to
book, though woe betide the slave whose complaints were found to be
groundless![157] In practice, especially in the outlying districts, cases of maltreatment or deprivation were seldom reported unless they caused the death
of the victim. And when a slave did die after being beaten by his master, his
death was held to be an accident unless it could be proved that his master had
deliberately set out to kill him; and his master would therefore not be
charged with murder, but with a lesser offense, for which the penalty might
be corporal punishment or a fine, 'according to the circumstances of the
case'.[158]

The slave code was not explicitly invoked in cases involving the maltreatment of Khoisan servants. However an examination of such cases suggests that it did indeed serve as a guide to magistrates investigating complaints of assault and brutalization. Thus only the most serious allegations
attracted the attention of the authorities: a whipping which did no permanent
physical damage was unlikely to invite inquiry and, as with slaves, a prosecution was rarely instituted unless at least one of the victims had died. The
charge in such cases, moreover, was usually 'impermissible punishment' or
'mistreatment', rather than murder, and the punishment was normally a
fine.[159]

---

153 Ross, 'Rule of Law', p. 7 and Fiscal Denyssen to Sir John Cradock, 16 Mar. 1813, Statement of the Laws
    of the Colony of the Cape of Good Hope Regarding Slavery, Article I, in G.M. Theal (ed.), *Records of
    the Cape Colony (RCC)*, vol. 9 (1901), pp. 143–61.

154 Theal, *RCC*, vol. 9, Article 9, p. 147.

155 *Ibid.*, Article 15, p. 148.

156 *Ibid.*, Articles 13 and 14, pp. 147–8.

157 *Ibid.*, Article 33, p. 152.

158 *Ibid.*, Article 30, p. 151.

159 Cf. CA, CJ 28, Minutes of Proceedings in Criminal Cases (1746), 3 Nov. 1746.

In 1746, for example, the soldier Hendrik Tessenaar, *knecht* of the Burgerraad Jan Louwrens Bestbier, was fined 50 rixdollars for the 'impermissible punishment' of a Hottentot named Stuurman.[160] Stuurman had openly defied the *knecht*, disobeying an order and dismissing Tessenaar's promise of a reward for a job well done with the words 'You are a cheat, you give me nothing'. The two had become embroiled in a hand-to-hand struggle which ended when Stuurman pinned Tessenaar to the ground and sat on his chest.[161] The following morning, with the assistance of a visitor named Anthony Minie, Tessenaar caught Stuurman, carried him bodily into the house and suspended him by his hands from a roof-beam, with his right foot tied to a pillar of the chimney and his left foot on the ground. Then, according to a witness,

> first Hendrik Tessenaar and shortly thereafter Anthony Minie each hit the Hottentot with a *sjambok* on his naked back and rear body for about half an hour.[162]

They stopped when the witness warned them that the Hottentot might die. It was already too late, however, for he died three days later. Minie, who said in his defence that he 'hadn't known it was not permitted to tie up and hit someone like that,' was fined 25 rixdollars.[163]

The judgement in this case was consistent with the attitude of the Court of Justice right up to the end of the period of Company rule. It was not until 1801, during the trial of Rudolph Brits, that a magistrate set out to prove 'murderous intent' in a case involving the whipping and subsequent death (from gangrene) of a Hottentot servant.[164] And it was not until well into the nineteenth century that such a charge was made to stick. Throughout the Company period, the heaviest punishment imposed on a European for the maltreatment of Khoisan servants was banishment from the colony. In 1744 Marthinus Spangenburg was banned for life for having molested and shot a servant of the widow Mouton, near the Piketberg.[165] In 1765 Jan Otto Diederikse, employed as *knecht* on the farm of Jacobus van Reenen in the Hantam, was charged with 'far-reaching excesses and maltreatment of the Hottentots living with him' and condemned to be 'tied to a pole and severely scourged with rods on his bare back, then to be banished for twenty-five consecutive years to Robben Island'.[166] And finally, in 1776, Carel Hendrik

---

160 CA, CJ 28, Minutes of Proceedings in Criminal Cases, 3 Nov. 1746.

161 CA, 1/SWM 3/10, Criminal Interrogatories, Statement of the soldier Hendrik Tessenaar, 10 Sept. 1746.

162 *Ibid.*, Statement of Coert Cnoetse, 16 Nov. 1746.

163 CA, CJ 28, Minutes of Proceedings in Criminal Cases (1746), 3 Nov. 1746.

164 CA, CJ 483, Documents in Criminal Cases (1801), Eisch ende Conclusie of F.R. Bresler, Landdrost of Graaff-Reinet, 28 May 1801.

165 Ross, 'Changing Legal Position of the Khoisan', pp. 80–1.

166 CA, CJ 47, Minutes of Proceedings in Criminal Cases (1765).

Buijtendag of the Bokkeveld was banished from the district of Stellenbosch after being found guilty on a similar charge.[167]

In all these cases, moreover, from the viewpoint of the authorities, there were aggravating circumstances. In the first and last cases, for example, the accused had not merely maltreated their *own* servants, they had also molested the servants of their neighbours, and this, given the timocratic ethos of Cape society, was a more serious offence, since it was as much an affront to the dignity of the master as it was an injury to his servant.[168] In the case of Diederikse, the aggravating factors are less evident, but it appears that at least one of his victims had links with an independent Khoekhoe kraal in the area and the authorities perhaps feared that his behaviour would provoke reprisals.[169]

'WHY ARE WE TO BE PLACED UNDER THE HEATHEN?'

It could be argued that to receive the same protection from the law as slaves was to receive no protection at all, that it merely went to show that there really *was* no difference in status between 'Hottentots' and slaves, and that the Boers, and more to the point, their merchant overlords, had entirely failed to implement the strategy of 'divide and partially enslave' which had been within their grasp. The second part of this statement is substantially correct, but to accept the first part uncritically would be to overlook not only the crucial ambiguities in the status of 'Hottentot' servants, which I have been at pains to document, but, more importantly, the determination with which they themselves exploited these ambiguities in their struggle against subjection.

We have already noted that they made energetic use of their right to complain. They complained not only of murder and assault, but also of wages unpaid, contracts dishonoured, parents and children detained and livestock misappropriated. 'But Master, what damage did I ever do you?' the Hottentot Kiewiet had said to Jan Schoeman,

> What did I ever get from you but a mouthful of meat, and otherwise nothing? I'm not a slave, you know. [*Ik ben immers tog ook geen slaaf.*][170]

---

167 N. Penn, 'Anarchy and Authority in the Koue Bokkeveld, 1739–79: The Banishing of Carel Buijtendag', *Kleio*, 17 (1985), p. 24.

168 For a discussion of the relationship between slavery, power and honour, see Patterson, *Slavery and Social Death*, ch. 3. One may note, apropos this issue, that when Hendrik Tessenaar had asked the burgher Coert Cnoetse to help him beat the Hottentot Stuurman, Cnoetse had replied: '*Hendrik, ik sal wel wijser weesen—jij weet wel dat ik een ander mans volk niet mag slaan.*'(CA, 1/SWM 3/10, Statement of Coert Cnoetse, 16 Nov. 1746.)

169 CA, 1/STB 3/11, Criminal Interrogatories, Statement of the Hottentot Coridon, 30 Nov. 1763. Brits was also banished, though only for 5 years. His crime was committed at a time when the authorities of Graaff-Reinet were endeavouring to pacify the rebellious Khoisan, and they may have wished to make an example of him, so as to convince the Khoisan of their good intentions.

In particular, 'Hottentot' servants used their access to the Landdrost and the courts to assert custodial claims in their parents and children. And to the extent that they succeeded, they were clearly set apart from slaves, who, according to the Roman Law, did 'not possess the right of disposing of their children, even if they be minors'.[171] They had, as we have seen in the case of the Bastard Hottentot Sara, to contend with the system of apprenticeship, and with the dogged tenacity of slaveholding masters; but a plaintiff who persevered had a good chance of receiving support from the Drostdy.

The story of the Khoekhoe Captain Ruiter Platje's efforts to be re-united with his family is a case in point.[172] In November 1791 Ruiter complained that his wife and child and two young relatives had been kidnapped by a party of Boers.[173] His wife had escaped soon afterwards, but had been obliged to leave her child and her livestock behind. Landdrost Woeke summoned the offending burghers to the Drostdy, but they ignored his summons and, by July 1792, Ruiter evidently felt it necessary to make a direct appeal to the government in Cape Town.[174] He was fortunate in that his visit coincided with the arrival of Commissioners Nederburgh and Frijkenius, who were immediately sympathetic to his cause, and by the end of that year his case had received a preliminary hearing in Graaff-Reinet, from which he may have received some satisfaction. In October 1793, however, he was arrested on suspicion of conspiracy and held for some time in Cape Town,[175] and on his release he apparently found that another burgher, this time the infamous Coenraad Frederik Bezuidenhout,[176] had got hold of two of his wives, together with their

170 CA, 1/GR 3/16, Criminal Interrogatories, Statement of the burgher Johannes Nel, Willemzoon, 15 Dec. 1790. See also the statement of the burgher Andreas Hendrik Krugel, 5 Jan. 1791, for a longer version of Kiewiet's declaration.

171 Denyssen to Cradock, 16 Mar. 1813, in Theal, *RCC*, vol. 9, p. 150. Cf. Patterson, *Slavery and Social Death*, p. 112.

172 Ruiter Platje was also known as Ruiter Beesje and as Benedictus. (Newton-King and Malherbe, *Khoikhoi Rebellion*, pp. 38, 62 (n. 102), 70, 71, 73 (n. 26 and 27). He was a grandson of the Hoengeyqwa Captain Ruiter, but by the end of the century he was usually referred to in the records as Gonaqua. Until 1791, when he moved onto the farm of Coenraad de Buys, he had lived 'on a certain stretch of veld next to the Bushman River,' that is, close to his grandfather's former territory. (CA, 1/GR 3/16, Statement of the Hottentot Captain Ruiter Platje, Nov. 1791.)

173 CA, 1/GR 3/16, Criminal Interrogatories, Statement of the Hottentot Captain Ruiter Platje, Nov. 1791. Ruiter's wife Hester and her child were kidnapped by Christiaan Kok, while Hester's cousin/niece Mietje and a young boy named Jantje Kaffer were carried off by Alewijn Rautenbag. Both burghers alleged in court that Hester and Mietje were runaways who had worked for them before. (CA, 1/GR 3/16, Statement of the female Hottentot Hester, 25 Nov. 1791; Statement of the burgher Theunis Botha Jacobuszoon, 7 Nov. 1792; Statement of the burgher Christiaan Kok, 7 Nov. 1792.)

174 Böeseken, 'Nederlandse Kommissarisse', p. 86.

175 CA, C 219, Resolusies (1793), 8 Nov. 1793, p. 258 ff; C 601, Incoming Letters (1793), Secretary of Swellendam to Sluyksen, 12 Oct. 1793.

176 During the war of 1793, C.F. Bezuidenhout had been singled out by the Zuurveld Xhosa as one of the chief provocateurs. He had allegedly 'taken their women and used them as...concubines' and had locked the Gqunukhwebe chief, Cungwa, in a flour mill 'and under severe threats ordered him to turn it in person'. (Marais, *Maynier*, pp. 28–9.)

children and livestock, so that the Landdrost was again obliged to take up his pen.[177]

The allegations against Ruiter were not necessarily unconnected with his untiring struggle for personal redress. For, despite their bravado in the face of authority, the Boers were acutely sensitive to the insecurity of their position. They were only too well aware that a 'faithful Hottentot', just like a captive Bushman, might at any moment be transformed, emerging as a rascal and an enemy. He might, like Van der Walt's servant Bakker, throw in his lot with the Bushmen, escaping alone, like Bakker,[178] or absconding in the company of others, like the 'Hottentots' who set out from the Roggeveld in 1791, taking muskets, powder and shot to their Bushman allies.[179] Alternatively, like the 'Captain of the Bokkeveld', he might warn the Bushmen of a commando's approach.[180] If he had no connections with the mountain raiders, he might choose the life of a 'vagabond', skulking in the interstices of colonial society, appearing unexpectedly to molest unwary travellers,[181] or terrorize a former master.[182] Worse still, at least for settlers on the borders of Xhosa country, he might make common cause with the Zuurveld Xhosa.

The Boers believed that the Xhosa chiefs deliberately encouraged the desertion of slaves and Hottentots, so that they might thereby acquire guns. However when the Veldwagtmeester, Lucas Meyer, had raised the issue with the Gqunukhwebe chief, Cungwa, the latter had told him the Boers should

> remain quiet about the slaves and Hottentots, seeing that it was not he that took them away from the farms—he had not enticed them away, so he need not return them.[183]

Both during and after the Second Frontier War of 1793 it was reported that Hottentots were 'daily absconding from the Boers' and joining the Xhosa,

---

177 CA, 1/GR 16/1, Part I, Secretary of Graaff-Reinet to C.F. Bezuidenhout, 20 June 1794.

178 See above, p. 248.

179 Penn, 'Labour, Land and Livestock', p. 18, n. 87.

180 Report of Field-Sergeant Willem Steenkamp, 3 Feb. 1778, in Moodie, *The Record*, part III, p. 74.

181 See, for example, the case of the runaway servants of Pieter and Stephanus Venter, in CA, CJ 69, Minutes of Proceedings in Criminal Cases, 22 Mar. 1787; 1/GR 3/17, Criminal Interrogatories, Statement of Petrus Pienaar, 7 Dec. 1786; Statement of Albertus Viljoen, 7 Dec. 1786; Statement of Pieter Venter, 9 Dec. 1786; C 563, Woeke to Governor, 10 Dec. 1786. See also 1/GR 15/71, Wynant Brijtenbach to Landdrost, 12 Nov. 1797; CJ 450, Case of the Bastard Hottentot Toontje; ZL 1/3/2 (LMS microfilm), Alberti to Vanderkemp, 7 Jan. 1804.

182 See above, pp. 246. See also the case of the runaway servants of Adriaan Louw in Moodie, *The Record*, part III, pp. 11, 13, 14, 17 and CA, CJ 403, Documents in Criminal Cases (1772) and, for a later example, V.C. Malherbe, 'Hermanus and his Sons: Khoi Bandits and Conspirators in the Post-Rebellion Period (1803–18)', in *African Studies*, 41 (1982), pp. 189–202.

183 Marais, *Maynier*, p. 26. The two major Xhosa chiefdoms in the Zuurveld at this time were the Gqunukhwebe under Tshaka and the Mbalu under Langa. (J.B. Peires, *The House of Phalo: A History of the Xhosa People in the Days of their Independence* (Johannesburg, 1981), pp. 48–51.)

and it seemed there was little their masters could do to stop them.[184]

In this context, the simple act of going to the Landdrost to complain could be construed as a dangerous threat to a master's authority—or even as a challenge to European dominion as a whole. And a complaint made in good faith could become a pretext for murder. For, having disregarded the restraining council of the authorities in Cape Town, and aborted what chance they might have had to win the loyalty of the Khoekhoe, the *veeboeren* were obliged to live in a state of constant apprehension. Daily life on the farms became a continual battle of wills, and suspicion lurked in every recess. So great was the Boers' fear of their Hottentot servants that they could never appreciate the wisdom of Company policy towards the Khoisan. The legal safeguards granted to the latter and their resultant access to the courts of Landdrost and Heemraden were consistently perceived as an intolerable affront. 'How dare you accuse me?' Jacobus Scheepers had asked his servant Jan Blaauw:

> You are the first Hottentot who has dared to testify against me [*die mij durft verklagen*], and I'll get you Hottentotje, I'll get you.

Three weeks later, Jan Blaauw was found dead in the veld, but since his body had been destroyed by wolves, no satisfactory case could be brought against Scheepers.[185]

As for the Landdrosts who 'opened their courts to the heathen', they were at best resented, as we have seen, and at worst, as in the case of Honoratus Maynier of Graaff-Reinet, painted in lurid colours as traducers of honest men and traitors to the Christian cause. Maynier's willingness to hear the complaints of the Boers' Hottentot servants was seen as an outright betrayal of European interests, rather than as a politic attempt to forestall the servants' total disaffection from their masters.[186] He might profess, explained the rebellious colonists in their *tesamenstemming* of February 1795, to have the public good at heart, but his real intention was to bring ruin to the district and subjugate the citizenry.[187] 'We ask', they continued in a later document,

> did we request this magistracy for us, or for the Hottentots? All know what schelms they are—and we may ask if, since the first foundation of the colony, so much Christian blood has ever been shed by the heathens as since the foundation of this district? ...Why are we to be placed under the heathen?[188]

184 *Ibid.*, pp. 48, 62.

185 CA, CJ 3387, Commission of Circuit, Uitenhage, 1812, Case no. 5. Statement of the Hottentot Candace, wife of Jan Blaauw, 24 Sept. 1810, and p. 497 ff. For further examples of hostile reactions to servants who complained, see 1/GR 3/16, Statement of Johannes Nel, Willemzoon, 15 Dec. 1790 and 1/GR 3/32, Statement of the Hottentot Piet Stamper, 1798.

186 Marais, *Maynier*, pp. 71, 73; CA, VC 68, Tesamenstemming, 29 Jan. 1795, p. 185.

187 CA, VC 68, Tesamenstemming, 29 Jan. 1795, p. 186.

188 CA, VC 871, Moodie's Afschriften, vol. 8, Klagtschrift, 16 Apr. 1795.

This was fertile soil for the growth of rumour. In the fevered imaginations of frontiersmen, a few disparate shreds of information could be woven together to form a dense blanket of fear. Thus it was that, in September 1793, Ruiter Platje found himself accused, together with the Hottentot Captain Kees and 33 others, of having formed 'a conspiracy…with the Hottentots of Namaqualand to burn down the Drostdy of Swellendam and lay waste the whole land'.[189]

The sequence of events which preceded these allegations was as follows: in March 1793, two Swellendam burghers, one a woman, had been murdered by unknown assailants.[190] Towards the end of March, Captain Kees, like Ruiter before him, had journeyed to the Cape to lay a complaint before the Council of Policy.[191] In April, during his stay at the Cape, Kees was engaged by Philip Albertus Meyburg, Captain of the Stellenbosch militia, to lead an expedition against a band of maroons living in the Hangklip caves.[192] To this end, Kees and his party (amongst whom were several of Meyburg's employees, including one Klaas Kees) were provided with sixteen muskets and a large quantity of powder and shot. Kees returned three weeks later with one recaptured runaway and all but a handful of the ammunition. The remaining ammunition had, according to Meyburg, been used to shoot *klipspringers*.[193]

This incident appears to have been the immediate catalyst for the agitation against Kees. In August it was reported from the Hantam and Roggevelden that 'the Bushman Hottentots had stolen a great number of cattle and murdered several shepherds,' and that the Veldwagtmeesters of these districts deemed it necessary to send a commando against them as soon as possible.[194] By September, the inhabitants of the Bokkeveld were in the grip of a 'general panic', and those of the Roggevelden, where the men were absent on commando against the Bushmen, were tremulously awaiting the arrival from Namaqualand of '500 revolted Hottentots', led or instigated by Captain Kees.[195]

189 CA, VC 65, Outgoing Letters (1793), Sluyksen to Commissioners, 25 Oct. 1793. See also C 219, Resolusies, p. 258, 8 Nov. 1793.

190 CA, C 219, Resolusies, 1793, p. 258 ff, 8 Nov. 1793. By Nov. 1793 the identity of the assailants was still unknown. The daughter of one of the victims said she had seen them from afar and counted 'fourteen or so'. (CA, 1/SWM 3/17, Statement of the burgher Johannes Jacobus Oosthuizen, 25 Nov. 1793.)

191 CA, 1/STB 10/7, Council of Policy to Landdrost, 1 Apr. 1793. 'The Hottentot Captain Kees complains bitterly of several injuries,' wrote the Colonial Secretary, 'amongst other things, that they are refusing to give his children back to him.'

192 CA, VC 66, Brieven en Bijlagen van den Commissaris A. J. Sluyksen, 1st Part, Statement of P.A. Meyburg, 2 Oct. 1793, pp. 191–2. For an account of the Hangklip maroons, see R. Ross, *Cape of Torments: Slavery and Resistance in South Africa* (London, 1983), ch. 5.

193 CA, VC 66, Statement of P.A. Meyburg, 2 Oct. 1793. A *klipspringer* is a species of mountain antelope.

194 CA, C 601, Incoming Letters (1793), Landdrost of Stellenbosch to Council of Policy, 28 Aug. 1793 and 10 Sept. 1793.

195 CA, VC 66, Brieven en Bijlagen van den Commissaris A.J. Sluyksen, 1st part, J.H. Wagener to Sluyksen, 24 Sept. 1793, 28 Sept. 1793, pp. 168–9, 173–4, 176.

During the course of September some 35 'Hottentots', including several of Philip Meyburg's servants, were detained by the burghers of Swellendam and Stellenbosch and handed over to the authorities. Among them was one named Dirk, who told how he had accompanied Kees on his return from the Cape, and had learnt that Kees and another Hottentot named Jantje Hermanus had been instructed by Commissioners Nederburgh and Frijkenius to make peace with the Bushmen, or, if that failed, to attack them. When they reached the interior, however, Hermanus had allegedly told Dirk that his real intention was 'to ravage the farms of the inhabitants and to murder them, and that Captain Kees also had this intention'.[196]

The authorities in Cape Town quickly came to the conclusion that there was no substance to these allegations.[197] Commissioner Sluyksen decided, however, to keep Captain Kees in custody at the Castle, 'until the country people have recovered from their fright'.[198] Alas, in the troubled atmosphere of the mid 1790s there was to be no recovery. If anything, the level of tension rose and the pressures faced by frontiersmen multiplied during the course of 1794. These pressures were both political and economic. On the political front, Bushman robberies, though occurring with decreasing frequency in the Camdeboo, continued unabated in the Sneeuberge and the Koup. In September 1794 Adriaan van Jaarsveld reported that the robbers from behind the Groote Tafelberg were appearing *met hele complotten* (in whole bands of conspirators) on the Sneeuberg.[199] According to figures compiled by Donald Moodie from the records of Graaff-Reinet district, a total of 1,546 cattle and 11,719 sheep were destroyed or driven off by the Bushmen between January and December 1794.[200] Moreover, the inconclusive battles between the Boers and the Zuurveld Xhosa in 1793 had left the latter firmly entrenched in the coastal forelands, and by 1795 Ndlambe's people, seeking refuge from the ire of their chief's rebellious nephew Ngqika, were pressing in on the inhabitants of Bruins Hoogte.[201] The proximity of the Xhosa, in turn, further emboldened the Boers' unwilling servants and encouraged a spate of desertions.[202] Indeed Maynier, for one, believed that much of the stock-theft reported from the

196 CA, C 601, Incoming Letters (1793), W.L. van Hardenbergh to Governor, 29 Sept. 1793.
197 Böeseken, 'Nederlandse Kommissarisse', p. 87. See also CA, VC 66, Statement of P.A. Meyburg, 2 Oct. 1793, pp. 191–2; Statement of Hermanus Engelbrecht d'oude, 20 Oct. 1793, pp. 193–4.
198 Böeseken, 'Nederlandse Kommissarisse', p. 87.
199 Gerrit Wagenaar, 'Johannes Gysbertus van Reenen-Sy Aandeel in die Kaapse Geskiedenis tot 1806' (MA thesis, University of Pretoria, 1976), p. 117; CA, VC 68, Adriaan van Jaarsveld to Maynier, 24 Sept. 1794. The Groote Tafelberg lies about 25 km south-east of present-day Middelburg, on the Middelburg-Cradock road.
200 Marais, *Maynier*, p. 65.
201 *Ibid.*, pp. 48–51 and 58–9; 1/GR 1/2, Minutes, 7 May 1795; Peires, *House of Phalo*, p. 51.
202 Marais, *Maynier*, p. 62.

Zuurveld in 1794 was the work of 'discontented Hottentots'.[203]

As though this were not enough, the economic difficulties of the *veeboeren* had also assumed critical proportions. By the mid 1790s the whole colony was caught in the grip of economic depression.[204] A falling off in demand, combined with the unsettled state of the interior, had at last enabled the Company's butchers (the Van Reenen brothers) to bring down the price of slaughter-stock to a level which suited them: by mid 1793 the Boers were receiving 9 or 10 *schellings* for sheep which in 1791 had fetched 16 *schellings* a head, and by the end of the following year the situation had not improved.[205]

At the same time, a shortage of specie in the colony's commodity markets was inducing the Company's butchers to suspend cash payments for livestock.[206] The *veeboeren* had a deep (and not ill-founded) distrust of the Company's paper money and they had always preferred to be paid in specie. They had, however, been prepared to accept the butchers' *briefjes*, or credit notes, provided the latter could be exchanged for cash in Cape Town. Now, however, the Van Reenen Maatschappij declared itself unable to provide cash in exchange for the notes; even those of their creditors who had been induced to part with stock at a price below the prevailing level, in return for a promise of prompt cash payment on presentation of the *slagters briefjen*, found themselves deceived. On arrival in Cape Town they were given the choice between waiting a further six months for payment, or exchanging the *briefjes* directly for trade goods, all too often at shops belonging to friends or business associates of the Van Reenen brothers.[207]

In addition, the butchers were given the job of implementing the VOC's new hardline rent policy.[208] Most of the loan-farm holders were in arrears with their rent, some by as much as 20 years.[209] By 1792 the total arrears on loan-farms amounted to the enormous sum of 376,360 rixdollars and by 1795 arrears due from the district of Graaff-Reinet alone amounted to 69,221 rixdollars.[210] Acting on the advice of Commissioners Nederburgh and Frijkenius, who had been deputed to find ways of reducing the colony's

---

203 *Ibid.*, pp. 62–3.

204 Wagenaar, 'Johannes Gysbertus van Reenen', p. 118. The depression had been precipitated by a fall in the number of foreign ships, especially British ships, calling at the Cape. See also Kirsten to Craig, Oct. 1795, in Theal *RCC*, vol. 1 (London, 1897), p. 170.

205 Wagenaar, 'Johannes Gysbertus van Reenen', pp. 112, 123–4.

206 *Ibid.*, pp. 96 and 116. The shortage of specie was at least partly due to the decline in the number of foreign ships calling at the Cape. British ships in particular had been a major source of hard cash.

207 Wagenaar, 'Johannes Gysbertus van Reenen', p. 116. See also *Ibid.*, pp. 120–2.

208 *Ibid.*, pp. 109–113; VC 68, Statement of the burgher Christoffel Aucamp, 25 Oct. 1793, enclosed in Wagener to Sluyksen, 30 Dec. 1793, pp. 636–7.

209 This is apparent from the liquidation accounts in the series CA, MOOC 13/1/5–13/1/36 (1760–1813).

210 Wagenaar, 'Johannes Gysbertus van Reenen', p. 110; Public Records Office (PRO), WO 1/324, Enclosure in Craig to Dundas, 18 Dec. 1795.

deficit, the Council of Policy instructed the butchers to collect three years' back rent annually from the *veeboeren* with whom they did business. To this end, the butchers' servants were to be provided with lists of debtors whom they would 'encourage' to part with slaughter stock in lieu of rent.[211] The *veeboeren* were scandalized by these arrangements and, by the end of 1793, many were refusing to sell any livestock at all to the Van Reenen brothers.[212] If Maynier had become the focus of their social and political insecurity, J.G. van Reenen, as his biographer observes, had become the personification of their economic grievances.[213]

It should come as no surprise, then, that the rumours surrounding Captain Kees could not be laid to rest, and further, that when these rumours were resurrected at the height of the burgher rebellion of 1795, J.G. van Reenen was named as one of Kees's co-conspirators, along with Colonel Robert Jacob Gordon (Commander of the Company's garrison) and the recently-evicted Special Commissioner, O.G. de Wet.[214] Gordon apparently came under suspicion because of his role in the recruitment of Khoisan for the newly-formed Hottentot Corps,[215] while De Wet, having been insulted and humiliated by the rebel *volkstem* and its leaders, had now sprung up from the collective unconscious, as it were, to wreak a fantastic revenge.[216] Moreover, the rumours surrounding Kees had grown in scope and fearfulness in proportion to the greater vulnerability of the citizenry: the district of Graaff-Reinet was now under the control of the rebel party and could expect no succour from Cape Town; even private shopkeepers had refused to extend credit to the 'people's representatives' and their citizen Landdrost.[217]

The first 'signs' of a new conspiracy were detected in July, 1795. On Saturday, 11 July, the Bastard Hottentot Louis was brought into a meeting of Landdrost, Heemraden and *volks representanten,* so that he might testify to his connection with Captain Kees.[218] His testimony, as recorded in the minutes, was less than satisfactory, but it was sufficient to serve as a foundation for the belief that Kees had left the Castle,[219] and that his accomplices in the

---

211 Wagenaar, 'Johannes Gysbertus van Reenen', p. 113.

212 *Ibid.*, p. 119.

213 *Ibid.*, p. 128.

214 Marais, *Maynier*, pp. 83–4.

215 CA, VC 887, Moodie's Afschriften, vol. 24, p. 687. See also CA, 1/GR 1/2, Minutes of Board of Landdrost and Heemraden, 11 July 1795 and CJ 2492, Raad van Justitie, Inkomende Brieven (1793–5), O.G. de Wet to Bletterman, 11 Aug. 1795. Gordon had allegedly despatched several Hottentot Captains into the interior to raise recruits for his new corps.

216 For a graphic description of the expulsion of O.G. de Wet, see CA, VC 68, pp. 138–51.

217 VC 887, Moodie's Afschriften, vol. 24, p. 700.

218 Possibly the same Louis who, in 1793, had been one of Kees' accusers, though he was then described as 'a slave of the burger Coenraad de Buijs'. (CA, C 219, Resolusies, 8 Nov. 1793.)

219 See above, p. 265.

interior were experimenting with ammunition and possibly also with magic.[220] The meeting may also have detected evidence of a possible collusion between Xhosa and Hottentot, inspired by Colonel Gordon.[221]

The Bastard Louis having been dismissed, a certain Johannes Reichard entered the Council Chamber and told how he had heard from Jan van Zyl at the Cogmans Kloof that

> there were three hundred male Hottentots lying in a kraal in the Roodeberg [Agter Renosterberg], with two knapsacks of powder and many guns; and that they were just waiting for the citizenry here to revolt so as to revolt themselves and attack the Christians.[222]

Having heard these witnesses, the Board determined that henceforth 'no Hottentot should travel more than an hour's distance from his master's place without a pass,' and closed the meeting.[223]

By August it had become clear to the people's representatives that the entire colonial government was ranged against them in a diabolical conspiracy: 'Sworn brothers,' wrote Gerrit Rautenbach,

> we must no longer doubt our country is betrayed ... the general presumption is that the greater number of the men in office are concerned: watch narrowly our appointed Landdrost [Carel David Gerotz], and as soon as treason is discovered, at once arrest him as a criminal, for he is suspected by many persons of judgment. Everything agrees, Captain Kees has left the Cape; we begin to collect together; be brave and honorable, and trust that God will not allow us to live under the heathens. One of Kees's men is taken in the Lange Kloof; he confesses that Ruiter Beestjes is gone to Outeniqualand. We have ordered as much powder and lead as can be fetched by three men, on account of the *volkstem*.[224]

In the event of these three men being arrested on arrival at Cape Town, Rautenbach added, the *volkstem* should be ready to proceed thither 'in a body', so as to arrest the chief conspirators.

As to the purported aims of the conspiracy, there were no doubt many variations, of which we unfortunately have no record. However Moodie has left us one account, which is as follows:

> The Hottentots were to have destroyed all the males of the white inhabitants, excepting Messrs De Wet, Gordon and Van Reenen, who were to be spared to manage their political concerns, and to be further rewarded by permitting each to select for himself three of the handsomest females previous to their general distribution among the Hottentots.[225]

220 CA, 1/GR 1/2, Minutes of Board of Landdrost and Heemraden, Saturday 11 July 1795.
221 *Ibid.*
222 *Ibid.* The Cogmans Kloof lies in the south-west Cape between present-day Ashton and Montagu, i.e. several hundred kilometres from the Roodeberg.
223 *Ibid.*
224 Rautenbach to Prinsloo, Bester and other representatives of the people, cited in CA, VC 887, Moodie's

It would seem then, that the dangers inherent in the enslavement of a native population *in situ* could all too easily overflow the bounds of the master-servant relationship, expanding inexorably to threaten the very foundations of colonial life on the frontier: the family and household, around which all life revolved.

Maynier, who had borne the first brunt of the burghers' paranoia, was no longer in Graaff-Reinet when the rumours surrounding Kees resurfaced.[226] He had retired to *de Kaap*, where he could reflect more calmly on the injudicious conduct of his erstwhile charges. 'I have continually endeavoured' he wrote some years later,

> to convince the peasantry of their error, but in vain; as long as they were with me they agreed with me, they were fully convinced; they promised to rely on government, and to join hands with the Landdrosts and Commissaries to promote the public good; but as soon as they meet with some or other ill-intentioned person, with some or other vagabond schoolmaster, or with some Butcher's worthless servant, they suffer themselves to be immediately imposed on by such sort of people, and everything done or said on the side of government is looked upon with distrust; and this is not only the case at present, but it has been the case for many years and will always remain so, as long as the people do not see with their own eyes and learn to know their own interest.[227]

Their own interest, Maynier was certain, lay in the fair and conciliatory treatment of their Hottentot servants and the preservation of the peace recently concluded with the Zuurveld Xhosa. Decent treatment was the only way, as he patiently explained to a man whose servants had recently absconded,

> to render the Hottentots faithful and prevent them from going away...although they are your servants it is best to treat them as we would wish to be treated, if in their place.[228]

The advice was excellent. Indeed, it has been the central argument of this chapter that the failure of the colonists to respect the free status of the Khoisan was bound to end in disaster, aggravating an already turbulent frontier conflict and rendering the master-servant relationship fundamentally unstable. In May 1799, as the burghers of Graaff-Reinet fled in panic before a combined 'confederacy' of Xhosa and 'vagabond Hottentots', Maynier could feel himself fully vindicated.[229]

We are returned once more, then, to the question with which we began:

Afschriften, pp. 699–700. The original was nowhere to be found, despite a fairly thorough search.

225 CA, VC 887, Moodie's Afschriften, vol. 24, pp. 701–2.

226 See above, p. 225.

227 Maynier's Provisional Justification, April 1802, in Theal, *RCC*, vol. 4, pp. 320–1.

228 Maynier to Jan Booysen, 1801, cited in Marais, *Maynier*, frontispiece.

229 See Newton-King and Malherbe, 'Khoikhoi Rebellion', pp. 18–22.

why, if Maynier's counsel was wise, could his subjects not follow it? What kept them from seeing what Maynier saw, and acting in their own best interest? I have tried in this chapter to examine what Barthes would call the 'consecutional' dimension of this problem—the pressure of events which, beginning with the taking of captives during commando raids on 'Bushman' camps, engendered an acute instability in master-servant relations and precluded the emergence of a paternalistic compromise, so that violence seemed the only resort of a threatened master class. However an examination of the circumstances under which a brutal system was born does not exhaust the search for its origins. There were other less visible factors which influenced the behaviour of Maynier's subjects—other interests of which even Maynier may have been unaware, since he was a Company employee and his subjects were not. The exploration of these factors must await another occasion.

10

SLAVERY & EMANCIPATION IN THE EASTERN CAPE

– CLIFTON CRAIS –

The winter of 1850 was unusually dry. The valleys of the eastern Cape had received little rain and the Winterberg Mountains lacked their mantle of snow which fed the streams and small rivers that snaked towards the Indian Ocean coast some 224 kilometres away. The drought came on top of other devastations. Three years earlier British troops had marched across the eastern Cape and into western Xhosaland, burning homesteads, capturing cattle, and sending a flood of refugees east into the colonial districts of Fort Beaufort, Somerset East, and Albany. The despotic actions of settlers and the local state accompanied the wreckage of war, forcing 'squatters' off the land and into service of white farmers. By the spring of 1850, the malnutrition that already had become a fixture of life among the poor and landless worsened. Then the summer rains failed.

In December, in the middle of the Cape summer, the days were hot and dry and the skies insistently refused to give up their moisture. A labourer by the name of Kautgong, who also went by the name of Africa April, sat down, perhaps around a fire, with 11 other men. They met on a prosperous wool farm where Kautgong laboured for a British settler. We have only the barest glimpse into their discussions, though we know that peasants, squatters and labourers across the region engaged in similar conversations, forming a web of communication across much of the eastern Cape. They probably spoke of the drought, of an earth gone barren, but also of a land over which they had little control.

There was, however, a related and more immediately pressing issue at hand. The men had received a fateful message. A messenger had come among them from the peasant community at the Kat River Settlement a short ride to the east. Kautgong had a relative at Kat River. His wife's brother, the soon-to-be-famous rebel commander, Willem Uithaalder, had settled there in

1828 as a peasant, cultivating grains and fruit trees and living in a small wattle and daub house.

The messenger spoke of the necessity of getting 'together' to fight the British. This was not flippant talk, and Kautgong and the others must have considered the weighty implications of the message for some time. The recent war had made clear once again the destructive power of the British army, and Africa April and the others knew well that white settlers in the region were willing to engage in acts of considerable and sustained violence. Nor was this discussion on a seemingly remote farm unique. Other messengers had spread the fighting talk to peasants, blacks living on white farms, and squatters who stubbornly claimed land on the edge of farms or fingers of waste land created by the folding mountains and hills of the eastern Cape. The entire region brimmed with gossip, rumour, and ponderous debate.

Kautgong and the others spoke of the message, and of the past and present, and they arrived at a momentous decision. They would leave the farm and head off towards the Kat River Settlement to join the revolt that was soon to shake the very foundations of the colonial order in South Africa. Kautgong, in fact, would become an important leader in the revolt, perhaps, in part, because of his relation to Uithaalder. In deciding to fight the British settlers, Kautgong spoke of how he had 'once' been a 'slave' and how he was willing to shed blood—to engage in organized and protracted armed struggle—to preserve his freedom. For Kautgong, the poverty-stricken Africa April, 'before he would again become' a slave 'it would cost blood'.[1]

Similar discussions and declarations unfolded across the region. Individuals and groups recalled the pain of bonded servitude and the freedom they had 'tasted' with the ending of forced labour. Peasants and the newly dispossessed reiterated the importance of independent access to land, and they spoke bitterly of the rise of avaricious farmers and the emergence of a coercive colonial state. The enormous power of memory, and the creation and maintenance of ties covering considerable geographic distances which it sustained, became crucial in transforming discordant anger into an organized violent conflict that would engulf the entire eastern Cape for three long years. Typically referred to as the 'Hottentot Rebellion' and assumed to have been restricted to the Kat River Settlement, the widespread rebellion of ex-slaves and ex-peons threatened to spread west into the rest of the Cape Colony. While other ex-slaves in the western Cape decided against taking up arms, in the east rebels joined forces with the Xhosa in the most widespread resistance the Cape Colony would witness for the next century.[2]

---

1   See Cape Archives (CA), AG 2798, evidence of Martin, 18 Sept. 1852; AG 2798, evidence of Petersi, 18 Sept.1852; AG 2798, statement of Peters, n.d. 1852; CA 1/UIT 14/37, case 44.

2   The war is discussed in detail in Crais, *White Supremacy and Black Resistance in Pre-Industrial South Africa: The Making of the Colonial Order in the Eastern Cape* (Cambridge, 1992), reprinted as *The*

Plate 11 Kat River Settlement, 1838, by Henry Butler. *South African Library.*

The revolt of the newly free represented the dramatic and violent culmination of processes unleashed by the British abolition of peonage and slavery in the eastern Cape. It also paralleled quite powerfully the wars and revolts that rocked the region in the twilight years of the eighteenth century.[3] The earlier conflict erupted out of the expansion of Dutch settlers, the enslavement of the Khoisan and, as Newton-King has demonstrated in this volume, the creation of an enormously violent system of unfree labour. But while the ex-slaves who participated in the rebellion of 1850–3 remembered the earlier conquest and the slavery that had accompanied it, the conflict of mid century was less about the creation of colonial supremacy than over the character of its reassertion. Nor was this resistance in an era of emancipation unique. Ex-slaves from Jamaica to South Carolina to the coast of Kenya resisted the attempts of ex-masters to reassert their control.[4]

However, the situation in the eastern Cape was, in some important respects, different from both that in the region to the west and, for that matter, from that in most other slave societies. For the settlers against whom Africa April battled were very much part of a new master-class. Many of the most prominent exploiters of unfree labour during the late eighteenth and early nineteenth centuries had left the region between 1838 and 1842 in what has since become known as the 'Great Trek'. The 1820 settlers from the British Isles took their place. They also brought with them new practices and sensibilities. In contrast to the 'Boers', the great majority of the new settlers, who established sprawling wool farms across much of the region, considered slavery an institution injurious to economic development and social progress. Moreover, these capitalists, who increasingly espoused the new racism of the nineteenth century, saw the colonial state as a central institution in the creation of a society that produced wealth but maintained control over the labourers who produced it.[5]

ON THE EVE OF EMANCIPATION

Slavery in the eastern Cape paled in comparison with that in its western neighbour. The number of slaves in the region had increased by close to 600

Making of the Colonial Order: White Supremacy and Black Resistance in the Eastern Cape, 1770–1865 (Johannesburg, 1992). See also, E. Bradlow, '"The Great Fear" at the Cape of Good Hope, 1851–2', *International Journal of African Historical Studies*, 22, 2 (1989), pp. 401–22, which focuses primarily on the western Cape.

3   See V.C. Malherbe and S. Newton-King, *The Khoikhoi Rebellion of the Eastern Cape: 1799–1803* (Cape Town, 1981).

4   See E. Foner, *Nothing But Freedom: Emancipation and Its Legacy* (Baton Rouge, 1983); T.C. Holt, *The Problem of Freedom: Race, Labor, and Politics in Jamaica and Britain, 1832–1938* (Baltimore, 1992).

5   See C. Crais, 'Slavery and Freedom Along a Frontier: The Eastern Cape, South Africa, 1770–1838', *Slavery and Abolition: A Journal of Comparative Studies*, 11, 2 (1990), pp. 190–215.

per cent between 1795 and 1834, from just under 1,000 to 5,765, but even at its height this sum represented only 15 per cent of the total slave population in the Cape Colony. Throughout the region whites outnumbered slaves, though there were important local differences. In Graaff-Reinet, which had the eastern Cape's largest slave population, in 1823 whites outnumbered their chattel by a ratio of almost 3.5:1. Only in the most densely European-settled areas with the strongest economic ties to Cape Town did slaves tend to outnumber the Khoisan or the white men who mastered over them, as in the field-cornetcies of Bruintjieshoogte and Bushman's River in Somerset East. Throughout the eastern Cape, Khoisan (noted in the records as 'Hottentots') tended to roughly equal the number of colonists; for example, in 1823 in Graaff-Reinet there were 5,924 'Whites' compared to 5,919 'Hottentots'.[6]

Chattel slavery unquestionably reigned over the social and economic landscape of the western Cape. The picture in the east, from the Zwartberg Mountains to the Great Fish River, was rather more complicated. For Dutch settlers the model of unfree labour remained similar to that of the patriarchal slavery of the more wealthy farms to the west. As Newton-King has argued, even though the Dutch East India Company (VOC) prohibited the formal enslavement of Khoisan, there was, nevertheless, a market for captives, and laws concerning the disciplining of slaves were applied to the other unfree inhabitants of the colonial farm. Certainly, when affordable, colonists purchased slaves who had been brought to the Cape via the export trade. When possible, they enslaved the local Khoisan. Where practical, when their control over an area was tenuous, colonists reluctantly allowed the unfree on their farms to own property and to have some independent control over their lives. And in some places Africans maintained an increasingly fragile existence: as Sparrman described it in the eighteenth century, Khoisan continued to live in their own 'small societies…where the colonists cannot easily come at them, and are sometimes in the possession of a few cows'.[7]

The organization of labour thus varied from outright slavery to, in some cases, a kind of colonial serfdom. During the course of the late eighteenth and early nineteenth centuries, these 'serf-like' tenants increasingly were the illegitimate offspring of European men and Khoikhoi women and, to a far lesser extent, slave women, and not the Khoisan who once lived independently in the area. Like earlier tenants, they lived 'by sufferance upon portions of farmers' places, giving a partial service for the privilege of pasturing their cattle'.[8] Referred to as 'Bastaard Clients', such tenants occupied a

6   The great exception is Albany, where some 5,000 British settled in 1820.

7   A. Sparrman, *A Voyage to the Cape of Good Hope…1772–6*, V.S. Forbes (ed.) (Cape Town, 1975), vol. 1, pp. 199–200.

8   CA, CO 362, Thomson to Cole, 28 Sept. 1829.

privileged if ambiguous place among the unfree members of the colonial farm. They sometimes possessed significant property, like Christian Groepe, by far one of the wealthiest of all 'Clients', who in 1829 owned 600 sheep and goats, 16 oxen, 40 cattle, 18 horses and a wagon.[9] Men such as Groepe were as wealthy as some of the poorer colonists living on the frontier, though colonists denied them the status of burghers and restricted their participation in the colonial market economy.

The other dependents of the colonial farm faced a far more oppressive world. In general, the late eighteenth century saw a painful levelling of colonial labour relationships, which more closely approximated the model of slavery in the western Cape. Many of the Khoisan who had lived as serfs in 'small societies' during the 1770s became, in later decades, debt-peons tied to the colonial master's house. Here the apprenticeship (*inboek*) system played a central role. Beginning in the 1780s with the indenturing of children to the age of 18 years, in the following decade colonial authorities extended the length of indenture to the age of 25 years. Culminating in the Caledon Code of 1809, the *inboek* system ensured the creation of a debt-ridden servile class.[10]

Whether enslaved in raids, or reduced to servitude through the encroachments of the colonial farmer, by the beginning of the nineteenth century the great majority of Khoisan ended up in a situation of debt-peonage and near slavery, '*slaaf Hottentoten*' who were 'hired' for their 'lifetime'.[11] Debt-peons, for example, increasingly were divided and transferred as property upon the death of the master, while forms of punishment such as branding reiterated assertions of private property rights in the bodies of others. Along with captives from raids in the interior, debt-peons or their children may have been illicitly elided into the category of slave, though our evidence on this illegal activity remains slim.

In the daily lives of many people on the farm, there was thus often precious little difference between the legal distinctions of slave and indentured apprentice. Indeed, peons and slaves increasingly formed a single class of the unfree. Living under the whip and gun of the colonial master, they assembled and maintained conjugal relations and engaged in an informal economy that produced a web of relationships beyond the farm and across the region. This creation of a sub-culture and what I have called elsewhere the 'domestic economy of the unfree' would, as we shall see, have profound implications for the collapse of unfree labour in the eastern Cape. Most important was the

---

9   Crais, *White Supremacy and Black Resistance*, p. 81

10   Also see V.C. Malherbe, 'Indentured and Unfree Labour in South Africa: Towards an Understanding', *South African Historical Journal*, 24 (1991), pp. 3–30.

11   On the transition from serfdom to debt-peonage and slavery, see Crais, *White Supremacy and Black Resistance*, p. 50.

emergence of a consciousness that sustained powerful links across a wide expanse of relatively sparsely-populated territory, bonds that are recalled in the archival record of Africa April. The defining idiom of this consciousness was the late eighteenth century expansion of unfree labour itself. Peons would thus recall how they or their parents had once lived as tenants where they had had 'large flocks of their own' but had been reduced to servitude by the violence and expropriations of the colonial farmer.[12] Others spoke of mothers tied to the master's house and branded and how they had been enslaved. In 1847 an impoverished woman remembered how her husband had been 'brought into the colony and *sold for a slave*'.[13] The creation of a single class and sub-culture of the unfree meant that the economic exploitation and patriarchal pronouncements of the master-class did not go unquestioned. Indeed, the very violence of the frontier was indicative of the frailty of colonial life in the eastern Cape.

The legislative destruction of peonage and slavery under Ordinance 50 of 1828 and the 1833 Abolition Act brought to the surface the unresolved and intractable issues of organization of labour. Escape had long been a possibility for slaves and the other unfree members of the colonial farm. The Dutch frontier farmer, in turn, pursued runaways for considerable distances. When found, they often suffered enormous punishments, often followed by death. More generally, the farmer typically relied on brute force, euphemistically referred to in the records as 'domestic correction', as a way of keeping his workers in line. The new British rulers of the Cape generally abhorred such violence and, throughout the first two decades of the century, progressively curtailed the severity of the punishments colonists could mete out to their dependents. With the ending of unfree labour, slaves and peons abandoned their white masters in enormous numbers, especially in the less densely-populated districts of Somerset East and parts of near-by Graaff-Reinet. On many farms from 1828 and well into the first half of the next decade, virtually the entire servile population deserted, frequently engaging in various acts of retribution ranging from theft to banditry and murder. In Somerset East, to take one example, the ex-servant David Pimple turned to banditry and threatened to 'shoot' whites 'dead'. Indeed, from the late 1820s and through the next decade, 'bands of loose Hottentots' left the farms to create small communities of bandits who largely depended on the plunder of white farmers.[14]

Others left for the towns and the mission stations. All of the London

---

12 Quoted in Giliomee, 'Processes in Development of the Southern African Frontier', in H. Lamar and L. Thompson (eds.), *The Frontier in History: North America and Southern Africa Compared* (New Haven, 1981), p. 83.

13 CA, SSE 8/89. Aldrich to Hudson, 29 Oct. 1847; CA, ACC 50, Meeting, 5 Aug. 1834.

14 See CA, LCA 6, Dreyer to Campbell, 18 Aug. 1829; CA, SSE 1/1A, Case no. 39 vs. Pimple, 24 Nov. 1828.

Missionary Society (LMS) stations in the eastern Cape reported increases during the third decade of the century, and most suffered from overcrowding. In Grahamstown, Uitenhage, and especially in Port Elizabeth, hundreds of ex-servants established small communities on the outskirts of the white town where the newly free erected habitations ranging from sheds 'among the bushes' to buildings of a more European design.[15] As late as 1845, a LMS missionary described to his superiors how in the town of Uitenhage ex-peons and 'emancipated slaves', who often migrated to towns because there was little available rural land after their apprenticeship period expired in 1838, had 'erected comfortable cottages and cultivated little gardens'.[16]

The emergence of peasant communities, which is discussed in greater detail in the next section, offered a third repudiation of the eastern Cape's master-class. Combined with a spate of legislation ranging from a re-working of the local state to changes in land tenure and the increasing dominance of British settlers, who tended to receive privileged access to land and who had the ear of colonial politicians, the emancipations forced a substantial number of frontier settlers to leave the Cape Colony in what later became mythologized in Afrikaner nationalism as the 'Great Trek'. The ending of slavery, as one trekker put it, had 'compelled' him 'to dispose of my property for half price'.[17] Certainly the monetary compensation due to slaveowners under the Abolition Act failed to meet the market value of their slaves. Nor, as was the case in the western Cape, were slaveowners in a position to invest their compensation monies in other economic activities.[18]

The ending of slavery and peonage thus constituted a fundamental disjuncture in the colonial world of the eastern Cape. Slaves and peons deserted the farms, often to return as social bandits, seeking retribution for earlier injustices or making claims to property. The newly free openly contested and repudiated an etiquette of oppressive race relations that had been assembled in the daily social relations of the farm from the late eighteenth century. Unable to protect their considerable capital investments in human flesh in the face of British policies and practice, and incapable of controlling the lives of the unfree who had laboured on the colonial farm, the fragile world the frontier Boers had made collapsed. There was, as many of those colonists who 'trekked' now saw it, 'no longer any justice for the burghers, but only for blacks'.[19]

---

15   See CA, 1/AY 9/6, Campbell to Bell, 29 Jan. 1830; *Graham's Town Journal*, 13 June 1833; CA, CO 2721, S. Bradshaw to Moodie, 6 Mar. 1830.

16   School of Oriental and African Studies, University of London (SOAS), LMS 21(2)C, Elliot to Tidman and Freeman, 13 June 1845.

17   CA, CO 2748, Jacobs to Meintjes, 20 May 1838. Also see CA, 1/AY 8/87, Retief to Campbell, 18 Apr. 1836.

18   See Meltzer, ch. 7 in this volume.

19   Quoted in J.B. Peires, 'The British and the Cape, 1814–34', in R. Elphick and H. Giliomee (eds.), *The*

RECONSTRUCTING WHITE SUPREMACY

Three major developments characterized the years between the abolition of unfree labour and the outbreak of war in late 1850. The first, ultimately rooted in the beginning of British rule at the beginning of the century, was the creation and increasing reach of the colonial state. Secondly, this period saw the development of settler capitalism in the eastern Cape and the emergence of a new colonial élite in the region; an élite which clamoured for control of the state. Unlike the Boers, British settlers—not to mention most Colonial Office bureaucrats—desired an economy based on free wage labour. They also desired an orderly society where the state assumed many of the disciplinary duties that had once been the privilege of the master. Thirdly, between the colonial state and white capitalist farmers stood a black peasantry composed of ex-slaves, ex-peons and, to a lesser extent, Africans from Xhosaland, whose small plots sometimes literally abutted those of the wealth wool estates.

We have already noted the ease with which peons and slaves deserted their white master's service in the period immediately after emancipation, turning to banditry or moving to mission stations or the burgeoning towns of the eastern Cape. The formation of peasant communities, a not unusual development in post-emancipation societies, constituted a third possibility for the recently free. As one missionary put it, on 'receiving their civil liberty' the recently free 'became anxious to also obtain some property'.[20] The most important 'property' was the land on which the emancipated believed their future freedom rested; for many land and freedom were synonymous. Blacks flocked to the increasingly overcrowded mission stations and urban locations because they offered access to land over which the white colonists had no control. In Port Elizabeth, for example, ex-peons preferred working in the harbour to labouring for farmers. The emancipated would simply 'not accept…employment'—they would 'not work'—and when they did they forced farmers into short-term contracts and cash wages, and thus maximized their control over the labour-process.[21]

In areas where land was more plentiful and the control of European colonists less secure, or in the government-sponsored Kat River Settlement, ex-slaves, ex-peons and Africans from all over southern Africa established peasant communities. Space permits only a short description of these communities, though some, particularly the Kat River Settlement, have been

Shaping of South African Society: 1652–1840 (Cape Town, 1989), p. 504.

20   SOAS, LMS 12(4)C, extract of letter from Read [?] to Campbell, n.d. Aug. 1831.

21   See SOAS, LMS 12(4)A, Robson to Directors of LMS, 6 Jan. 1831; SOAS, LMS 11(1)B, Edwards to Arundel, 1 May 1828; SOAS, LMS 6, Memorial of the inhabitants of Pacaltsdorp mission station, n.d. 1834.

discussed in detail elsewhere.[22] There were at least four such communities in the district of Somerset East, ranging from six families to more than 150 people; most were located on the edge of white farms or on unclaimed or marginal land. The most successful peasant community in the district was that of Damon, a Bechuana chief who collected a group of refugees from the interior and who, in 1833, obtained an ill-defined concession of land from the colonial government. The community grew well into the following decade, attracting Xhosa and ex-peons and ex-slaves, and engaging in substantial wheat and maize production in which the peasants sold 'many muids' on the colonial market economy.[23]

There were similar marginal communities of peasants in upper Albany and in the district of Fort Beaufort typically populated by the newly free. In was, however, along the Kat River that peasant production took root most forcefully. Established in 1829, the Kat River Settlement has long captured the attention of historians, from the vilifying and racist account of Cory to the liberal work of Marais, and the newer work of Kirk.[24] Unlike the other communities which dotted the region, the Kat River Settlement was large, conspicuous and, from the beginning, embroiled in controversy. Two years after its founding, for example, some 3,300 people pastured thousands of animals and engaged in the extensive cultivation of fruits and grains. In the mid 1840s the population of the settlement and the Blinkwater community which bordered it had topped 6,000. The peasants owned close to 20,000 animals and yearly produced some 50,000 pounds of hay, 22,000 bushels of grains and over 45,000 pounds of fruit.[25]

More than any other community in the eastern Cape, the peasants of Kat River were most able to withstand the growth of settler capitalism and the spread of white supremacy that characterized particularly the fourth and fifth decades of the century. If black peasants engaged in cereal and fruit production for the local market, British settlers engaged in the more lucrative, but potentially more unstable, production of wool which ended up on the looms of an industrializing Britain. The beginnings of an agrarian capitalism lay in the late 1820s and in the shift from the frontier trade to commodity

---

22   See T. Kirk, 'The Cape Economy and the Expropriation of the Kat River Settlement', in S. Marks and A. Atmore (eds.), *Economy and Society in Pre-Industrial South Africa* (London, 1980), pp. 226–46; Crais, *White Supremacy and Black Resistance*, pp. 64–86, 147–88.

23   See, for example, CA, SSE 8/89, Hart, grant to Damon, 19 Mar. 1833; SSE 10/2, RM and CC for Somerset East to Hudson, 31 Aug. 1842; SSE 10/2, Ziervogel to Hudson, 8 Dec. 1841;, and Marillier to Hudson, 27 Apr. 1842; SSE 8/89, Return, 21 Sept. 1847; SSE 8/73, Stretch to Hudson, 8 Aug. 1842; CA, 8/32, Hudson to Chase, 10 Jan. 1848.

24   See Kirk, 'The Cape Economy'; J.S. Marais, *The Cape Coloured People: 1652–1937* (Johannesburg, 1957).

25   These estimates are based on James Read Jr., *The Kat River Settlement in 1851* (Cape Town, 1852); Marais, *The Cape Coloured People*, pp. 216–45; SOAS, LMS 15 (2)B, Barker, 'Report', 16 Dec. 1836. See also Crais, *The Making of the Colonial Order*, pp. 64–86, 147–72.

production. Many settlers reinvested profits, made through exchange with the Xhosa, in the acquisition of land and sheep. As early as the 1830s wool had become the colony's single most important export commodity, and it would continue to dominate the colonial economy of the region until the late 1860s and the discovery of diamonds in Griqualand West. The most impressive growth occurred in the 1840s when wool production soared some 500 per cent to 5,500,000 pounds per annum in 1851. As one official put it in an 1855 report, the district of Fort Beaufort included 'every convenience for a pastoral life' and 'many handsome and substantial mansions'.[26]

Compared to the colonial frontier economy of the late eighteenth and early nineteenth centuries, capitalist wool production was economically vulnerable to shifts in world commodity prices and consumed much more land and labour. Wool production also required a more disciplined and skilled working class—inept shearing, for example, could halve profits—and the emergent rural bourgeoisie well knew that the sites of resistance expanded beyond the usual theft and desertion of earlier decades and into the labour-process itself. In response to these challenges, wool farmers struggled to transform land and labour into commodities, and blacks into a dependent and, for the most part, landless working class. Moreover, in contrast to the colonists of the late eighteenth century who maintained little social distance between master and servant, the new élite sought the creation of a culture of domination which would allow them to retreat from the site of production and struggle and into the placid and insular world of a colonial bourgeoisie.[27]

To do so required the state, which increasingly assumed many of the disciplinary duties that had once been the privilege of the Dutch master. The abolition of unfree labour, a political act instituted from London, was supposed to make much of the world a better, or at least more moral, place. Now the colonial state was required to make the eastern Cape safe for settler capitalism. The state was never simply the tool of avaricious capitalists, and even in its most cooperative moments there were a number of tensions and contradictions.[28] Despite the contradictory position of the Civil Commissioner and Resident Magistrate, however, during the fourth decade of the century the rising élite in much of the eastern Cape nonetheless captured the local state and, in the on-going debates on representative rule, expected to enlarge and extend its power. This increasing control manifested itself in a number of ways, from the appointment of magistrates more sympathetic to the development of settler capitalism, to the establishment of

---

26   See CA, 1/FBF 6/1/3/2/1, Stringfellow, Report for 1854, 5 Jan. 1855; Kirk, 'The Cape Economy'; Crais, *White Supremacy and Black Resistance*, pp. 147–72.

27   This is covered in more detail in Crais, *White Supremacy and Black Resistance*.

28   See Crais, *White Supremacy and Black Resistance*. See also B. Berman, *Control and Crisis in Colonial Kenya: The Dialectic of Domination* (London, 1990).

livestock pounds, labour legislation and laws such as Ordinance 2 of 1837 which prohibited what settlers and the state considered were the unauthorized locations of black peasants and squatters. In the various towns of the region, where white residents had gained much more power from the late 1830s, for example, the authorities extended greater control over the increasingly populous black locations, enforcing building standards, reducing access to commonage, charging rents and rates, and arresting individuals on the often dubious charge of vagrancy. One missionary believed such practices were designed to 'force persons of color into contract service'.[29]

The intervention from above by the local state intersected with the onslaught of capitalist farmers who increasingly displaced blacks living on lands which whites now claimed to own. Farmers limited the number of stock blacks living on their farms could own and restricted the size of the community, depriving them of access to productive resources and further reducing them to the ranks of a rural proletariat. Farmers in Albany and Uitenhage bought up the land surrounding mission stations and impounded black-owned livestock with much enthusiasm. In Bethelsdorp in 1844, for example, 'many Hottentots possess waggons and cattle, but have no lands'. Such individuals increasingly had little other choice but to seek work from white farmers.[30]

The growth of capitalist production and the enlargement of the control of settlers which increasingly became inseparable from the actions of the local state represented South Africa's first 'enclosure movement'. These processes engendered considerable resistance, of which theft and flight were the most common expressions. Solid factual data are hard to come by, but judging from reports in the *Graham's Town Journal* and memorials there is considerable evidence which suggests that the number of thefts dramatically increased from the late 1830s, and particularly during the second half of the following decade. Many blacks managed to avoid farm labour altogether by migrating to the peasant settlements of the region, by forming squatter communities or by joining the growing urban working class. Others lived a more precarious existence, maintaining access to small parcels of land and engaging in irregular labour with white farmers. Settlers were not surprisingly incensed when, for example in 1846, Africans stole three spades and seven sacks from one farm, only to go to another farm where the thieves filled the sacks with maize and wheat.[31]

29   See SOAS, LMS 20(1)C, Elliot to the Commissioners of the Municipal Government, 12 Feb. 1844; CA, 3/AY 3/1/1/1, Latham, mem. of the Commissioners for the Municipality for Graham's Town, 7 Aug. 1843.

30   See SOAS, LMS 20(3)C, Kitchingman to Tidman and Freeman, 31 Dec. 1844; Crais, *White Supremacy and Black Resistance*, esp. pp. 147–72.

31   CA, 1/AY 8/96, Hewson to Hudson, 28 Feb. 1846.

Particularly in the 1840s—just over a decade after Ordinance 50 and a few years after the abolition of slavery—with the help of the local state, white farmers not only extended their control over land and labour, which were necessary preconditions for the development of agrarian capitalism, but they also initiated a frontal attack on the peasants of the eastern Cape. In large part this was because such communities bottled up labour that otherwise could have been employed on the settler farm. Farmers moreover believed that the destruction of independent black communities was necessary in order to attain a hegemonic position in the political economy of the region. From the second half of the 1830s politicians in the Cape and in London had discussed the nature of political society and representation in the Cape Colony. By the early 1840s it was already clear to most prominent eastern Cape settlers that the Cape would receive representative rule; the nagging question was the position of blacks in a new political system.[32]

In the 1840s, wealthy white farmers captured effective control of the local state throughout much of the eastern Cape. For peasants and squatters the decade was one of dispossession and misery. Blacks living on mission stations in Albany and Uitenhage lost access to land, and 'in order to obtain subsistence' increasing numbers had little choice but to seek employment as 'farm servants'.[33] The poor communities at Gaba, Kaba and Bush Fontein in Somerset East, and at Caffre Drift and Trompetter's Drift in Fort Beaufort, appear to have virtually disappeared in the fourth decade of the century, as a result of problems internal to the communities such as population growth, but especially from the use of livestock pounds and the buying up of land by white farmers. Damon struggled to avoid conflicts with farmers and local officials, but settlers hassled his people and the authorities destroyed the huts of blacks who sought refuge in the community and 'ordered' them 'to enter into service'. In 1842 the state looked into the 'alarming' increase in the 'irregularities committed' by the people of Damon's location. Surveillance by the local state increased throughout the decade. By 1848 the state had resolved to charge rents retroactively, and three years later it decided to destroy the community and sell the land.[34]

Communities such as Damon's were relatively easy to destroy. Such was not the case with the Kat River Settlement and its adjoining squatter

32   See B.A. Le Cordeur, *The Politics of Eastern Cape Separatism: 1820–54* (Cape Town, 1981), esp. pp. 227–36.

33   See SOAS, LMS 20 (1)C, Taylor to the Foreign Secretary of the LMS, 10 Jan. 1844; SOAS, LMS 20 (3)C, Taylor to the Foreign Secretary of the LMS, 7 Nov. 1844.

34   On the developments in Damon's community, see CA, SSE 10/2, Marillier to Hudson, 27 Apr. 1842; SSE 10/2, Marillier to Hudson, 15 Aug. 1842; SSE 8/89, Aldrich to Hudson, 6 Jan. 1848; CA, CO 2849, Hudson to Chase, 10 Jan. 1848; SSE 8/89, Alrich to Hudson, 19 Aug. 1847; SSE 8/89, Alrich to Hudson, 22 Apr. 1847; SSE 8/3, Montagu to Civil Commissioner of Somerset East, 29 Feb. 1850; SSE 10/47, Hudson to Stephenson, 6 Sept. 1852.

communities of the Blinkwater and Fuller's Hoek. A community of only 880 people in 1829, by 1831 the population of the Kat River Settlement had almost quadrupled. Population growth continued throughout the decade and into the 1840s, owing to the growth of peasant families and the migration to the community of blacks, including ex-slaves, from throughout the colony. By 1845, the Kat River Settlement and adjoining communities were home to more than 6,000 people who occupied some 312 square kilometres. As many as half of these people fell under the colonial definition of 'illegal squatters' because they did not have formal legal title to land. The majority had been, or at least their fathers and mothers had been, peons. Ex-slaves also sought refuge in the communities, as did the growing numbers of Xhosa whose lands had been conquered by the British. Not surprisingly considerable economic stratification characterized the settlements at Kat River and the Blinkwater. While in 1845 peasant production reached some 50,000 pounds of hay, over 20,000 bushels of grains and 50,000 pounds of fruits and vegetables, not to mention the thousands of farm animals, the bulk of this wealth was concentrated in perhaps as few as 750 to 1,000 hands. This stratification expressed itself sub-regionally—the poorest areas tended to be in the south—and between and within families. Particularly from the second half of the 1830s, the sons of peasants found it increasingly difficult to obtain land and, with other poor peasants and squatters, faced a future of rural labour on the estates of white farmers which surrounded the communities.[35]

Like Damon's community to the west, in the 1840s the peasants and squatters faced an onslaught of white farmers and the local state. Collecting taxes became a preoccupation of officials; so did the enforcement of livestock pounds. The widespread use of Ordinance 2 of 1837, and the decision to sell to white farmers land which was used by peasants and squatters but not formally owned by them, resulted in the wholesale destruction of villages. The 1847 appointment of the conservative T.J. Biddulph as Justice of Peace over the Blinkwater and Kat River Settlement made matters even more tense, and while LMS missionaries were successful in forcing Biddulph to resign, his successor T.H. Bowker was, in most respects, worse. Bowker began arresting blacks whom farmers accused of using 'threatening language' and confiscated the livestock of individuals he believed were thieves. With the strong reinforcement of the conservative Colonial Secretary Montagu, from 1848 Bowker and others actively destroyed communities throughout the Blinkwater, Fuller's Hoek and in the southern portions of the Kat River Settlement. Additional lands on which peasants and squatters had lived were sold to white farmers.

This piece by piece construction of white supremacy in the eastern Cape

---

35   See Crais, *White Supremacy and Black Resistance*, pp. 147–88.

reached a head in 1850. Throughout the Cape colonists were busy extending their control over land and labour and reducing the freedoms the slaves and peons had won and struggled for in the years following the emancipations. In Cape Town, discussions progressed on the creation of a new colonial state once London granted the colony representative rule. At the very core of these discussions was the franchise. Eastern Cape farmers almost unanimously argued for a restricted franchise based on enough wealth to effectively disenfranchise the vast majority of blacks.[36] The Legislative Council, which tended to be dominated by the agrarian élite, tabled a Squatters Ordinance which was designed to prohibit 'idle and ill-disposed persons' from 'refusing labour'.[37]

At roughly the same time, the council established the Fuller's Hoek and Blinkwater Commission to look into the relations between whites and blacks in the area around and including the Kat River Settlement, and to advise the council in developing appropriate 'squatter' legislation. The commission consisted of four of the most conservative settlers in the eastern Cape, and among the most conservative colonists in the entire colony. All of them owned land in the vicinity of the Kat River Settlement, and all were stalwart supporters of the Squatters Ordinance. When they went into Fuller's Hoek and Blinkwater they confiscated guns, kicked over cooking pots and ransacked the belongings of peasants and squatters.[38]

CONCLUSION

A month after the commission reported its findings to the Legislative Council, Kautgong, the Africa April whom we met at the beginning of this chapter, sat down with the 11 other men and decided to take up arms against the British. The rebellion and frontier war that engulfed the entire eastern Cape and which threatened to spread west into the midlands and western Cape would constitute the most widespread conflict the Cape Colony would see for a full century. While statistics are, for the most part, non-existent, there is considerable evidence to suggest that approximately 75 to 90 per cent of the rural workers in the districts of Albany, Fort Beaufort and Somerset East revolted. Most of the residents of the Theopolis and Shiloh mission stations rebelled, as did almost the entire Blinkwater, and much of Fuller's Hoek and the Kat River Settlement. In the western Cape workers by

---

36 Discussions of representative rule can be found in Le Cordeur, *The Politics of Eastern Cape Separatism*; T. Kirk, 'Self-Government and Self-Defence in South Africa: The Inter-Relations Between British and Cape Politics, 1846–54' (D.Phil. thesis, Oxford University, 1972).

37 A draft of the ordinance is located in *BPP* 1636/52–3, Smith to Grey, 12 Feb. 1852.

38 SOAS, LMS 26 (4)C, Read to [?], Thompson, collection of letters re: Kat River Settlement, 11 July 1850.

and large remained in the fields, though whites there greatly feared an explosive race war.[39]

A year after the outbreak of the war, Governor Smith, who considered the rebellion 'the most important event that ever occurred in this colony', wrote to his superior in London that the conflict had 'arisen out of the direct relations...of the two classes forming the great bulk of the inhabitants of this colony, the white and the black or in other words the master and servant'.[40] Kautgong would have agreed with the governor. Rebels often spoke of fighting against a return to slavery.[41] They were acutely aware of the importance of land, that land insured freedom, that land protected them from having 'to submit to daily labour or monthly service under the white man'.[42] They also greatly feared the promulgation of coercive vagrancy legislation which, in fact, had just been tabled before the Legislative Council. Rebels were thus cognisant of the discussions on representative rule taking place in Cape Town and in London, and of the future implications of a colonial state controlled by the propertied and the white.

The history of the eastern Cape in the almost three decades between Ordinance 50 of 1828 and the granting of representative rule in 1853, however, involved not the return of old masters but the creation of a new and more modern form of colonial domination in South Africa. For the conflict which roared on for three bloody years was directly related to two developments of fundamental consequence to the history of South Africa: the emergence of settler capitalism and the creation of a coercive colonial state. More precisely, Africa April and his comrades were fighting against the emergence of a labour-repressive political economy in the eastern Cape.

Like many stories of the struggles of the newly free elsewhere in the world, the history of emancipation in the eastern Cape was exemplary for its inability to live up to the promises of abolition. Emancipation did not bring freedom. But our fragmentary knowledge of the life of a single rebel is instructive not only for demonstrating the daily and, often heroic, struggles of the poor. Nor is the past of the region during the first half of the nineteenth century important for constituting yet another example of the failure of what Holt has referred to as the 'mighty experiment' of emancipation.[43] Both, of course, are important. But the story does not end here.

Almost three decades ago, Barrington Moore Jr. argued in his *Social Origins of Dictatorship and Democracy* that labour-repressive economies

39   See Bradlow, 'The "Great Fear" at the Cape of Good Hope'.

40   Public Records Office, London, PRO 135/2, Smith Papers, Smith to Montagu, 5 Mar. 1851; CA, GH 23/20, Smith to Grey, 12 Feb. 1852.

41   For a discussion of the aftermath of the war, see Crais, *White Supremacy and Black Resistance*.

42   CA, LG 592, Warner to Southey, 27 Dec. 1856.

43   Holt, *The Problem of Freedom*.

'provide an unfavorable soil for the growth of democracy and an important part of the institutional complex leading to fascism'.[44] Moore's thesis had a powerful impact on historians analysing agrarian transformations and South Africa's 'Prussian Road' to capitalism, who by and large focused primarily on the relationships among wealthy capitalist farmers, industrialists, and the state in the era after the discovery of diamonds and gold. What was crucial for Moore—the relationship between economy and political culture—sadly has remained largely unexplored.[45]

By whatever road capitalism arrived at the southern tip of Africa, it has become axiomatic in much historical writing to point out the unusually coercive nature of a state which, often in collusion with capital and almost always acting in the interests of wealthy white settlers, played a central role in the creation of a 'labour-repressive' economy.[46] The story of emancipation in the eastern Cape helps to isolate the violent moment when this political economy, a political economy which would persist well into the twentieth century, first emerged. The oppressive world which white farmers and the state made was neither located in an earlier era of slavery as an unfortunate anachronism of a more distant past, nor the result of the South Africa's economic revolution of diamonds and gold. Instead it emerged in the very era that saw slavery's destruction at the hands of the liberal British.

Africa April and the other rebels were cognisant of this fateful moment in South Africa's history, of the forging of a capitalist order and the formation of what Marais aptly described as a 'parliament of masters'.[47] Does an acknowledgement that these signal developments unfolded during they heyday of liberalism suggest that the life and memories of Kautgong serve as a cautionary tale for the Africas and the Aprils of today?

---

44 B. Moore Jr., *Social Origins of Dictatorship and Democracy: Landlord and Peasant in the Making of the Modern World* (Boston, 1966), p. 435. See also S. Hahn, 'Class and State in Postemancipation Societies: Southern Planters in Comparative Perspective', *American Historical Review*, 95, 1 (1990), pp. 75–98; H. Bradford, 'Highways, Byways and Culs-de-Sacs: The Transition to Agrarian Capitalism in Revisionist South African History', *Radical History Review*, 46/7 (1990), pp. 59–88.

45 See W. Beinart, P. Delius and S. Trapido (eds.), *Putting a Plough to the Ground: Accumulation and Dispossession in Rural South Africa, 1850–1930* (Johannesburg, 1986.) See also Bradford, 'Highways, Byways and Culs-de-Sacs' which includes a critique of the 'Prussian Road' to capitalism in South Africa.

46 See Bradford, 'Highways, Byways and Culs-de-Sacs'.

47 Marais, *Cape Coloured People*, p. 205.

Plate 12 Meeting at 'the Stone' to celebrate the anniversary of emancipation, 1903. *South African Library.*

11

MEANINGS OF FREEDOM
SOCIAL POSITION & IDENTITY AMONG EX-SLAVES & THEIR DESCENDANTS IN CAPE TOWN, 1875-1910

— VIVIAN BICKFORD-SMITH —

This chapter explores what freedom—in terms of social position and identity—meant for those who shared a heritage of slavery in an urban context at the Cape. Although there is little research on the social history of Cape Town between emancipation and the 1870s, the years 1875 to 1910 have recently been examined in two doctoral theses.[1] Economic and political developments in this period provided possibilities of social improvement for those who had suffered bondage. In the event 'the traditional system of class and race relations' in the city, in terms of white dominance and black subordination, was challenged but left virtually intact before 1910.[2] What did emerge between 1875 and 1910 were new forms of social and political identities among freed slaves and their descendants, most notably the idea of being 'coloured'. These identities were inevitably built on those that had emerged in the era of slavery. This chapter attempts to demonstrate that an understanding of this process can be gained by analysing occasions when black Capetonians commemorated emancipation and celebrated New Year, the traditional slave holiday.

SOCIAL POSITION

Analysing the social position of freed slaves in late nineteenth-century Cape Town naturally depends on being able to identify which citizens were of slave descent. There is, as yet, no detailed family reconstitition to help

---

1 E.B. van Heyningen, 'Public Health and Society in Cape Town 1880–1910' (Ph.D. thesis, University of Cape Town, 1989); J.V. Bickford-Smith, 'Commerce, Class and Ethnicity in Cape Town, 1875 to 1902' (Ph.D. thesis, Cambridge University, 1989).

2 This quotation is from G.R. Andrews, *The Afro-Argentines of Buenos Aires 1800–1900* (Madison, 1980), pp. 204–5. Andrews argues that in Buenos Aires, and elsewhere in the Americas, such traditional systems were challenged by economic growth.

historians in this respect. But, given the approximate correlation between colour and status before accelerated manumission and emancipation, it is possible to assert that the majority of ex-slaves and their descendants were entered into censuses as 'Coloured' in 1865 and 'Other than European or White' in 1875.[3] This later label was further divided by the 1875 census officials (who viewed themselves as 'European or White') into 'Malay', 'Hottentot', 'Kafir and Betshuana', 'Fingo' and 'Mixed and Other'.

According to this later census, which provides detailed information on Cape Town, there were 19,236 'Other than Whites' (for which we shall use the term 'blacks') in the city's population of 44,803. If the small number of people in the 'Hottentot', 'Fingo' and 'Kafir and Betshuana' categories are excluded, it seems fairly safe to assume that the majority of the remaining 18,996, or the vast majority of blacks, were of slave descent. If this assumption is correct, and allowing for the fact that some of the more economically successful and paler probably 'passed' into the White category,[4] it would seem as though ex-slave accumulation and social mobility had been limited in the four decades after emancipation.

Only 315 'Malays' and 'Mixed and Others', of nearly 13,000 in occupations specified in the 1875 census, could readily be described as bourgeois or petty bourgeois.[5] Of these, 272 were men and 42 were women. One was a doctor named A.C. Jackson; but Jackson was an immigrant, and therefore not of Cape slave descent.[6] Of the remaining 314, the ·vast majority were minor retailers. A few teachers, clergymen and boarding- or eating-house keepers made up the numbers. There may have been other candidates for bourgeois status among 'Malay' or 'Mixed and Other' artisans and fishermen. These could have included successful independent craftsmen and fishermen/fish-curers, but the census does not distinguish them from the less successful in such categories.

Among artisan occupations, there were 1,541 'Whites' and 1,397 'Malays' and 'Mixed and Others'.[7] Many crafts were almost evenly divided between the two, such as shoemaking or painting. But there is reason to believe that whites received higher wages in at least some of these crafts, such as carpentry, because they were trained in more specialized work.

---

3   *Cape Parliamentary Papers (CPP)* G20–1866, 'Cape Census for 1865'; *CPP* G42–1876, 'Cape Census for 1875'. The quantitative analysis of the social position of freed slaves that follows in this chapter is drawn from statistics in the 1875 census.

4   See G. Lewis, *Between the Wire and the Wall* (Cape Town, 1987), pp. 9, 13.

5   For explanation of this use of terminology and which occupations are included within the categories 'bourgeois' and 'petty bourgeois', see Bickford-Smith, 'Commerce', ch. 2, where there is a detailed analysis of Cape Town's social structure in the mid 1870s based, in large part, on the 1875 census.

6   Van Heyningen, 'Public Health', p. 78.

7   Again see Bickford-Smith, 'Commerce', ch. 2, for a breakdown of which occupations I include under artisan.

Occupations least liable to casualization, like watchmaking or mechanical engineering, were dominated by whites according to the census. The corollary was that 82 per cent of the 1,500 people categorized only as 'unspecified labourers' were of slave descent.

With just a couple of exceptions, artisans and labourers were men. But occupations dominated by women witnessed a similar correlation between colour and status, whether the latter is defined in terms of income or the servile nature of the work. About 70 per cent of dressmakers and seamstresses were white, while a similar percentage of domestic workers and 90 per cent of washerwomen were of slave descent.[8]

These statistics should be taken only as a guideline in terms of their occupational descriptions. Divisions of labour, particularly among lower-paid occupations, were far from rigid. Many black workers swapped or took on additional occupations if they could, according to demand or opportunity. Certain illegal occupations, such as liquor selling or prostitution, were not mentioned or were seriously under-counted in the census.[9]

But the census does tell us that few ex-slaves or their descendants were in positions of economic or political power in 1875. Almost 90 per cent of Cape Town's combined grand and petty bourgeoisie was 'European or White'.[10] The Governor of the colony, as well as central and local government legislators, were whites; so were most merchants, professionals, those of 'independent' means and 'capitalists'. The upper echelons of the civil service, as well as the imperial and colonial defence forces, were the monopoly of the same group. All but one member of the police force was white.

De facto white supremacy would appear to have continually characterized Cape Town's social structure from the 1830s to the 1870s. The nature of economic activity, together with the reality of both white and black Capetonians in almost all gradations of the 'underclasses', had thus far prevented a society rigidly ordered according to colour/appearance. Nor were there rigid divisions of labour along these lines. Nonetheless, an approximate correlation would appear to have existed between lighter colour, male gender and better-paid jobs.

The erosion of slavery in Cape Town in the first three decades of the nineteenth century, and eventual emancipation, had still left most slave descendants among the city's lower classes 40 years later. Why this was so can only be adequately answered by a detailed social history of the intervening period. J.S. Marais' suggestion, that after slavery they (his term 'Cape

---

8   The 1875 Census gave 560 white and 261 'Malay' and 'Mixed and Other' as dressmakers and seamstresses. The corresponding figures for female domestic servants were 572 and 1,384, and for washerwomen/laundresses 94 and 935.

9   For a lengthier discussion see Bickford-Smith, 'Commerce', ch. 2.

10   Or 2,988 out of 3,304 listed in relevant occupations in the Census.

Coloureds') were 'allowed to find their level', is not exactly enlightening.[11] This statement obscures the fact that 'level' in Cape Town, and wider Cape, society was in part a legacy of the power relations that existed under slavery. This legacy is part of the explanation of continued white dominance, as previous chapters dealing with rural areas have already suggested.

In his important emphasis on the extent of economic, social and psychological space captured by Cape Town's underclass before emancipation, Bank has had little room for the limits and gradations of such gains—along lines of gender, occupation, class and colour.[12] Shirley Judges' work on the 1830s suggests that the majority of ex-slave Free Blacks had been poor before emancipation, with many families having earnings under the poverty datum line. Most of those slave-apprentices freed in 1838 were even poorer. Few 'Other than Whites' had access to much capital at this stage.[13]

Certainly there had been some blacks in Cape Town who were slave and property owners.[14] We need to know more about their history, before and after emancipation, to confidently explain why so few black merchants or substantial property owners emerged in the mid nineteenth century. One possibility, already suggested, is that many of those ex-slaves or their descendants who were fairly light-skinned and successful, 'passed' into the 'European' category in official statistics. In addition, Meltzer has helped to explain why capital in the city, like land in the countryside, remained largely in the hands of whites. The bulk of compensation money went to whites and was invested in property and joint-stock companies. British merchants used their London connections to put themselves at an advantage in these transactions, and a credit network evolved between London, and Cape merchants and farmers. Credit was extended by the Cape of Good Hope Savings Bank, established in 1831, only on fixed property, largely owned by whites.[15]

Meltzer can quote the editor of Cape Town's *Commercial Advertiser* in 1848 as saying that 'people of European descent' were in 'the widest sense the ruling class'. He correctly predicted (save for the existence of a few black voters) that under representative government, 'both the electors and the elected would be of their body'.[16] Despite examples of ex-slave accumulation[17] and a

---

11 J.S. Marais, *The Cape Coloured People* (Johannesburg, 1968), p. 281.

12 See Bank, ch. 3 in this volume, and also A. Bank, *The Decline of Urban Slavery at the Cape, 1806–34*, Centre for African Studies, University of Cape Town, Communications, no. 22 (1991).

13 S. Judges, 'Poverty, Living Conditions, and Social Relations-Aspects of Life in Cape Town in the 1830s' (MA thesis, University of Cape Town, 1977).

14 Bank, *Decline of Urban Slavery*, p. 193, where he talks of 130 Free Black slaveholders; Judges, pp. 159–60.

15 See Meltzer, ch. 7 in this volume, and Meltzer, 'The Growth of Cape Town Commerce and the Role of John Fairbairn's *Advertiser* (1835–59)' (MA thesis, University of Cape Town, 1989), esp. pp. 65–7, 107–20.

16 Meltzer, 'Cape Town Commerce', p. 133.

low, colour-blind franchise at local and central political levels, blacks still
could pose little threat to white political domination before the 1870s.[18]

Many occupations that could have provided means of accumulation for
black Capetonians, in retailing or transport, often required considerable capital outlay on licences—apart from any consideration of expenditure on
equipment, stock or premises.[19] Many of the major economic activities in
Cape Town which employed slave descendants—fishing, building, con-
veyancing of goods, and production of foodstuffs and clothing—could be
affected by the weather, the season, the number of ships in Table Bay and so
on. Earnings were intermittent and often insufficient. Other major employers, domestic service and laundering, were badly paid.[20]

Nigel Worden has shown how their years as apprentices did not mean
access to artisanal skills for ex-slaves.[21] At least from the 1860s, education at
the superior non-denominational government schools was *de facto* for the
light-skinned. Mission schools provided a limited education, often 'neglect-
ing secular subjects', for the children of the poor be they black or white.[22]
Most freed slaves were unable to afford to give their children more than a
basic education in reading and writing; many were unable to afford even
that. The result was that by 1875, 69 per cent of black Capetonians over the
age of 15 years could neither read nor write compared to 9 per cent of
whites. In the 5 to 15 year age group the respective figures for blacks and
whites were 88 per cent and 26 per cent.[23]

For many of slave descent, the early nineteenth-century erosion of

---

17   See, for instance, D. Grant, 'Bokkoms, Boycott and the Bo-Kaap: The Decline of the Rogge Bay Fishing
     Industry between 1890 and 1920' (MA thesis, University of Cape Town, 1991), pp. 21–3, for some
     examples within the fishing industry. Lady Duff Gordon, *Letters from the Cape* (Cape Town, 1925),
     p. 38, refers to two slaves who bought their freedom and in the early 1860s were running a fruit shop.
     They sent their son 'Abdul Rahman' to Cairo University. His son was Dr Abdullah Abdurahman, leader
     of the African Political Organization, the first significant coloured political organization in Cape Town:
     see later in this chapter and in L.G. Green, *Growing Lovely, Growing Old* (Cape Town, 1975), p. 185.

18   R. Davenport, *South Africa: A Modern History*, 4th edn. (London, 1991), pp. 88–98, provides a brief
     overview of the Cape franchise and politics before Union.

19   Judges, 'Poverty', p. 8, shows that a baker's licence in the 1830s cost £3 15s., while butchers had to rent
     part of the town slaughterhouse; on the other hand, a fruit seller's licence was comparatively cheap, at
     7s. 6d. D.P. Warren, 'Merchants, Commissioners and Wardmasters: Municipal Politics in Cape Town,
     1840–54'(MA thesis, University of Cape Town, 1986), p. 124, establishes that liquor licences required
     an annual fee of £20 in the mid nineteenth century; Van Heyningen, 'Public Health', pp. 65–6, confirms
     that the Colonial Medical Committee controlled licences for physicians, surgeons, chemists and druggists
     from the 1830s; *Cape Times*, 1 Jan. 1886 shows that cab licences were between £2 and £1. 10s. by that
     date.

20   E.B. Van Heyningen, 'Poverty, Self-Help and Community: The Survival of the Poor in Cape Town,
     1880–1910', *South African Historical Journal*, 24 (1991), pp. 128–43; Bickford-Smith, 'Commerce',
     chs. 2 and 5.

21   N. Worden, 'Slave Apprenticeship in Cape Town', *Studies in the History of Cape Town* (hereafter
     Studies), 7 (1994), pp. 32–44.

22   Marais, *The Cape Coloured People*, pp. 269–70.

23   *CPP* G42–1876, 'Education', pp. 75–6.

slavery, or emancipation itself, may have made little material difference before the twentieth century. The majority were still subject to poverty and high mortality rates up to 1910. As Elizabeth van Heyningen's work has shown, 'a very large number of families depended on good health, temperance, good management and good fortune to keep their financial heads above water', and few were continuously successful in this regard.[24]

In addition, workers in Cape Town, as in the countryside, continued to be subject to suitably named Masters and Servants Acts in this period. These Acts helped circumscribe personal freedom acquired by emancipation. Although they gave some rights to the 'servant', such as the possibility of taking an employer to court for non-payment of wages, they were heavily weighted in favour of the employer. A wide range of behaviour on the part of the worker, such as 'careless work', or 'absence', was defined as a misdemeanour. These definitions had originally been adapted from the Slave Codes. They were sufficiently vague to allow magistrates to punish, with fines or imprisonment, virtually any behaviour on the part of a 'servant' that threatened an employer's authority.[25]

Freed slave women were, on the whole, worse-off than their male counterparts in the late nineteenth century. Gender discrimination in Cape Town's labour market had worked in favour of men before emancipation and continued to do so thereafter.[26] Perhaps the women who suffered most were those in domestic service. Correspondence to the newspapers, court records and select committee reports in the 1880s and 1890s, describe their meagre wages and 'absence of personal freedom'.[27] They lived not unlike slaves, virtual prisoners on the premises of their employers, often suffering from insufficient food and poor amenities, including no proper sleeping places or washing facilities. One correspondent argued that bad conditions provided by employers were the result of 'old habits', presumably formed during slavery: 'the mistresses begin to expect decent girls of pure white blood to put up with the slatternly modes that suited the blacks and browns they have only known'.[28] Not surprisingly perhaps, there is at least some evidence that a

---

24 Van Heyningen, 'Poverty', p. 131.

25 C. Bundy,'The Abolition of the Masters and Servants Act', *South African Labour Bulletin*, 2, 1 (1975), pp. 37–46. Warren, 'Merchants', p. 41. *CPP* A15–1856, 'Rights and Duties of Masters, Servants and Apprentices Act'; *CPP* A18–1873, 'Masters and Servants Act'.

26 P. Van Der Spuy, 'Slave Women and the Family in Nineteenth-Century Cape Town', *South African Historical Journal*, 27 (1992), pp. 50–74.

27 *Cape Times*, 19 Jan. 1880, leading article.

28 *Cape Times*, 1 Mar. 1880, letter from 'A Colonist' which also talks of the dullness of the work routine. Correspondence about domestic service is frequent in Cape Town newspapers in the late nineteenth century. The majority of letters are from dissatisfied employers, but many reveal the bad pay, lack of freedom and other poor conditions in which domestic servants were expected to work and live. Apart from the one already cited, see for example *Cape Times*, 12 Oct. 1896, 'One Who Speaks From Experience'; *Cape Argus*, 4 Mar. 1893, letter from 'A Slavey'; *Cape Times*, 12 Sept. 1896, letter from 'A Mistress'.

contemporary colloquial term for domestic servants was 'slavey',[29] and some women opted for prostitution as an alternative means of employment to the rigours and low pay of domestic service.[30]

The Mineral Revolution did bring investment in infrastructure, mechanization of production, and expansion of retail. While these developments may have threatened the existence of some occupations, they also brought new or enhanced entrepreneurial and employment opportunities for black and white Capetonians. Most notably, a growing number of small factories provided occupational opportunities for women outside the domestic sphere.[31] While no study has yet examined how this affected standards of living in Cape Town, it is possible that many black workers did enjoy increased real earnings. A few black Capetonians 'who had nothing but a mission school education are now very well off', an Anglican minister reported to a commission in 1903,[32] and the size of the black bourgeoisie undoubtedly increased.[33]

But it is also true that the approximate correlation between better pay, lighter colour and male gender continued to characterize Cape Town's labour market. This was partly because of state-aided immigration schemes that favoured the importation of white male artisans,[34] as well as the developing segregation in Cape education.[35] It was also furthered by the fact that the majority of southern African migrants to the city were black, and often perforce took the worst jobs such as working with coal at the docks.[36] But individual employers often, if by no means always, appear to have found some benefit in imposing rigid colour and gender divisions at their place of work.[37] Equally some, if not all, white male artisans succeeded in practising

CPP G39–1893, 'Labour Commission', gives considerable information on the wages and other circumstances of domestic servants, see esp. evidence of Father Osborne; for court cases that reveal something about the limitations imposed on domestic servants' freedom of movement, see e.g. Cape Times, 8 Dec. 1876, Lantern, 5 July 1884, Cape Argus, 7 Nov. 1895, 9 July 1897, 29 Sept. 1897.

29 Cape Argus, 23 June 1892, Police Court Column, has heading, 'Courting the Slavey'; Cape Argus, 4 Mar. 1893, the letter from 'A Slavey'.

30 G39–1893, evidence of Dr J. Waterstone, p. 69; E.B. Van Heyningen, 'Prostitution and the Contagious Diseases Acts: The Social Evil in the Cape Colony, 1868–1902', Studies, 5 (1984), p. 96.

31 Bickford-Smith, 'Commerce', pp. 99–102, 210, 264–72. K. Ward, 'Catering for Taste in Late Victorian Cape Town' (paper, Cape Town History Project Workshop, University of Cape Town, 1991).

32 South African Native Affairs Commission, vol. 2 (Pretoria, 1905), p. 188.

33 Lewis, Between the Wire and the Wall, p. 12.

34 Bickford-Smith, 'Commerce', pp. 102–4, 272–7.

35 Ibid., pp. 310–14.

36 Ibid., p. 397.

37 CPP A6–1906, 'Select Committee on the Factory Act' gives information about some employers who segregated their workers in different parts of factories or in terms of access to different toilet facilities: p. 53, J.J. Hill and Co, confectioners; p. 80, United Tobacco Company; pp. 142–3, Garlick's Clothing Factory.

colour and gender exclusivity in stonemasons', carpenters' and plasterers' unions in the 1900s.[38]

Despite increased black prosperity, and larger numbers of poorer whites, the dominance of whites in Cape Town society remained. This occurred not just because whites continued to dominate the economy, but also because economic and social domination was kept in place by the imposition of *de facto* and *de jure* segregation. Cape Town's white bourgeoisie extended segregation aimed at retaining exclusive access to facilities such as theatres and hotels. Understandably, Jackson had seen the exclusion of blacks from the new roller skating rink in 1879 as a 'relic of slavery'.[39] Such exclusions occurred, as Fredrickson implicitly suggested, when the number of 'facilities' in Cape Town wherein exclusion was deemed necessary also increased—beyond the schools and churches where it had existed in various forms before the 1870s.[40]

A *Cape Times* leader of December 1889, using the occasion of the fifty-fifth anniversary of emancipation to discuss the position of blacks at the Cape, stated:

> As a matter of experience black passengers are not commonly met with in the saloons of steamships, or in first-class railway carriages, or in the reserved seats of the theatres, or in the best pews in churches or chapels, or in bathing machines and bathing houses, or at hotel tables, or even in the rooms of the Young Men's Christian Association.

It went on to say that there was no need to mention particular instances when the above had been 'brought home severely to the black man of European education travelling in this country'.[41] Social intermingling of black and white would appear to have been a lower class phenomenon.

The maintenance of white supremacy in Cape Town, and in the Cape as a whole, had also been facilitated by the granting of Responsible Government to the Cape in 1872. Local whites had been handed the political means to continue to dominate economically and socially, despite the maintenance of an overtly non-racial franchise. Successive Cape governments and their administrations, with mineral enriched revenues from the 1870s, had the will and the means to bring about, or maintain, segregation in institutions under their control in the next three decades. Segregation was enforced in prisons and hospitals. Apprenticeship at the Salt River railway works was reserved for whites. Educational segregation from the late 1880s was overtly aimed at benefiting poor white children, who were to be rescued from 'black' mission

---

38   J.V. Bickford-Smith, 'Protest, Organisation and Ethnicity among Cape Town Workers, 1891–1902', *Studies*, 7 (1994), pp. 84–108.

39   *Lantern*, 23 Aug. 1879.

40   G.M. Fredrickson, *White Supremacy* (Oxford, 1981), pp. 257–68.

41   *Cape Times*, 7 Dec. 1889.

schools. Eventually *de jure* segregation of all schools (including technical training colleges and the mission schools) was achieved in 1905. Whites were now, by legal proscription, given compulsory, free and superior education to blacks.

When white legislators believed that blacks were going to mount a political challenge to white supremacy in the 1880s and 1890s—because their electoral numbers were increasing or they had put up a candidate who stood some chance of election to the House of Assembly—the central state changed the franchise or electoral rules in favour of whites, even if they balked at legislating black political exclusion by name.[42] The Cape Town municipality, faced with ex-slaves who were 'a bigger problem than pure bred Natives',[43] attempted much the same—although one slave descendant, Dr Abdullah Abdurahman, did become a town councillor before 1910.[44] The Act of Union in 1910 put political, and thereby economic and social, domination of South Africa unequivocally in the hands of whites. The franchise was denied to blacks in the other provinces of the Union and no blacks could stand for Parliament.[45] The chains of white political supremacy would not be broken before the 1990s.

SOCIAL IDENTITY

Thus far our exploration into the meaning of freedom for Capetonian slave descendants has taken little account of their own views. Unfortunately black voices that describe their lives and opinions are heard only sporadically in the archival records. When present they are often in white-controlled media, or translated and transcribed by whites. Nevertheless, one window into the experience of slave descendants is provided by occasions when black Capetonians commemorated or celebrated freedom, even if they were described by whites. These occasions reveal something of both the enduring and changing meanings of freedom for those who shared a slave heritage. They also provide clues to the complex and changing nature of black social identities in Cape Town at this time.

Perhaps the most visible celebrations took the form of processions and music. One occasion for festivity was the annual anniversary of Emancipation Day. Some of the proceedings of 1 December 1885 were

---

42   J.V. Bickford-Smith, 'A "Special Tradition of Multi-Racialism"? Segregation in Cape Town in the Late Nineteenth and Early Twentieth Centuries', in W. James and M. Simons (eds.), *The Angry Divide* (Cape Town, 1989), pp. 47–62.

43   *Cape Times*, 7 Dec. 1889.

44   Lewis, *Between the Wire and the Wall*, p. 27. J.V. Bickford-Smith, '"Keeping Your Own Council": The Struggle Between Houseowners and Merchants for Control of the Cape Town Municipal Council in the Last Two Decades of the Nineteenth Century', *Studies*, 5 (1984), pp. 188–207.

45   Davenport, *Modern History*, pp. 222–5.

commented on by a reporter of the *Cape Times*:

> Yesterday was the anniversary of the emancipation of slaves in this colony in 1834. Some of their descendants expressed their appreciation of the blessings of freedom by all that was exasperating in the way of processions, accompanied with hideous noises.[46]

Emancipation Day had first been celebrated by music and procession on the day of abolition, 1 December 1834:

> Large bodies of the 'apprentices', of all ages and both sexes, promenaded the streets during the day and night, many of them attended by a band of amateur musicians.[47]

It would appear as though 'coloured bands' paraded the streets of Cape Town even before emancipation, in festivities that celebrated New Year, a slave holiday at the Cape. New Year celebrations in the form of street processions and music may have occurred by 1823.[48] By the 1870s, many street paraders were organized into singing and sporting clubs distinguished by different costumes, such as firemen's uniforms.[49] The *Cape Times* reported on 4 January 1886, that there were large and 'frivolous groups of coloured people...dressed most fantastically, carrying guys, and headed by blowers of wind and players of stringed instruments'. Songs performed included variations of 'Rule Britannia' and the 'Old Hundredth'. Costumes were made, on the strength of twentieth century evidence, by families engaged in tailoring and paid for on a 'set-aside' system during the year.[50] There were three kinds of paraders: 'Malay choirs' or *'nagtroepe'* (night bands); 'Christmas choirs' (who demanded alms for their churches) and 'Coon' troupes.[51]

At some stage between emancipation and the Mineral Revolution whites had begun referring to Muslims, whatever their actual ancestral origins, as 'Malays'. In fact, Malay had become virtually a synonym for Muslim, in the mouths of whites, by the 1850s.[52] In the 1870s, if not before, the term Malay was adopted by numbers of people so categorized to describe themselves, at least in their dealings with whites.[53] By 1875, according to the census, there

46   *Cape Times*, 2 Dec. 1885.

47   Meltzer, 'Cape Town Commerce', p. 48.

48   G. Stone, 'The Coon Carnival' (paper, Abe Bailey Institute of Interracial Studies, Cape Town, 197–), p. 2. Also mentioned, without reference, in D. Coplan, *In Township Tonight* (Johannesburg, 1985), p. 11.

49   Stone, 'Coon Carnival', pp. 2–3.

50   S. Jeppie, 'Aspects of Popular Culture and Their Expression in Inner Cape Town, c.1939–59' (MA thesis, University of Cape Town, 1991), ch. 3.

51   Stone, 'Coon Carnival', p. 2.

52   R. Shell, 'Rites and Rebellion: Islamic Conversion at the Cape, 1808 to 1915', *Studies*, 5 (1984), pp. 46–78. Duff Gordon, *Letters from the Cape*, p. 33. J.S. Mayson, *The Malays of Cape Town* (Manchester, 1955). G42–1876.

53   *CPP* A2–1875, 'Select Committee Report on Cemeteries Bill', p. 183: Abdol Burns, a cab owner and a fairly prominent figure in Cape Town political circles, replied 'yes' when asked by a white member of

were 7,656 Malays in Cape Town.

It is probable that the vast majority of Malays/Muslims were ex-slaves and their descendents. Most of the people brought to Cape Town from the Malay archipelago had been slaves. Islam would appear to have united the vast majority of Free Blacks, and thus freed slaves, in the early 1820s. In Bank's estimation, there were 1,896 Free Blacks in Cape Town in 1822.[54] Shell suggests that about 1,600 of them were Muslims.[55] Of a total slave population in the town of 7,160 at this date, close to 1,300 were also converts to Islam.[56] Some of these conversions, by slaves not owned by Muslims, were presumably possible because of the extent of economic, social and psychological space that they had gained in the early nineteenth century (and quite possibly earlier). It would seem likely that there was a consequent gender dimension to conversion to Islam, tied to greater occupational opportunity amongst male slaves. Two-thirds of Muslim slaves were male at a time when male slaves formed only about 55 per cent of the slave population. Conversion to Islam, which took place at an impressive rate between the 1820s and 1870s, can at least in part be seen as an affirmation of freedom desired or obtained, even if gender partly determined its extent. With its rituals, institutions (such as mosques and madrassas) and practices that differed from white-dominated Christianity, Islam aided the process of giving slaves or their descendants psychological 'self-ownership'.[57] Membership of the Muslim community provided material support for the poor and social status for the wealthier, which was denied to them in the wider society. Islam, distinctive dress, culinary and medical practices, as well as choral bands—such as The Star of Independence Malay Club which participated in the New Year celebrations of 1887—became part of an available Malay identity for many of Cape Town's freed slaves.[58]

---

this Committee whether he belonged to the 'Malay Community'. *Cape Times,* 14 Sept. 1878, 'a Moslem' wrote a letter hoping Samuel 'a Malay man', was innocent of forgery. In the 1880s many letters were written to the English-language papers by people who described themselves, and fellow Muslims, as Malay. It seems likely that all of these factors were important in the emergence of a 'Malay' ethnicity as an available identity chiefly for Cape Town's Muslim population, at least in the 1870s and 1880s.

54   Bank, *Decline of Urban Slavery,* p. 236.

55   Shell, 'Rites', p. 7.

56   See A. Bank, ch. 3 in this volume; Shell,' Rites', p. 7.

57   E. Foner, *Nothing But Freedom: Emancipation and its Legacy* (Baton Rouge, 1983), p. 6, for a further discussion of self-ownership. Shell and Bank provide the information on Islam and slavery in early nineteenth-century Cape Town. A Davids, '"The Revolt of the Malays": A Study of the Reactions of the Cape Muslims to the Smallpox Epidemics of Nineteenth Century Cape Town', *Studies,* 5 (1984), p. 60, argues that belief in Islam had provided slaves with hope since 'they sincerely believed that to die as a Muslim was to die free'. He based this view on the evidence of Imam Muding who told a Commission in 1825 that he and other Imams taught this belief.

58   Van Heyningen, 'Poverty', pp. 134–4, 139; A. Davids, 'Politics and the Muslims of Cape Town: A Historical Survey', *Studies,* 4 (1984), p. 184; Davids, 'Revolt', pp. 66–7; Judges, 'Poverty', p. 161; I.D. du Plessis, *The Malay Quarter and its People,* (Cape Town, 1953); E. Rosenthal, *Fish Horns and*

The existence of Christmas choirs among New Year paraders was testimony to the Christian evangelism that began among Cape Town's underclass at the time of emancipation, and to which we shall turn shortly. An important influence on the appearance of the Coon troupes was that of American minstrel groups, who first visited the city in 1848.[59] By 1906, if not before, the term 'coon' was attached to the name of two New Year troupes, and by later in the century the New Year festivities were popularly known as the Coon Carnival.[60] Particularly important in these developments had been the visit in 1887 of Orpheus M. McAdoo's Jubilee Singers, several of whom stayed in Cape Town with the Dantu family. The five Dantu brothers had founded one of the singing and sporting clubs, the Cape of Good Hope Sports Club. On 1 January 1888, members of this club appeared in American minstrel costumes and with blackened faces.[61] This adoption of black Americans' ideas on costume and appearance may not have been purely an aesthetic whim. It suggests, perhaps, that descendants of South African slaves had compared notes on their social positions and experiences with their American brothers; that they had seen some point beyond aesthetics in following sartorial suit.[62]

The New Year and Emancipation Day parades contained a number of similarities. Both commemorated and celebrated occasions of freedom, be it a one day holiday or emancipation itself, as carnivals have done in other places, including elsewhere in Africa.[63] They were occasions of fun and excess, where the immediate experience of participants was probably not self-reflection but sheer enjoyment before the toiling and lean months ahead; similar to the carnival of Shrove Tuesday before the deprivations of Lent. But the forms that they took were forged in the era of bondage and were further shaped by post-emancipation experience.

As Bank has shown, the growth of a vibrant inner-city 'underclass'

Hansom Cabs: Life in Victorian Cape Town (Cape Town, 1977), pp. 100–1.

59 Stone, 'Coon Carnival', p. 3.

60 *Cape Times*, 9 Nov. 1906: 'The Jolly Coons Masquerade Troupe', and the 'Jolly Coons'; Jeppie, 'Popular Culture', ch. 3.

61 Stone, 'Coon Carnival', p. 3.

62 See V. Erlman, '"A Feeling of Prejudice", Orpheus M. McAdoo and the Virginia Jubilee Singers in South Africa', *Journal of Southern African Studies*, 14, 3 (1988), pp. 331–50, who suggests a link between the minstrels and the African Methodist Episcopalian Church, established in South Africa in the 1890s, and for further details of the visit. Erlman says that there is no evidence that black professionals or members of the petty bourgeoisie saw the political message of the American minstrel songs, but the adoption of the Coon style perhaps argues that Carnival participants did make a connection between their position in Cape society and that of Afro-Americans in their's. It is not clear from available evidence which, if any, American minstrel songs were sung by Cape Town troupes, although 'A troupe of minstrels' were reported as singing 'Marsa's in de cold, cold ground' and 'De old banjo' in the Good Hope Theatre in 1909: *Cape Times*, 2 Oct. 1909. For a somewhat different American influence on the nature of the troupes, the *Cape Times*, 9 Nov. 1906 reported that one was called the Woodstock Mohawk Minstrels.

63 D. Birmingham, 'Carnival at Luanda', *Journal of African History*, 29 (1988), pp. 93–103.

64 Foner, p. 6.

culture, participated in by slaves, reflected the accelerating erosion of slavery in early nineteenth-century Cape Town. The rich records of personal testimonies available to historians of emancipation in the United States have suggested that the freedoms most immediately desired by slaves were 'self-ownership';[64] 'unrestricted movement';[65] 'reaping the fruits of our own labour' and the possibility of developing a 'richer social life'.[66] Street parades were celebrations of such freedoms gained, albeit to a far greater extent by men than women. From the era of bondage to the present, with some interruptions because of state interference, New Year parades have involved the noisy occupation of public space by an underclass, most of whom have shared a slave heritage. As Pinnock has written of the Coon Carnival, as celebrated after the Second World War, it:

> entailed the annual symbolic storming of the city by the poor, an act which clearly unnerved both the city authorities and the police. Thousands of noisy street brothers were demanding freedom of the streets, lampooning 'respectable' citizens and actually being seen.[67]

Both New Year and Emancipation Day celebrations were occasions 'in which people rejoiced…[celebrations of]…an identity with neighbours and kinfolk…of defiance before the uncomprehending bourgeoisie'.[68] They were practised by people with a shared history of bondage and, at least in the case of the emancipation parades, would obviously have reminded those involved of that heritage. The emergence of street parades and their musical bands was a consequence of the growth of kinship and occupational ties, incorporating slaves, that had bound members of the pre-emancipation underclass, as defined by Bank.[69] Establishing those ties was itself part of a passage to freedom.

Although it is not often clear what songs were sung at particular festivities during the nineteenth century, it is likely that *ghoemaliedjies* (literally drum songs) predominated. These songs were also known as *straatlied* or 'Malay picnic songs', and would appear to have originated as slave songs in Cape Town. They were sung to the accompaniment of the skin-covered drum (*ghoema*) and a guitar.[70] *Ghoemaliedjies* were, as Winberg has said, 'part of an oral tradition…bound to change over the years',[71] but one in which there

---

65   A.H. Taylor, *Travail and Triumph—Black Life and Culture in the South since the Civil War* (Westport, 1976), p. 4.

66   I. Berlin, *Slaves Without Masters* (New York, 1974), p. xiii.

67   D. Pinnock, 'Stone's Boys and the Making of a Cape Flat's Mafia', in B. Bozzoli (ed.), *Class, Community and Conflict* (Johannesburg, 1987), pp. 421–2.

68   Birmingham, 'Carnival at Luanda', p. 102.

69   See Bank, ch. 3 in this volume.

70   C. Winberg, 'The "Ghoemaliedjies" of the Cape Muslims: Remnants of a Slave Culture' (paper, University of Cape Town, 1992). I would like to thank Chris Winberg for permission to use this material and her translations of the *ghoemaliedjies*.

is the possibility of suggesting some kind of chronology through linguistic analysis and contemporary allusions. They were often (sometimes sexually crude) parodies or burlesques of Dutch folksongs, and satirized figures respected by owners or employers. Some *ghoemaliedjies* contained veiled threats towards the latter. Others offered comment on events, sometimes in satirical form. An example is this one. It is obviously from the late nineteenth century, and just might have been that variation of 'Rule Britannia' mentioned by the reporter of the *Cape Times*:

> King Pluto said to England:
> 'Look beyond the blue seas;
> I'll place the Transvaal in your hand.'
> And the gold fields sing along:
>
> [refrain]
>
> Come Britannia, the civilizing one,
> Make the nations into slaves
>
> People not as crazy as you,
> Must slowly learn your laws...
>
> Your tyranny will soon humble
> Those that call this land their own...
>
> O foggy Island, what a lot of
> Crazy rogues you have by the hand.[72]

New Year festivities were a celebration of inner-city community for their participants. The spatial dimensions of 'underclass' or, post-emancipation, working-class communities were not extensive. In the first half of the nineteenth century, the outer boundary ran approximately from the shore below Signal Hill, along its side, then below the Public Gardens and to the west of the Castle, back down to the sea. In the second half of the century, the area expanded towards the east into the developing suburbs of Woodstock and Salt River, and included 'Kanal Dorp'/District Six, between the Castle and Woodstock.[73] At least some of the lyrics of *ghoemaliedjies* overtly expressed, and furthered, communal consciousness:

> Listen to what the people are saying,
> The people of Canal Town.[74]

By 1910, families were camping out for New Year in the main thoroughfares

71   *Ibid.*, p. 3.

72   *Ibid.*, pp. 25–6.

73   Bickford-Smith, 'Commerce', pp. 43–4, 277–9.

74   'Kanal Dorp' was another name for District Six in the late nineteenth-century. See Winberg, 'The "Ghoemaliedjies" of the Cape Muslims', p. 17.

of District Six.[75] But paraders, rather than onlookers or supporters, remained almost exclusively male. Consequently the processions remained, predominantly, celebrations of male identity.[76]

The celebration of emancipation became an established practice amongst descendants of slaves, or ex-slaves, in Cape Town, into the early twentieth century. On what was obviously an informal celebration in 1886 a dock 'coolie', Omaar Hendricks, drank with fishermen at the Queen's Hotel because, 'we were keeping up the first of December'.[77] The venue and the company suggest that this was a further example of space gained and valued predominantly by male slaves before emancipation, and predominantly by their male descendants 50 years after abolition.

In contrast to these male-dominated celebrations, George Manuel has written that 'each year on December 1...the washer-women of Platteklip [a stream that ran down from Table Mountain and a traditional washing-place from the slave era] made merry with song and dance under the trees'.[78] The washing that took women to Platteklip Gorge was that rare form of women's work that afforded them not only relative freedom from immediate employer surveillance, but also from male supervision. This had been true even in the era of slavery. This female space had enabled a different kind of emancipation celebration to evolve. It is unfortunate that we do not know more about the exact 'song and dance' that took place over the years. But in their celebration the washerwomen were undoubtedly furthering a sense of occupational group identity, informed by a sense of a shared slave heritage, as the fishermen may have been doing when drinking in the Queen's Hotel.

Certainly there was something of a community of people, numbering close to 1,000, who lived from the proceeds of the fishing industry in the crowded lanes near Rogge Bay, Cape Town's beach.[79] Members of this community fought for the preservation of their way of life, and thereby for the preservation of their community, when threatened by municipal and central government interference from the 1870s. In a petition to the Council in 1878, their leaders wrote:

> We were always under the impression that we were emancipated in the reign of our most Gracious Majesty Queen Victoria, and freed from tyranny, but it seems that we are mistaken, as our rulers (perhaps without intention) are depressing us [sic]; surely it is without the proper knowledge of the extent of our misfortunes.[80]

---

75 Stone, 'Coon Carnival', pp. 3–4.

76 Jeppie, 'Popular Culture', ch. 3 explores the gender dimension of the Carnival as it existed in his period.

77 Cape Archives (CA), 1/CT 6/192, 'Cape Town Resident Magistrate's Records', case of Asardien Lewin, 3 Dec. 1886.

78 *Cape Times*, 6 Nov. 1971, 'District Six wash-house closes its door for the last time'.

79 Bickford-Smith, 'Commerce', p. 63; Grant, 'Bokkoms', p. 12.

80 *CPP* A4–1878, 'Select Committee on the Rogge Bay Nuisance', appendix G, p. ix.

Washing and fishing or fish-curing, as we have seen, were numerically among the most significant employers of slave descendants in this period. Together with tailoring/dressmaking, they were the major occupations that underpinned communal networks, culture and identity among slave descendants in Cape Town. These networks were doubtless complex and interwoven. They imbued, and were imbued by, the institutions and ideologies of popular religion, be they in Islamic or Christian form.

In 1838 an ecumenical Christian mission had been established in Cape Town, under the jurisdiction of St. Andrew's Presbyterian Church, with the intention of ministering to the freed slaves. After an internal dispute, one of the ministers set up the separate Dutch Reformed Church Mission congregation of St. Stephen's, Riebeek Square: 'the members with only very few exceptions are from the "Coloured classes", the former slave population, a few Moslems and some negro slaves captured by men-of-war and liberated here.'[81]

By the 1890s, emancipation celebrations occurred in the form of Christian services. Perhaps some ex-slaves and their descendants took part in both these services and the street parades. It would seem that the services took place on 2 December rather than 1 December. In 1896, for instance, the Anglican Canon Lightfoot presided over a commemorative service attended by 1,000 people 'nearly all coloured'.[82] From 1859 Lightfoot had been involved in establishing day schools, adult night schools and benefit societies associated with St. Paul's Mission in the western part of inner Cape Town, on the slopes of Signal Hill. In 1878 the foundation stone was laid of St. Paul's Church, which would appear to have had a largely, or wholly, 'coloured' congregation. The latter had contributed £1,000 towards the building of the church. Members of the benefit societies, such as the Cape Town English Church Friendly Society and St. Paul's Benefit Society, went in procession to the ceremony.[83]

There would seem to be little doubt that the majority of those attending the service on 2 December 1896 were united by a shared heritage of slavery, kinship and occupational ties. They, like Muslims in Cape Town, also benefited from the supportive networks, institutions and rituals conferred by congregational membership. Christmas choirs, parading the streets of Cape Town, were helping to keep these networks alive.

Similar considerations help to explain the growth of Christian mission

---

81   G.C. Cuthbertson, 'The Impact of the Emancipation of Slaves on St Andrew's Scottish Church, Cape Town, 1838–78', *Studies*, 3 (1984), pp. 49–63. On p. 56, Cuthbertson quotes the Revd J.A. Stegmann, who was in charge of St. Stephen's at the time.

82   *Cowley Evangelist*, Jan. 1897.

83   H.P. Barnett-Clarke, *The Life and Times of Thomas Fothergill Lightfoot, BD, Archdeacon of Cape Town* (Cape Town, 1908), esp. pp. 110–85.

institutions as the area of the inner city grew eastwards into District Six in the second half of the nineteenth century. Thanks to the *Cowley Evangelist* we have lengthy descriptions by Anglican missionaries of how their institutions were established. St. Philip's Mission was started in 1884 on the slopes of Devil's Peak, to reach the newly-developed parts of the city. [84] The majority of the inhabitants of this area were 'Dutch speaking brown people...from the country', and the population of the District grew from about 1,500 in 1884, to about 6,000 in 1896.[85] The Christian institutions offered them a means by which they could create new social connections and identities in the city.

For almost 20 years, before a church was built, services in both English and 'Dutch patois' (Afrikaans) were held in houses belonging to 'coloured' people, like Mrs Holmes or the ex-slave Lydia.[86] It would seem as though many people came to the area with their own forms of Christianity, and this, together with the active assistance of some, helped the Mission to grow. Lydia rang a handbell to call congregants to service at her cottage. After 1900, when St. Philip's Church was built, Lydia's cottage was allowed to fall into disrepair and Lydia was forced to move.[87]

Lydia had been reported in 1893 as 'keeping with festival the anniversary of the proclamation that abolished slavery, and bears still on her back the marks of the slave whippings she got in her youth under Dutch regime'.[88] She allowed her cottage, in the Dry Docks area of District Six, to become the venue for the first Cowley Evangelist services in 1884,[89] and was baptized a Christian some time after abolition. On 2 December 1901:

> The one-roomed church and cottage was decorated with hanging boughs and flowers, and pigs and swans and birds and sweets hung on nails, which children's eyes gazed lovingly at. We passed through troops of children just at tea, provided by the common contributions of the invited guests—self-invited a good part of them, I expect—and entering the cottage...found Lydia seated within, with a court of ladies all with white handkerchiefs on their heads, seated around; ...Lydia told us her story [one of considerable suffering as a slave]...she is getting old, and at this feast she would like some hymns sung, for it might be the last. So we sang three Dutch hymns, Mr Watkins interpreted into Dutch a little address and a few prayers, and then Lydia asked if she might say a prayer for those who were absent. We all stood, for there was no room to kneel. Lydia then knelt down and poured out her heart in a prayer. Then as she knelt, I gave her the

84 *Cowley Evangelist*, 1893, p. 105; 1904, p. 83.

85 *Cowley Evangelist*, 1896, pp. 185–9. The quotation is from *Cowley Evangelist*, 1893, p. 105.

86 *Cowley Evangelist*, June, 1885 and 1893, p. 105.

87 *Cowley Evangelist*, 1901, pp. 126–8; 1910, pp. 180–1.

88 *Cowley Evangelist*, Sept. 1893.

89 *Cowley Evangelist*, 1901, pp. 125–6.

parish priest's blessing and we departed.[90]

This festival, like street processions, was also an occasion of 'identity with neighbours and kinfolk', if on a far smaller scale and hardly 'defiant'. Indeed it can be argued that the missionaries were the most important conveyors to black Capetonians of Victorian notions of respectability (which necessitated cleanliness and thrift) and deference. When Lightfoot was asked what coloured children gained by schooling, he replied 'manners...habits of diligence...and order, and also respect and reverence'.[91] Another Anglican minister asked the headmistress of St. Philip's Mission school in 1901 whether any change had come over the children and people in the area in the last 15 years. She replied:

> It is most clear; fifteen years ago the people in this district were very rough and coarse in tone and manners; ...today I see a very happy change in the children in school, which implies a corresponding change in their homes; they are cleaner in dress and habits; they have improved in respect for, and affection towards, their teachers.[92]

Lydia died in 1910 and with her, it would seem, Lydia's Day. The *Cowley Evangelist* reported her death saying:

> Lydia kept this day with great fervour, for she herself had been a slave, and a married one; and besides other rigours, had known what it was to have her child taken from her. So on that day young and old, and every coloured neighbour or relation of every sort, were gathered in and around the cottage, and much store of cakes was contributed by sympathisers, or provided by the hostess, who was reimbursed by a collection; and one of the Fathers and Mr Watkins without fail attended to...conduct a short service. Now the politicians amongst the coloured people have taken up Emancipation Day, and the day of Lydia's fervent simplicity has passed.[93]

The writer was referring to the fact that, from 1903, politicians connected with John Tobin's Stone meetings in District Six had helped organize celebrations with an overtly political agenda. The Stone was 'a huge grey boulder' at the top of a circle of smaller stones on which people sat and listened to speeches by Tobin (a café owner whose mother had been a slave), and others, which emphasized coloured or black 'race pride' as well as being occasions for discussing political events of the day. Apparently a slave bell had once stood nearby. As a reporter commented: 'To-day the black men come and assert their rights as freemen on the altered scene of the slave

---

90   *Cowley Evangelist*, 1902, pp. 36–7. This reference states that Lydia 'always has observed...the Feast of the Release of the Slaves'.

91   *South African Native Affairs Commission*, vol 2, p. 191.

92   *Cowley Evangelist*, 1901, p. 125.

93   *Cowley Evangelist*, 1910, pp. 180–1.

days.'[94] On the morning of 1 December 1903, cameras recorded a commemorative gathering at the Stone and there was a service given at the African Methodist Episcopalians' Bethel Institute. In the afternoon a fête was held for children. In the evening 'an extremely large gathering' at the Bethel Institute heard an address by Tobin, himself a slave descendant, which included his comment that 'up to the present day the black man has always managed to get the Bible and the white man to get the land.'[95]

The Stone meetings were part of a process of political organization among the descendants of slaves in Cape Town that began in the 1880s. The first major initiatives in this process were taken by members of the Muslim/Malay community. This community had borne the brunt of state policies that threatened Islamic practice, and a barrage of white English-speaking racism, from the late 1870s. Stereotypes of Malays in the English language press became increasingly antagonistic, climaxing in vitriolic attacks during the 1882 smallpox epidemic for which they were made scapegoats. Malays were described as being dirty, independent, profligate, ignorant and unruly, and residential segregation was one proposed solution. In response, considerable numbers of letters were written to the newspapers by people describing themselves as, and defending, Malays.[96] For instance, Abdol Soubeyan wrote defending Malay 'independence' saying: 'independence is the aim of everyone who is a little above grovelling in the mud'.[97]

Malay ethnicity, it would seem, became temporarily salient in the 1880s for virtually all members of an embattled Muslim community. Most Malays, of every status, took part in protests against the Cape government's impending closure of Muslim cemeteries in Cape Town. These protests, as Elizabeth van Heyningen has shown, brought together 'inherent' and 'derived' ideology in defence of perceived rights. They culminated in 1886 in a series of incidents of defiance of state authority and skirmishes with the police that have become known as the Cemetery Riots, or the 'Revolt of the Malays'. These happened just two weeks after the New Year festivities. It is likely that the anti-authoritarianism and communal solidarity displayed in the period of 'Big Day' celebrations fed into the subsequent events during the 'illegal' burial of a Muslim child on 17 January.[98]

It was in the wake of this, ultimately unsuccessful, campaign to prevent the closure of Muslim cemeteries, that élite members of this community apparently determined, in 1889, to put up their own candidate, Achmat

94 *South African News*, 28 Nov. 1903.

95 *South African News*, 2 Dec. 1903. For more details of Tobin and the politics of his Stone meetings, see Lewis, *Between the Wire and the Wall*.

96 Bickford-Smith, 'Commerce', chs. 4 and 8.

97 *Lantern*, 23 Sept. 1882.

98 Van Heyningen, 'Public Health', ch. 4; Bickford-Smith, 'Commerce', pp. 356–63.

Effendi, for the next parliamentary election in Cape Town. This election was not held until 1894. In the meantime, the raising of the franchise qualifications and the Cape government's ongoing moves to bring about *de jure* segregation in education (as well as in other social and occupational spheres), ensured that Christian descendants of slaves began to seek common political cause with their Muslim counterparts. The British *volte-face* on equal rights for black and white after the Anglo-Boer War added urgency to these initiatives.[99]

The differing forms that subsequent initiatives took have been chronicled at length elsewhere.[100] Of significance for social identity, forms of political mobilization became part of a process that saw the emergence of coloured ethnicity. This identity had meaning for many slave descendants by the twentieth century.

If Malay was a term coined by whites in Cape Town as a synonym for Muslims, coloured or the coloured races was a term they often used for the wider category of 'Other than White' in the decades after 1838.[101] For much of the nineteenth century the vast majority of people so described were of slave descent and spoke Creole-Dutch that developed into Afrikaans. This language—if with variations of dialect—became a medium of communication between slaves, Free Blacks and ex-bonded migrants from the countryside, as well as many owners and employers, before and after emancipation in Cape Town. This medium changed during the course of the nineteenth century to reflect the ongoing interaction of different dialects and exposure to other languages in Cape Town.[102] *Ghoemaliedjies* reflected such change.

The participants in street processions and emancipation celebrations spoke a language which marked the heritage and communal bonds they shared. Islamic and Christian institutions that we have described, such as the benefit societies, helped to maintain those ties. But so too in its own way did extended segregation.

The appellation 'Coloured' was eventually adopted by the élite of those so described because of discrimination against them by whites, but also because, as 'Coloureds', they were wanting to distinguish themselves from Bantu-speaking Africans. Many new social and sporting organizations were created in the late nineteenth century, and their white exclusiveness gave rise

99   Bickford-Smith, 'Commerce', pp. 363–93.

100 Most notably in Lewis, *Between the Wire and the Wall.*

101 See, for instance, the Cape Blue Books of the 1840s to 1860s, or the 1865 Census cited above.

102 H. den Besten, 'From KhoeKhoe Foreigner Talk Via Hottentot Dutch to Afrikaans: The Creation of a Novel Grammar', in M. Putz and R. Derven (eds.), *Wheels Within Wheels: Papers of the Dutsburg Symposium on Pidgin and Creole Languages* (Frankfurt, 1989), pp. 207–49. I would like to thank Prof. Raj Mesthrie, of the Department of Linguistics, University of Cape Town, for bringing this paper to my attention. See also A. Davids, 'Words the Cape Slaves Made: A Socio-Linguistic Study', *South African Journal of Linguistics*, 8, 1 (1990), pp. 1–24.

to the growth of parallel institutions along the divide of 'White' and 'Other than White', such as the Order of Good Templars and Order of True Templars respectively. There was also a black Baptist church, the black Wesleyan Forward Movement and a Cape Town branch of the African Methodist Episcopalian Church of America.

Situated in Cape Town, these black organizations, like other Christian and Islamic institutions already described, consisted largely of Afrikaans-speaking descendants of slaves, even if the educated élite could also speak English. Members may have called themselves black, brown or coloured, on occasion. Colour was only one potential means of self-identification.

But by the early 1890s, overtly coloured political organizations began to emerge to fight white discrimination and were active among communities of slave descendants in Cape Town. During the next decade it became clear that whites were singling out Bantu-speaking Africans for specific discrimination, including residential segregation and prohibitory liquor laws. The number of Africans, categorized as 'Kafirs' or 'Natives' by whites, was increasing rapidly in Cape Town at the time. 'Coloured' became an acceptable self-description for many slave descendants in Cape Town to distinguish them-selves from 'Natives' for pragmatic reasons. But also because such distinc-tion made sense at the time in terms of existing kinship, occupational and communal ties, the culture these supported, and because new divisions of labour were tending to confirm a tri-partite division of Cape Town's social formation into 'white', 'coloured' and 'native' as migration of the latter into the city increased.

By the end of the decade, several parallel black organizations had been founded which called themselves 'Coloured'. These included the Coloured Young Men's Christian Association, Western Province Coloured Athletics Association and Cycling Union and Western Province Coloured Rugby Football Federation.[103] By 1902 the African Political Organization (APO) was formed in Cape Town. Despite its name, and the fact that one of its aims was to promote unity among all the 'coloured races', the APO was estab-lished to defend specifically the 'Coloured people's social, political and civil rights'.[104] From its actions, membership and newspaper, it is clear that the APO meant by 'Coloured people' descendants of the ex-bonded, many of whom were bound together by networks of community and culture, already described. The creation of the APO, like that of other overtly coloured or-ganizations, was premised on the existence of these networks.

The point is that both organizations and networks emerged in particular historical circumstances. Their convergence, and subsequent developments

103 Bickford-Smith, 'Commerce', pp. 366–93.
104 Lewis, *Between the Wire and the Wall*, p. 20.

in South Africa's political economy, paved the way for the emergence of coloured ethnicity among slave descendants. Coloured ethnicity came to have greater salience for slave descendants as an available social identity than, say, the putative black ethnicity suggested in the discourse of emancipation commemorations organized around the Stone meetings. This was a complicated process, and a far from inevitable or unchangeable one. But analysing it may help to explain why there was more to coloured identity than categorization by whites, or political opportunism by coloureds, under apartheid regimes.

EPILOGUE

Occasions of commemoration and celebration begin to reveal something of the way in which ex-slaves and their descendants experienced freedom. Part of this experience was the forging of kinship, occupational, and communal ties, of social identities with attendant cultural forms, which included these celebrations. Such ties and identities provided material, spiritual and psychological support for many against poverty and discrimination. But they were also shaped by that poverty and discrimination and articulated by dominant class culture, just as the latter was articulated by their aspirations.

On Tuesday, 22 June 1897, a large procession wound its way through the streets of central Cape Town, passing in front of Sir Alfred Milner, the Governor of the Cape Colony. The occasion was Queen Victoria's Jubilee. Leading the procession were mounted policemen, followed by contingents of Imperial troops. Towards the end were local regiments, members of the Jubilee Committee and the Town Council, with the Mayor a few paces behind. Bringing up the rear were more horses and men, in the form of a detachment of the Duke of Edinburgh's Own Volunteer Rifles.

In the middle of the procession were members of a wide range of civilian organizations, interspersed with an occasional float ('HMS Victory', 'Model rink on decorated car', to name but two). Present were members of the Society for the Prevention of Cruelty to Animals and those proponents of temperance, the Order of Good Templars and the Order of True Templars. Members of cycling clubs wheeled by, reflecting the emergence of a new form of leisure activity among a middle class swollen by the economic and demographic expansion resulting from the Mineral Revolution. Dominating the middle of the procession, albeit split by eight wagon-loads of workers from the railway works at Salt River, were members of a large variety of Friendly Societies, including those of the English Church, St. Paul's and St. Stephen's. At their rear was a group of 'Malay Hadjes [sic], with camels'. Almost at the very centre of the whole parade, placed either side of a 'Statue of Her Majesty', were two sets of 'Malay gim cracks'—one representing the year 1837 'Slavery', the other the year 1897 'Freedom'.[105]

The Jubilee procession was a pageant of British hegemony in all its eccentric glory. Onlookers and members of the procession would have been able to read the occasion as symbolic of the social order they inhabited. But they could do so, of course, in different ways. The 'Malay Hadjes with camels', or 'Malay gim cracks', may have represented one person's communal pride and another's vignette of orientalism.

What had become a linchpin of British hegemony at the Cape after slavery, and was clearly represented in the parade, was the association of 'freedom' with British rule. On 1 December 1834 the British flag had been unfurled from the Commercial Exchange in front of processions of the emancipated.[106] Queen Victoria came to the throne shortly before the freeing of the slave-apprentices in 1838. The symbolism of Malay gimcracks representing 1837 and 1897 in her Jubilee pageant, like the refrain of the song 'Rule Britannia', were reminders that Victoria/Britannia continued to guarantee freedom.

In return, ex-slaves and their descendants were expected to be grateful and patriotic to Britain. A plethora of imperial rituals, such as royal visits or frequent military parades, maintained encouragement in this direction, as did more direct appeals in the press, pulpit or schoolroom. Many ex-slaves and their descendants did take part in displays of patriotism from the 1830s onwards, be they in organized or more spontaneous forms. In 1838, a witness to the celebrations ending apprenticeship said that he saw processions of coloured people 'singing a Dutch song, in which every verse ended "Victoria! Victoria! Daar waai de Engelschen Vlaag"'.[107] During Victoria's Jubilee in 1887 'even the poorest of the Malays in the back streets illuminated their tenements'.[108] An Anglican missionary noted approvingly during the Boer War: 'All the poor coloured people know who Queen Victoria is, and something of what we owe to her.' This was demonstrated to his satisfaction when 'everyone' put on signs of mourning when the Queen died in 1901.[109] In the same year the ex-slave, Lydia, had on her walls not only religious portraits but also one of the new monarch, Edward VII.[110] A Union Jack was hoisted at the Stone meeting's commemoration of emancipation in 1903.[111]

---

105 CA, 3 CT 1/7/1/2, Mayor's Minutes, p. 17.

106 See Meltzer, ch. 7 in this volume.

107 J.G. Steytler, 'Remembrances from 1832–1900', *Quarterly Bulletin of the South African Library*, 25, 1 (1970), p. 25.

108 *Excalibur*, 24 June 1887.

109 *Cowley Evangelist*, 1901, pp. 58–9.

110 *Cowley Evangelist*, 1901, p. 126.

As Bill Nasson has warned us, such popular displays of loyalty to Britain or the crown 'should not be interpreted as the product of a simple, unmediated absorption of an imperial creed'. Rather 'own meanings' were imposed on patriotism by ex-slaves and their descendants.[112] Patriotism could have characterized the emergence of community and marked the attainment of that ubiquitous Victorian virtue, respectability. Its meaning, like the meaning of freedom, was contested.

The fishermen we quoted earlier had used part of the discourse of patriotism, used deference to the Queen, while struggling to maintain their own interests. The 'Rule Britannia' *ghoemaliedjie* clearly satirized British Imperialism. 'Malay gim cracks' were presumably Coon troupes arrayed in appropriate fashion for the Jubilee Parade. If so, their understanding of what 'Freedom' symbolized, what emancipation had meant, may have been somewhat different to that of white observers or participants.

---

111 *South African News*, 2 Dec. 1903.

112 B. Nasson, *Abraham Esau's War* (Cambridge, 1991), p. 62.

12

LINKS IN THE CHAIN
COMMUNITY, IDENTITY & MIGRATION IN MAMRE
1838 TO 1938

– KERRY WARD –

There was a hotnot, a Hottentot er captain. He used to stay at Louwskloof…a kraal was there… And when Mamre started, the missionary started here in Mamre, a lot of people stays in Louwskloof… And so those days, then you've got the Hottentots, and then, the Boesmans. Die Strandlopers was hier. In the Western Province, they were here, when, when…this whites came here. These people were here. So my people, my, our Hottentot people, they were here. They're from South Africa. And we are intermarriage… My father's mother, she was from Saint Helena. And my oupa was a hotnot… In those days, there was a mix children. And my oupa, was a hotnot, er a farmer and a hotnot. The Johannes they were mos white, and farmers. There was a whole intermarriage business. That's why we are coloured today![1]

This oral narrative of Mamre's origins, which links the present to the past, is part of a story often told by Adam Pick to his fellow Mamriers. Adam Pick, born in 1927, was told the story as a child by his grandfather, Petrus August Pick. Both Adam Pick and his grandfather before him were lay preachers in the Mamre community, so their story, which constitutes part of the collective oral tradition of Mamre, has been told to generations of Mamriers. Like all oral traditions, it has been constructed and altered to explain how the present has come about. In doing so, the story conceals parts of the community's history which does not concur with Mamriers' vision of themselves. While it highlights the evolution of the apartheid category of 'coloured', Mamriers' collective oral history in the 1990s is silent about the community's slave heritage.[2]

---

1 Interview with Adam Pick, 10 July 1991, pp. 49–50. All interviews and page numbers refer to the interview transcripts which are lodged in the Western Cape Oral History Project, University of Cape Town. See also, K Ward, 'The Road to Mamre: Migration, Memory and the Meaning of Community c.1900–92' (MA thesis, University of Cape Town, 1992).

2 My research in Mamre partly involved interviewing the oldest generation of Mamriers, those born before the Second World War, and recording their life histories. I also helped to organize a community history

This chapter forges a link between the archival record of Mamre's history from emancipation in the 1830s and Mamriers' oral history of their lives and community until the end of the 1930s.[3] It explores how Mamriers constructed identity and a notion of community during this period, and how the oral history of Mamre in the 1990s has been shaped by the generation of Mamriers who were born in the early twentieth century. These people are now the oldest generation in the community, and their memories and the stories they tell about their parents and grandparents constitute the collective memory of the community's history. Through their memories, the period between the two world wars is seen as the turning point when Mamre's orientation shifted permanently away from the countryside towards the city. After the Second World War, daily commuting between Mamre and Cape Town changed the structure of the community. There is a focus on the perspective of the people who came to identify themselves not only as Mamriers, but also as 'coloured' in the increasingly stratified society at the Cape.

Mamre, named Groenekloof until 1854, was established in 1808 as a Moravian mission station in the heart of the Swartland wheat-farming district.[4] The land was granted by the British at the Cape under the governorship of Lord Caledon, at a time when mission activity was being encouraged in an attempt to halt the spread of Islam amongst Cape slaves. Groenekloof was also intended as a mission station for free Khoi soldiers and their families. The Moravian missionaries had been active at the Wynberg military camp of the Cape Corp because many of the Khoi soldiers were from the rural Moravian mission of Genadendal. The government therefore considered the Moravian missionaries to be most suitable to establish a new settlement in close proximity to Cape Town.[5] The grant incorporated the land at Louwskloof which belonged to a Gouraiqua Khoi settlement under the leadership of Captain Hans Klapmuts. The early mission at Groenekloof was,

group which researched aspects of Mamre's history and presented these in an exhibition to the community. Themes around the collective memory and identity of the Mamre community emerged in these dialogues, upon which this chapter is based. My interview with Adam Pick was particularly significant as he has a reputation in Mamre as someone who 'knows about Mamre's history', and his perceptions of Mamre's history hold weight in the community. Not only did he tell me about his own life, but he shared with me the stories he tells about Mamre's history.

3   I am greatly indebted to Helen Ludlow for sharing her research on Groenekloof in the mid nineteenth century, which forms the basis for the early part of this chapter. See E. Ludlow, 'Missions and Emancipation in the South Western Cape: A Case Study of Groenekloof (Mamre), 1838–52' (MA thesis, University of Cape Town, 1992).

4   The Swartland was one of the main wheat-growing districts of the western Cape, and one of the wealthiest farming areas. It encompassed the magisterial districts of Malmesbury, Darling and Koeberg, although the area is sometimes referred to as extending to Namaqualand. J. Blaauw, *Malmesbury—Grepe uit die Geskiedenis van die Dorp en Distrik* (Malmesbury, 1960).

5   B. Kruger, *The Pear Tree Blossoms: The History of the Moravian Church in South Arica, 1731–1869* (Genadendal, 1966), pp. 96–8.

Plate 13   Mamre inhabitants in 1991. Photograph by Kerry Ward.

according to Kruger, a heterogeneous community admitting free Khoi of various backgrounds.[6] Most of the Klapmuts clan had been absorbed into the mission by the time of emancipation, when there was a further influx of several hundred people, many of whom were ex-slaves with their extended family networks.[7]

Mission stations like Groenekloof were one of the main sites where ex-slaves were able to negotiate meaningful freedom. But even the choice to migrate to Groenekloof or one of the other missions came with both opportunities and constraints, determined by the social world which emerged in the western Cape in the post-emancipation era. Freed people who flocked to Groenekloof in the few years following emancipation primarily sought to create and control their private worlds through the family.[8] Helen Ludlow's meticulous study of Groenekloof shows that people coming into the mission did so mainly in family groups. The period immediately following emancipation was a time in which family and community networks between ex-slave apprentices and free 'Hottentots' on the farms in the region were united within the sanctuary of the mission station.

There was a generally stable slave population in the western Cape which had facilitated the growth of these links over generations. In fact, it is impossible to make a firm distinction between the Khoi and slave communities of the Swartland in the nineteenth century because the ties between them were so strong. The Klapmuts clan at Louwskloof certainly had bonds with the local slave population, and many worked on the farms under similar conditions. By the early nineteenth century most of the slaves working on the Swartland farms had been born locally. Thus it is not surprising that a quarter of the 'newcomers' who came to Groenekloof after emancipation already had kinship ties with people living in the mission.[9] Moreover, the familial relationships between masters and slaves were also recognizable, even if they were rarely acknowledged.

Not all ex-slaves sought entry into the missions: many moved to Cape Town or rural villages, or attempted to squat on government land. There was one group of squatters on the farm Wittezand who survived by burning and selling charcoal.[10] It is not clear whether anyone from these squatter

6   B. Kruger, *The Pear Tree Blossoms*, p. 103.

7   B. Kruger, *The Pear Tree Blossoms*, pp. 100–5; J. de Boer and E.M. Temmers, *The Unitas Fratrum: Two Hundred and Fifty Years of Missionary and Pastoral Service in Southern Africa (Western Region)* (Genadendal, 1987), pp. 40–1.

8   See Scully, ch. 8 in this volume, and 'Liberating the Family? Gender, Labor, and Sexuality in the Rural Western Cape, South Africa, 1823–53' (Ph.D. thesis, University of Michigan, 1993).

9   E. Ludlow, 'Missions and Emancipation', ch. 2; R. Shell's work supports this evidence of stable slave and underclass networks in the western Cape, see his *Children of Bondage* (Middleton, 1994), esp. ch. 4.

10   E. Ludlow, 'Missions and Emancipation', p. 54.

11   B. Kruger, *The Pear Tree Blossoms*, p. 197.

communities moved to Groenekloof after emancipation, although links with the mission were established at the time. The missionaries at Groenekloof started an out-station at Wittezand in 1839.[11]

Thys Loock, born in 1918 on Wittezand, recalls that his father, Mathewis, and his grandfather, Samuel Loock, were born on the same farm.

> All the time they lived there, first, and then they were old they moved from there to Pella [a Mamre out-station]… They were the first people, I think, in South Africa that delivered [charcoal] now.[12]

It would appear that this family lived on the same farm for over a century. Later, we will hear about the Loock family's final departure from Wittezand in the 1930s as a result of the declining use of charcoal as a fuel source in the city and then later also in the country towns.[13]

Helen Ludlow calculates that the majority of newcomers to Groenekloof actually came from Cape Town.[14] It is likely that many freed people migrated to town after emancipation but were unsuccessful in gaining a livelihood in the city, so returned to the rural areas over the following few years. Ludlow traces the pattern of movement of freed people, contracting themselves as wage labourers over a series of farms, as they made their way towards the mission. Some stayed and established themselves at Groenekloof, others moved on to town or to rural employment elsewhere.

Many other freed people remained on the farms where they had been enslaved, working for their ex-owners, negotiating new relationships between themselves and their masters. As Liz Host has shown, Frederick Duckitt, the owner of the farm, Klaver Valley, neighbouring Groenekloof, apparently went to considerable effort to prime his apprentices with gifts prior to emancipation in 1838 in order to foster their loyalty. This paternalistic relationship between master and apprentices was a strategy on the part of Duckitt to ensure that his labourers would not desert him when they were free to do so. When the day of emancipation arrived, some of the ex-apprentices asserted their freedom by going to town for a month or so, but most returned to engage themselves as wage labourers on Duckitt's farm.[15] Clearly, they had been unsuccessful in establishing themselves in town, and returned to Duckitt's employ because he was a comparatively benevolent master, and because they wanted to come back to a familiar world.

12   Interview with Thys Loock, 8 Nov. 1990, pp. 1–2.

13   Interview with Thys Loock, 8 Nov. 1990, pp. 1–3.

14   E. Ludlow, 'Missions and Emancipation', pp. 67–68.

15   E. Host, 'Capitalization and Proletarianization on a Western Cape Farm: Klaver Valley 1812–98' (MA thesis, University of Cape Town, 1992), pp. 112–14. Host constructs an argument about changing modes of paternalism between farmer and workers over the period from the 1820s to 1890s on the farm Klaver Valley which remained in the possession of the same family.

16   E. Ludlow, 'Missions and Emancipation', pp. 62–3.

The example of Duckitt's paternalistic relationship with his workers on Klaver Valley did not alter their attempts to minimize the farmer's control over their private lives. People living on nearby farms in the years immediately before and after emancipation often sought to have relatives or friends in Groenekloof foster their young children prior to their own arrival, in order to prevent their children from being bound over to farmers. Klaver Valley apprentice, Rachel le Fleur, arranged to have her baby son fostered with Groenekloof church servants, Jonathan and Concordia Conrad, in September 1839, while Rachel only followed two years later.[16] Clearly Duckitt's attempts to control the labour of his ex-slaves' children were resisted wherever possible. Yet Duckitt maintained close links with the Mamre community both in his capacity as a Justice of the Peace, and as a major employer of mission residents in the district.[17]

Frans Carls, Nanto September and his wife Spasi, had been living on the farm Draaihoek before they entered Groenekloof in September 1840.[18] These people had obviously formed close relationships during their enslavement which spanned several farms in the area. Their prime incentive in the first flush of freedom was to re-establish these close relationships and an environment in which they could live together. The growth of Groenekloof was partly the reconstitution of existing family and community ties already established in the region.[19]

On arrival at Groenekloof, the newcomers were likely to have been met by one of the mission overseers. These church officials were members of respectable established families in the community, and were the main links between the missionaries and people settling at Groenekloof. As these numbers of new arrivals increased rapidly, the overseers' role and influence also grew. They assisted the missionaries in deciding who should be allowed to become a member of the community, and were likely to have had daily contact with the newcomers and have assisted them in socializing into the mission community.[20] An essential part of becoming a member of the community was the experience of a conversion to Christianity. For the Moravians this was a gradual process of attaining faith over a period of time through accepting Christian teaching and being granted membership of the congregation. Being a Moravian brought with it beliefs and codes of

---

17   E. Host, 'Capitalization and Proletarianization', pp. 24–5.

18   E. Ludlow, 'Missions and Emancipation', appendix B, pp. 214–34 and Figure 2.6 'Diagram Representing 8 Farms which were Birthplaces of Newcomers to Groenekloof'.

19   E. Ludlow, 'Missions and Emancipation', pp. 71–2; R. Shell, 'Domestic Slave Market', in *Children of Bondage*.

20   Discussion at the Conference on People, Power and Culture: The History of Christianity in South Africa 1792–1992 (University of the Western Cape, Aug. 1992), raised the issue of the role of church intermediaries as an under-researched area in mission history.

21   E. Ludlow, 'Missions and Emancipation', pp. 35–45.

behaviour which became the basis of a common bond in the community.[21]

However, in negotiating the creation of the Groenekloof community, the missionaries accepted the validity of relationships which had been established prior to entry into the mission that were not sanctified by marriage. Spasi September and her husband, Nanto, were both baptized into the church as Hermina and Joshua, within three years of arriving at Groenekloof in 1840 with their children. Yet they did not marry in the church for another ten years. *De facto* relationships like that of the Septembers were acceptable in this era.[22] The children of newcomers, however, were far more likely to marry in the church.

By the early twentieth century, the wedding procession down the main road of Mamre to the church had become an important public event in the community. Maggie Johannes, a Mamrier born in 1921 who trained in Cape Town to be a schoolteacher and then returned to Mamre, remembers her mother Rebecca's recollection of her wedding day in 1910. 'Dit was 'n baie groot wedding. Klomp strooimeisies... Die hele skool, daai tyd was getuie gewees... Dit was mos...die vooraanstaande mense, wat hier die geld gehad het...'[23]

The creation of a Moravian community in Groenekloof involved a public commitment to the church. Ceremonies like weddings and annual church festivals became more important over subsequent generations from emancipation onwards, as they became a public display of respectability and participation in the life of the community. These ceremonies, and membership of various church structures such as choirs and prayer groups, were fundamental to the creation of community and identity in Mamre from emancipation to the early twentieth century. Membership of the community depended on maintaining ties through active participation in the public life of Mamre.

Church overseer, Samuel Pick, who had arrived in Groenekloof before the mid 1820s, was thus considered an 'old-timer', in contrast to the 'newcomers', those who had arrived later. He was a highly-respected leader who 'had a good name in the community as a church servant. He had a reputation for taking special care that the young members of the community as well as all new members were taught the church regulations.'[24] In the period after emancipation, the division between old-timers and newcomers took on an extra layer of meaning in referring not only to length of residence but to

---

22   *Ibid.*, pp. 77–90.

23   Interview with Magdalena Johannes, 26 Feb. 1991, pp. 4–10. 'It was a very big wedding. Bunch of flower-girls... The whole school witnessed it... It was...the prominent people from here, who had money...'

24   W.F. Belcher, *Benigna van Groenkloof of Mamre: Een Verhaal voor de Christen Kleurlingen van Zuid Afrika door een Hunner Leeraars* (Genadendal, 1873, translated into Afrikaans by P.D. Johannes, Louwskloof, 1968), p. 76.

25   E. Ludlow, 'Missions and Emancipation', pp. 40, 66.

non-slaves and ex-slaves.[25]

As one of the old-timers, Samuel Pick was also in a privileged economic position. He was one of the wealthiest people in the community, along with some members of the Adams, Conrad, and Johannes families. At the time of emancipation some of these old-timers had been small commercial farmers employing other Groenekloof residents as labourers. Samuel Pick had been the only stock farmer in Groenekloof at the time. As well as being the wealthiest families, these families also held positions within the Moravian Church. Nine out of twelve of the wealthiest people in Groenekloof in 1825 were church overseers by 1840. Power and privilege were linked within the community which had already established clear lines of hierarchy.[26]

Some newcomers had links with the wealthy old-timer families. We have already seen how Rachel le Fleur from Klaver Valley fostered her child with one of the Conrad couples. Newcomers also married into old-timer families and became part of the wealthier élite of the community. There were early links made between ex-slave Rachel Liedeman's children and old-timer families. Two of her children went on to marry into the Pick family, creating patterns of wealth amongst families in Groenekloof which existed throughout the nineteenth century, some even persisting to the present.[27]

Newcomers were far less likely to be able to establish themselves as independent farmers. As the western Cape missions like Mamre became more crowded after emancipation, they were less able to support their residents without their involvement in wage labour. Mamre was becoming a reservoir of seasonal casual labour for the surrounding farms, and, increasingly throughout the nineteenth century, wage labour for the city.[28] Ludlow argues that 'what is, in fact, most striking about the new arrivals is their almost complete failure to become established as mission-based producers'.[29] Only those who had arrived at the mission with either artisanal skills or with resources such as wagons and oxen were able to escape the pressure to enter wage labour on the farms outside the mission from the 1840s.[30]

---

26 Hendrick Abrahams, Christlieb Adams, Immanuel Adams, Mathews Adams, Hiob Conrad, Petrus Dambra, Henoch Esau, Nathanael Johannes, Samuel Pick, Davis Vertyn, Gottlieb and Jeremias Vister were the 12 wealthiest people in Groenekloof in 1825. See E. Ludlow, 'Missions and Emancipation', pp. 128–9.

27 E. Ludlow, 'Missions and Emancipation', pp. 90, 109.

28 S. Trapido, 'The Friends of the Natives: Merchants, Peasants and the Political and Ideological Structure of Liberalism in the Cape, 1854–1910', in S. Marks and A. Atmore (eds.), *Economy and Society in Pre-Industrial South Africa* (London, 1980), pp. 247–74; J. Marincowitz, 'Rural Production and Labour in the Western Cape, 1838–88, with Special Reference to the Wheat Growing Districts' (Ph.D. thesis, University of London, 1985), see esp. ch. 3.

29 E. Ludlow, 'Missions and Emancipation', p. 117; J. Marincowitz, 'Rural production and labour', ch. 4.

30 E. Ludlow, 'Missions and Emancipation', ch. 4.

31 E. Ludlow, 'Missions and Emancipation', ch. 3 and pp. 204–8.

The missionaries' explanation as to why they changed the mission's name from Groenekloof to Mamre in 1854 reveals a great deal about their role in encouraging a coherent community identity which distinguished between insiders and outsiders. At the same time, the division between old-timers and newcomers at emancipation diminished as the mission population stabilized and became more interwoven and integrated into the church.[31] Francke wrote in the Mamre diary at the time that

> every farmer in our immediate neighbourhood has the name of Groenekloof on his wagon. Besides, the Hottentots and others run up accounts with trades-people in Cape Town, under the impression that they belong to us. Afterwards when sought here, no such persons were to be found. Again, when an intoxicated black was seen in a wagon, bearing the name Groenekloof, he was sure to be considered an inhabitant of this place.[32]

The blurred boundaries between the mission and the outside world was closer to reality than the closed self-contained and regulated community which the Moravian missionaries had had as their ideal. Mamriers, as mission residents became known, were never isolated from the surrounding rural economy and, towards the late nineteenth century, pressure on mission resources pushed more and more people into labouring on the surrounding farms, and increasingly into urban migration. As opportunities for economic independence on the mission had been declining since emancipation, mission res-idents had had to rely on wage labour to survive. In a sense, the missionaries paved the way for the smooth transition from slave to rural wage labourer by nurturing the Calvinistic work ethic as part of being a respectable church and community member.[33]

Mamriers were able to negotiate from a position of relative strength in the labour market because of their permanent home base at the mission. They used this leverage to choose from amongst potential employers on the farms and in town, to extract advance wages from farmers, to withhold women and children from farm work, and to invoke contractual obligations contained in the Masters and Servants Act to challenge their employers in court. Anton (David) Carls and Joshua (Nanto) September, employed on Louis Greef's farm, Zomerveld, took Greef to court for non-payment of wages in 1848. The use of courts as a means of redress was a strategy which had continued from the days of the Slave Protector, and in Mamre the same phrase of 'going to complain' persisted into the new forms of labour relations.[34]

32   Mamre, 25 Nov. 1854, *Periodical Accounts*, vol. XXI, 1855, cited in E. Ludlow, 'Missions and Emancipation', p. 208.

33   J. Raum, 'The Development of the Coloured Community of Genadendal Under the Influence of the Missionaries of the Unitas Fratrum, 1792–1892' (MA thesis, University of Cape Town, 1953).

34   E. Ludlow, 'Missions and Emancipation', pp. 160–72.

35   R. Ross, 'The Origins of Capitalist Agriculture in the Cape Colony: A survey', in W. Beinart *et al.*,

Robert Ross has argued that in the decades following emancipation, the western Cape rural labour force was bifurcated into a large, mobile, seasonal casual labour contingent and a small, permanent labour force living on the farms. In this emerging system, mission stations were labour reservoirs which 'fulfilled this role as the rubber in the elasticity of labour utilization'.[35] It was on these grounds that, in 1854, Frederick Duckitt M.P., the farmer at Klaver Valley, defended the continued existence of the missions which were being pressured by farmers suffering from labour shortages.[36] Along with these emerging relations of production in the commercial farming areas, came attempts by farmers to impose controls over their labourers to prevent them from moving about freely. The Masters and Servants Acts legislated in favour of increasing employers' control over their workers by extending the range of work offences punishable by criminal law.[37] This was accompanied by other means of control in the rural areas, like indebtedness through advancing wages and the dop system, which encouraged alcohol dependence as a means of diffusing resistance.[38]

In 1879 the Governor of the Cape, Frere, observed of Mamre:

> It is of much interest, as one of the oldest missionary station for the education and civilisation of Natives established in this part of Africa more than 70 years ago by the Moravian Brethren, and...it has steadily flourished and advanced in prosperity up to the present time. It has always been more or less a labour supply for the whole of the neighbouring country. As far as I am aware, the Moravian Brethren are among the first to recognize the duty of teaching all converts to work for their living, and this principle appears to have been steadily kept in view throughout their subsequent proceedings.[39]

By the early 1890s farmers were still complaining of labour shortages. Jakob van Reenen, M.P. for Malmesbury, again defended Mamre's continuation but suggested that the missionaries be required to force 'idle' people on the missions to work on the farms.[40] The missionaries maintained their position of not interfering in labour contracts and wage negotiations of their residents.[41] Yet, the farmers complaints had changed over the 50 years from emancipation. They perceived their main competition for labour as being the

---

Putting a Plough to the Ground: Accumulation and Dispossession in Rural South Africa 1850–1930 (Johannesburg, 1986), p. 85. See also Ross, ch. 6 in this volume.

36   Cape of Good Hope, Report of the Select Committee in Granting Lands in Freehold, 1854. Evidence by Frederick Duckitt.

37   C. Bundy, 'The abolition of the Masters and Servants Act', *South African Labour Bulletin*, 2 (1975), pp. 37–47.

38   J. Marincowitz, 'Rural production and labour', ch. 2; S. Trapido, 'Friends of the Natives', p. 260; E. Host '"Die Hondjie Byt": Labour Relations in the Malmesbury District *c.*1880–*c.*1920' (BA Hons. thesis, University of Cape Town, 1987), and also E. Host, 'Capitalization and Proletarianization'.

39   Letter by Frere, Governor of the Cape, after a visit to Mamre in 1879. CA, GH 23/36, p. 359–63. Letter dated 22 Nov. 1879.

state itself through the extension of the railways and roads, and other public works. They also complained about rural labourers going into town to seek higher wages instead of remaining on the farms.

Mamriers were in a strong position to take advantage of expanding employment opportunities in Cape Town. Not only were they relatively close to town, an overnight walk, but those who had managed to escape indebtedness to farmers were mobile and able to explore the options available in the expanding urban economy. In the 1894 Labour Commission, two Mamre church wardens, Johannes April and Wilhelm Johannes, gave evidence about the patterns of employment and household strategies devised by Mamriers.

One must be wary of this evidence, as the Mamriers were clearly aware of how they were being perceived by the commissioners and answered accordingly. In reply to one commissioner's provocative question, 'Which is more customary, to lie at the station or to seek work?' Johannes April replied: 'Everyone who hears of a master wanting labour, goes thither'.[42] Again replying to an ambiguously racial question about whether Mamre women drank alcohol, Wilhelm Johannes quipped: 'Yes; at Mamre as throughout the world.'[43]

Nevertheless, the evidence reveals the choices and constraints, and the strategies adopted by Mamrier households in negotiating the rural and urban economies. Johannes April observed:

Many go to Cape Town and the wine farmers, in fact to any place where they will be employed. Men permanently employed by farmers remain with them. [There are] better wages in Cape Town and men prefer to go there than to the farmers... The man cannot leave the farm because he is in debt to the farmer. The longer he stays the deeper he sinks and frequently has to put his children in the field too, to aid in clearing his liability. As soon as they are free, they go to Cape Town, if not they must remain on the farm.[44]

Indebtedness was also tied to alcohol abuse, both of which were encouraged by some farmers to retain their labourers. 'They ask their master for a few shillings and he gives them an order on the canteen. In this way they become drunkards... The man goes backwards and the family suffers from want.' April, responding to questions about women and children working on the farms said 'I do not let my minor children work. Is not a child of eight years a minor?... I cannot let [my wife] go out, she works in my garden.' He also said that he would not allow his daughter to work unless she was of a

40   1893/94 Labour Commission, Evidence by Jakob van Reenen, p. 209.

41   1893/94 Labour Commission, Evidence by Revd Frederick Kunick, p. 238.

42   1893/94 Labour Commission, Evidence by Johannes April, p. 239.

43   1893/94 Labour Commission, Evidence by Wilhelm Johannes, p. 241.

44   1893/94 Labour Commission, Evidence by Johannes April, p. 239.

'serviceable age'. Mamriers resisted sending their womenfolk onto the farms and, as the century progressed, they chose instead to send their daughters into domestic jobs arranged in town.[45]

Wilhelm Johannes linked the flow of labour from the farms to the towns to the seasonal nature of farm employment and the poor wages offered to permanent farm workers.

> When it is not harvest time, many being out of employ come to the station. Their wages do not go on. The farmer does not want them until it has rained. Then his family has to be fed daily. So the man gets into debt and many cannot get out of it again... Some farmers do not give enough food to satisfy man's hunger... I think that the treatment [on the farms] in general is worse. You referred to children of twelve years of age. They were formerly capable of working at that age, but now they are not, as their parents do not give them food enough. Especially when the man is in debt with the farmer, he must put his children to work too early.

He concluded about the farmers' complaints of labour shortages:

> The good ones do not come into prominence as they are always well supplied with labourers. I have experience of this in our neighbourhood.[46]

Within these statements by Mamriers, both change and continuity from the period of emancipation to the end of the nineteenth century is clear. The Swartland farmers were divided into a few capitalizing commercial and many small struggling farmers. By the end of the nineteenth century, land consolidation had increased, and many large farms had poor white bywoners and foremen. It was particularly those farmers who were closest to Mamre who were in the best position regarding labour.[47] Farmers like Van Reenen, who were within walking distance of Mamre, continued to rely on the mission as a pool of seasonal casual labour.

Mamre families still resisted sending their children, especially young women, on to farms. Yet many had no choice. Increasingly, families relied on sending both men and young boys on to farms as labourers. Women generally stayed on the mission to tend the household garden plot and raise the children, specifically avoiding permanent domestic service on the farms. Since emancipation this 'shortage' of domestic servants had been one of the chief complaints of farmers, and remained so.[48] The missions did not provide independence from wage labour for most Mamriers but, at best, allowed them to choose from the available options. Often this meant that members of families worked in separate spheres for much of the time, and choices about

---

45   1893/94 Labour Commission, Evidence by Johannes April, pp. 239–40.

46   1893/94 Labour Commission, Evidence by Wilhelm Johannes, p. 241.

47   E. Host, "Die Hondjie Byt", pp. 1–31.

48   1893/4 Labour Commission. See, for example, evidence of Jakob van Reenen, but almost every farmer giving evidence echoes the cry of the unwillingness of mission women to enter into domestic service on the farms.

work were often channelled along gender and age lines. It is to the choices about various forms of work and migration from the late nineteenth century that we now turn our attention.[49]

Mamriers had been migrating into Cape Town from the inception of the community in 1808. In a sense, Mamre has always had links with the urban economy. The expansion of the urban economy and infrastructure in the late nineteenth century had provided major opportunities for Mamriers to seek alternative work. During the 1880s and 1890s employment on the railways and roads was at its peak, while after 1900 the growth of industrial manufacturing in Cape Town expanded the horizons of Mamriers seeking work.[50]

Complaints by farmers in the 1894 Labour Commission centred on the railways and public works as the chief culprits in 'stealing' their labour. Swartland farmer, Frans Schroeder, suggested that the government should 'get men out [immigrants or contract labourers] for their works and release our farm hands, who would then return to the farmer'.[51] Many farmers showed a perception of the labour market which was rooted in slavery, or, at least, could not accept a situation where their workers could exercise their own freedom. They often made recommendations which focused on punitive and coercive measures to induce labour to remain on the farms when giving evidence to the various Labour Commissions in the late nineteenth century. Many suggested that the state should restrict urban employers from hiring 'farm hands'. Some wanted a 'strop bill' (corporal punishment) introduced to bypass the inconvenience of court appearances under the Masters and Servants Act, and the reintroduction of compulsory child indenture.[52]

By the 1870s there were so many Moravians from the various rural mission stations living and working in town that, in 1886, the Moravian missionaries set up a city congregation to gather together their dispersed members. Moravian Hill in District Six became the focal point of rural migrants in the city. From their links with the church, a vibrant Moravian community developed, which brought together Moravians scattered all over the city. There was some concentration of people living in cottages and boarding houses around the chapel at Moravian Hill. Many of these were bought by the

---

49 K. Ward, 'The Road to Mamre', see esp. ch. 3.

50 K. Ward, '"Catering for Taste" in Late Victorian Cape Town: An Investigation into the Emergence of Factory Production in Selected Consumer Industries' (unpub. paper, Cape Town, 1991); V. Bickford-Smith, 'Commerce, Class and Ethnicity in Cape Town, 1875–1902' (Ph.D. thesis, University of Cambridge, 1988); D. Kaplan, 'Industrial Development in the Western Cape, 1910–40: Composition, Causes and Consequences' (unpub. paper, Cape Town, 1986); A. Mabin, 'The Making of Colonial Capitalism: Intensification and Expansion in the Economic Geography of the Cape Colony, South Africa, 1854–99' (Ph.D. thesis, Simon Fraser University, 1984).

51 1893/94 Labour Commission, Evidence by Frans Schroeder, p. 214.

52 K. Ward, 'Employers' Perceptions of the Labour Market in the Late Nineteenth Century Western Cape: With Reference to the 1893/94 Labour Commission' (paper presented at the Cape Slavery and After Conference, University of Cape Town, June 1989), pp. 1, 25–7.

church between 1886 and 1894 to encourage people to leave accommodation shared with Moslems. The area also served as a community for people from the missions who were living and working elsewhere in the city, as a place to congregate, not only for church, but to socialize with friends.[53]

The extent of migration can be seen through the value of remittances from members of rural mission stations working in town. The missionary at Moravian Hill transferred over £2,000 to people at the various rural missions in 1894, and this would have been only a proportion of the total. Mamre was third on the list, after Genadendal and Elim, with just over £220. But the relatively small amount transferred to Mamre reflected its closer links with Cape Town rather than the number of Mamriers working in town.[54] We do not know the exact numbers of mission residents living in town. But considering that the average monthly wage of black female domestic workers between 1893 and 1907 was approximately 30 shillings, and that of male day labourers between 18 and 21 shillings, several hundred must have been working in town to have remitted such large amounts of money.[55]

Mamriers' experiences of the urban job market differed according to their gender. Men and women had different opportunities and constraints placed upon them as members of the Mamre community. These expectations shaped not only the type of work they chose, but also their perceptions of what was respectable work and behaviour. Women increasingly had moved out of permanent farm work, including domestic work, from emancipation onwards. Yet they were strongly encouraged to find work as live-in domestic servants if they were alone in the city, in order to be 'protected' in a 'home' environment. If Mamre women were living with family or friends in town, they worked as day servants. There was a definite unofficial censure about women working in factories.[56] Men who sought to leave permanent farm work could choose from the available options, and where they lived in town was not an issue. In the late nineteenth century this often meant combining seasonal urban and rural labour, but by the early twentieth century many men were choosing to work permanently in town, or on the construction of roads. On the other hand, there was a strong incentive for men to find permanent pensionable jobs, whereas there was no censure against women domestic workers changing employers at will.[57]

---

53   J. de Boer and E. Temmers, *The Unitas Fratrum*, pp. 83–4; B. Kruger and P. Schaberg, *The Pear Tree Blossoms*, pp. 19–20; K. Ward, 'The Road to Mamre', ch. 3.

54   B. Kruger and P. Schaberg, *The Pear Tree Blossoms*, p. 39.

55   Evidence compiled from 1893/94 Labour Commission, Cape of Good Hope, Statistical Registers, 1898–1907.

56   See K. Ward, 'Employers' Perceptions', for an analysis of negative perceptions of women factory workers reflecting Victorian notions of respectability and womanhood, pp. 27–31.

57   E. Host, '"Die Hondjie Byt"' pp. 30–40; K. Ward, 'The Road to Mamre', pp. 76–7.

Mamriers relied on the network of mission station residents in town to get access to work and accommodation. At the turn of the century, Simon Petrus Magerman, Petrus August Pick and Andreas Johannes were three Mamriers working and living in town. Petrus worked in a shop in Hanover Street, District Six, and during the week stayed with the Johannes family in Waterkant Street. Simon Magerman worked as a labourer down the road at a saw-mill near the docks. Mr Johannes, who owned the house in Waterkant Street, worked at the E.K. Green Distillery in Somerset Road. His brother was employed there too, but he stayed in Upper Ashley Street with the Facolyn family, who were also Mamriers.[58]

The pattern of men taking a variety of jobs persisted throughout the twentieth century. Men tended to test the options and then settle on a job which offered a pension scheme and some hope of training and promotion. Mamriers favoured jobs on 'the Council' either in the city or working for one of the local authorities. Often these jobs came through local networks which were important sources of information and inside recommendations for employment.[59]

Christlief Adams, born in 1923 in Mamre, remembers that his father and grandfather worked on the Council. He was sent, as an adolescent, to work on one of the neighbouring farms until the age of 21 when he was considered old enough to take up work with his brothers on the Council. '[It was] almost a way of life in Mamre... Most of the men worked on the Council from Mamre... Most work there now...'[60]

Hennie Adams was born in Cape Town in 1912, while his Mamrier parents were living and working there. But his family ties with Mamre were so strong that, during the 1918 flu epidemic, he was sent to Mamre and continued to stay there for the remainder of his childhood, visiting his parents in town. After finishing school in Mamre in the 1920s, he went to town to look for work.

> The first job, I went there [to town], I worked at the Docks. Go carry the bags, the mail from the mail ships...and then from that, there was the Opera House [as an usher]. I remember, I used to try everything you know—I get [a job at] a harness-making place in Harrison Street, there was a Jewish place. There I worked a couple of years. I was a boy there. So you make saddles and so on. And from there I get a job from my uncle, near the Docks. There I work, I will say, about 25 years—[starting as] a labourer. My uncle was a foreman. But from there I go into the joinery shop... I was first in the yard where the wood is, then you come into the joinery shop. When the day when [we moved] out to Ndabeni, then...we were only two coloured men when moved with the Duitsman to Ndabeni.[61]

58   K. Ward, 'The Road to Mamre', pp. 40–1. See also interviews with Adam Pick, 10 July 1991, pp. 1–4; Magdalena Johannes, 26 Feb. 1991, p. 4; Simon Magerman, 6 May 1991, pp. 3–4.

59   Men who worked for the various local authorities include Samuel Arends b. 1896, employed from 1911

Women, too, relied on family to arrange jobs for them in town. Particularly in the early twentieth century when women began working in town as 'nurse girls' from as young as 11 years old. Simon Petrus Magerman's daughter, Amalia, born in 1908, started work as a domestic servant as a young girl in the early 1920s. Her mother's seven sisters were already working and staying in town and had arranged work for her.

> They went to work into town, because everyone always went to work in Cape Town... You see, people were very poor. They worked for very little on the farms... Can you see, that's why you go to town, you don't like to work on the farm... You get food, and you get a sleeping place, and everything. You can send [your wages] here. You can send it home.[62]

Domestic workers had extremely restricted leisure time, and so women from the rural mission stations tended to congregate together in their spare time. Amalia remembers:

> Then I go and visit my family, in the afternoon. You get off Wednesday afternoon, till ten o'clock. Ten o'clock you must be in. Sundays we go to church. Then from church we just walk to Adderley Street, just up and down, till it's time to catch the train to Sea Point [where she worked].[63]

Church at Moravian Hill was a focal point of their leisure and community ties in town. Charlotte April, whose father Andreas started a general store in Mamre in 1920, was sent to live with an aunt at Moravian Hill where she attended school and a teacher training college. She remembers life at Moravian Hill in the early 1930s.

> But let me tell you, those servants they came very regularly to church. We had services on Wednesday evenings and Saturday evenings, they couldn't get away. But Wednesdays and Sundays, and whenever we had a Church festival, the Church was, as they say, 'chock-and-block'... We had very many of those girls coming to our place. They'd come there, maybe before the service, they would be very early. They'd just come and sit for a cup of tea and a chat. They'd wait till the service started then they'd go there and after church they'd leave again... [Our house] was sort of a meeting place for everybody who was Moravian and who came from Mamre. All the Mamriers would come there. Not only they, but people from Genadendal and they'd bring their friends there.[64]

until retirement at 65 years; Adam Titus b. 1914, from 1932 until retirement; Alexander September b. 1911, from 1927 until retirement; Christlief Adams b. 1923, from c.1945 until retirement; Isak Witbooi b. 1905, from 1926 until retirement; Simon Magerman b. 1910 and Thys Loock b. 1918, from c.1945 until retirement. See also UG 54, 1938, Report of the Willcox Commission of Enquiry into the Cape Coloured People, p. 63, which discusses the range of employment opportunities available to coloured men on the City Council and Divisional Council of the Cape.

60   Interview with Christlief Adams, 20 May 1991, pp. 20–1.
61   Interview with Hendrick Adams, 21 Feb. 1991, pp. 7–8.
62   Interview with Amalia Collins, 4 Mar. 1991, pp. 3–4.
63   Interview with Amalia Collins, 4 Mar. 1991, p. 3.
64   Interview with Charlotte April, 4 June 1990, pp. 13–14, 26.

Domestic servants in town were either young single women who contributed to their family income, or married women who left their own children with their grandparents or relatives in Mamre. Mamre women also tended to marry locally. Maggie September, born in 1917, who worked in town as a domestic servant, remembers:

> But I always said, when I catch a man one day, he'll be a farm man... We didn't have boyfriends from town. Usually outside, Mamre boys. Or perhaps Pella, you see. But I can't remember anyone from town.[65]

There was a strong incentive to marry men from home in order to maintain ties with the community and, as Maggie September said, they could never be too sure whether their town boyfriends were already married, but they could at least check on the local men.

Married women often interspersed work in town with child rearing in Mamre. Some were able to stay in Mamre without working, or had accommodation in town with their husbands. Mamre men could be working in any number of different areas, on the farms, in town, or spanning the space between the two by working on construction of the roads. Remittances from wages supported family members living in Mamre, although men often came home to Mamre on the weekends and took food, which had been produced in the family garden plot, back with them for the week.[66]

Adam Pick explains how Mamriers were linked with town in the period until World War Two:

> The people stayed in town... Worked in town. I can't tell you exactly where, all over they worked. You pop up, you see a Mamrier works here, you know... They worked in service, the ladies. And the men, er people, that came to stay in town, and worked in town, then Moravian Hill was the church they go to... The church had a lot of houses in front of the church. That's why there was a strong community... You came from Mamre, you go to Moravian [Hill] Church, you stay in town... So, they sometimes they build their house [in Mamre] and then when they get old in years, and then they come out. And when they retire, they come out home, and stay home. And then people will do their little gardening, and on the land, some people were still busy with their lands, you know. This was in the old days.[67]

Most Mamriers working in town had family living back in Mamre. Families were usually split between a number of living and working contexts, with Mamre being their 'home base'. Mamriers developed a fluid notion of community which transcended time and space. Being a Mamrier meant maintaining ties with the rural community, usually by having one's

---

65   Interview with Magrieta September, 22 Nov. 1990, p. 17.

66   K. Ward, 'The Road to Mamre', pp. 94–102.

67   Interview with Adam Pick, 10 July 1991, pp. 24–7, 54–5.

family home there. Those Mamriers who worked in town visited home as often as possible, even if it was only for Easter and other religious festivals.

These were the established patterns of the community. Although there had been a shift from alternating seasonal work in town and on the land, to permanent work in town, Mamriers made sure their links with the community were renewed periodically. As early as the 1890s domestic workers from Mamre had negotiated their working lives to suit their community obligations. Mary Lancaster, a domestic servant agent operating in Cape Town, said in evidence to the 1894 Labour Commission:

> But there is a general exodus to their homes at Easter and at Christmas. Many mistresses who know the ways of the country give their Mamre girls paid holidays to retain them.[68]

In 1938, 100 years after emancipation, the Willcox Commission of Enquiry into the Cape Coloured People summarized the consolidation of the trend over the century.

> The introduction of machinery and increased fencing on the farms, the better opportunities for employment and social life in the towns, and a growing desire for the better education of their children, induced many of the coloured rural population to seek a living in urban centres.[69]

The Report reached general conclusions about the move from permanent farm work which did not take into account the ability of Mamriers to negotiate from a secure base on the mission. This enabled Mamriers to choose from available options with more flexibility than people based on the farms. The family life cycles of Mamriers had begun to change by the end of the 1930s, with men seeking permanent employment in town instead of seasonal work between town and farms, or permanent farm work.

The Loock family had lived on the farm, Wittezand, for generations, working as labourers and charcoal makers, and selling their charcoal in Cape Town until the mid 1920s. They then redirected their trade to the rural villages of Malmesbury and Darling where charcoal was still in demand for steam mills. But this became a dying trade by the 1930s as a result of the spread of electricity and fuel-driven engines. Thys Loock, born in 1918, went to live with his sister who was working in town, and found a job as a store hand on his first day. In his first year he also met his wife, Maria Johannes. Maria was a Mamrier and it was in Mamre that they built their home, raised their family and, in the 1980s, retired.[70]

---

68 1893/94 Labour Commission, Evidence by Mary Lancaster, pp. 7–8.

69 UG 54, 1938, Report of the Willcox Commission of Enquiry into the Cape Coloured People, p. 33. See also A. Walker, 'Out on a Limb—The Economy of Cape Town, 1934–41' (unpub. paper, Cape Town History Project, University of Cape Town, Sept. 1990).

70 Interview with Thys Loock, 8 Nov. 1990, pp. 10–11.

Although many Mamriers followed a family life cycles similar to that of the Loocks, Mamre was not just a place to which one retired. Many women lived there while raising their children, and there were a few Mamriers whose employment was based in Mamre. There were only about five bona fide farmers left in Mamre, including Anna Liedeman and her husband Theodore, whose family had been one of the farming élite in Mamre for generations.[71] Anna did not ever work in town; after leaving school she worked for the mission store before marrying. Then her job was to help run the farm by preparing food for the day labourers that her husband hired from amongst local residents. Farmers' wives regulated the working rhythms of the day by calling the workers for tea and meal breaks. Sometimes they prepared the food in the fields, or would walk from their homes carrying large pots of food out to the labourers.

Andreas April had expanded his economic interests from farming and had opened a general store and butchery by 1920. His wife helped to run the farm lands by preparing food for the Mamriers they hired as day labourers. April also hired a permanent assistant for his store, and relied on his children, including Gustav and Charlotte, to work in the store on weekends and after school. Family labour was an important part of the household economy throughout the period to the early twentieth century, and children contributed to the family income through chores or work, and then supported their parents in their old age.

In the nineteenth and early twentieth centuries, mission residents who owned a cart and oxen, mules, or horses were able to earn a living as self-employed transport drivers. A number of Mamre men had been employed by the British as transport riders during the South African War.[72] Ox-carts were still a familiar sight on the roads to Cape Town until the 1920s. But by the 1930s, transport riders were being replaced by young men with automobile licences. Willie 'Poswen' Johannes remembers getting his licence, on 1 January 1938, as a turning point in his life. Although Willie's family were farmers in Mamre, he was one of the few people who earned his living driving, as the district postman. In the 1930s car ownership in Mamre started to increase. People could drive to work in town in the morning and return to Mamre at night. But it was towards the end of the 1940s, when three Mamre men started a daily bus service into town, that working and commuting patterns in the community were revolutionized.[73]

---

71   Other bona fide farmers included Frederick Carlse's father, Gustav April's father, and Willie Johannes' father.

72   W. Nasson, 'Moving Lord Kitchener: Black Military Transport and Supply Work in the South African War, 1899–1902, with Partial Reference to the Cape Colony', *Journal of Southern African Studies*, 11 (1984), pp. 25–51.

73   Interview with Willie Johannes, 6 Dec. 1990.

Over the century, from emancipation in 1838 to the brink of World War Two in 1938, the Mamre community had evolved a unique identity which spanned both city and country.

Throughout the second half of the nineteenth century, patterns of wealth remained constant in the village, giving old-timers with their prior access to resources the edge. As land became a scarce commodity, more and more Mamriers were forced into wage labour. But as the century progressed, they increasingly explored the expanding options offered by public works and in the city. By the late nineteenth century, Mamriers often alternated seasonal rural labour with urban employment. This, in turn, was replaced by permanent urban employment by the end of the 1930s, when even those Mamriers who had been working on farms tended to move into urban employment. Within this broad overview, women experienced the transition from slavery to freedom as a removal from the farms into domestic work either in the village, or as servants in town. As the influx of rural mission residents expanded, the Moravian missionaries responded by creating a city congregation in District Six, which became known as Moravian Hill. A vibrant community life at Moravian Hill enabled Mamriers to keep their ties with Mamre through remittances home organized by the missionaries, and by meeting up with other Mamriers in town.

Family links formed the bridge between the two milieux, and participation in broader community life in Mamre was the cement which strengthened the bonds of community identity. Easter was the key festival for Mamriers. Liz Host documents how Klaver Valley farmers, over several generations in the nineteenth century, had been unable to prevent their Mamre labourers from returning to the mission for Easter.[74] Mamrier Charlotte April, born in 1915, echoes across the century when she remembers that 'everybody would go home at Easter-time. Nobody—no mistress—or nobody could keep them in town at Easter time… We always said "Easter…like the Malays go to Mecca, now the Moravians go to Everyplace!" That's their Mecca!!'[75]

Mamriers manipulated the range of options open to them at any one time, using the village as a home base from which to negotiate. In one sense, Mamriers were never homeless. Even if they did struggle with poverty and unemployment, in Mamre there was always a house and garden plot for subsistence, as well as family and neighbours for sustenance.[76] Adam Pick, whose story of the history of Mamre introduced this chapter, a lay preacher and church warden like his forebear Samuel, who helped to integrate newly-arrived ex-slaves into the mission, articulates the sense of community in

---

74   E. Host, 'Capitalization and Proletarianization', p. 139.

75   Interview with Charlotte April, 4 June 1990, p. 13.

76   See also, D. Cohen and E. Atienio Odhiambo, *Siaya: The Historical Anthropology of an African Landscape* (London, Nairobi and Ohio, 1989).

Mamre which still exists:

> Here we stay as a community...and the people all knows each other. They all know their problems. They all know they have, you know, their friends, and all, they like to stay as a community'[77]

The distinction between old-timers and newcomers at emancipation, which also defined non-slaves from ex-slaves, had given way by the beginning of the twentieth century to a division between *ingebores* and *inkomers*. Mamriers were born and not made. As slaves in the Swartland, people had had few rights to community, home and family. In freedom, this had became the essence of being for Mamriers.

But at the same time, the evolving identity of Mamriers over generations had been accompanied by the dissolving identification with slavery. This process seems to have been part of the process of community formation in Mamre. Indeed, both free and freed people were reborn as part of their conversion to Christianity and their identity as Mamriers was reinforced by their adoption of new names. Mamriers born in the early twentieth century often told me that they were not allowed to ask their elders questions about their lives. The oral history of slavery has been lost partly because of this, but also because there was a stigma attached to having had slave origins.

Very few Mamriers know whether their forebears were slaves, and over generations the collective memory of slavery has faded. Perhaps this is not surprising for a community which has suffered continued racial discrimination under apartheid. The new generation of Mamriers, growing up within a rapidly-changing society in South Africa, are sure to ask different questions of their history.

---

77   Interview with Adam Pick, 10 July 1991, pp. 24–5.

- INDEX -

H

Heemraden 28, 33–4
Heideman, Carfrae & Co. 188, 189
hierarchy, social
    and women 222
    maintenance of 9, 14, 207
hiring out
    of 'Prize Negroes' 105
    of slaves 11, 14, 76n, 79
        in Cape Town 82–3, 84, 104
        income from 105, 110
historiography 8, 15, 27, 160, 202
honour, importance of in community
    38–42
hospitality of Boers 56–7
'Hottentot' 49n
    free people? 254–5
    rebellion 272, 285–6
    servants, victims of Khoisan 251–2
    status 260
    see also Khoisan
hours of work, of apprentices 124,
    125
housing 185, 194

I

imports 79, 183–4
inboek system *see* indentureship
indenture(s) 103
    of 'Prize Negroes' 110, 112, 114
    of children 142, 211–14
indentureship 211n
insolence 52, 56, 62, 64, 68
    criminal offence 222
interest rate 184–5
Islam 11, 90–1, 112–3, 115, 299,
    314
    slave converts 87

J

Jamaica 13, 90, 120, 131, 133, 151
    ex-slaves in 274

slave population 1, 152, 157
joint stock companies 16, 176,
    196–7
jury system 10, 28, 42n

K

Kat River Settlement 19, 164,
    279–80, 283–4
    population 280, 284
    revolt 272–4
Kautgong 271–2, 277, 285, 286, 287
Kees, Captain Klaas 264–5, 267–9
Khoekhoe *see* Khoikhoi
Khoi *see* Khoisan
Khoikhoi *see* Khoisan
Khoisan 17, 203, 227, 251, 275–6
    and Ordinance 50 13, 133, 145,
        154, 161–2
    and Vagrancy Ordinance 162–3
    as serfs 148–9, 275–6
    complaints by 256–8
    deprived of land 146, 149
    in 'Bushman war' 229, 230, 250
    labourers 18, 122, 123, 146
    revolt 4, 18, 149
    see also 'Hottentot'
kinship 11, 32, 90, 205, 206, 316
Klapmuts, Captain Hans 314, 316

L

labour
    bifurcation of 15, 17, 161–6, 322
    compliant, state design for 12–13
    control of post-1834 5, 144,
        162–3
    patterns, post-emancipation 14, 15,
        17, 167, 326
    rural 221, 323
    seasonal 14, 165–6, 322
    shortages 86, 322, 324
    sources of 148
Labour Commission (1894) 323,
    325, 330

Y

Z